Leonard and Virginia Woolf, the Hogarth Press and the Networks of Modernism

Leonard and Virginia Woolf, the Hogarth Press and the Networks of Modernism

Edited by Helen Southworth

Edinburgh University Press

© in this edition Edinburgh University Press, 2010, 2012
© in the individual contributions is retained by the authors

First published in hardback by Edinburgh University Press 2010

Edinburgh University Press Ltd
22 George Square, Edinburgh EH8 9LF

www.euppublishing.com

Typeset in 10.5/13 Adobe Sabon
by Servis Filmsetting Ltd, Stockport, Cheshire, and
printed and bound in Great Britain by
CPI Antony Rowe, Chippenham and Eastbourne

A CIP record for this book is available from the British Library

ISBN 978 0 7486 4227 4 (hardback)
ISBN 978 0 7486 4714 9 (paperback)

Contents

PART THREE   Marketing Other Modernisms

List of Figures

Acknowledgements

I would like to thank all of the contributors to this collection for their fine work, their patience and their help putting the volume together.

Thanks to Roger Hubank and the late Mercer Simpson who travelled to the International Virginia Woolf conference in Birmingham in June 2006 to hear me deliver the paper on their uncle, John Hampson, that represents the starting point of this project. Also thanks to Roger and Joy for hosting me at their house in Loughborough and to my friend, Emma Hall, husband Simon and to Leo and Charlie for giving up their room to Helen from America.

Gratitude goes to the Woolf community for help and support, to Stuart Clarke, Suzette Henke, Laura Marcus, Alice Staveley and those at Molly Hite's New/Renewed Woolf seminar at the Modernist Studies Association conference in Nashville, among many others. Thanks also to the many other people I've contacted with questions and queries regarding Hogarth Press authors, little magazines, modernist presses and more, including Andrew Thacker, Stephen Rogers, Patrick Collier and Tony Brown. Trevor Bond of Manuscripts, Archives and Special Collections at Washington State Universitiy Libraries was wonderfully generous and helpful.

I would also like to acknowledge Random House and the Society of Authors as the literary representative of the Estate of Virginia Woolf for granting permission to reproduce citations from Woolf's work.

I would like to thank Paul Peppis for his willingness to share ideas, and my colleagues at the Robert D. Clark Honors College at the University of Oregon for their collegiality. Thanks also to the Oregon Humanities Center and the Honors College for their support of this project.

EUP editor Jackie Jones's contributions to this project have been invaluable. Thanks go also to the EUP staff.

Thanks to my friends and families in the US, in England and in Holland. My husband, Caleb Southworth, provided invaluable emotional, professional and much needed technical support. His energy continues to inspire me.

A Hogarth Press Timeline

1915 The Woolfs decide to buy a printing press and Hogarth House at Richmond.

1917 (1 title) purchase of printing press; hand print 134 copies of *Two Stories* (with Dora Carrington woodcuts).

1917–23 Hogarth Press publishes almost exclusively literature (Willis 213).

1918 (2 titles) Mansfield's *Prelude* (68 pages); Woolfs are approached by Harriet Shaw Weaver regarding Joyce's *Ulysses* (they refuse it).

1919 (4 titles) VW's *Kew Gardens*; Woolfs use commercial printer for the first time for second edition; Hogarth Press publishes first poetry, Eliot and Murry; the Press begins travelling books more seriously; closure of Omega Workshop (in operation since 1913).

1920 (4 titles) Forster's *Story of the Siren*; translation of Gorky's *Reminiscences of Tolstoy* (printed by Pelican Press; according to Willis, the Woolfs' first commercial enterprise; with this, Willis writes, the Woolfs became 'a small scale international publisher' (80)). Ralph Partridge taken on as assistant (–1923); first Hogarth Press advertisements (in the *Nation, TLS*); first real profits.

1920–23 (27 titles) 8, or nearly one-third, of which are Russian translations.

1921 (6 titles) the Hogarth Press establishes a relationship with Harcourt Brace in the USA. The Woolfs purchase a Minerva platen printing press. LW's *Stories of the East*; VW's *Monday or Tuesday*, Gorky's *Notebooks of Tchekhov*.

1922 (6 titles) 5 years! VW's first Hogarth Press novel, *Jacob's Room* (first book to be printed by R. & R. Clark of Edinburgh); Bunin's *The Gentleman from San Francisco*; more commercially printed books than hand printed for the first time; first pictorial Hogarth Press dust jacket by Vanessa Bell (her first for the Press); merger offers rejected.

1923   (11 titles, 5 hand set) Eliot's *The Waste Land*; Forster's *Pharos and Pharillon*; Read; Bell; Graves (first of 3 books of poetry and 3 of criticism); Marjorie Joad joins the Press; LW becomes literary editor at *The Nation and Athenaeum* (–1930).

March, 1924   Move to 52 Tavistock Square.

Mid 1920s–mid 1930s   Continue with literature, and over 50 books and pamphlets on domestic social and economic issues added to Press' list (Willis 239).

1924–30   VW dominates at the Press, according to Willis.

1924–late 1930s   8 pamphlets on Russia, communism and Marxism.

1924   (17 titles, 3 hand set) F. M. Mayor's *The Rector's Daughter* (on a commission basis); Sackville-West's *Seducers in Ecuador*; publish first socio-political title, Norman Leys' *Kenya*; begin Hogarth Essays series (1928, 35 titles); begin relationship with International Psycho-Analytical Library (IPL); decide against publishing a translation of Gide by Dorothy Bussy; Dadie Rylands joins the Press (stays only 6 months).

1925   (27 titles, 4 hand set) LW's first non-fiction Hogarth Press publication, *Fear and Politics: A Debate at the Zoo*; Muir's *First Poems* and 8 other volumes of poetry; first of 11 titles on women (Willis 244) (Willa Muir's *Women: An Inquiry* followed by *Leisured Women* in 1928); first of 3 titles on India (Thompson's *The Other Side of the Medal*); VW's *Mrs. Dalloway* and *Common Reader*; Mrs Cartwright joins the Press as manager. Sylvia Beach is stocking Hogarth Press titles at her Shakespeare and Co. in Paris.

1925–6   Hogarth Press publishes 3 of J. M. Keynes' shorter works.

1926 onwards   Only one or two hand-set books per year.

1926   (30 titles) Plomer's first novel *Turbott Wolfe* (Hogarth Press' eighth novel); first cheap edition (third edition of Leys' *Kenya*); second in series of publications by Katherine Innes on international politics for young readers; first in series of publications on peace and disarmament (by Philip Noel-Baker); first of 2 publications by Laura Riding.

1927   (38 titles) Lectures on Literature (–1934, 16 titles); first of annual Merttens Lecture on War and Peace (at Hogarth Press 1927–30; 1934–6); Freud's *Ego and Id*; Muir's *The Marionette*; 'Virginia Woolf's greatest artistic and commercial success [and] peak years for the Hogarth Press' (Willis 134), Kauffer's first cover and new logo for Hogarth Press; Hogarth Press begins a relationship with the Garden City Press in Letchworth (chief printer, among more than 30, for the Press). Alice Ritchie joins the Press as a part-time traveller.

1928   (36 titles) VW's *Orlando* (best-seller); Living Poets series edited until 1932 by Dorothy Wellesley (–1937, 29 titles).

1929 (30 titles) Uniform Editions of VW's books (Willis says this 'marked one more stage in the evolution of the Hogarth Press into a commercial publishing house' (155)). First of number of titles on education (Starr's *Lies and Hate in Education*).

1930s Press issued an average of 8 titles per year on a variety of political and social issues (Willis 259); following Russian translations in the 1920s, translations of Svevo and Rilke appear in the 1930s.

1930 (29 titles) launch Day to Day Pamphlets; Sackville-West's *Edwardians* (best-seller). Margaret Llewelyn Davies' *Life as we have known it*. Maximum profits in 1930 and 1931 of approximately £2,300 (exceeded only in 1937).

1931 (35 titles) Lehmann joins the Press and his poems are published; Easdale's *A Collection of Poems*; Kitchin's *The Sensitive One*; Hampson's best-selling *Saturday Night at the Greyhound*; Letters series (–1933, 12 titles); LW's *After the Deluge*; VW's *The Waves*.

1932 (36 titles) the Woolfs cease hand printing; Lehmann departs Press. Michael Roberts' *New Signatures* in the Living Poets series (Auden, Spender); Plomer's *The Case Is Altered*.

1933–6 Political books outnumber literary (Willis 213).

1933 (20 titles) Michael Roberts' *New Country*; Mussolini's *The Political and Social Doctrine of Fascism* (Day to Day Pamphlet); Derrick Leon's middlebrow *Livingstones*.

1934 (24 titles) Laurens van der Post's *In a Province*; Parmenas Mockerie's *An African Speaks for his People*.

1935–7 Only 6 volumes of poetry.

1935 (24 titles) Isherwood's *Mr Norris Changes Trains*; LW's *Quack, Quack!*

1936 (23 titles).

1937 (20 titles) World-Makers and World-Shakers (4 titles); VW's *The Years*; death of press manager Margaret West, replaced by Dorothy Lange then Norah Nicholls (1938–40); first salaried book traveller, Barbara Hepworth.

1938 (17 titles) Lehmann returns to the Press as partner and managing director (–1946), brings *Folios of New Writing* to the Press; Isherwood's *Lions and Shadows* (sold 1699 copies in first three months); Upward's *Journey to the Border*; VW's *Three Guineas*.

1939 (23 titles) mid August 1939 Hogarth Press moves to Mecklenburgh Square; Lehmann launches Sixpenny Pamphlets (5 titles, first of which is Forster's *This I Believe*) and Poets of Tomorrow (–1941, 3 titles); Henry Green's *Party Going*; Christopher Isherwood's *Goodbye to Berlin*.

1940   (10 titles) Lehmann launches New Hogarth Library (–1941, 6 titles); VW's *Roger Fry*; paper rationing introduced.

1941   (8 titles) In March, VW's death; *Between the Acts* published posthumously; translation of Rilke's selected poems.

1942   In April, LW and Lehmann reject Sackville-West's novel *Grand Canyon*.

Works cited

Willis, J. H. *Leonard and Virginia Woolf as Publishers: The Hogarth Press, 1917–41*. Charlottesville: University Press of Virginia, 1992.

Introduction

Helen Southworth

In 1922 Leonard and Virginia Woolf considered selling, or seeking a partner for, their five-year-old Hogarth Press. One of the challenges the Woolfs faced was finding the right person to take on what Leonard Woolf describes as their 'commercial hippogriff', as '[the] very curious type of business we were trying to create' (*Downhill All the Way* 79, 78). Although professionalisation seemed inevitable, the Woolfs wanted to retain an element of amateurism, an openness and a non-exclusive quality, that they felt might be lost if they ceded control. Leonard writes '[w]e felt to these writers and their books the responsibility of the commercial publisher to the author' (78). Like the wizard in Ariosto's *Orlando Furioso*, coincidentally an intertext for one of the most successful of the Hogarth Press' publications, Virginia Woolf's own *Orlando* (1928), the Woolfs ultimately decided to keep hold of the reins and to cultivate what remained their hybrid Press or hippogriff.[1]

The essays that comprise *Leonard and Virginia Woolf, the Hogarth Press and the Networks of Modernism* track the Woolfs' Press from its beginnings as a hobby in 1917 through its transformation into a commercial enterprise, still in operation at Virginia Woolf's death in 1941. In its infancy the Press relied on hand printing, mostly fiction penned by friends and family. The mature operation produced high-quality, professionally printed books on topics ranging from politics to art to science.[2] The essays in this volume reassess the Woolfs' contributions to twentieth-century literary and artistic culture and to modernism. They investigate the networks of ideas, people and institutions of some of the more than 450 works and their authors that the Woolfs published over a twenty-four-year period, and the nexus of professional relationships that the Press generated.

Existing studies of Leonard and Virginia Woolf's coteries and associations have focused mainly on the Bloomsbury Group, albeit in some very interesting ways. Jennifer Wicke, for example, looks at the 'free-floating social ties of Bloomsbury', at Bloomsbury as 'an invented community' as she 'investigates the degree to which Woolf's writing is inflected with and by its Bloomsbury context as an experiment in coterie consumption, which means both the consumption of art by a coterie, the "Bloomsberries", and the marketing and consumption of their art (and thought and lifestyle) as produced by a celebrated coterie' (110). Sara Blair reads Bloomsbury 'not as a movement or group or coterie or junta but as a local world', she 'explor[es], in the fullness of their complication, the specific circuits of production and exchange in which [Bloomsbury's] work and works participate, the geocultural landscape in which they unfold' (813). While conceptions are becoming more nuanced, as Wicke's and Blair's work (and that of Caws & Bird, Chapman & Manson and Laurence) suggests, attacks on Bloomsbury elitism and insularity persist even today.[3] The authors here shift the emphasis onto the networks generated and intersected by the Hogarth Press, dispelling misconceptions about the dominance of Bloomsbury Group authors at the Press; they create another context, a group broader than the Bloomsbury Group, in terms of which to evaluate the Woolfs' contributions to the making of modernism. Widening and multiplying the Woolfs' circles, these studies follow recent work on Virginia Woolf's contemporary reading audiences, such as Anna Snaith's edition of letters sent by readers of *Three Guineas* to Woolf, Beth Daugherty's edition of fan mail sent to Woolf and Sybil Oldfield's *Afterwords*, a collection of condolence letters written on Virginia Woolf's death.

The essays in this volume consider the Woolfs and those who worked with them at the Press in their role as publishers and editors, as mediating agents, and their Press as an institution. In this way, these essays credit the Woolfs with greater agency in terms of early twentieth-century cultural production than is often the case. They portray the Woolfs as risk takers and innovators, and as individuals attempting to direct, and often defy, public taste and public opinion.[4] With this emphasis, there is more interest in this volume in the period after 1922, when the Press became involved in the broader publishing scene, than in its first years when limited, hand-printed editions were its purview. Attention is paid, however, to the often disconcerting mix of professional and amateur practices, the way in which the Press maintained the amateurism with which it began, and to the difficulties of reconciling the insider quality of a small press with its commercial aspects. Indeed the hybrid quality of the Press – an aspect emphasised again and again by Leonard Woolf in his autobiography – is one of the major conceits of this book.

I begin this introduction by considering the birth and the evolution of the Hogarth Press alongside several other presses of the period, both small-scale presses oriented toward niche markets and mass-market commercial. To this end, I focus first on the 1922 turning point in terms of the future of the Press as an ideal place from which to consider the type of enterprise the Hogarth Press ultimately became.[5] Nineteen twenty-two was an especially significant year for the Press with the publication of *Jacob's Room*, Virginia Woolf's first major work to appear under the imprint of the Hogarth Press, the subtext of which involves access to writing. This was a move that, according to Sally Dennison, 'made possible [Woolf's] change from a commercial to an experimental writer' (193). It was also the year that works by Freud and Dostoevsky appeared at the Press. Nineteen twenty-two is also of course modernism's most popular, although oft contested, *annus mirabilis*, a watershed in terms of revolutionary changes on the broader literary and artistic scene that saw the publication of Joyce's *Ulysses* and Eliot's *The Waste Land* as well as the founding, by Eliot, of the magazine the *Criterion*.

In the second section of this introduction, I explain the rationale behind a focus on the output of the Press and the network of relationships that grew around it, especially those involving the lesser-known agents, institutions and books produced by the Press. I locate this study in terms of work undertaken in the field of modernist publishing and, more specifically, in terms of the modernist periodical. I make a case for a network approach, a focus on links, connections and intersecting spheres – historical and sociological in tone – as a fruitful new way in which to study the modernist/small press.

Leonard and Virginia Woolf and the Hogarth Press

The Woolfs' decision in 1915 to buy a printing press and to learn the art of printing was no doubt somewhat influenced by the 'private presses' or 'small presses' fashionable at the turn of the century, the best known among them William Morris' Kelmscott Press.[6] In operation for seven years, from 1890 until Morris' death in 1896, Kelmscott produced fifty-three editions in sixty-six volumes. Inspired by experiments with type font design and by a failure to find reliable hand printers, Morris' aim in launching Kelmscott, named, like the Hogarth Press, for his home(s), ' "in a small way" ' was to ' "re-attain a long-lost standard of craftsmanship of book printing" ' (qtd in Cave 104). Following the tenets of the Arts and Crafts movement, Morris believed that ' "a work of utility might also be a work of art" ' (qtd in Naylor 110) and that

> [a] book … should be conceived as architecture, each detail contributing to the whole, so that the paper, the ink, the type-faces, the word and line spacing, the placing of the margins and the integration of illustration and decoration all had to be considered in detail, and in relation to the complete book. (Naylor 111)

Morris' ' "little typographical adventure" ' (qtd in Cave 106) inspired many other private presses interested in 'the Book Beautiful' (Ashbee qtd in Naylor 111), including St John Hornby's Ashendene Press (1894–1935), which published mostly editions of classics, also Henry James, Robert Bridges and Oscar Wilde; Cobden Sanderson's Doves (1900–16), which closed its doors just a year before the Hogarth Press published its first title (Ransom 103); and Lucien and Esther Pissarro's Eragny Press (1884–94) among others. Roger Fry's Omega Workshops (1913–19), a model for the early Hogarth Press, which produced books as well as furniture, pottery and textiles, was also certainly influenced by Morris; however, as Judith Collins points out, Omega's 'regard for the present', rather than 'nostalgia for the past', sets it apart from its predecessor (6).[7]

On a similar scale to Morris, but with less of a clear vision of what they were trying to do, the Woolfs launched their Press in 1917 as a sideline, 'a manual occupation … which, in say the afternoons, would take [Virginia's] mind completely off her work' (Leonard Woolf, *Beginning Again* 233). Many small presses folded in their first five years of operation; however by 1922, with approximately twenty titles and names ranging from T. S. Eliot, Maxim Gorky and Sigmund Freud to little-known poets Frank Prewett, a Canadian, and Ruth Manning-Sanders, a Welshwoman, the Woolfs sought to distance themselves from operations like Kelmscott. Writing many years later, Leonard Woolf distinguishes the Hogarth Press from Kelmscott and also from Nonesuch Press in terms of a privileging of the inside of the book over the outside, and in terms of a desire to free art and literature from the grip of the educated and privileged few:

> We were interested primarily in the immaterial inside of a book, what the author had to say and how he said it; we had drifted into the business with the idea of publishing things which the commercial publisher could not or would not publish. We wanted our books to 'look nice' and we had our own views of what nice looks in a book would be, but neither of us was interested in fine printing and fine binding. We also disliked the refinement and the preciosity which are too often a kind of fungoid growth which culture breeds upon art and literature; they are not unknown in Britain and are often to be found in cultivated Americans.

And he continues in terms of the possible 1922 takeover: 'It was because [James] Whittall seemed too cultured and might want to turn the

Hogarth Press into a kind of Kelmscott Press or Nonesuch Press that we turned him down' (*Downhill* 80).[8] Virginia Woolf words it slightly differently in her diary but, like Leonard, emphasises their shared desire to have the Press be something more than a coterie press producing limited editions for a small group of friends (to work outside of Pierre Bourdieu's restricted field): 'I am a little alarmed by the social values of Mr [Whittall] for we don't want the Press to be a fashionable hobby patronised & inspired by Chelsea. Whittall lives only two doors off Logan' (*D2* 189–90). Logan was Logan Pearsall Smith, Whittall's father's cousin and Woolf's sometime Chelsea nemesis.

Consistent with the rejection of the overly cultured American Whittall and the Kelmscott and Nonesuch models, the Woolfs' operation also parted ways at this point with small presses in Paris and London, operated in the interwar period. The Hogarth Press does resemble these, such as Nancy Cunard's The Hours Press (1928–31) and Harry and Caresse Crosby's Black Sun Press (1925–36), in that it published the works of its owner–editors and, at least to start, those of a select coterie of contributors.[9] Like these other small presses, the Hogarth Press also maintained a distinctive editorial imprint, that is, its list reflects the personalities of its writer–editors; however, the life and output of the Hogarth Press – more than four hundred and fifty titles over the twenty-four years until Virginia Woolf's death, and many more beyond this – far exceeds those of other small presses which averaged approximately five titles per year and approximately five years.[10]

At the same time that Whittall's offer was declined, and the idea of the Hogarth Press as a fashionable hobby rejected, the Woolfs also turned down offers from several larger commercial publishing houses. These offers suggest that publishing firms oriented toward the mass market recognised the potential of the Hogarth Press based on its first five years' work. The first involved a merger with Constable at the suggestion of Pearsall Smith – Constable was his own publisher – against which then Hogarth Press assistant, Ralph Partridge, fought in the name of English literature, somewhat disingenuously according to Virginia Woolf (*D2* 212). The second was an offer of 'a kind of partnership or "association"' from Heinemann, again involving Whittall, by that point a reader for Heinemann (Leonard Woolf, *Downhill* 79). Heinemann's proposal meant their 'tak[ing] over the whole business management of the Hogarth Press, distribution, accounting, advertising, and, if [the Woolfs] wanted it, printing and binding. [The Woolfs] should be left complete autonomy to publish or not to publish any book [they] liked' (*Downhill* 79).

Constable and Company Limited (1890–), run by Michael Sadleir and

Otto Kyllmann and, in a lesser capacity, William Maxsee Meredith in the 1920s, had a varied list that featured George Bernard Shaw, Walter de la Mare, W. E. B. Du Bois, Hilaire Belloc, Woodrow Wilson, and Neville Chamberlain. Katherine Mansfield followed *Prelude*, her 1918 Hogarth Press publication, with five titles over the 1920s at Constable. Important American authors included John Dos Passos, Damon Runyon and Theodore Dreiser. Harold Nicolson was among the company's most successful contributors, joining the Press in 1921; however, suggesting that he had nothing to do with Constable's offer to merge with the Hogarth Press, the association of Nicolson and his wife, Vita Sackville-West, with the Woolfs and the Press post-dated this proposal. Reflecting the division of labour at the Hogarth Press, but also providing a contrast to it, as the dividing line was not so rigid at the Hogarth Press, the more extravagant Sadleir, like Virginia Woolf, dealt with the creative side of the operation and made decisions on the manuscripts, while the more conservative Kyllmann, like Leonard Woolf, oversaw the finances.[11] Despite Sadleir's daring, Sondra Miley Cooney describes Constable as 'pursu[ing], during its seventy years of independent existence, a basically conservative and traditional publishing philosophy' (66). Indicating that Bloomsbury/the Hogarth Press and Constable were working along similar lines, from 1921 Constable published the periodical *Nineteenth Century and After* (1877–), home to the work of several Hogarth Press authors, including R. M. Fox; Virginia Woolf and E. M. Forster published 'The "Censorship" of Books' here in April 1929. Constable also briefly published *Life and Letters*, which had been, under Desmond MacCarthy's editorship (1928–34), a vehicle for Bloomsbury writers (Cooney 68).

In its thirty-second year of operation in 1922, Heinemann was a well established commercial operation with, at the time of William Heinemann's death in 1920, a list that included 'new books by more than five hundred writers, half of whom were novelists' (Fritschner 153). Heinemann had opened his business in 1890 with £500 and two rooms in Covent Garden and, by the end of 1893, the Press had more than one hundred books on its list. Heinemann's first book was the romantic novel *The Bondsman* by Hall Caine, a book neither Caine's existing publishers, Chatto and Windus (1873–1987), nor Cassell (1883–), would take (Fritschner 151). Heinemann's 1890 fiction list included the work of Henry James, Rudyard Kipling and Wolcott Balestier, H. G. Wells' best-known titles (several lesser known were published by the Woolfs), E. F. Benson, works by D. H. Lawrence, George Moore, Robert Louis Stevenson, the periodical *The New Review*, and Conrad's *Nigger of Narcissus* (1897). Other important authors for Heinemann included John Galsworthy and Somerset Maugham, both of whom began publishing with the Press in the early 1910s. Heinemann was also an early champion of Ibsen. After Heinemann's death, authors included Graham Greene, James Elroy Flecker and Edward Upward. Other areas covered by Heinemann included art books, expedition books, the Loeb Classical library (1912–) and medical books (1917–). Important to Heinemann's success was a series of translations, selected with the help of Edmund Gosse, like Pearsall Smith, a Woolf nemesis and possible source for *Orlando*'s Nick Greene, and a Great Educators series. In both of these regards, we see similarities between Heinemann and the Hogarth Press: well known for its Russian translations and less well known for its series of educational books about the League of Nations and biographies for children. Although it had a reputation as a publisher of 'cosmopolitan' works, Heinemann also had a strong list of popular, 'best-selling' fiction (Fritschner 152). Sackville-West, who, like a number of Hogarth Press authors, also published with Heinemann, would fulfil this role at the Hogarth Press.

According to Leonard Woolf, he and Virginia decided against Heinemann, and also likely Constable, 'for the simple reason: *timeo Danaos et dona ferentes*, I fear the Greeks, especially when they offer me gifts. We felt that we were really much too small a fly to enter safely into such a very large web' (*Downhill* 81). Leonard's characterisation of Heinemann's offer as a Trojan horse, with a quote in Latin from Virgil's *Aeneid*, suggests that they feared that it represented a takeover rather than a partnership. Size mattered to Leonard Woolf.[12] According to Virginia Woolf's diary of 3 December 1922:

> The Hogarth Press is in travail. Heinemanns made us a most flattering offer—to the effect that we should give us [*sic*] our brains & blood, & they would see to sales & ledgers. But we sniff patronage. If they gain, we lose. Our name has to be coupled with theirs. In the opinions of Desmond [MacCarthy], Clive [Bell], Roger [Fry] & I think Vanessa [Bell], the exchange would be capitulation. We are both very willing to come to this conclusion, & have decided for freedom & a fight with great private glee. (D2 215)

Confirming their commitment to amateurism and to 'freedom & a fight with great private glee', while at a meeting with Heinemann at the 1917 Club 'in the midst of ... negotiations and conversations and hesitations', when the Woolfs overheard a rather dishevelled-looking young stranger (soon identified as Marjorie Thomson, later Joad) express her decision to leave her teaching position and become a printer, the first woman printer, she boasted, with uncharacteristic spontaneity the Woolfs set about hiring her on the spot (*Downhill* 81).

Reflecting the fact that independence and freedom were to remain important considerations for the Woolfs, when Heinemann came up again ten years later in 1933, this time as a competitor for the hand of Vita Sackville-West, Leonard's opinion had not changed very much. In a letter in response to Sackville-West, then among the Press' best-selling authors, Leonard argues that the sales of her books would not be adversely affected if she were to stay with the Hogarth Press, a name at this point as reputable and as likely to draw buyers as that of its competitors, and Leonard lists Chatto [and Windus], Faber, Constable, Heinemann and Secker (1910–35), the latter a smaller press like Hogarth. Here Leonard drew on his and Virginia's prior work with presses, as well as their experience weighing lucrative offers for Virginia's work from competitors. Leonard had published with Edward Arnold, E. M. Forster's primary publisher, the Hogarth Press, his secondary. Virginia Woolf's first novels appeared with Duckworth. In its capacity as a highly successful press led by her half-brother, Gerald, Duckworth must have influenced the Woolfs' work at the Hogarth Press, despite Virginia Woolf's relief at escaping what represented for her a problematic conflation of the personal and the professional.[13] As well as several Woolfs (Virginia, Bella, Philip and Cecil) and Leslie Stephen, Duckworth, with Edward Garnett's help, published Henry James, W. H. Hudson, Charles Doughty, W. H. Davies, Hilaire Belloc, Chekhov, Gorky, Andreev, Strindberg, Ibsen, D. H. Lawrence, Dorothy Richardson, Knut Hamsun, Ford Madox Hueffer, Evelyn Waugh and the Sitwells. Leonard admits to Sackville-West that the offer of a hefty advance from Heinemann and other similar commercial presses must prove appealing to an author, and he concedes that it made sense for the Press to extend these kinds of offers, using William Plomer, a recent Hogarth Press loss to Jonathan Cape, as an unnamed example; however, setting the Hogarth Press apart, Leonard refuses to enter the fray and 'gamble' in this fashion (in Spotts 316–18).

The Woolfs wanted *complete* editorial freedom and they recognised as early as 1922 that, despite the commitment entailed in running all aspects of the Press almost single-handedly, freedom could not be maintained if they surrendered the business side of the Press to a larger, commercial operation. As many of the essays here demonstrate, what the Hogarth Press offered authors was precisely either a passage into or an alternative to the commercial press. Such a commercial affiliation was a compromise or an opportunity that other contemporary editors and readers negotiated with mixed success. Individuals who might serve as good comparisons with the Woolfs include Edward Garnett, who read for Duckworth, Unwin and then for Cape for sixteen years until his death (1921–37), and who is generally considered, like the Woolfs, to have acted more as the author's 'broker' or agent than the 'publisher's reader'; William Plomer, Garnett's successor at Cape; and T. S. Eliot, who took a job at Faber and Faber in 1925 (McDonald *British Literary Culture* 31).[14]

Simultaneous with the fashionable hobby and the commercial merger proposals, a third offer arrived, this one from inside, from their assistant, Ralph Partridge, whose future with the Press was unclear in 1922. According to Virginia Woolf, Partridge was lumpy, grumpy, slovenly and stupid, but also nice, strong, fundamentally amiable and well connected (*D2* 189); he was attached to them and to the Press 'like a drone' (*D2* 210) but refused to really commit to it. Partridge suggested that the Hogarth Press become a company with Noel Carrington as London manager, Lytton Strachey, Leonard and Virginia as partners and Partridge himself 'remaining as he is' (*D2* 215). Noel Carrington had experience in the world of publishing, having recently worked at the Indian branch of Oxford University Press, and he would go on, in 1939, when editor for Country Life Books, to come up with the idea for Puffin Books. He was an insider in his capacity as the younger brother of Dora Carrington (known as Carrington), whom Partridge had married in 1921, although she was in love with Strachey. Carrington had become involved with the Press in its early days when she provided woodcuts for the very first Hogarth Press publication, Leonard and Virginia Woolf's collaborative *Two Stories*. Although Strachey was a close friend of the Woolfs, his only writing for the Press was an introduction to George (Dadie) Ryland's *Words and Poetry* (1928). A number of other Stracheys, however, do appear on the Hogarth Press list, including Alix, E. J., James, Julia, Marjorie and Ray.

The Woolfs rejected this third option in many respects due to a combination of the previous two sets of issues: this solution would create an operation that was at once too small and too insular – these were friends with complicated Bloomsbury-type relationships – and too big – Noel Carrington had worked for a commercial press and would want to take the Hogarth Press in a similar direction. The Woolfs foresaw that they would 'have to keep N.C. in work, be ready to tackle an enormous commercial success, & fall more & more, so we suspect, into readers & advisers to the firm of Partridge & Carrington, who would become by force of circumstances, commercial mainly with only a dab of Hogarth gold left on top.' 'At this moment', Virginia Woolf concludes, 'we incline to Miss Tomson [*sic*] & freedom' (*D2* 215). Perhaps suggesting that the Woolfs did the right thing, Strachey's and Partridge's subsequent attempt to launch their own Tidmarsh Press failed (c. 1922–3).[15]

This 1922 turning point, just one of a number identified by scholars as critical to the Press' identity, illustrates well the degree to which the Hogarth Press remained a hybrid operation, 'an alternate press' (Rosenbaum 24), or, to return to Leonard Woolf's characterisation, a 'commercial hippogriff', unique in its successful combination of the risk-taking of a smaller press and the professional production work of a commercial press.[16] This crossroads highlights the extent to which the Woolfs deliberately took a third, less conventional route, loathe to give up the freedom which control of the Press allowed them, but determined nevertheless to compete in terms of reviews and sales with their commercial counterparts. John Lehmann captures the mixed identity of the Press when he describes his learning experience there:

> I learnt the essentials of publishing in the most agreeable way possible: from a man who had created his own business, had never allowed it to grow so big that it fell into departments sealed off from one another, and who saw it all as much from the point of view of an author and amateur printer as of someone who had to make his living by it. (*In My Own Time* 110)

The Woolfs' determination to hold on to the reins of their 'great horse', to ride it 'in a spirited and independent way' and to remain connected to all aspects of the Press is largely responsible for the wide variety of books, authors and artists that we find over the next twenty years at the Hogarth Press (*D2* 259). While readers recognise many Bloomsbury-affiliated names on the list, although these are often connected to less well-known titles, perusal of Howard Woolmer's *A Checklist of the Hogarth Press* produces many puzzling questions, some of which are answered in this volume. Less constrained than their commercial competitors in terms of financial success and largely unfettered by the tyranny of friendship or coterie sentiment, the Woolfs were in a position to open their doors to 'all sorts of people', 'tramps and du[ch] esses', 'plumbers and Prime Ministers' (Leonard and Virginia Woolf, 'Are too Many Books Written and Published?' 241). Thus, following nine titles in 1922, the Woolfs produced twelve in 1923 and eighteen more in 1924, including their first in the politics and society category, Norman Leys' *Kenya*. Nineteen twenty-five was a bumper year with twenty-eight additions to the list, among them C. H. B. Kitchin's satirical novel *Streamers Waving*, which Kitchin would follow with a best-selling detective novel, *Death of My Aunt*, in 1929, and John Maynard Keynes' short pieces on the economy and Churchill and on Russia. The Press reached a peak with thirty-seven books and pamphlets in 1927 and thirty-six in 1928. By this time the Woolfs were publishing work on topics ranging from music to education and politics, and from art, domestic and international, to war and peace, as well as the literary works (poetry, novels, literary criticism) with which they had begun. The late 1920s and 1930s also saw the inauguration of various important series that suggest both the Woolfs' reach and status and their continued commitment to innovation: to name just a few, the International Psycho-Analytical Library (1924–), the Hogarth Living Poets series (1928–37), and the socio-political Day to Day Pamphlets (1930–9).

The Networks of Modernism

The second section of this introduction takes up the third term of the collection's title, 'the *networks* of the Hogarth Press', and addresses how an investigation of the names and titles on the Press' list, a look at the networks that developed at the Press and around it, and sometimes even in opposition to it, contributes to a deeper understanding of early twentieth-century literature and culture. I begin with a brief overview of scholarship in the field of modernist publishing and modernist periodicals. I argue that emphasis in the field of book history on networks or maps of production and consumption provides a useful framework for the current study of the Woolfs' Hogarth Press as it highlights the degree to which the Press shaped twentieth-century literature and culture. Further, I use the recent shift in focus in modernist publishing, and particularly in periodicals studies, away from canonical authors and ideas onto lesser known figures, providing for more inclusive portraits of the institutions that published their work, to show the value of this broad-ranging collection and to suggest a direction for future work on other modernist/small presses.

The essays in this collection draw on work in the field of print culture to examine what has been variously called 'the sociology' (McKenzie), the 'communications circuit' or 'life cycle' of the text (Darnton 110–11; McDonald *Literary Culture* 11) or the 'literary field' (Bourdieu). In the 1980s, in response to a perceived overspecialisation in the field of book history, D. F. McKenzie argued for a broader approach that took into consideration 'the human motives and interactions which texts involve at every stage of their production, transmission and consumption [and] the roles of institutions, and their own complex structures, in affecting the forms of social discourse, past and present' (15). Later proponents of this approach describe their object of study as an exploration of the ways in which the 'material conditions of the production and transmission of texts' impact 'the practice of authorship' 'in the context of . . . critical editing and literary biography' (Willison et al. xii).

Attention to the life cycle of the text has proved particularly interesting to scholars of modernism as they attempt to unravel the fraught relationship of the modernist writer to the emerging mass market in the 1890s and the early twentieth century, and, as they have responded to Andreas Huyssen's and John Carey's claims about 'the great divide' separating modernists from the public, the 'intellectuals' from the 'masses' (see Dettmar & Watt 5–6). One of the best-known volumes in this field is Lawrence Rainey's *Institutions of Modernism* (1998) and in particular his often anthologised chapter on Eliot's *The Waste Land*, 'The Price of Modernism'. The essays in this collection take up Rainey's provocative charge and explore the Hogarth Press as a 'site[] of production' or a 'staging venue[]' for modernism (Bornstein 1; Rainey 5). They provide support for Rainey's contention that 'modernism [is] more than a series of texts or the ideas that found expression in them [but is, rather,] a social reality, a configuration of agents and practices that converge in the production, marketing, and publicisation of an idiom, a shareable language in the family of twentieth-century tongues' (4–5).

While acknowledging Rainey's contribution to the field of modernist publishing, Peter D. McDonald takes issue with *Institutions*' failure to consider the late Victorian period. McDonald believes that Rainey overstates his case when he describes as quintessentially modernist the 'tactical retreat into a divided world of patronage, collecting, speculation, and investment' (Rainey 5). In an essay mostly focused on Rainey's book, McDonald groups the Hogarth Press with little magazines, such as the *Dial* and *Rhythm*, and small presses, such as Sylvia Beach's Shakespeare & Company. He acknowledges that these are modernist publishing venues 'outside or on the margins of the market economy' that 'made the modernist movement viable by providing (temporary) refuge from censorship; by creating a space relatively free from the various constraints of large-scale commercial publishing; and by becoming centres of association, cultural solidarity, and self-promotion' ('Modernist Publishing' 228). However, he counters Rainey's claim about retreat when he emphasises that while small and exclusive, the Hogarth Press, like contemporary presses Elkin Mathews, John Lane and Faber, was not a coterie or private press working apart from the commercial marketplace (229). The essays in this collection confirm McDonald's broader characterisation as they emphasise the eclectic work and the variety of authors published by the Woolfs. In their early edited collection *Marketing Modernisms*, Kevin Dettmar and Ian Watt advocate a more inclusive definition of modernism via a study of the marketing of modernism with a set of essays that 'reconsider the critically suppressed relationship between canonical modernists and the commercial marketplace, and . . . provide a metacommentary on other exclusionary and political effects devolving from such a pristine conception of modernist poetics, its dense and mysterious "purity" ' (3). The essays in this volume similarly deploy the study of networks to problematise the parameters of conventional definitions of modernism.

A number of critics have also found troubling what McDonald calls Rainey's 'hierarchical division of labour', where '[r]eading is for critics and theorists' and 'the study of publishing provenance is for bibliographers, scholarly editors, and cultural historians' ('Modernist Publishing' 230), summed up in Rainey's bold claim that 'the best reading of a work may, on some occasions, be one that does not read it at all' (Rainey 106), this more diplomatically reformulated by Aaron Jaffe as one that 'read[s] other things and interpret[s] by other means' (6). While several of the essays in this volume do focus exclusively on the material conditions of the work, most combine an exploration of the text's production and consumption with a close reading, especially important due to the obscurity of some of the material dealt with here. In his own *British Literary Culture and Publishing Practice 1880–1914* (1997), covering the thirty years preceding Rainey's period, McDonald uses Darnton's work on 'communications circuits' and Pierre Bourdieu's work on the literary field to frame his own discussion of the early publishing careers of Conrad, Bennett and Conan Doyle and the transition of literary culture to greater commercialism in the period 1890–1914. McDonald acknowledges the value of Darnton's 'holistic view of the book as a means of communication', but finds his more functionalist approach limiting (Darnton qtd in McDonald, *Literary Culture* 11). (Darnton's theory takes into consideration, for example, how agents function in the circuit, but not 'their status in the intricately structured field' (McDonald, *Literary Culture* 11)). McDonald finds in Bourdieu a 'satisfyingly inclusive methodological framework which embraces, and even transcends, many traditional divisions within cultural and literary studies' as it weds ' "internalist" modes of reading' 'focus[ed] on textuality *per se*' with ' "externalist" modes, which [when exercised alone] threaten to dissolve the text into its non-discursive context' (172). McDonald's approach anticipates that of many of the essays in this volume.

A growing subfield within the area of modernist publishing is that of the modernist magazine. Spurred, in part, by the availability of new digital resources offering full-text versions of the magazines, including front and back material traditionally excised from bound library editions (see Latham & Scholes), scholars have moved away from the 'practices of strip-mining' modernist magazines for articles by or about the best-known names of modernism, or treating them 'simply as useful anthologies of modernist material', and have begun considering individual magazines in their own right (Churchill & McKible 4, xv). Among the first books to take up this approach are Morrison's *The Public Face of Modernism* and Paul Peppis' *Literature, Politics and the English Avant-Garde*; subsequent titles include Jason Harding's book length study of the *Criterion*, Adam McKible's look at the Russian Revolution in a series of New York-based little magazines, and Suzanne Churchill's study of Alfred Kreymborg's *Others*.

Focus on the magazine itself has meant increased attention to the lesser-known names and ideas of modernism and early twentieth-century literature and culture, to what John Sutherland calls the 'human infrastructure' in terms of his study of Victorian writers (152), Harding, in his work on the *Criterion*, the 'undergrowth' of the periodical (5), and Jaffe 'upstream' and 'downstream' production, the work traditionally not 'on display in modernism's canonical *masterpieces*' (88–93, 96–7). The pressure on the parameters of conventional definitions of 'modernism' that has resulted from this contextual look at early twentieth-century culture demonstrates the degree to which the growing field of modernist magazines represents 'a pressing challenge to existing paradigms for the investigation of . . . modern cultures' (Latham & Scholes 517). Thus, in her study of *Others*, Churchill argues that to return to the magazine itself (even the 'drivel') 'enables us to recover the range of modernist poetry: the intermixing of high and low, serious and absurd, breathtaking and banal' and that '[l]ittle magazines like *Others* provide a record of the undecided, heterodox character of the avant-garde before it was simultaneously reduced to and aggrandized as "Modernism"' (8).

This collection makes a similar claim for the modernist small press.[17] It argues that if we consider presses as 'social forums for writers of different genders, races and nationalities', as 'loci of identification and difference', they become spaces in which scholars are able 'to recover lines of connection, influence, conflict, and resistance that entangle the many strands of modernism' (Churchill & McKible 4). Modernist small presses were places where established authors encountered first-time authors and where old ideas met new. Like magazines of the period they 'belonged to a nexus out of which an ongoing campaign for artistic, intellectual, and broadly political values were launched and launched again' (Brooker & Thacker 3). Because the small presses were spaces somewhat free from the constraints of commercial publishing, such as censorship and financial success, like the modernist periodical, they offered potential for innovation and experimentation during the early twentieth century. With a mandate to publish 'young, unknown writers whose work might not attract the publishing establishment' (Leonard

Woolf, *Downhill* 130), the Woolfs were exemplary in their effort to break new ground, their list, as the essays in this collection demonstrate, highlighting the impossibility of 'mak[ing] the many Modernisms into one thing' (Levenson 7). At just over four hundred and fifty titles between 1917 and 1941, the Woolfs' list approximates a periodical in a run of, say, thirty issues, fifteen pieces per issue. In this regard the Hogarth Press represents an excellent test case for such a network approach.

While J. H. Willis' history of the Hogarth Press (1992), the only book-length study of the Press to date, is comprehensive in its assessment of the Woolfs' role in the building of their publishing operation, it mostly leaves out the complex and fascinating histories of the diverse network of authors, artists and workers involved with the Woolfs and the work that they produced.[18] Taking their lead from recent work on the 'European dimensions' of the Hogarth Press and on Russian translations (Marcus and Clarke & Marcus), on Hogarth Press novelists C. H. B. Kitchin and John Hampson (Gillespie and Southworth, respectively) and on Hogarth Press manager Norah Nichols (Staveley), these essays shift attention away from the better-known names and titles, the Nobel prize winners, Freud and the Woolfs, for example, onto the lesser-known and often unexpected. As they open the Press out onto the larger scene of writing, these essays trouble not only our understanding of Leonard and Virginia Woolf's role in the making of early twentieth-century literature and culture, but also call into question a series of other commonly held beliefs about modernism and the avant-garde. In this way the essays in this volume answer Michael Levenson's call for 'richer, thicker' accounts of modernism as they re-evaluate the scene of writing and of publishing one hundred years on, on the eve of the centenary of the founding of the Hogarth Press in 2017 (1).

What comes into better focus with a look at the lesser-known authors and artists published by the Press is the degree to which experiment, risk, idiosyncrasy, hybridity and 'heterogeneity', as Laura Marcus has described it, were keywords for the Press, rather than the ease and comfort so often celebrated in terms of Virginia Woolf's experience publishing her own work at her own press (Marcus, 'Virginia Woolf and the Hogarth Press' 128, 129). Collaboration and reciprocity were also indispensable to the unique personality and the success of the Press. Thus, the contributions to this volume cover the Woolfs' commitment to young, first-time authors (Young, Hussey, Southworth), their efforts to bring working-class voices to middle-class readers (Southworth) and to entertain unconventional treatments in conventional publishing categories, such as religion and poetry (Gillespie, Hussey). They document the Woolfs' provision of 'an alternative publishing arena' for middlebrow women writers (Sullivan) and a principle venue for others (Barkway, Hussey). They see the Woolfs engaged with the marketplace and questions of (visual) art and commerce (Barkway, Willson Gordon, Southworth), and they uncover the Woolfs' commitment to radical politics (Mills) and to anti-colonial sentiment (Snaith), their contributions to international modernism (Mills, Young, Snaith) and their work at the edge of empire, both domestic and international (Southworth, Snaith). These essays reintroduce to the history of the Press little-studied figures, such as American artist E. McKnight Kauffer, child poet Joan Easdale, socialist factory worker and conscientious objector R. M. Fox and Welsh collier poet Huw Menai, and they cast well-known individuals in less familiar roles: Classics scholar Jane Harrison and poet Hope Mirrlees as Russian translators, Indian writer Mulk Raj Anand as press worker, middlebrows Rose Macaulay and E. M. Delafield as highbrows, poet William Plomer as modernist novelist and Virginia Woolf's friend and lover Vita Sackville-West as professional client, for example. In this way, the Press becomes more than the 'incidental location of a canonical text's original publication', and instead a lively counterpublic sphere peopled by a network of innovators (Churchill & McKible 9).

This set of chapters is unified by its attention to the life cycle or the networks of production, creative and commercial, of Press publications. This includes a concern for the networks of actors and ideas, understood as webs of ties, links or connections that grew up at and around the Press, with the Press functioning as a hub of sorts. Examples include social networks of like-minded writers, networks of writers of a similar class, political leaning or cultural disposition who might not necessarily have been tied socially, publishing or periodical networks and networks of texts on similar topics or ideas. Most of the essays in this volume entertain questions about how the Woolfs shaped Press publications. Most also speculate about the impact of Press publications on both Leonard and Virginia Woolf's own writing. In this sense they record at once 'a voyaging in' and 'a voyaging out' of ideas. Thus, Virginia Woolf does not sit at the centre of this volume in her capacity as canonical modernist. Instead what we see is a network of authors and artists challenging or disrupting the exclusiveness often associated with the Press, authors, such as C. L. R. James and Mulk Raj Anand for example, who sought at the Press 'non-conventional sites of highbrowism' (see Snaith in this volume).

A focus on networks suggests itself as a particularly appropriate approach in terms of the recuperative effort, a return to the untold stories of the lesser-known authors, artists and workers of the Hogarth

Press, being undertaken in this volume. Network study emphasises dynamism and reciprocity; it undoes the myth of the individual artist working alone as do Bruno Latour and Michel Callon's Actor Network Theory and the broader field of social network analysis with its focus on 'actors and their actions . . . as interdependent rather than independent, autonomous units' (Wasserman & Faust 4). As prior studies suggest, the network constitutes an extremely useful tool or metaphor in terms of looking at traditionally marginalised groups, such as women writers and colonial writers. Examples include Bonnie Kime Scott's 'Tangled Mesh of Modernists', Susan Stanford Friedman's 'geographics', Marina Camboni's 'networking women', Jaffe's 'promotional networking' and Simon Gikandi's description of 'the relationship between the institution of modernism and these other [non-western] cultural spaces' as 'dynamic [and] dialectical' (Gikandi 420). Network study underscores the collaborative nature of modernism, ground covered by the large and invaluable body of historical work on modernist coteries, salons, movements and institutions, such as bookstores and publishing houses, and on texts such as Ezra Pound's *Cantos* and Eliot's *The Waste Land*. As it reintroduces lesser studied figures into the story of modernism, network study supports Jaffe's contention that 'modernist cultural formations are predicated on dependency', and that 'the most celebrated modernist work is leveraged on the less esteemed work of financing, publishing, and publicity' (96).[19]

The essays in this collection are divided into three sections; however, reflecting the collaborative quality of the work undertaken at the Press, several different configurations suggest themselves in terms of grouping these chapters. In the opening section, 'Class and Culture', Mark Hussey, Melissa Sullivan and Diane F. Gillespie counter conceptions of the Woolfs' and the Hogarth Press' highbrow cultural and class biases with studies that uncover their involvement with networks of middlebrow writers and readers and their engagement in debates over mainstream cultural issues. Hussey documents Virginia Woolf's and the Hogarth Press' sponsorship of the unconventional writing of child poet Joan Easdale in the face of opposition from press manager and Auden generation poet and publisher John Lehmann. Hussey pits a network that includes Easdale, Naomi Mitchison, Stevie Smith and Virginia Woolf herself, in her capacity as Easdale mentor, against that of 'W. H. Day Spender'. He moves beyond an analysis of the difficult alliance of Lehmann and the Woolfs, in particular Virginia, by interrogating the perspective of each one on modern poetry, using Lehmann's unpublished diaries and letters and Woolf's lesser-read writings on poetry. By revealing the story behind Easdale's appearance at the Hogarth Press,

Hussey connects her work with what we now understand to be 'thirties poetry'. In so doing, he makes a case for the seriousness of Easdale's contribution to the contemporary poetry scene and demonstrates how the Hogarth Press represented an important site of encounter for a variety of schools of poetry in the 1920s and 30s. As does Hussey, Sullivan locates the Hogarth Press in the broader landscape of early twentieth-century women's writing; like Hussey, she shows the degree to which the Press' circles intersected with other circles conventionally considered outside its purview. Sullivan's chapter suggests that the Woolfs broke with mainstream publishing practices as they provided a venue for the more strictly academic work of middlebrow women writers Rose Macaulay and E. M. Delafield. In this way, she argues, the Press enabled Delafield and Macaulay, *and* the Woolfs, to challenge entrenched notions about class and culture as the Press acted as an in-between space or 'contact zone', where the Woolfs played with their own prejudices and preconceptions as well as those of the general reading public. In the last chapter in this section, Gillespie charts the Hogarth Press' highly varied and unconventional publications in the category of religion, this a good example of the way in which the Woolfs intervened, often in unexpected ways, in public debate on social issues of the day. Gillespie demonstrates how material came to the Woolfs in the 1920s via both social networks (Logan Pearsall Smith's satirical and whimsical *New Testament Stories*) and periodical networks (Braithwaite's write-up of the results of a survey initiated by Leonard Woolf in the pages of the *Nation*). The addition to the Press' 'religion' texts in the 1930s of semi-strong tie Rose Macaulay's contribution to the Lectures on Literature series (in an analysis which supplements Sullivan's discussion of Macaulay's involvement with the Press and reminds us of the different hats individuals wore at the Press) and socially not connected, but well qualified, churchman J. C. Hardwick's to the Letters series, suggests a strengthening of the Woolfs' networks and a willingness to entertain an ever broader range of ideas. The degree to which the Woolfs provided a forum for ideas in the field of religion often antithetical to their own supports the claim that the Press functioned as a vibrant, dialogic space or network. All of the chapters in this section see the Press not as a closed elitist institution, but as a place where class bias and cultural norms are continually interrogated.

In 'Global Bloomsbury', Anna Snaith, John K. Young and Jean Mills look at the Woolfs' engagement in international networks, in India, the Caribbean, Africa and Russia, via their work at the Press. Insider-outsiders in their capacity as colonial subjects, but both also recipients of a solid British education and, at least initially, anxious to experience the magic of the metropolis, West Indian C. L. R. James and Indian Mulk Raj Anand's accounts of their experiences in Bloomsbury and their involvement with the Hogarth Press and Bloomsbury networks 'typify', for Snaith, 'the conflicted yet transformative exchanges which occurred between colonial and British writers in modernist London'. James' pamphlet on self rule in the West Indies came to the Press, Snaith speculates, via the Woolfs' friend, himself a Hogarth Press author, Lord Sydney Haldane Olivier; Anand came to the Press as a proof-corrector, via University College London and via the BBC in the late 1920s, returning as an author in John Lehmann's *New Writing* journal in the late 1930s. Snaith shows how 'the physical presence of colonial intellectuals, interacting in a wide variety of literary and political networks [including those represented by the Hogarth Press] invariably altered the trajectory of their activism[,] their fictional and non-fictional writing.' She demonstrates, in turn, how the Woolfs', Bloomsbury's and London's imperialism changed in response to the colonial intellectuals' presence, highlighting 'the creative and critical conjunctions of modernism and empire'. Young's chapter explores the Hogarth Press' transnational status with an analysis of their six-year-long professional relationship with William Plomer. Young argues for the somewhat neglected Plomer as a 'noteworthy figure in new histories of modernism for his role in the international scope of that movement'. He shows how the launch and promotion of Plomer's career by the Woolfs implicates the Press in this same movement. He suggests that Plomer's work 'in its Hogarth Press phase' parallels the Press' 'transition from a coterie Bloomsbury handpress to a proper publishing business' and shows how his South African fictions suggest a 'Bloomsbury sensibility . . . willing to question racial and sexual foundations of empire'. Young also demonstrates how Plomer's more mainstream, and highly lucrative, *The Case is Altered* reflects the Woolfs' efforts in the 1930s 'to locate themselves inside the mainstream of the literary market', generating necessary profits to finance the 'more challenging texts' appearing at the Press in the 1930s. Mills uses the 1924 publication of a translation of the first Russian autobiography, *Avvakum*, a text neglected in accounts of the Hogarth Press' engagement with Russian literature and culture (often centred around their best known Russian connection, co-translator and Russian teacher Ukrainian S. S. Koteliansky), to illustrate the Woolfs' commitment to radical left-wing politics and to underscore the 'internationalist outlook' of the Press. Mills' chapter maps the connections between the network of actors involved in the Hogarth Press publication of the book, which found its way to the Press via Virginia Woolf's mentor, the classicist Jane Harrison, who co-translated the book with her lover,

Hogarth Press poet Hope Mirrlees, and via the Woolfs' lesser-known Russian connection D. S. Mirsky, author of *Avvakum*'s preface. These three chapters suggest the range of international collaboration enjoyed by the Press: this emphasised by the fact that there is surprisingly little overlap in terms of networks of actors in each of the case studies. At the same time, they highlight the degree to which the international contributions are criss-crossed by other issues and are, in this way, brought into dialogue with some of the other essays in the collection, in terms, for example, of Plomer's homosexuality, James' British provincial connections, and the mix of personal and professional behind the publication of *Avvakum*.

In the final section of the collection, entitled 'Marketing Other Modernisms', Elizabeth Willson Gordon, Helen Southworth and Stephen Barkway explore the Woolfs' engagement in the early twentieth-century book market via their exploitation of visual artists, and their promotion of working-class writers and of best-seller Vita Sackville-West. Willson Gordon uses the career of Hogarth Press cover and logo designer, American artist E. McKnight Kauffer, his experience in the world of book production and his connections with Bloomsbury figures such as Roger Fry, to frame a discussion of Hogarth Press publicity practices. Willson Gordon argues that by adding to their list Kauffer, whose work she characterises as appropriate to the Hogarth Press in its 'useful ambivalence', 'productively engaged with art and commerce, books and market', 'the Press added a different yet compatible discourse about artistic purpose and productions'. Southworth considers the Woolfs' engagement with working-class writers and working-class topics in both the society and politics and the fiction categories. She identifies a growing Hogarth Press network in the 1930s and an effort at inclusiveness, of workers' perspectives and of northern views, on the society/politics side. Alongside this, she charts a complex set of negotiations on the fiction and poetry side between writers, such as Welsh poet Huw Menai and Birmingham Group novelist John Hampson, who wanted to downplay their working-class roots and publishers who saw profit in promoting them. Using previously unpublished letters, Barkway closes the volume with a detailed analysis of Vita Sackville-West's largely unexplored business relationship with the Woolfs as publishers. Barkway uses the Woolfs' astute negotiations with their friend Sackville-West, among the Press' most prolific and important writers in terms of sales, publishing sixteen titles between 1924 and 1941, to show their investment in best-selling fiction and their understanding of the commercial advantages of middlebrow institutions like the British Book Society and of limited editions. Fitting as the closing essay of the volume, Barkway challenges readings of the Hogarth Press as 'altruistic' and 'pure' in its motives and as uninterested in 'the book's physicality'. As do all of the essays in this volume, Barkway's shows the Woolfs networked into and knowledgeable about contemporary fields of writing and book production.

Far from exhaustive, this study of just a handful of names and titles nevertheless gives a good sense of the ways in which the Hogarth Press, as an idea, a physical institution and a site of cultural capital, became a node that linked together writers as disparate as Anand, Easdale, Menai and Sackville-West with emergent cultural formations like the middle-brow and globalism. These intersections are important, this collection suggests, because they allow one to think about cultural production as a collaborative process, outside the limits of any given text and beyond the control of any single agent. Functioning as a starting point, these essays aim to encourage further work on the Hogarth Press and to suggest new directions in the neglected field of modernist presses.

Notes

1. A hippogriff is part horse, part griffin (see Ariosto Canto IV, XIX).
2. Willis describes the shift as one from a private press to a small publishing house (3).
3. John Xiros Cooper suggests that 'Bloomsbury was able to maintain, especially early on, a sense of "family" solidarity within an English context but also effect with the passage of time the inevitable transition to a group defined less and less by social and family relations and more and more by common purposes, shared antipathies, artistic pursuits, and styles' (246). In his *The Intellectual Life of the British Working Classes*, Jonathan Rose attacks the Woolfs for their elitism. Raymond Williams' early essay 'The Bloomsbury Fraction' offers a more balanced view.
4. Aaron Jaffe cites Stephen Spender: ' "Other than Eliot the only two older writers who made themselves *present* to contemporaries twenty years younger were E. M. Forster and Virginia Woolf" ' (15).
5. See Willis (64–6) or Quentin Bell (86–7) for an alternative account of these events.
6. Lehmann writes that his interest in printing began with William Morris (106). Wicke contrasts Morris with Bloomsbury: whereas Morris 'resolutely opposed the capitalist mass production and structures of social living . . . Bloomsbury was not so flagrantly antitechnological nor nostalgic for what amounted to the craft production techniques of a far distant Merrie Olde England' (112). Willis notes the Stephen family's general disinterest in Morris (6–7).
7. See Rosenbaum for a discussion of the connection between the Omega Workshops and the Hogarth Press (14–17).
8. The Nonesuch Press was set up in 1923 by Sir Francis Meynell. Ties with

Nonesuch include David Garnett, and designers E. McKnight Kauffer and Duncan Grant.

9. In a similar fashion to the Woolfs, Nancy Cunard began printing alone (then with Henry Crowther and a printer) in a stable with 'an [almost 200-year-old] Belgian Mathieu press' purchased from Bill Bird after the closure of his Three Mountains Press. Like the Woolfs, who had published Cunard's poem 'Parallax' in 1925 and who famously discouraged Cunard's undertaking, telling her ' "your hands will always be covered with ink!" ' (8), her aim in establishing the Hours Press was to make available work that might otherwise not find a publisher.

10. See Ford, and Morrisson's 'Modernist Publishing' for a list of small presses.

11. Sadleir contributed an essay to *Books and the Public* (Hogarth Press, 1927).

12. Highlighting the difference in output of the Hogarth Press and competitor operations, while in 1926, Cape's sales, according to Rose, 'exceeded fifty thousand pounds' (53) the Woolf's net profit, according to Willis, amounted to just £53 18s 2½d (Appendix B).

13. See Rosenbaum for a discussion of how Duckworth's enterprise 'inspired' the Woolfs (13).

14. Edward Garnett stands out as one of the few commercial press editors to have enjoyed a freedom comparable to that of the Woolfs. Garnett began his career with Duckworth, where he recommended Woolf's *The Voyage Out*, before moving to Bodley Head with John Lane and then Cape. Garnett's nurturing of talent resembles that undertaken by the Woolfs. Rose describes Garnett's cultivation of H. E. Bates, getting his stories published, inviting him to his house and finding him work.

15. See Virginia Woolf on Tidmarsh Press (*D2* 224).

16. Other turning points include the 1924 move to Tavistock Square or the Woolfs' engagement of Francis Meynell's Pelican Press in 1920 to print Pearsall Smith and Gorky, marking the Press' move from 'a hobby to a commercial publisher' (Gaither 158). Marcus argues that this 'mark[s] the moment at which the Press became a small publishing house' ('Virginia Woolf and the Hogarth Press' 126). Rosenbaum singles out 1923 when the Woolfs gave up their subscription system. At this point the Woolfs became, according to Leonard, 'more or less ordinary publishers selling our books mainly to booksellers at the usual discount' (qtd in Rosenbaum 7).

17. Existing studies of presses tend to focus on press operators and are largely biographical. Titles include first-hand accounts such as Nancy Cunard's *These were The Hours* (Southern Illinois University Press, 1969), Caresse Crosby's *The Passionate Years* (Dial, 1953), and Sylvia Beach's *Shakespeare and Company* (Plantin, [1959] 1987). Histories of other small presses include Hugh Ford's *Published in Paris* (Pushcart, 1975), Geoffery Wolff's *Black Sun* on the Crosbys (Vintage, 1976), Gifford Lewis' *The Yeats Sisters and the Cuala* (Irish Academic Press, 1994), *Dear Miss Weaver* by Jane Lidderdale and Mary Nicholson (Viking, 1970) and *Harold Monro and the Poetry Bookshop* by Joy Grant (University of California Press, 1967). On larger presses of the period see *William Heinemann: A Memoir* by Frederic Whyte (Doubleday, 1929), *Edward Garnett: A Life in Literature* by George Jefferson (Cape, 1982), Ruth Dudley Edwards' *Victor Gollancz: Biography* (Gollancz, 1987) and John Attenborough's *A Living*

Memory: Hodder and Stoughton Publishers (Hodder and Stoughton, 1978). James G. Nelson's book on Bodley Head, *The Early Nineties* (Harvard, 1971), and its companion study on Elkin Mathews (Wisconsin University Press, 1989), are broader than the strictly biographical study. Volumes 105 and 106 in the *Dictionary of Literary Biography* on British publishing houses are immensely useful. Recent press-related work includes Mary Ann Gillies' *The Professional Literary Agent in Britain, 1880–1920* (Toronto, 2007).

18. Other shorter studies of the Hogarth Press include David Porter's ' "We All Sit on the Edge of Stools and Crack Jokes": Virginia Woolf and the Hogarth Press' in *Book Illustrated: Text, Image and Culture* (Oak Knoll, 2000) and his *Virginia Woolf and the Hogarth Press 'Riding a Great Horse'* (Bloomsbury Heritage, 2004). Exhibition catalogues include 'Seventy Years at the Hogarth Press', Hugh Morris Library Special Collection Department, University of Delaware (1987); 'Virginia Woolf and the Hogarth Press: from the Collection of William Beekman exhibited at the Grolier Club, New York', (2004); and Elizabeth Willson Gordon's *Woolf's-head Publishing: The Highlights and New Lights of the Hogarth Press*, Bruce Peel Special Collections Library, University of Alberta (2009). See also Laura Marcus, S. P. Rosenbaum, and Trevor Tolley's work on John Lehmann.

19. Other network studies include Lucy McDiarmid's 'A Box for Wilfrid Blunt' *PMLA*, 120.1, 2005: 163–180, Catherine Clay's *British Women Writers 1914–1945: Professional Work and Friendship*, Ashgate, 2006 and Georgina Taylor's *H.D. and the Public Sphere of Modernist Women Writers 1913–1946: Talking Women*, Oxford University Press, 2001.

Works cited

Ariosto, Ludovico. *Orlando Furioso*. Trans. Barbara Reynolds. London: Penguin, 1975.

Bell, Quentin. *Virginia Woolf: A Biography*. New York: Harcourt Brace Jovanovich, 1972.

Blair, Sara. 'Local Modernity, Global Modernism: Bloomsbury and the Places of the Literary'. *ELH* 71.3, 2004: 813–38.

Bornstein, George. *Material Modernism: The Politics of the Page*. Cambridge: Cambridge University Press, 2001.

Bourdieu, Pierre. *The Field of Cultural Production: Essays on Art and Literature*. Ed. Randal Johnson. New York: Columbia University Press, 1993.

Brooker, Peter and Andrew Thacker, eds. *The Oxford Critical and Cultural History of Modernist Magazines: Volume I: Britain and Ireland 1880–1955*. Oxford: Oxford University Press, 2009.

Camboni, Marina, ed. *Networking Women: Subjects, Places, Links, Europe-America*. Rome: Edizioni di Storia e Letteratura, 2004.

Cave, Roderick. *The Private Press*. New York: Bowker, 1983.

Caws, Mary Ann and Sarah Bird. *Bloomsbury and France: Art and Friends*. Oxford; New York: Oxford University Press, 2000.

Chapman, Wayne and Manson, Janet M. *Women in the Milieu of Leonard and Virginia Woolf*. New York: Pace University Press, 1998.

Churchill, Suzanne. *The Little Magazine Others and the Renovation of Modern American Poetry*. Aldershot; Burlington: Ashgate, 2006.

—and Adam McKible, eds. *Little Magazines and Modernism: New Approaches*. Aldershot: Ashgate, 2007.

Clarke, Stuart and Laura Marcus, eds and Intro. *Translations from the Russian. By Virginia Woolf and S. S. Koteliansky*. London: Virginia Woolf Society of Great Britain, 2006.

Collins, Judith. *The Omega Workshops*. Chicago: University of Chicago Press, 1984.

Cooney, Sondra Miley. 'Constable and Company'. *British Literary Publishing Houses 1881–1965. Dictionary of Literary Biography*. Vol. 112. Detroit: Gale, 1991: 66–70.

Cooper, John Xiros. *Modernism and the Culture of Market Society*. Cambridge: Cambridge University Press, 2004.

Cunard, Nancy. *These Were the Hours*. Carbondale: Southern Illinois University Press, 1969.

Darnton, Robert. *The Kiss of Lamourette: Reflections in Cultural History*. New York: Norton, 1990.

Daugherty, Beth Rigel, ed. *Woolf Studies Annual*. Vol. 12. New York: Pace University Press, 2006.

Dennison, Sally. *[Alternative] Literary Publishing*. Iowa City: University of Iowa Press, 1984.

Dettmar, Kevin and Ian Watt, eds. *Marketing Modernism: Self-Promotion, Canonization, Rereading*. Ann Arbor: University of Michigan Press, 1996.

Ford, Hugh. *Published in Paris*. New York: Pushcart, 1975.

Fritschner, Linda Marie. 'William Heinemann Limited'. *British Literary Publishing Houses 1881–1965. Dictionary of Literary Biography*. Vol. 112. Detroit: Gale, 1991: 151–7.

Gaither, Mary. 'The Hogarth Press'. *British Literary Publishing Houses 1881–1965. Dictionary of Literary Biography*. Vol. 112. Detroit: Gale, 1991: 157–62.

Gikandi, Simon. 'Preface: Modernism in the World'. *Modernism/modernity*. 13.3, 2006: 419–24.

Gillespie, Diane F. 'Virginia Woolf, The Hogarth Press, and the Detective Novel'. *South Carolina Review* 35.2, 2003: 36–48.

Harding, Jason. *The Criterion: Cultural Politics and Periodical Networks in Inter-War Britain*. Oxford: Oxford University Press, 2002.

Jaffe, Aaron. *Modernism and the Culture of Celebrity*. Cambridge: Cambridge University Press, 2005.

Latham, Sean and Robert Scholes. 'The Rise of Periodical Studies'. *PMLA* 121.2, 2006: 517–31.

Laurence, Patricia. *Lily Briscoe's Chinese Eyes: Bloomsbury, Modernism and China*. Columbia: University of South Carolina Press, 2003.

Lehmann, John. *In My Own Time: Memoirs of a Literary Life*. Boston: Little, Brown, 1969.

Levenson, Michael. 'Introduction'. *The Cambridge Companion to Modernism*. Cambridge: Cambridge University Press, 1999: 1–8.

McDonald, Peter D. *British Literary Culture and Publishing Practice 1880–1914*. Cambridge: Cambridge University Press, 1997.

—. 'Modernist Publishing: "Nomads and mapmakers."' In David Bradshaw, ed. *A Concise Companion to Modernism*. Oxford: Blackwell Publishing, 2003: 221–42.

McKenzie, D. F. *Bibliography and the Sociology of Texts*. Cambridge: Cambridge University Press, 1999.

McKible, Adam. *The Space and Place of Modernism: The Russian Revolution, Little Magazines and New York*. New York: Routledge, 2002.

Marcus, Laura. 'The European Dimensions of the Hogarth Press'. In Mary Ann Caws and Nicola Luckhurst, eds. *The Reception of Virginia Woolf in Europe*. London and New York: Continuum, 2002: 328–56.

—. 'Virginia Woolf and the Hogarth Press'. In Ian Willison, Warwick Gould and Warren Chernaik, eds. *Modernist Writers and the Marketplace*. New York: St. Martin's Press, 1996: 124–50.

Morrisson, Mark S. 'Modernist Publishing'. In David Bradshaw and Kevin Dettmar, eds. *A Companion to Modernist Literature and Culture*. London: Blackwell, 2006: 133–42.

—. *The Public Face of Modernism: Little Magazines, Audiences, and Reception 1905–1920*. Madison: University of Wisconsin Press, 2001.

Naylor, Gillian. *The Arts And Crafts Movement: A Study of its Sources, Ideas and Influence on Design Theory*. Cambridge: MIT Press, 1971.

Oldfield, Sybil. *Afterwords*. New Brunswick: Rutgers, 2005.

Peppis, Paul. *Literature, Politics and the English Avant Garde*. Cambridge: Cambridge University Press, 2000.

Ransom, Will. *Private Presses and their Books*. New York: Bowker, 1929.

Rainey, Lawrence. *Institutions of Modernism: Literary Elites and Public Culture*. New Haven: Yale University Press, 1998.

Rose, Jonathan. *The Intellectual Lives of the British Working Classes*. New Haven: Yale University Press, 2001.

—. 'Jonathan Cape Ltd'. *British Literary Publishing Houses 1881–1965*. *Dictionary of Literary Biography*. Vol. 112. Detroit: Gale, 1991: 50–65.

Rosenbaum, S. P. 'Leonard and Virginia Woolf at the Hogarth Press'. Austin: Harry Ransom Center, 1995.

Scott, Bonnie Kime, ed. *The Gender of Modernism: A Critical Anthology*. Bloomington: Indiana University Press, 1990.

Snaith, Anna. 'Wide Circles: The *Three Guineas* Letters'. *Woolf Studies Annual*. Vol. 6. New York: Pace University Press, 2000.

Southworth, Helen. ' "Outside the magic (and tyrannical) triangle of London-Oxford-Cambridge": John Hampson, the Woolfs and the Hogarth Press'. *Woolfian Boundaries: Selected Papers from the Sixteenth Annual Woolf Conference*. Ed. Anna Burrells et al. Clemson: Clemson University Press, 2007: 43–50.

Spotts, Frederic, ed. *Letters of Leonard Woolf*. San Diego: Harcourt Brace Jovanovich, 1989.

Stanford Friedman, Susan. *Mappings: Feminism and the Cultural Geographies of Encounter*. Princeton: Princeton University Press, 1998.

Staveley, Alice. 'Marketing Virginia Woolf: Women, War and Public Relations in *Three Guineas*'. *Book History* 12, 2009: 295–339.

Sutherland, John. *Victorian Fiction: Writers, Publishers, Readers*. New York: St Martin's Press, 1995.

Tolley, Trevor, ed. *John Lehmann: a Tribute*. Ottawa: Carleton University Press, 1987.

Wasserman, Stanley and Katherine Faust. *Social Network Analysis: Methods and Applications*. Cambridge: Cambridge University Press, 1994.

Wicke, Jennifer. 'Coterie Consumption'. In Kevin Dettmar and Ian Watt, eds. *Marketing Modernism: Self-Promotion, Canonization, Rereading*. Ann Arbor: University of Michigan Press, 1996: 109–32.

Williams, Raymond. 'The Bloomsbury Fraction'. *The Raymond Williams Reader*. London: Wiley-Blackwell, 2001: 229–48.

Willis, J. H. *Leonard and Virginia Woolf as Publishers: The Hogarth Press, 1917–41*. Charlottesville: University Press of Virginia, 1992.

Willison, Ian et al. *Modernist Writers and the Marketplace*. London: Macmillan, 1996.

Woolf, Leonard. *Beginning Again: An Autobiography of the Years 1911 to 1918*. New York: Harcourt Brace Jovanovich, 1967.

—. *Downhill All the Way: An Autobiography of the Years 1919 to 1939*. New York: Harcourt Brace Jovanovich, 1967.

—. and Virginia Woolf. 'Are too Many Books Written and Published?' *PMLA* 121.1, 2006: 235–44.

Woolf, Virginia. *The Diary of Virginia Woolf*. Ed. Anne Olivier Bell. 5 vols. New York: Harcourt Brace Jovanovich, 1978.

Woolmer, J. Howard, ed. *A Checklist of the Hogarth Press 1917–1946*. Revere: Woolmer/Brotherson, 1986.

Part One

Class and Culture

Chapter 1

'W. H. Day Spender' Had a Sister: Joan Adeney Easdale

Mark Hussey

> Let me imagine, since facts are so hard to come by, what would have happened had Shakespeare had a wonderfully gifted sister . . . For it needs little skill in psychology to be sure that a highly gifted girl who had tried to use her gift for poetry would have been so thwarted and hindered by other people, so tortured and pulled asunder by her own contrary instincts, that she must have lost her health and sanity to a certainty. . . . if we face the fact, for it is a fact, that there is no arm to cling to, but that we go alone and that our relation is to the world of reality and not only to the world of men and women, then the opportunity will come and the dead poet who was Shakespeare's sister will put on the body which she has so often laid down.
>
> *A Room of One's Own*

Travelling books for the Hogarth Press in October 1939, John Lehmann took the opportunity to have lunch in Cambridge with Nicholas Moore, the philosopher G. E. Moore's son. 'People of his age seem already to be saying no to the things we [?] wanted', Lehmann wrote in his diary that evening; 'They don't even seem to find "W.H. Day Spender" the rage any more. Shocking.'[1] Lehmann was in his second stint at the Hogarth Press, having walked out without a word in 1932; he had returned at the end of the 'Red Decade' of the 1930s. That W. H. Auden, Cecil Day Lewis and Stephen Spender had been 'the rage' was in large part due to Lehmann's efforts.

Virginia Woolf wrote to Vita Sackville-West on New Year's Day 1931 that 'a charming young man, John Lehmann, brother of Rosamund, wants to become our manager.' Though she was rather suspicious of 'charming young men who write poetry', she thought Lehmann might be just what she and Leonard needed to help with the increasing workload the Press imposed. For example, she continued to Vita, 'our spring season must be worked. Easdale, the 17 year old poetess, wants us to bring Dotty' – i.e., Dorothy Wellesley, sponsor of the Hogarth Living Poets series – 'to see her act a play in a shed in the garden' (*L4* 272).

Lehmann (1907–87) and Joan Adeney Easdale (1913–98) thus appear in the Woolfs' orbit at roughly the same time.

A Collection of Poems (written between the ages of 14 and 17) was published in February 1931 as number nineteen in the Hogarth Living Poets series. 'The girl poet is my discovery,' Woolf wrote in April to Hugh Walpole; 'She sent me piles of dirty copy books written in a scrawl without any spelling; but I was taken aback to find, as I thought some real merit' (*L4* 311). Despite Woolf's confidence in her discovery, subsequent critics have dismissed Easdale, apparently without having read her work. Historian of the Hogarth Press, J. H. Willis, pointed out that *A Collection of Poems* was already in production when Lehmann began work on 21 January 1931 and 'must have confounded Lehmann, a committed poet' (185). Others take a similar line: Hermione Lee finds the decision to publish Easdale 'peculiar' (606); Adrian Wright, in his biography of Lehmann, says: 'The first few months had Lehmann overseeing the publication of titles the Woolfs had accepted before his arrival, such as the flapper-poet Joan Easdale . . . (Lehmann was distinctly unconvinced)' (52). A reviewer of Tony Bradshaw's *The Bloomsbury Artists* in 1999 remarks of Easdale's work, 'As with any publishing house the Hogarth Press published some dross' (Rosenthal). Willis archly comments that perhaps it was the marvellous oddness of the poems that attracted Woolf to them, and wonders what 'regular Hogarth readers' thought. But, Willis says, 'No comments survive' (186).

Reviews do survive, however, and *A Collection* was well received by critics. *Bookman* named Easdale one of the five 'poets of the year' (qtd in Robertson 48). Woolf invariably referred to Easdale's youth whenever she mentioned her, and that fact was emphasised both by the *Collection*'s subtitle and by its arrangement of contents according to the year in which the poems were written. Nevertheless, reviewers were struck by the assurance and insight of the teenager.

In the *Saturday Review*, Geoffrey Grigson, the dogmatic editor of the poetry magazine *New Verse*, acknowledged that the poems proclaimed their author 'a girl of unusual ability', noting that Christina Rossetti and Abraham Cowley also had been successful poets in their youth. But the 'real surprise of these poems has to do not with adolescent precocity but with positive virtues.' Grigson quoted in full 'The Mad City', written when Easdale was 14, and singled out for praise 'Aunt Vera's Questions'. When Easdale submitted her work to the Press the poems were accompanied by her drawings, but it was decided not to include these in the book. Given how reminiscent her work often is of that of Stevie Smith, whose whimsical cartoons often accompany her poems, this is a loss.[2]

For Grigson, Easdale's 'notable gifts' included a 'rare objectivity . . .

an interest in character and states of mind, an unusual irony, and', he concluded, 'a power of sensitive word painting with a simple, unforced economy of words' that reminded him of Edith Sitwell 'with the glittering nonsense and affectation knocked out'. The comparison to Sitwell, whose *Poetry and Criticism* was published in the Hogarth Essays series in 1925, would be made at several points in Easdale's career.

In *The Spectator*, Richard Church, literary editor of the Independent Labour Party's *New Leader*, noted that in the opening poem of the *Collection*, 'Round the Room Walked the Duchess', Easdale showed that she had 'already discovered the drama of adult life'. Faced with this poem's 'terrifying' knowledge, Church wrote, 'the critic turns tail and runs, crying out over his shoulder to the publisher "Why hasn't Mrs. Virginia Woolf stepped in between with an ameliorating introduction?"' As an example of 'another bombshell into the adult world', Church quoted 'Two Talking', a poem he found 'reminiscent of the elliptical genius of Emily Dickinson'. Church was also reviewing a number of other new volumes of poetry, including works by Vita Sackville-West, Sylvia Lynd and Margaret Adamson, as well as another Hogarth publication, the *Anthology of Cambridge Women's Verse*, which he dismisses as having 'an atmosphere of arty-shops, of leaping sandalled into the dawn, and of a grudge against the world of men'. The Cambridge women come off poorly in his review in comparison with 'a genius like Joan Easdale' who can 'break through the clumsiness of inarticulate youth'. The *Times Literary Supplement* also quoted from 'Aunt Vera's Questions' and 'Two Talking', and described the poems as 'sharp and sometimes even harsh, seldom in the least imitative', expressing 'the pungent individuality of an unlearned mind' and observing the adult world with a disquieting detachment ('Youthful Poems').

Clearly, then, Easdale's first book received reviews that would thrill a publisher, contradicting the impression created by Willis, Lee and others that Woolf's judgement of poetry was eccentric, particularly in comparison with Lehmann's sound seriousness. Recovering the work of Joan Easdale prompts a revaluation of the canon of 1930s poetry, and suggests that the Hogarth Press poetry list reflects a willingness on the part of Leonard and Virginia Woolf to take risks on behalf of a writer who seemed out of step with the dominant mode of poetry at the time.

There was already a network of family and Bloomsbury connections between Woolf and the Easdales. Mrs Easdale's close companion, Mark Rutherford, a minor Victorian man of letters who used the pen name Hale White, had known Leslie and Julia Stephen, Woolf's parents (Woolf, *L5* 95). Joan married James Meadows Rendel, son of Lytton

Strachey's nephew, Richard Meadows, and Judy Marshall, the sister of Frances Partridge. Joan's uncle, Bernard Adeney, was, according to Woolf, a 'bad painter' (*L4* 379): a founding member of the London Artists' Association, he had shown in the Second Post-Impressionist Exhibition, of which Leonard Woolf was secretary, and worked with Roger Fry, Duncan Grant and Frederick Etchells on the Borough Polytechnic murals. He was married to Thérèse Lessore, who later married Walter Sickert. The publication of *A Collection* inaugurated a relationship between Woolf and the Easdale family that would last until Woolf's death in 1941 (Joan's mother, Gladys, continued to correspond with Leonard Woolf and with Vita Sackville-West into the 1960s). In July 1931 Woolf attended a concert at Wigmore Hall where Joan read five of her poems to the accompaniment of her brother Brian's music.[3] The *Times* found the 'recitation of five poems . . . for speaking voice with six instruments . . . a complete failure as the balance of tone was all wrong' ('Recitals'), but Woolf recorded no verdict. As Stephen Barkway has detailed, taking on Joan as her protégée meant that Woolf opened herself to the adoration of Mrs Easdale. Perhaps to diffuse its intensity, she planned to take Vita with her on a visit to the Easdales' home in the summer of 1931. Vita, however, had tonsillitis and therefore had to experience the afternoon vicariously through one of Woolf's inimitable letters (*L4* 379–80). Despite her sometimes cruel mocking of Gladys, Woolf clearly was struck by her daughter, as she wrote to Vita: 'Joan is the mystery—She looks like a chocolate box flapper, talks like one . . . and yet produces those strange poems' (*L4* 379).

Joan Easdale was not the kind of poet John Lehmann thought the Hogarth Press should be publishing. He told Leonard Woolf in a note at the end of April 1931 that he had written to Easdale 'suggesting she should wait until her new long poem is finished before submitting it to us. The book hasn't moved much, I'm afraid.'[4] He had come to the Hogarth Press on a mission to revitalise what he saw as the moribund state of poetry and to bring attention to exciting new poets who were not – in his opinion – widely enough known. In a long reflection in his diary in mid-November 1931 he urged himself to 'find new values':

> The poet must now look into the future, and help in the creation of the new world – we must either recreate or die . . . I am beginning to believe that the poet must be 'political' for a while – for his own salvation & the salvation of poetry – with exhortation, with pity, with irony, with satire, above all with vision, must throw himself into the battle . . .
> I will leave the old values, will take the train away, but will take Shakespeare across the frontier with me.[5]

Lehmann had enlisted Virginia Woolf in his mission, inviting her to discuss with him not only his own work, *A Garden Revisited*, published in the Hogarth Living Poets series that September, but also the work of his contemporaries Auden, Day Lewis and Spender. Woolf agreed that she must 'go into the question of poetry' (*L4* 383) and thought his idea of a 'letter to a young poet' 'most brilliant' (*L4* 381). Lehmann's influence on the Hogarth poetry list was felt almost at once with the publication in February 1932 of the landmark *New Signatures*, edited by Michael Roberts and including poems by Auden, Julian Bell, Day Lewis, Richard Eberhart, William Empson, Spender, A. S. J. Tessimond, William Plomer and Lehmann himself (see Lehmann, *Thrown* 17–20). In its introduction, Roberts sounded a note similar to that Woolf herself had sounded in 'Modern Novels' in 1919: 'new knowledge and new circumstances have compelled us to think and feel in ways not expressible in the old language at all' (Roberts 7). Discouraged by the dominance of science and technology, Roberts went on, the intellectual has become a 'detached and pessimistic observer of the democratic process' (9). It was time for the poet to assume the role of a leader. In *New Signatures*, its editor wrote, 'poetry is . . . turned to propaganda, but it is propaganda for a theory of life which may release the poet's energies for the writing of pure poetry, as well as provide him with standards which may make simple and direct satire possible again' (19). Julian Bell's long poem 'Arms and the Man' expressed what would become a familiar theme of young male intellectuals in the 1930s. Those who shrank 'from rough, tedious business', wrote Bell, to 'feebly twist the painted strings of art' would find that they 'share their gas and famine with mankind' (46).

In *A Letter to a Young Poet* (published first in June 1932 in the *Yale Review* and then in England in July as part of the Hogarth Letters series), Woolf seemed directly to take issue with Roberts' call for poets to be 'leaders':

> once you begin to take yourself seriously as a leader, or as a follower, as a modern or as a conservative, then you become a self-conscious, biting, and scratching little animal whose work is not of the slightest value or importance to anybody. (9)

In 'Poetry, Fiction and the Future' (1927), Woolf had adumbrated some of the ideas she would return to in the *Letter*, describing in the earlier article how poetry had failed to serve the needs of contemporary society: 'the lyric cry of ecstasy or despair' (429) is inadequate to modern experience, poetry has been 'frightened away' by the modern mind's openness to and interest in sordidness and ugliness (434). Prose, she wrote in 1927, has already 'taken over some of the duties which were once discharged by poetry' (434). She returned in the *Letter* to this theme of poetry as a medium ill equipped to convey life as it was now, something the novel could do with ease. Ordinary life, which she personifies in the *Letter* as 'Mrs. Gape', is apparently a 'hard and hostile object' upon which rhythm is smashed to pieces (12). Yet, when she turns to the work of young contemporary poets, she admits that 'the common objects of daily prose' (13) are to be found there. Quoting from Auden's 'Which of you waking early' (a poem 'on which Auden's second (and final) thoughts were that it was "pompous trash"' [Mendelson 141]), from Lehmann's 'To Penetrate that Room', Day Lewis' 'From Feathers to Iron XI' and from Spender's 'Never being, but always at the edge of Being', she notes how the young poet seems at pains to incorporate ugliness and the everyday, but that these qualities are at odds with the aesthetic satisfaction she looks for in poetry. Confronted by the jarring difficulty of writing poetry about Mrs Gape, Woolf argues, the poet has turned to writing about himself and 'is much less interested in what we have in common than in what he has apart' (18). The young poet seems to her 'shut . . . up in one room, alone, by yourself' (21).[6] Her advice to the young poet was to hold off on publishing so as to avoid worrying about what other people would say: 'publish nothing before you are thirty' (26).

The thirties literary scene was a 'youth boom' (Cunningham 107); many of those who came to prominence began their literary careers very young. Certainly Woolf herself had championed in Joan Easdale the poetry of someone well below the age of thirty, and in the month following the publication of *New Signatures*, the Hogarth Press issued Easdale's second volume of poetry, *Clemence and Clare*. Easdale was 18.

In *The Observer* in April 1932, the Irish poet Austin Clarke reviewed several new volumes of poetry including both *New Signatures* and *Clemence and Clare*. The poets of *New Signatures*, he wrote, 'are in revolt against the advanced modernists, who have got rid of definite articles, capital letters, and old-fashioned adjectives'; 'These poets have taken the troubles of the modern world upon their shoulders.' If this was to be the tenor of contemporary poetry, the fantastic world of Easdale's narratives would struggle to find an audience: 'Miss Joan Easdale', he wrote, 'lingers in a fairy-tale world of staid lovers, formal engagements, and tearful tiffs.' *The Poetry Review* quoted about thirty lines from the title poem and dismissed the rest as 'mostly too "imagist" to be impressive; they merely startle' (E. D. B.). Although the *Times Literary Supplement* did find an individuality similar to that noticed by reviewers of Easdale's first volume, its notice was lukewarm. The *TLS* did, however, single out the last poem, 'Revelation', as of particular interest ('Review').

Clemence and Clare's title poem, dedicated to Virginia Woolf, tells a tale of the love affair between Clare and the much older Clemence, whose masculine sister, 'Mrs. Blank', is almost indistinguishable from him. At the centre of the poem is a great carp swimming in a lake. The poem is pervaded by a fairy-tale atmosphere reminiscent of Rossetti's 'Goblin Market'. As in *A Collection*, there are also children's poems and poems about damp and miserable creatures called 'scoolshes' that derive from the childhood fantasy world Easdale and her brother created that bears comparison to the Angria and Gondal fantasies of the Brontë siblings. One of the poems in this volume, 'Chintz', had been published (with some very minor differences in punctuation) in the BBC's magazine, *The Listener*, in December 1931. In its imagination of a world alive in the fabric of a sofa, it is similar to a story Woolf wrote for her brother Adrian's daughter, Ann Stephen, 'Nurse Lugton's Golden Thimble', which describes the animals in a design coming alive while the woman who has been sewing it sleeps.[7] This is a common device in Victorian and subsequent children's literature, and Easdale created her fantasy vividly, again with evident allusion to Rossetti's 'Goblin Market'. Two of the poems in the second collection – 'On a Walk' and 'A Sad Story' – might be described as 'unwritten novels', poems that are suggestive of a much richer narrative, of possibilities to be explored and developed, similar to the narrative in Woolf's own 'An Unwritten Novel'.

Although *Clemence and Clare* does not have the consistent appeal and freshness of Easdale's first collection, its voice is idiosyncratic. The final poem, which the *Times Literary Supplement* singled out for praise ('Review'), introduces a mystic element that Easdale would develop throughout the 1930s and realise in her final publication with the Hogarth Press in 1939. Subtitled 'A Dream Poem' and dedicated to Easdale's mother, 'Revelation' describes a 'negro' who leads the speaker along a lush avenue 'Of shrouded trees, where glossy dates/Fell in showers/On sickly flowers/That wafted death with each hot breath.' She witnesses a wild dance, and is led back down the avenue to a shrine where her guide tells her to pray: 'I felt my consciousness suspended/ In one long line/Of thought divine,/Until the mystic trance had ended.' After taking her back to where she began her journey, the 'negro' tells her that 'the soul, once having known/Can never lose what it was shown.' This poem is dated 15 July–2 October 1931, the only one apart from the longer title poem that indicates it was written over an extended time. It signals the direction in which Easdale's thinking would move in the 1930s, away from the sharply observed interactions of men and women, youth and age, and away from the imaginative world of child-hood towards a mystical apprehension of the visionary reality underly-ing the external world. As such, 'Revelation' was the antithesis of what Lehmann considered to be the direction in which poetry should be moving. Given that Woolf had published *The Waves* in October 1931, however, it is not surprising that she would have been drawn to the mystical elements in Easdale's work.

At the Hogarth Press, Lehmann was becoming increasingly embittered, at odds in particular with Leonard Woolf who he felt was not interested in his ideas about poetry. To his diary in July 1932 he confided:

> The rat goes on gnawing in my mind (about the H. P.) I might say this: you have kept me only because you were afraid, afraid of the talk that would follow my departure, afraid too that I would lead a secession. You have kept me in a way that makes me purely a profit-sharer (I believe you know I didn't want that). In a way that makes it far easier for you to sidetrack me, to evade my plans and ideas and stifle my enterprise (and instinctively you hate that, though your voice says Yes). . . . I am warned now . . . and when the crisis comes will make the break swiftly, and without words.[8]

And this is precisely what Lehmann did, walking out in August 1932. 'That egotistical young man with all his jealousies & vanities & ambi-tions, his weakness and changeableness', wrote Woolf in her diary, 'is no loss' (*D*4 123).

Woolf and Lehmann had before this, however, continued to discuss the state of poetry and in particular what he viewed as her inadequate understanding of what the Auden group was all about. She agreed that the quotations she had used in her *Letter* might not have been well-chosen – a point recent critics have emphasised[9] – but reiterated her argument that 'the young poet is rather crudely jerked between realism and beauty, to put it roughly' (*L*5 83). What she looked for in a poet, she implied, was beauty, a quality that had little to do with argument, propaganda, or descriptions of 'Mrs. Gape'. 'Poetry' to Woolf was a quality of imagination rather than a technique, and her references to poetry invariably stress its sensory and sensual aspects. For example, in 'Impassioned Prose', a 1926 essay on DeQuincey, she says, 'prose writer though he is, it is for his poetry that we read him and not for his prose' (32). DeQuincey was one of those artists *sui generis* who, finding no ready means to express his vision, invented his own 'modes of impas-sioned prose' in which the best passages are 'not lyrical but descrip-tive . . . they are descriptions of states of mind in which, often, time is miraculously prolonged and space miraculously expanded' (39). Writing to Lehmann at the end of July 1932 in defence of her *Letter to a Young*

Poet, Woolf acknowledged that her dissatisfaction with the poets' effort to include ordinary life might in fact be 'some of the ill effects of my own struggles the other way round—writes poetry in prose' (*L5* 83).

In October 1935, Joan Easdale read aloud to Woolf from her work in progress, *Amber Innocent*, a long poem she had begun in March 1932. Among Woolf's unpublished reading notes is a scrawled page, very hard to decipher but noting elements of the poem's plot and phrases such as 'religious motifs', 'revelation of eternity'.[10] Woolf had written in 1934 to Stephen Spender that she wanted to 'read nothing but poetry' (*L5* 315). Her reading notes from this period on Spenser's *Faery Queen* (for an essay that would not be published until after her death[11]) emphasise again Woolf's attention to the sensual qualities of poetry: 'Perhaps all our first impressions of poetry are visual.'[12] Discussing T. S. Eliot's plans to write a play about Thomas à Becket, she records him telling her that 'he could not like poetry that had no meaning for the ear' (*D4* 288). When she read his play, Woolf said she first ran through it '& tested my colour sense' (*D4* 323), expecting it to be good. In her reading notes she reiterated the point that in reading poetry the 'colour sense' was first roused: 'Thus in Murder in the Cathedral I am stirred—my senses quickened—first by the purple bullfinch . . . by the white sail on the grey sea.'[13] She wrote to Julian Bell in October 1935, about two weeks after hearing Easdale's new poem, 'do you find that your mind works oddly, about poetry? I can read it for an hour with rapture but without understanding a word. And the first of my senses to wake is the colour sense' (*L5* 437).

Given these stray remarks about poetry and her antagonism to the emphasis on argument and content in the work of many of the poets championed by Lehmann, I suggest that what attracted Woolf to Easdale's poetry was what she would have called its beauty as well as its impersonal yet individual voice. In 1939 Woolf wrote to Robert Trevelyan, whose *Collected Poems* the Press had just published, that she wanted to try and explain why she liked them so much: 'Its as though all superfluities had been consumed and whats left is very satisfying. That is a quality I admire very much, and don't find often among the moderns. And often there's a special colourless (perhaps I mean unexaggerated, or impersonal) beauty that I find also lasting and possessing—not surprising, but stealing over one' (*L6* 348). Woolf's insistence that her Press publish not just the work of political young men but also poetry that was distinctly un-modern gave the Hogarth poetry list characteristics rarely associated with received opinion about 'thirties poetry': beauty, mysticism, the domestic, for example.

Lehmann was reconciled with the Woolfs in 1935, resuming a

relationship both business and personal that would again profoundly influence the Hogarth Press. In 1936 he published the first issue of *New Writing* with Bodley Head, a vehicle for his vision of publishing interesting unknown writers from many countries alongside those who were already better established. This vehicle would go through a number of name changes and also reside for a time at the Hogarth Press, to which Lehmann returned in 1938 under an agreement that explicitly acknowledged the fact of his providing a connection between the Press and what Woolf soon began to call the 'New Writing . . . gang' (*D5* 138). Indeed, the impression that literary success in England was in the hands of a gang or racket became commonplace. Woken to action by the Spanish Civil War, poets 'explod[ed] like bombs', in Auden's memorable phrase; the generation championed by Lehmann and other publishers believed in the necessity of a directly political art.

In 1938 the prolific Scottish poet and novelist Naomi Mitchison wrote to Woolf about her recently published *Three Guineas*, and then brought up her close friend Joan Easdale:

> Joan Easdale has been staying with me, and has re-started on poetry, which is a good thing. Like so many of us, she has been discouraged by the gang of young men who run the poetry racket just now, and needs a lot of encouraging. I think her long epic poem, Amber Innocent, is extraordinarily good; but that may be that I have seen so much of its birth. She's a remarkable young woman, anyhow; a bit mad, but then so is everyone who is poetically sensitive. She is lazy too, or perhaps it is that she does things slowly, and apparently can't learn to spell; I spend my time poking and pinching her and making her get on. She's worth taking trouble about. (Mitchison, 'Letter')

Robertson describes Easdale's friendship with Mitchison as 'the most important' of her life. Easdale and her husband, James Rendel, who worked for Mitchison's brother, the pioneering geneticist J. B. S. Haldane, stayed often with Mitchison at her house, Carradale, in Scotland. When Mitchison's newborn baby died in July 1940 she wrote in her diary that she wished 'there was a chance of my making contact with any of my friends who are doing the same kind of thing as I am. If I could have a few hours with Storm [Jameson], or Margaret [Cole] or Stevie [Smith] or Joan [Rendel]—diverse enough people . . . I might be able to work something out' (*Among* 72). In February 1941, on a visit to London, Mitchison visited Easdale, Smith and Cole (*Among* 116). A couple of months after hearing from Mitchison in 1938, Woolf mentioned in a letter to Joan's mother that she had not seen her 'for an age, but was glad to hear of her from Miss Mitchison & hope the poem <is> growing slowly' (Barkway, 'Letters' 30). Mitchison's friend Stevie

Smith wrote to her of her own publishing troubles around this time: 'Well, your old battle axe on the *New Statesman* won't have me, nor John Leighman [*sic*], nor Spender, nor Ian Somebody on *The Spectator*, nor Ackerley on *The Listener*. Only *Punch* will sometimes if they are funny' (qtd in Mitchison, *You May Well* 157). As Cunningham remarks, 'the '30s belonged to boys ... Boys were clearly the preoccupation of *New Writing*. "Four Boys Alone" was the editor John Lehmann's description of four little fictions about males in No. 3 (Spring 1937)' (110). Furthermore, he says, 'The smell of a racket was everywhere, and not only in the newspapers. It had penetrated the offices of publishers. The young John Lehmann at Hogarth, the young Anthony Powell at Duckworth, Uncle Tom Eliot, all endeavoured to grant the youths prompt access to the book trade' (119).

Woolf had quoted in *Three Guineas* from memoirs and letters to describe the typical upbringing and education of young men, arguing that it led to war as an experience that they craved. Also published in 1938 was Louis MacNeice's *Modern Poetry: A Personal Essay* where he described his poetic education in explicitly gendered terms. MacNeice recounts how he was given Palgrave's *Golden Treasury* at school and was attracted by 'the flashier heroics' (41). He suggests that the narrow range of the Palgrave selection could be improved for boys by the addition of 'a quantity of light verse and of modern folk-poetry, such as the ballads of American cowboys'; as an example of what he has in mind, he refers to *The Poet's Tongue*, an 'anthology for boys ... recently ... compiled by John Garrett and W. H. Auden' (42). Among works by writers of the English canon, folk songs, carols and nursery rhymes in this volume there are just three poems by women, one by Edith Sitwell and two by Emily Dickinson.

MacNeice called for a diction that was 'masculine but not exhibitionist. After the feminine writing of the nineteenth century ... and after the neuter writing of the Georgians we are working back towards the normal virile efficiency of Dryden or Chaucer' (152). Hopkins, he writes, is 'the most masculine of our poets; his style and his rhythms lay the strongest stress of all our literature on the naked thew and sinew of the English language' (152). Lest anyone imagine he was using 'masculine' and 'feminine' only as technical terms of prosody, we should note that in commenting on extracts from works by Emily Dickinson and Christina Rossetti, MacNeice suspects 'that in both these mystically minded women their fondness for using jewellery and clothes stuffs as images represents a repressed desire for the actual things' (94).

In concluding, MacNeice echoes what many of the young men of the 1930s said in one way or another:

for the production nowadays of major literature on a large scale, a sympathy is required in the writer with those forces which at the moment make for progress. The important events outside him must penetrate him in the same way as Euripides was penetrated by the Peloponnesian War or by the intellectual discoveries of the sophists. (204)

In 'The Leaning Tower' two years later, Woolf would implicitly take issue with this point of view, and MacNeice would be the most hostile of her respondents (MacNeice, 'The Tower').[14]

Lehmann had returned in 1938 to the Hogarth Press, buying out Woolf's share and entering into a contentious business relationship with Leonard that would stagger on until 1946. In suggesting the terms of their partnership, Leonard had raised the issue of turning the Press into a private company. 'It might be possible', he wrote, 'to combine such an arrangement with a loose attachment to the Gang, in the shape of an advisory Board' (Woolf, *L6* 201). Nothing came of this plan in the sense of any formal connection between those writers at the core of the *New Writing* 'gang' and the Press, but Lehmann's new position embodied their de facto presence in discussions about how the Press would proceed.

Reflecting towards the end of the year on his new position, Lehmann confided to his diary that he believed he had

> a real role to play, but only the shape the battle takes can determine what precisely it is. It is necessary now as never to seek power. At moments I feel so urgently convinced of this that I am like a machine roaring aimlessly out of gear; at others I feel I am inflating myself into a grossly exaggerated confidence and powers, and want someone to make a joke in order that I can laugh at my absurdity.
>   But again I feel that my part as rallying point for the younger writers and intellectuals—particularly those who care about politics as well as art—defines itself always more clearly, and I mustn't shirk my responsibilities.[15]

He was explicit in his diary about why he had taken the position at the Hogarth Press: 'I went into it quite clearly for one reason (though I need a job, I believe I could also have found that elsewhere), which was to give myself more scope to expand . . . New Writing . . . And in fighting for the H. P. I am fighting for that . . . and intend to go on doing so.'[16] Lehmann was anxious that Woolf contribute to *New Writing*, but she was wary about writing for a publication with declared aims: 'Why lay down laws', she asked him, 'about imaginative writing?' (*L6* 252).

In January 1939, just before giving up her official role at the Press, Virginia Woolf wrote to the daughter of Edward McKnight Kauffer, an artist who had designed several jackets for Hogarth Press books. Ann, who was at the time twenty-four, had submitted poems to the Press, and Woolf wrote to advise her 'to put these poems away and write a great many more and re-write them before you try to publish them.' Although she liked the poems, Woolf went on, 'there is a lot of work to do before one can make a poem express one's feeling completely for other people' (*L6* 313). Given her advice to young poets of 1932 not to publish before they were thirty, her letter to Kauffer is unremarkable; but it points to the singularity of her interest in and support of Easdale. Willis notes that Easdale's 1939 *Amber Innocent* was 'published over John Lehmann's objections', and suggests that 'perhaps Virginia's feminist sympathies were engaged in sponsoring Joan and giving her a room of her own through publication' (187). Willis' implication that Woolf's literary judgement was clouded by her 'feminist sympathies' can be refuted by the record of her correspondence with other prospective Hogarth authors who happened to be women, such as Ann Kauffer. In support-ing Easdale, Woolf not only was encouraging a writer in whose work she heard an individual and original voice, but also was ignoring her own rather snobbish disdain for the circle with whom Easdale became connected – Mitchison, Naomi Royde Smith and John Middleton Murry, for example.

Amber Innocent was published in September 1939 in a run of 1,000 copies. Given the economic circumstances at the beginning of the war, and the imminent threat of paper rationing, such a run is a remark-able testament to the Woolfs' faith in Easdale's art. Vanessa Bell drew the cover image for *Amber*, the only one she did for Hogarth that year (reproduced in Roberts). (Replying to Easdale's letter thanking her, Vanessa said she had been 'intrigued & interested in your poem & thought much of it lovely' [qtd in Barkway, 'An "incredible goose"' 19].) On the dust jacket, the Woolfs expressed their long-standing support of their young poet:

> Eight years ago, the Hogarth Press published Joan Easdale's first book of poems, now out of print. Its title was A Collection of Poems, and its sub-title recorded the fact that it had been written between the ages of 14 and 17. Many people agreed with the view of the publishers that these poems were a remarkable achievement in view of the author's age, but that they were some-thing more; they were not merely the work of an infant prodigy; they were not and could not be great poetry, but they had a streak in them of real and individual poetry. The author's second volume, published in 1932, *Clemence and Clare*, confirmed this view, though it was still obviously an 'early work.' Joan Easdale's third book which is now published is a long poem; she began it in 1932 and finished it—after considerable pauses—in 1939. The impulse to write it came from a dream, but, as the author herself says, the poem 'springs only from what I have observed in everyday life and relationships, and things I cannot remember.'

A scribbled note in the Hogarth Press archive records Lehmann's initial response to Easdale's long poem: 'I think it has a most remarkable quality . . . but 1. a bit too Tennyson, 2. terribly long, 3. nobody buy it?' (qtd in Robertson 84). Travelling books in September 1939, Lehmann expressed surprise in a memo to Leonard that the Ancient House Bookshop in Reigate had taken '2 copies of Amber Innocent!'[17] In a letter to Joan's mother that October, Woolf reminded her that the war was delaying reviews, and hoped 'Joan isn't disappointed. They will come in time; and we are selling more books than we expected' (*L6* 365). Vita Sackville-West wrote to thank Lehmann for the copy of *Amber Innocent* he had sent her. She was 'much impressed by it although I am not sure that I quite grasp all its implications and symbolism' (qtd in Robertson 93).

Easdale had told Naomi Mitchison that the pressure of impending war had made her feel 'one must throw out one's own small cry upon the wind without delay' (Robertson 81). She felt, according to Mitchison, that 'she was on a small island of sand with everything cut off before and behind' (*Among* 36). Mitchison was determined to help her friend get noticed, and wrote a brief review for the *New Statesman and Nation* titled 'A New Poet'. She emphasised Easdale's work as a 'new turn' in poetry that would give its reader a 'jolt out of time which is extremely salutary to this clock-bound culture'.

A month earlier, the novelist and literary editor of the *Westminster Gazette*, Naomi Royde Smith, had reviewed *Amber Innocent* in *Time and Tide* under the title 'The New Verse Novel'. Describing *Aurora Leigh* and *The Ring and the Book* as 'two great English psychological novels of the nineteenth century', Royde Smith positioned Easdale's poem as a similarly genre-crossing work. It belonged, she wrote 'definitely to the novel class: but to quite another class of novel. If Mrs Woolf had, early in her career, decided to write in verse this is very much the kind of book she might have produced.' The reviewer for the *Times Literary Supplement* described the poem as 'an unusually original attempt to crystallise the meaning and movement of a girl's life, the unfolding pattern of her self-awareness at a new and deeper level', and also placed Easdale in the context of her publisher's own art: Easdale 'may owe something in her exploration of this new dimension to the pioneer work of Mrs Woolf and others, but her discoveries are as much her own as is the sensuous refinement of her imagery and the somewhat sombre reflections upon life which filter through it' ('Crooked Cross').

Geoffrey Grigson, who had admired Easdale's first book, was unmoved. Writing in the first number of *Horizon*, he complained that 'this long poem is too like a novel: it is like a dew-on-the-grass first novel by a daughter of a member of the Book Society's panel who has mixed her *Wuthering Heights* with some Maeterlinck and some Lolly Willowes.' He quoted three lines and then concluded: 'No' ('New Poetry').

The rejection of Eliotic obscurity and arcane allusion that was announced in such prominent places as the introduction to *New Signatures*, and the call to arms heard from Spain by so many artists of the 1930s, had to a great extent drowned out the quieter notes of an 'upsurge of interest in the possibility of reconciling Christianity and socialism' during that decade (Hoskins 9). Lehmann sensed in 1939 that the propagandistic and political poetry he had helped so much to promulgate was giving way to a new desire: 'There is a growing feeling in my mind', he wrote on Christmas Eve 1939, 'that the Zeitgeist is moving towards a new kind of philosophy, or religion, to be discovered by poets and novelists.'[18] Given this statement, it is surprising that he could not recognise *Amber Innocent* as an example of precisely this movement.

Amber Innocent is a narrative poem of sixty pages in twenty sections. The opening describes a curious scene: Amber has her face pressed into the heavy curtains of a room in her brother-in-law Mark's house and is conscious of him looking her up and down. She is not 'in the world' where Mark, a widower who has been damaged by the First World War, sits opposite the chair where his late wife used to sit, wearing the carpet away with her feet.

> Speaking into the folds of the curtain,
> She would not be able to hear in her voice
> The height of the ceiling nor the width of the room.
> 'Dusk has come,' said Amber.
> And afraid lest a small chink might reveal
> A ribbon of sky more grey
> She drew the curtains closely together.
>
> The warmth of her breath on the velvet
> Made in the shadow a momentary bliss.
> Deeper she buried her face and her face
> Seemed all of her. Her lashes brushing the pile were part
> Of some sequestered woodland dark.
> She lived in her face. Her body might be
> A negative pillar alone.
>
> She knew that her brother-in-law sat
> In a chair behind in the world.
> Most likely his eyes were sizing her shape
> From her neck's dun curve down to her still shoes.
> But Amber was all in her forest's shade,
> It was only her face that held herself. (9)

When Mark speaks, Amber is forced back into the world. She has been disembodied, living only in her face, but now re-enters the world and her body. Mark indicates that she should bring a lamp into the dark room, and as she fetches one from the hall she hears the cry of a sick child – Megathy, her niece. Reflected in the hallway table, under the lamp, she sees the 'wide, anxious face of a mother', perhaps indicating her similarity to her sister, or that she has assumed a maternal role now that her sister is dead (10).[19]

Amber goes to see the sick child who is in a room at the top of a turret. As she climbs the winding staircase, Amber contemplates suicide at each window, but then withdraws from the thought as 'a voice from her blood' tells her not to go 'heavenward' yet: 'Assertion of self was no less a pain/Than the frozen limb that feels again' (13). We abruptly shift to the point of view of the sick child: 'Her tears made gold wheels round the candle flame' (14). The image-making power and strange, idiosyncratic imagination of Easdale's earlier work has now settled into a mature vision in a work that retains the fairy-tale atmosphere of many of those early poems yet also gradually develops a provocative philosophy.

In Megathy's room, Amber pours water into a basin to wash: 'She leant over the water and met her face,/A little removed she watched herself./The familiar when met is stranger than strangers' (14–15). From her bed, Megathy observes shadows cast by the flickering candle that look like 'Old men in capes/Were saying prayers, hypocritically bowing' (15). On the wall is a nail that is either 'God's watchful eye,/Or a hornless snail' (16). Rather than see these as influences or allusions, I suggest that Easdale is drawing on an image-world mapped out by Virginia Woolf. Among discrete examples are the way that Megathy's tears cause the light to wave in a way similar to that described at the opening of *Jacob's Room* when the world 'undulates' from the tearful Betty Flanders' perspective; the threatening shadows on the wall that appear like old men, similar to the scenes of Rachel's illness in *The Voyage Out*; the mark on the wall.

David Eberly has recently discussed how the centrality of the face in the ethics of Emmanuel Levinas can help us understand the narrative of trauma embodied in *Between the Acts*, where the 'characters search for relief in the responsive face-to-face encounter of an attentive and listening other. It is in the circumstance of the audience of the other that Woolf seeks in her novel to discover a community that will alleviate the anxiety of the traumatized self and offer respite, if not recovery, from the repercussions of trauma' (205). Amber's complex relation to her face and the faces of others recalls the figure in Woolf's work whom she most resembles, Rhoda in *The Waves*:

'That is my face,' said Rhoda, 'in the looking-glass behind Susan's shoulder—
that face is my face. But I will duck behind her to hide it, for I am not here. I
have no face. Other people have faces; Susan and Jinny have faces; they are
here. Their world is the real world.' (29)

At the centre of the poem, Amber, who has travelled to London, experiences a visionary collapse after knocking on a door that seems familiar
to her. When the occupant of the house opens the door, Amber does not
cross the threshold but steps *into* it and has a vision of eternity:

> There is a space called the threshold,
> Immeasurably long or unaccountably short,
> But it is crossed, and all that is remembered
> Is where we have left and where we have arrived.
> But Amber did not cross, she stepped in to the threshold.
>
> 'Have you journeyed long?'
>
> 'Yes, and Christ how tired I am.'
>
> The light switched on. A burning white
> Slew the values of her sight.
> A quick omniscience, an utter blankness,
> Revealed eternity rolled in a second.
> The man, the hall, the stairs and all
> Had diminished beyond the reach of vision,
> Or else enlarged till atoms were
> Holes within holes—again, oblivion.
> And this is all there is to know.
>
> ... Amber had fallen upon her face—
> The floor was so cold and lovely a place. (36–7)

Strongly reminiscent of moments of blankness and vision in *To the
Lighthouse*, *The Waves* and *Between the Acts*, this passage had already
been published in 'Holes', an article Easdale wrote for *The Adelphi*
magazine in May 1937.

By 1936, Easdale was living in London and had participated in a
summer school run by the *Adelphi* the previous year, meeting there
writers and other intellectuals with whom she would remain in contact
for several years. Her brief essay 'Holes' is helpful in understanding the
thinking behind *Amber Innocent*.

With remarkable faith in the commonness of poetic vision, 'Holes'
begins:

> I suppose that every one of us, at some time or another, experiences a vision
> of eternity. Once we have perceived it, the whole world becomes a single

utterance so provident and transparent that we feel ourselves to be no less, but rather more, than an 'Einstein Observer'. (326)

As Wai Chee Dimock has pointed out, Einstein's special theory of relativity 'demolishes the traditional conception of time as an absolute metric that unifies all incidents and chronologies' (1065). Easdale continues by recounting her own 'vision of eternity', which 'came to me about three years ago, accompanied by a conviction. The conviction I named "Reconciliation of Opposites", and the vision chose "focus" for its elucidation.'

> If an object were magnified to an exaggerated degree, it would become nothing, and likewise, I told myself, if it were diminished down to the *n*th degree again there would be nothing. I looked down at my knee, and in the weave of my dress I saw the same theory illustrated. There were more holes between each thread of material, and could I but see, I should find more holes within each thread, and the threads around those holes would contain more holes. Somehow I felt that in the end the holes would win. Likewise, I was full of holes, the table beside me was full of holes, everything and everybody were really just one hole—not w-h-o-l-e, but h-o-l-e. So-called reality was only a matter of focus. That table and myself were at the same focus, we both had the same frequency of holes—that was why we seemed real to each other, why I might touch the table and feel myself in contact with something hard instead of my hand passing through and out the other side. (326)

In this account of the self's reciprocal relation to the object-world, Rhoda of *The Waves* again comes to mind: 'Unless I can stretch and touch something hard, I shall be blown down the eternal corridors for ever. What then can I touch? What brick, what stone? and so draw myself across the enormous gulf into my body safely?' (115).[20]

Easdale reports in her article going about her domestic routine in a state where she can see through solid objects, accepting this uncertainty of the world's solidity. She resolves 'to draw upon myself all the natural bounties that were owed to me and other men and women' (327) by this world of 'numerous and invisible energies which must live and generate within the space just beyond my focus' (326). The vision was not, though, fully realised until her character Amber had also experienced a similar enlightenment; at this point she quotes in the article the passage from her work in progress where Amber experiences her vision of eternity by stepping into the threshold of the house. Easdale links Amber's experience with one of her own when she fainted after slicing off the tip of her finger. Coming to on the floor, she recalls how she 'regarded the biscuit tins under the kitchen table with an abounding love such as I had never felt for them before' (328).

At the end of the poem, after a ghostly visit from Megathy, Amber has a vision of wholeness similar to that Woolf describes in both 'Sketch of the Past' and *Between the Acts*. In her memoir, Woolf recalls 'looking at the flower bed by the front door; "That is the whole", I said. I was looking at a plant with a spread of leaves; and it seemed suddenly plain that the flower itself was a part of the earth; that a ring enclosed what was the flower; and that was the real flower; part earth; part flower' (71). The moment is recreated in the child George's experience early in *Between the Acts* (8). Amber links her own vision of interdependence to peace:

> 'Say that we are scribes to the written page,
> Yet what we write shall never be blotted out.
> Say that we are here and that we have gone before
> And as we shall be are we now and were we.
> So should we be more careful.
>
> Say that the bread upon the table is also in the van,
> And the wheat in the bread is also in the field
> And in our mouths as it is sown.
> Then would men not despise the moment, which is also eternity.
> Not until we acknowledge the moment as eternity
> Shall war cease and life have meaning.' (53)

She now feels ready to return to Mark's house, to 'the garden she had known' (55). When she arrives, the gardener tells her that Megathy has killed herself. In a final confrontation with her nemesis, Mark dies and Amber battles his emanation, a white lion. As she had earlier, she climbs to the turret room at Mark's house and again struggles with the temptation to suicide, but in the last line of the poem she decides, 'No, I have to live' (60).

In a rough poem 'On Hearing of the Death of Virginia Woolf' that Joan Easdale sent to Leonard Woolf with a letter of condolence in August 1941, she quoted lines from her poems and tried to explain the importance to her of being heard, of Woolf having been her receptive audience (Oldfield 59–61). She imagined Woolf as a mountain 'which listened and spoke and echoing not was echoed by many' (Oldfield 60). From *Amber Innocent*, she included the lines 'Everything speaks of death to those who hear,/In all life lies elegy, singing.'

With the loss of her mentor, Easdale's career as a poet was over. Woolf had written in September 1940 to Mrs Easdale that she had seen in the paper the notice of the birth of Joan's first child, and sent her congratulations: 'only we hope she won't stop writing' (*L6* 425). By May 1944, Naomi Mitchison was describing in her diary how Easdale was battling '[t]his hellish business of being a woman always with half an ear for babies or husbands or god knows what' (*Among* 283).

The history of Easdale's mental decline has been expertly told by her granddaughter Celia Robertson, who includes as an appendix to her biography a facsimile of *Amber Innocent*. In the mid 1960s, Joan's mother wrote to Leonard Woolf that her daughter had been missing for many months. 'We found her', she wrote; 'it is not Joan, a stranger inhabits her.'[21] Two decades earlier in an argument with John Lehmann about the poetry the Hogarth Press should support, Leonard Woolf wrote that 'the name and standard of the Press, such as they are, have been established by ... independent judgment by two people as to whether in their opinion any publication is or is not up to standard.'[22] Until now, Lehmann's judgement about what was the most significant and important poetry of the 1930s has been endorsed by literary history. If anyone has taken notice of Easdale, it has been as an example of how out of touch Virginia Woolf was with the world of contemporary poetry. But the Hogarth Press, as Leonard explained to his antagonistic partner in 1943, was the expression of his and Virginia's 'independent judgment'. That the Woolfs believed Joan Adeney Easdale's poetry was 'up to standard' is reason enough to re-read the work of this particular incarnation of Shakespeare's sister.

Notes

1. John Lehmann, Journal. 27 October 1939. Lehmann Family Papers, Princeton University Library. Permission to quote from the diary and correspondence of John Lehmann in the Lehmann Family Papers held by the Manuscripts Division, Department of Rare Books and Special Collections at Princeton University's Firestone Library is gratefully acknowledged.
2. Robertson reproduces some of Easdale's drawings.
3. Brian Easdale (1909–95) was a composer of opera and orchestral music who also had success writing film scores. He won an Oscar for his score for *The Red Shoes* in 1948.
4. John Lehmann to Leonard Woolf, 30 April 1931. Lehmann Family Papers, Princeton University Library.
5. John Lehmann, Journal. 16 November 1931. Lehmann Family Papers, Princeton University Library.
6. Nicholas Moore's 'Proud as a Hawk', in *Poets of Tomorrow* (London: Hogarth Press, 1940), is worth noting in this regard: 'Proud as a hawk and empty as a stone/I sit in a room of books and write my rhymes, . . .' (47).
7. The story was first published in the *Times Literary Supplement* in 1965, published by the Hogarth Press in 1966, and published under the title *Nurse Lugton's Curtain* by Harcourt in 1991.

8. John Lehmann, Journal. 8 July 1932. Lehmann Family Papers, Princeton University Library. And see Lehmann's much blander account of this period in *Thrown* 35–8.
9. For example, Hermione Lee in her introduction to the *Hogarth Letters* says (erroneously) that Woolf 'noticeably ignores Auden' (Lee xx), a point repeated by Liesl Olson (45 n16).
10. See Silver, Reading Notebook X. Quoted from Holograph RN1.10 in The Berg Collection of English and American Literature at the New York Public Library in Hussey.
11. In *The Moment and Other Essays*. New York: Harcourt Brace Jovanovich, 1948.
12. Notes entitled 'Four Voices/Faery Queen' Reading Notebook XLV in Silver. Quoted from Holograph MH/B2.m, Monks House Papers, University of Sussex Library in Hussey.
13. See Eliot: 'set the white sail between the grey sky and the bitter sea'; 'the purple bullfinch in the lilac tree'. Woolf Reading Notebook XLV in Silver.
14. Woolf had, of course, already addressed such masculinist arguments in *A Room of One's Own*, for example in her remarks comparing the life Tolstoy was able to lead with that led by George Eliot (69–70).
15. John Lehmann, Journal. 19 September 1938. Lehmann Family Papers, Princeton University Library.
16. John Lehmann, Journal. 4 December 1938. Lehmann Family Papers, Princeton University Library.
17. John Lehmann to Leonard Woolf, 15 September 1939. Lehmann Family Papers, Princeton University Library.
18. John Lehmann, Journal. 24 December 1939. Lehmann Family Papers, Princeton University Library.
19. The child's curious name might have something to do with the process known as 'harmomegathy' by which pollen grains respond to changes in the water availability of their environment, a suggestion that may not seem so far-fetched when we take into account that Easdale married a geneticist in 1938 and lived communally with scientists working for J. B. S. Haldane after her marriage. Later in the poem plant biology plays a sinister role.
20. Similar instances where characters question the solidity of matter occur, for example, in *To the Lighthouse* (204) and in *Between the Acts* (135).
21. Gladys Easdale to Leonard Woolf (n.d.). Easdale Family Papers, Reading University Library.
22. Leonard Woolf to John Lehmann, 8 June 1943. Lehmann Family Papers, Princeton University Library.

Works cited

Barkway, Stephen. 'An "incredible goose" and a "country flapper"': Virginia Woolf and the Easdales'. *Bulletin of the Virginia Woolf Society of Great Britain* 28, 2008: 5–24.
—, ed. 'Letters to Mrs. G. E. Easdale'. *Bulletin of the Virginia Woolf Society of Great Britain* 28, 2008: 31–5.
Bell, Julian. 'Arms and the Man'. In Roberts, ed.

Church, Richard. 'Music from Leucadia'. *The Spectator* 16 May 1931.

Clarke, Austin. 'Cross Currents and Clear Streams'. *The Observer* 24 April 1932: 5.

'The Crooked Cross'. [Anon.] Review of *Amber Innocent*. *Times Literary Supplement* 4 November 1939: 644.

Cunningham, Valentine. *British Writers of the Thirties*. Oxford and New York: Oxford University Press, 1988.

Dimock, Wai Chee. 'A Theory of Resonance'. *PMLA* 112.5, 1997: 1060–71.

Easdale, Gladys Ellen, Papers of. University of Reading.

Easdale, Joan Adeney. *Amber Innocent*. London: Hogarth Press, 1939.

—. 'Chintz'. *The Listener* 16 December 1931: 1046.

—. *Clemence and Clare*. London: Hogarth Press, 1932.

—. *A Collection of Poems (Written between the ages of 14 and 17)*. London: Hogarth Press, 1931.

—. 'Holes'. *The Adelphi* May 1937: 326–9.

Eberly, David. 'Face-to-Face: Trauma and Audience in *Between the Acts*'. In Suzette Henke and David Eberly, eds. *Virginia Woolf and Trauma: Embodied Texts*. New York: Pace University Press, 2007: 205–22.

E. D. B. 'Review of *Clemence and Clare*'. *The Poetry Review* 24, 1933: 389–90.

Eliot, T. S. *Murder in the Cathedral*. London: Faber, 1935.

Grigson, Geoffrey. 'New Poetry'. *Horizon* 1.1, 1940: 57–61.

—. 'Three New Poets'. *The Saturday Review* 11 April 1931.

Hoskins, Katharine Bail. *Today the Struggle: Literature and Politics in England During the Spanish Civil War*. Austin: University of Texas Press, 1969.

Hussey, Mark, ed. *Major Authors on CD-ROM: Virginia Woolf*. Woodbury: Research Publications, 1995.

Lee, Hermione. 'Introduction'. *The Hogarth Letters*. Athens: University of Georgia Press, 1986: vii–xxviii.

—. *Virginia Woolf*. New York: Alfred A. Knopf, 1997.

Lehmann, John. 'To Penetrate that Room'. In Roberts, ed.

—. *Thrown to the Woolfs: Leonard and Virginia Woolf and the Hogarth Press*. New York: Holt, Rinehart & Winston, 1978.

Lewis, C. Day. 'From Feathers to Iron XI'. *From Feathers to Iron*. London: Hogarth Press, 1931.

MacNeice, Louis. *Modern Poetry: A Personal Essay*. New York: Haskell, [1938] 1969.

—. 'The Tower That Once'. *Folios of New Writing*. Ed. John Lehmann. London: Hogarth Press, Spring 1941: 37–41.

Mendelson, Edward. *Early Auden*. New York: Farrar Straus Giroux, 1981.

Mitchison, Naomi. *Among You Taking Notes ... The Wartime Diary of Naomi Mitchison, 1939–1945*. Ed. Dorothy Sheridan. London: Victor Gollancz, 1985.

—. Letter. *Woolf Studies Annual*. Vol. 6. New York: Pace University Press, 2000: 48–9.

—. 'A New Poet'. *The New Statesman and Nation* 18 November 1939: 732.

—. *You May Well Ask*. London: Victor Gollancz, 1979.

Oldfield, Sybil, ed. *Afterwords: Letters on the Death of Virginia Woolf*. Edinburgh: Edinburgh University Press, 2005.

Olsen, Liesl M. 'Virginia Woolf's "cotton wool of daily life"'. *Journal of Modern Literature* 26.2, 2002–3: 42–65.

'Recitals of the Week'. *The Times* 3 July 1931: 12.

'Review of *Clemence and Clare*'. *Times Literary Supplement* 7 April 1932: 354.

Roberts, Michael, ed. *New Signatures*. London: Hogarth Press, 1932.

Robertson, Celia. *Who Was Sophie? The Lives of my Grandmother: Poet and Stranger*. London: Virago, 2008.

Rosenthal, Thomas. 'Blooming of a Square Set'. *Times Higher Education Supplement* 26 November 1999. http://www.timeshighereducation.co.uk.asp ?storyCode=157409&sectioncode=20.

Royde Smith, Naomi. 'The New Verse Novel'. *Time and Tide* 28 October 1939: 1390–1.

Silver, Brenda R. *Virginia Woolf's Reading Notebooks*. Princeton: Princeton University Press, 1983.

Spender, Stephen. *Twenty Poems*. Oxford: Basil Blackwell, n.d.

Willis, J. H. *Leonard and Virginia Woolf as Publishers: The Hogarth Press 1917–41*. Charlottesville: University Press of Virginia, 1992.

Woolf, Virginia. *Between the Acts*. Annotated and with an introduction by Melba Cuddy-Keane. San Diego: Harcourt, [1941] 2008.

—. *The Diary of Virginia Woolf*. Ed. Anne Olivier Bell. 5 vols. New York: Harcourt Brace Jovanovich, 1977–84.

—. 'Impassioned Prose'. *Granite & Rainbow. Essays*. New York: Harcourt Brace Jovanovich, [1958] 1975: 32–40.

—. 'The Leaning Tower'. *The Moment and Other Essays*. New York: Harcourt Brace Jovanovich, [1948] 1974: 128–54.

—. *Letter to a Young Poet*. London: Hogarth Press, 1932.

—. *The Letters of Virginia Woolf*. Ed. Nigel Nicolson and Joanne Trautmann. 6 vols. New York: Harcourt Brace Jovanovich, 1975–80.

—. *To the Lighthouse*. Annotated and with an introduction by Mark Hussey. San Diego: Harcourt, [1927] 2005.

—. 'Poetry, Fiction and the Future'. *The Essays of Virginia Woolf*. Vol. 4: 1925–1928. Ed. Andrew McNeillie. London: Hogarth Press, 1994: 428–41.

—. *A Room of One's Own*. Annotated and with an introduction by Susan Gubar. San Diego: Harcourt, 2005.

—. 'A Sketch of the Past'. *Moments of Being*. 2nd edn. San Diego: Harcourt, 1985.

—. *Three Guineas*. Annotated and with an introduction by Jane Marcus. San Diego: Harcourt, [1938] 2006.

—. 'An Unwritten Novel'. *Monday or Tuesday*. London: Hogarth Press, 1921.

—. *The Waves*. Annotated and with an introduction by Molly Hite. San Diego: Harcourt, 2006.

Wright, Adrian. *John Lehmann: A Pagan Adventure*. London: Duckworth, 1998.

'Youthful Poems'. [Anon.] Review of *A Collection of Poems (Written between the ages of 14 and 17)*. *Times Literary Supplement* 30 July 1931: 596.

Chapter 2

The Middlebrows of the Hogarth Press: Rose Macaulay, E. M. Delafield and Cultural Hierarchies in Interwar Britain

Melissa Sullivan

In 1938 the Hogarth Press published Margaret Cole's *Books and the People*, under the *Day-to-Day Pamphlets* series.[1] A socialist and supporter of comprehensive education who was linked to the Woolfs via the Fabians and the Labour Party, Cole boldly challenged the elitist relationship between culture and class within the literary field. She argued that the British literary establishment imposed the preferences of Oxford, Cambridge and London upon the reading public, and that this system led readers to consider their tastes shameful and view themselves as outsiders within their own culture. Cole advocated recognising the impact of education, class and travel upon tastes, and suggested that an imminent 'real revolution' in publishing will address the inequalities in the current system. According to Cole, the rise of libraries and book clubs, as well as the availability of affordable books, such as those published by Penguin, are 'the opening stage of a real revolution, a revolution which has been economically overdue for a long time, in the world of English book-production, and . . . its effects are going to be much more far-reaching than anyone in the earlier controversies had fully realized' (6).

Many of Cole's arguments appear to implicate the editors of the very press with which she is publishing. She claimed that 'the public schoolboy . . . who has access to a little money and wants an occupation which will amuse him, takes to publishing as the county schoolboy opens a garage', but is generally 'too highly educated' to address the concerns or desires of the general reading public (9). Leonard Woolf, 'the public school boy', and Virginia Woolf did initially begin the Hogarth Press as a 'hobby' to be 'practised . . . in [their] spare time', but their goals for the Press quickly expanded to include publishing some of the most exciting and revolutionary literature of the 1920s

(Leonard Woolf, *Downhill* 16). Yet during the 1920s and, especially, the 1930s, the Press addressed the changing needs and tastes of the British reading public through its work on politics and education and, although rarely mentioned, its engagement with a network of middlebrow women writers.

Prevailing portraits of the Hogarth Press tend to position it as an elite literary institution and a leading figure within Euro-American modernism. As J. H. Willis, Jr. explains, 'the novels of Virginia Woolf gave the Press its most important identity', and its reputation as a press for high modernist fiction and poetry, progressive political ideas and studies on psychoanalysis added to the Press' lustre (212). Hermione Lee has shown that the Press' prestigious reputation can lead to an emphasis upon it as a 'private' enterprise, which drew on 'old friends and family for its publications', most of whom moved within the highbrow sphere (362). In contrast, middlebrow culture was aligned with popular films and periodicals, best-sellers, leading commercial publishing houses, the middle class and literature that was simultaneously intellectual and pleasurable. Many middlebrow women writers published popular fiction both because they did not wish to write modernist fiction and because they could not support themselves through their academic non-fiction studies. Throughout the late 1920s and 1930s, however, the Hogarth Press increasingly published the work of middlebrow women writers who could not find an outlet for their academic interests in the mainstream literary public sphere, including Rose Macaulay (1881–1958) and E. M. Delafield (1890–1943). These changes parallel Leonard Woolf's growing involvement in politics and the evolution of Virginia Woolf's feminist principles on women and writing.

In *A Room of One's Own* (1929), Virginia Woolf challenged women to 'write all kinds of books, hesitating at no subject, however trivial or however vast … write books of travel and adventure, research and scholarship, and history and biography, and criticism and philosophy and science' (107). The borders between high- and middlebrow culture were 'permeable and shifting', as Lawrence Levine puts it, and Leonard and Virginia Woolf were active participants in illustrating these fluid boundaries for the sake of encouraging new intellectual work (8). The Hogarth Press enabled middlebrows Macaulay and Delafield to self-position as intellectuals within a multifaceted and privileged social forum, rather than accepting static portraits of themselves as middlebrow writers without refined interests. Macaulay and Delafield drew upon the juxtaposition of their cultural capital and that of the Hogarth Press to challenge culturally constructed boundaries between high- and middlebrow spheres and to argue for the recognition of middlebrow literature as 'legitimate culture' (Bourdieu, *Distinction* 323). Leonard and Virginia Woolf's work with middlebrow culture indicates that they increasingly used the Hogarth Press to craft a new portrait of the literary field that included a heterogeneous modernism and a hybrid middlebrow; this accounted for the diverse tastes of the reading public and created new opportunities for women writers to refigure the contentious concerns over interwar cultural hierarchies.

Leonard Woolf claimed that when selecting publications for the Hogarth Press, he and Virginia Woolf 'were interested in young, unknown writers whose work might not attract the publishing establishment' (*Downhill* 130). Many of the Press' early publications, such as Katherine Mansfield's *Prelude*, T. S. Eliot's *The Waste Land*, and Virginia Woolf's *Kew Gardens*, are now considered emblematic representations of high literary modernism. Virginia Woolf certainly recognised the impact of the Hogarth Press upon her own career, for, as she proclaimed in her diary, she was 'the only woman in England to write what [she] like[d]'; all others were forced to think of 'series and editors' (*D3* 43). The Press was a forum for predominantly experimental authors to publish their work, and thus gain access to the mainstream literary public sphere. The alternative for many writers who published with the Hogarth Press was either to leave their work unpublished and unread, as Leonard Woolf maintained would happen, or to acquiesce to the demands of the editors of the 'publishing establishment', much like Virginia Woolf's many female contemporaries.

Portraits of the Hogarth Press are often dominated by Leonard and Virginia Woolf's highbrow theories on art, cultural hierarchies and education, as well as their roles within Bloomsbury and Virginia Woolf's position as a high modernist. As Aaron Jaffe has argued, leading modernists 'transformed the textual signature itself into a means of promotion' (3); like the names 'Virginia Woolf' or 'T. S. Eliot', the label of the 'Hogarth Press' was established as distinguished and exclusive, and so granted desirable cultural capital upon its publications. And much of the Woolfs' work during the 1920s – both as publishers and as authors – does seem to support boundaries in what Virginia Woolf called 'the battle of the brows'.[2] Texts such as Leonard Woolf's 'Hunting the Highbrow' (1927) did uphold the figure of the 'genius' in the literary field and also discredited middlebrow writers who achieve sudden fame within the literary marketplace but are then forgotten by later generations. And while Virginia Woolf did not publish 'Middlebrow', 'Three Characters' or 'Bloodless Middlebrow' during her lifetime, the posthumous publication of the first often overshadows her own efforts to support a network of interwar women writers through her friendships, her work in publishing and her feminist arguments in *A Room of One's Own*. For Lee, 'she was not an especially generous champion of her women contemporaries', although, as is the case with Rose Macaulay, Virginia Woolf's criticisms of women writers could be accounted for by jealousies or insecurities (373).

As editors, Virginia and Leonard Woolf approached middlebrow women's studies in more academic interests far differently from their imaginative fiction. Melba Cuddy-Keane's work on Virginia Woolf's role as a 'democratic highbrow' who 'took the intellectual into the border zone where professional and common reader/writer meet' (8) persuasively establishes Woolf's commitments to issues of education, reading publics and the dissemination of high culture. Virginia and Leonard Woolf's participation within middlebrow culture, however, illustrates their alternative forms of feminist and democratic activism and offers an unusual perspective to their successful management and manipulation of cultural hierarchies. Indeed, as Pierre Bourdieu explains, when considering the successful negotiation of the 'hierarchically structured' literary public sphere, '*places*—galleries, theatres, publishing houses—make all the difference ... because these sites designate an audience which, on the basis of consumption, qualifies the product consumed' (*Field* 95). And in the case of the Hogarth Press, the cultural capital of middlebrow women writers was doubly rewarded, for they were first approved by the audience of their editors, the highbrow Woolfs, and then integrated within the network of readers, contributors and supporters of the well-respected Press. As I will show in two separate studies of their work below, the Hogarth Press gave Rose Macaulay and E. M. Delafield an alternative publishing arena that contrasted sharply with Macaulay's work with Collins or Delafield's work with Macmillan. With this focus, we find the Woolfs challenging both the operating procedure of a network of commercial presses and the preconceptions of the broader reading public on what constitutes the relationship between modernism and the middlebrow.

Middlebrow women writers were often considered insider-outsiders to 'legitimate culture', an issue that Macaulay and Delafield addressed repeatedly in their fiction, popular essays and academic studies. They often moved within highbrow networks because of their commitments to politics, feminism and education, yet their work was circumscribed by the limited opportunities for female writers within the mainstream publishing sphere and their own financial constraints. Essentially, this meant that their witty journalism, best-selling novels and 'light' essay collections superseded their experimental or problem novels, poetry and literary or social criticism. As Bourdieu explains, 'the most heteronomous cultural producers . . . can offer the least resistance to external demands', and thus have the fewest opportunities to shape the trajectory of their careers (*Field* 41). Indeed, following the demands of their editors and publishing such a vast array of popular novels, essays and journalism did prove problematic for Macaulay and Delafield when they tried to attain more prestigious positions in the literary field. But unlike many other middlebrow women writers, they did have many clear advantages, including access to the Hogarth Press and the name-value which it provided. Macaulay's and Delafield's work with the Press explores 'a more richly heterogeneous record of early twentieth-century cultural debates about the arts', as Ann Ardis calls for (408). Moreover, it emphasises how the 'position-takings' (or movements within the field of cultural production) of Macaulay, Delafield and the Woolfs were 'semi-conscious *strategies* in a game in which the conquest of cultural legitimacy . . . is at stake' (Bourdieu, *Field* 137). While they could not control all aspects of the reception of their publications or the cultural capital of the Press itself (hence the 'semi-conscious' nature of their efforts), they did work to create a network of diverse writers that helped to shape interwar legitimate culture in the face of the 'battle of the brows'.

In the 1920s, however, Virginia Woolf still approached this work with ambivalence, for such a bold trajectory for the Press would also impact her own cultural capital. Woolf's diary entries and letters concerning Macaulay show that Woolf mistrusted the middlebrow's journalism, popular novels and many of her friends, yet still found that Macaulay was 'just on the intellectual side of the border' (*D3* 61–2). Just as Jaffe shows that 'Eliot's name represented more than the sum of those intimate works' (72), the names of Macaulay and Delafield were 'cultural signifiers' for a range of assumptions about the middlebrow and the complexity of their positions within cultural hierarchies. Publishing the academic work of middlebrow women writers through the Hogarth Press was a decision to use the cultural capital of both the Press and middlebrow women writers to publicly portray the fluid boundaries between highbrow and middlebrow spheres. When members of the reading public saw the names of Rose Macaulay or E. M. Delafield upon Hogarth Press books, or when Macaulay or Delafield created links between their middlebrow and highbrow publications, the relationships between the two were exposed and the representations of each within the literary public sphere were changed.

Middlebrow Women Writers and the 'Battle of the Brows' at the Hogarth Press

Many interwar women writers working 'outside' modernism strate-gically performed multiples roles within the literary public sphere. According to Alice Gambrell, reading the complexities of intellectual women writers' forms of 'self-revision' illuminates the important ways in which they responded to modernist representations of them as 'other' or, for my purposes, middlebrow. Indeed, 'if modernist configurations of otherness tended to be static and coherent . . . then the process of con-stant self-revision can also be read, in part, as a strong effort to renegoti-ate these kinds of misreadings' (Gambrell 34). Macaulay, for example, explored similar ideas on class, gender and politics in a procession of historical fiction, essays, satires, adventure tales and detective fiction. E. M. Delafield is known best for her comic *Provincial Lady* series, but many of her more serious novels and her witty journalism from *Time and Tide* form the foundation of the popular series. Macaulay and Delafield thus challenged generalisations of their public positions through revi-sions that exposed the complexities of the middlebrow sphere; they used the Hogarth Press to further this work and to show how both writers and readers could navigate culturally constructed divides between the high- and middlebrow spheres. Both women were thus keenly aware of how the names of the Hogarth Press and the Woolfs were 'promotional vehicles' for increased cultural capital for any work attached to them (Jaffe 17).

Moreover, the Woolfs recognised that middlebrow women writers were often frustrated or inhibited by the literary establishment and sought to use their own name-value to ease such circumstances. Many middlebrow women writers attended university,[3] pursued diverse politi-cal interests[4] and were continually aggravated by their limited pub-lishing opportunities as cultural hierarchies tightened throughout the 1920s and early 1930s. When Macaulay and Delafield published with the Press, their work clearly built upon their own interests (language for Macaulay and the Victorian period for Delafield), rather than the desires or demands of Leonard and Virginia Woolf. There was, in fact, an array of women writers working with the Press during the interwar period, although the range of neglected or obscured women writers appears to increase after the publication of *A Room of One's Own*. Contributors such as writer Gertrude Stein (1874–1946); poet and critic Edith Sitwell (1887–1964); poet Laura Riding (1901–91); or feminist and editor Lady Rhondda (1883–1958) are not surprising choices for Leonard and Virginia Woolf. Yet they also published neglected poet

Ida Graves (1902–99); journalist, feminist and middlebrow novelist Winifred Holtby (1898–1935); and quasi-middlebrow historical novelist Naomi Mitchison (1897–1999), to name just a handful of the women working with the Hogarth Press. As my work on Macaulay and Delafield below will show, the Press became an increasingly liberating space for middlebrow women writers' academic work as Leonard and Virginia Woolf's anxieties about upholding cultural hierarchies lessened – and these concerns diminished as the Press published more work on socialism, education, and women's history and culture.

This work was often done through academic studies and series, and the middlebrow women writers' texts alongside established highbrow writers emphasises the 'heterogeneity' of the Hogarth Press, as Laura Marcus puts it. Yet as my work shows, the Press' 'broad and heterogeneous list' did not merely help 'move "Bloomsbury" to a more central position in intellectual and cultural life' (Marcus 129); it also moved middlebrow women writers to such prominent and academically stimulating positions. The *Hogarth Letters* (1931–3) series, for example, included contributions from a wide range of authors, from Virginia Woolf's *A Letter to a Young Poet* and E. M. Forster's *A Letter to Madan Blanchard* to Rebecca West's *A Letter to a Grandfather*, Rosamond Lehmann's *Letter to a Sister* and the middlebrow Hugh Walpole's *A Letter to a Modern Novelist*.

The Press' forays into children's literature were perhaps even more innovative and daring, for its highbrow name was coupled with a genre that is often dominated by struggling women writers. The texts of the World-Makers and World-Shakers series were sold for 1s. 6d. each and served as introductions to the lives of historical figures for children. The catchy and playful title of the series, the descriptive chapter titles and the carefully planned attempts to engage readers through exciting, rather than academic or highly intellectual writing, indicate that World-Makers and World-Shakers participated in the tropes of middlebrow novels.[5] The Press was thus keen to attract a broad readership and to use their prestigious intellectual reputation to enter the profitable children's literary field, which women writers from Frances Hodgson Burnett (1849–1924) to Mary Noel Streatfeild (1895–1986) used to support themselves. But the Woolfs also used the World-Makers and World-Shakers line to grant women writers a space to explore their academic interests. Naomi Mitchison, for example, co-authored a biography of Socrates for the Press and so pursued work on ancient Greece in a different (if still limiting) genre than her historical novel *Cloud Cuckoo Land* (1925).

In general, however, Leonard and Virginia Woolf performed this remapping of the literary field without compromising their aesthetic preferences, for many best-selling and leading middlebrow women writers' novels, such as those of Macaulay, Delafield, Margaret Kennedy, Stella Gibbons or Winifred Holtby, are noticeably absent from Hogarth Press publications. Aside from Julia Strachey's satiric *Cheerful Weather for the Wedding* (1932), the immensely successful novels of Vita Sackville-West were the exception to this rule. Sackville-West's novels were extremely popular among the middlebrow reading public,[6] and she was, often, an outsider within Bloomsbury. Indeed, Leonard Woolf described Sackville-West as 'an honest, simple, sentimental, romantic, naïve, and competent writer', who would have been a more successful best-seller if she was not so detached from the British middle-class (*Downhill* 158).

Middlebrow women writers did submit their work to the Hogarth Press, but, as was the case with Ivy Compton-Burnett (1884–1969), Leonard and Virginia Woolf did not seek to publish fiction which they found too traditional or without 'genius'. Even after Compton-Burnett's *Brothers and Sisters* (1929) became an acclaimed best-seller, Virginia Woolf was confident in her decision against publishing it. She maintained that while the Press 'ought to have done *Brothers and Sisters*' there was 'something bleached about Miss Compton Burnett', and she preferred to publish authors such as T. S. Eliot and Katherine Mansfield (*L4* 92). Virginia Woolf's decision to reject Compton-Burnett indicates the extent to which Woolf disliked fiction that appeared to be too middlebrow during the late 1920s.[7]

Keeping Up Appearances with the Hogarth Press

For many middlebrow writers, the Hogarth Press thus remained an elusive space during the 1920s. Aside from Vita Sackville-West, Rose Macaulay was the only best-selling middlebrow writer to publish under the Hogarth Press until the Hogarth Letters series (1931–3). Much like many interwar women writers, Macaulay published popular fiction because she did not wish to write modernist fiction and because she could not support herself through academic nonfiction studies or devote adequate time to what she considered to be more 'serious' fiction, such as her historical novel *They Were Defeated* (1932). Throughout the 1910s, 1920s and 1930s, she negotiated between the highbrow sphere, which could limit her aesthetic tastes, and the middlebrow publishers, which often circumscribed the intellectual range of her work. Yet she also sought to refigure the imperfect middlebrow sphere to suit her needs and was successful in some important ways through strategic position-takings. From 1920 on she wrote primarily satiric realist novels on modern women and the British middle class, but her scholarly interests in language, the English Civil War, religion in literature and modern fiction were rarely pursued directly in her imaginative literature. The Hogarth Press published Macaulay's *Catchwords and Claptrap* (1926), on language 'use and misuse', *Some Religious Elements in English Literature* (1931) and *The Writings of E. M. Forster* (1938).

At first glance, Leonard and Virginia Woolf's decision to publish Macaulay is not particularly shocking, for Macaulay attended Oxford, was an award-winning novelist, was the daughter of a Cambridge Don and, much like Virginia Woolf, was a descendent of the 'intellectual aristocracy'. Macaulay was also, however, a witty and satiric novelist and journalist with some disdain for high modernist literature, as evidenced by her satiric portraits of it in the novels *Potterism* (1920) and *Crewe Train* (1926). Such a perplexing combination of high- and middlebrow attributes complicated Woolf's and Macaulay's relationship as it progressed from a tense acquaintanceship during the early 1920s to a close friendship during the 1930s. Macaulay had the greatest esteem for Woolf, yet did not seek to join her friend's Bloomsbury world, while Woolf found her friend to be a pitiable and paradoxical figure. She writes that Macaulay 'has the beautiful eyes of all of us distinguished women writers; the refinement; the clearness of cut; the patience; & humbleness. It is her voice & manner that make one edgy' (*D3* 61–2). Ironically, throughout much of the 1920s Woolf was also envious of Macaulay's successes in the literary field.[8]

Catchwords and Claptrap was a part of the second series of Hogarth Essays, a collection dealing with literature, the arts, publishing and modernity. Leonard Woolf found that the Hogarth Press pamphlets were a unique way of introducing the British reading public to otherwise obscure thoughts and ideas in modern literature, poetry, art, philosophy or history. He claimed that 'those which we published by T. S. Eliot, Roger Fry, Virginia, Maynard Keynes, J. A. Hobson, were remarkable . . . All the others were, I think, well worth publishing' (*Downhill* 162). From the start of Macaulay's *Catchwords and Claptrap*, her writing indicates that she recognised the privilege of publishing with the Hogarth Press. Rather than present herself as a confident highbrow writer, she begins rather timidly, making excuses for her ideas by asking her audience to indulge her 'private taste'; this apology is unique to Macaulay's work. The language of the essay, particularly in the introductory paragraphs, is complex and at times almost convoluted, as if she were writing to impress her audience. Sarah LeFanu attributes this 'intellectual anxiety' to 'a lack of ease with the abstract argument she is pursuing' (177). This seems highly implausible, however, given Macaulay's life-long fascination with this subject and her 'constant' use of her father's *Oxford English Dictionary* in all of her writing projects (Emery 213).

The 'intellectual anxiety' is instead, I would contend, based upon Macaulay's discomfort with her insider-outsider position to literary modernism and her trepidation about this bold self-positioning within the highbrow publishing sphere. *Catchwords and Claptrap* was published with a coveted Vanessa Bell cover alongside Gertrude Stein's *Composition as Explanation* and Leonard Woolf's *Hunting the Highbrow*.[9] Macaulay's text is clearly crafted to appeal to a highbrow audience, for it creates a binary between her presumed elite readers and 'the masses'. In the essay, Macaulay complains that popular and uneducated writers have the 'lazy and sentimental desire to convey an effect by using catchwords' (*Catchwords* 10). Here, she effectively mocks writers who do not have her advantages in education or her (semi-) respectable position within the literary marketplace. She also expands upon her hatred of the sentimental, attacking it because it is uneducated and 'lazy' (10). Because the Hogarth Press was detached from her mainstream publications, Macaulay used this alternative social forum to pursue her work on literary criticism and language and participate in conversations on modern literature and culture with the leading figures of her day.

Macaulay's argument, however, is not fully developed – in part because she recognises the Hogarth Press as a heterogeneous, but still modernist, space during the 1920s, and so she does not explore why writers resort to the sentimental in literature. Indeed, through self-censoring she effectively suppresses her own knowledge about the relationship between writing (art) and publication (sales), a move which anticipates Bourdieu's discussions on the difference between mainstream and avant-garde publishing houses (*Field* 99–100). Her novels suggest that she had a more pragmatic understanding of the sentimental in fiction, and the need for incorporating aspects of romance or sentimentalism within imaginative literature. Indeed, in much of her middlebrow work, Macaulay seems to have anticipated Bourdieu's claim that middlebrow culture is 'defined' by its public, although she would not have supported his argument that this is the sole foundation for its production (Bourdieu, *Field* 125). In 'Problems of a Writer's Life' (1925), published in her essay collection with the mainstream publishing house Methuen, Macaulay advises 'wise' authors to 'exercise compulsion' and add 'what the public wants', especially a 'love interest' ('Writer's Life' 49). The contradictions between this essay and *Catchwords* highlight Macaulay's own struggles with conforming to the standards of both highbrow (or modernist) and middlebrow literature. Her harsh and judgemental tone in *Catchwords and Claptrap* corresponds with many ideas found in her novels from *The Secret River* (1909) and *The Lee Shore* (1912) to *Crewe Train* (1926) and *The Towers of Trebizond* (1956). But in nearly all of her novels a 'love interest' is evident, and so clearly Macaulay has 'exercise[d] compulsion' in order to comply with the demands of her editors. Macaulay's work within the high- and middlebrow spheres was thus a constant refinement of her own public personae and a strategic manipulation of the cultural capital and expectations of the social forums comprised of her publishers and reading publics.

Rather than pursuing exclusively highbrow publishing ventures after *Catchwords and Claptrap* (1926), Macaulay effectively committed herself to the middlebrow sphere and attempted to refine it to suit her tastes. She did not abandon intellectually stimulating work but she did insist that women's literature could incorporate elements of satire, comedy, history and realism without excessively pandering to sentimental tastes; as the Woolfs would have recognised, the cultural capital earned by publishing within the highbrow sphere, undoubtedly, helped her to maintain such standards with mainstream publishers. Macaulay also used *Catchwords and Claptrap* to emphasise the connections between literature deemed highbrow and that considered middlebrow. Her aptly named *Keeping Up Appearances* (1928) serves as a companion text for *Catchwords and Claptrap*, for her novel offers an alternative theorisation of the 'battle of the brows' and the middlebrow women writers' role within it.

The novel's garish blood-red dust jacket, with advertisements for other middlebrow novels, detective fiction and 'Wild West Novels',[10] as well as the catchy and descriptive chapter titles, position the book within the middlebrow literary marketplace. The text avails itself of many stereotypically middlebrow themes: this witty novel comes complete with a love affair, references to reading cultures and other middlebrow writers, and discussions on the dynamics of middle-class English daily life in the 1920s, all of which must have pleased Macaulay's mainstream publishers. Yet, as Alice Crawford argues, it also has a 'concentration' of modernist themes and techniques (104), a tactic which, as I would suggest, forcefully positions the text within highbrow public discourse and shows the hybridity of the middlebrow for privileged writers. By incorporating modernist tropes within a book that is formulaically and physically middlebrow in many respects, Macaulay visually represents the permeable boundaries between culturally constructed hierarchies – and her own work with the Hogarth Press further supports these efforts.

Building upon her Hogarth Press publication, Macaulay subtly weaves her own highbrow theories, published by elite and powerful literary writers and editors, within her literature labelled middlebrow. And she does so through a character whose identity is literally torn in two by the pressures of cultural hierarchies. The novel revolves around journalist Daphne Daisy Simpson, as she seeks to reconcile her highbrow life as the flirtatious and bold Daphne with the middlebrow world of the slightly sentimental and timid Daisy. In *Keeping Up Appearances*, Macaulay argues that a middlebrow text can openly discuss supposedly highbrow ideas through the fragmented Daphne/Daisy's fascination, and irritation, with the ways in which words 'possess activity' (61). 'Daisy' claims that negotiating the differences in phrasing and accent between her family members in (lower-middle-class) East Sheen and (upper-middle-class) Holland Park is like 'knowing intimately two languages' (61). These differences in languages further illuminate some of Macaulay's own ideas in her Hogarth Essay – ideas that were originally presented for a predominantly highbrow audience. Discussing sexism in the English language in *Catchwords and Claptrap*, Macaulay claims that the word 'spinster, originally meaning a woman who spins and then an unmarried woman, seems to have acquired (outside its legal use) some opprobrious cant sense, and to be used often with reference to some regrettable qualities, or to advanced age, or both' (*Catchwords* 20).

Macaulay continues this conversation in *Keeping Up Appearances*, again in terms of education and sexism, but in her novel she also considers differences in culture and class. In Bloomsbury society, 'spinsterhood was merely the feminine counterpart of bachelordom, and no more discreditable', but in the 'simple and homely circle' of East Sheen, 'it savoured of disgrace, of having tried and failed' (*Keeping* 139). Spinsterhood is a failure in the latter circle because the average lower-middle-class and middlebrow East Sheen young woman cannot successfully support herself in the manner of a bachelor – and because the male middlebrow publishers and writers, 'the masters, never the slaves, of language', have defined it as such (162). Within the Hogarth text, Macaulay did not venture to discuss this middlebrow gendered reality or the implications of a historical shift in meaning for the life of a single woman; similarly, in her popular novel, Macaulay avoided judgements of her mainstream reading public and favoured more direct and simple language.[11]

By continuing the conversation she began in *Catchwords and Claptrap*, Macaulay demonstrates that a middlebrow text can explore the same ideas as one marketed towards highbrow readers. Moreover, the same author can disseminate these ideas to a broad audience, and so extend her reading public and the network of the Hogarth Press. She thus argues for all of her work to be recognised as modern 'legitimate culture', even if it is not technically highbrow. To accomplish this end, Macaulay's counternarrative must challenge stereotypes about high- and middlebrow cultures and show that the middlebrow novel has goals distinct from those of the highbrow sphere. The cultural capital of both the highbrow Hogarth Press and the middlebrow Macaulay illustrates that participants within the literary field could challenge cultural hierarchies in order to craft new forms of modern literature, even if they could not control them. And in doing so, Macaulay and Leonard and Virginia Woolf, via the Hogarth Press, helped to guide their trajectories within the literary field and remapped the boundaries of the high- and middlebrow spheres.

The Provincial Lady in Bloomsbury

Virginia Woolf's novels and criticism, Freudian psychology, political commentary and modern poetry are often considered the most enduring and prominent publications of the Hogarth Press, but the 1930s were a period of dynamism and experimentation across cultural divides. During this time, many publishers fretted about book clubs and the rise of new publishing ventures such as Penguin Books. As Cole explains in *Books and the People*, 'the booksellers—with one or two exceptions—hated the Book Clubs; the publishers again with some exceptions, looked askance at the sixpennies. There was a considerable outcry . . . persons prophesied the immediate bankruptcy of Mr. Lane and Mr. Gollancz, or the ruin of all other publishers, or of bookshops, or of authors, of all those things at once' (5). Leonard and Virginia Woolf, however, built upon their projects within the middlebrow literary public sphere by seeking a broader reading public and endorsing a more democratic literary marketplace that acknowledged value in texts outside of a traditional highbrow sphere. This work included several publications on education and the aforementioned ventures into the children's literary marketplace – a space with few academic or high modernist attributes but a long history of middlebrow women contributors. The Hogarth Press also participated in a predominantly middlebrow revival of interest in Victorian literature and culture, an act that defies Virginia Woolf's earlier work to 'place [herself] in opposition to Victorian social and moral standards' and literary styles, as Lois Cucullu puts it, in order to claim her status within the high modernist field (6).

By encouraging academic and popular discussions on Victorian lives and literature during the mid 1930s Leonard and Virginia Woolf were supporting Virginia Woolf's work on women's literary history in *A Room of One's Own*. But Victorian literature was also the direct predecessor of realist middlebrow literature for, as Humble explains, 'the stylistic and thematic blueprints of the sort of literature that became seen as middlebrow . . . are little different from the conventions that dominated the mainstream novel throughout the nineteenth century' (11). While best-selling middlebrow novels during the 1920s focused upon bohemianism or postwar gender roles, such as Rose Macaulay's *Dangerous Ages* (1921), Margaret Kennedy's *The Constant Nymph* (1924) or Michael Arlen's *The Green Hat* (1924), the middlebrow reading public of the 1930s was increasingly interested in Victorian literature and culture. And E. M. Delafield, an 'heir of Jane Austen' (31), as Rachel R. Mather deems her, combined the tendency for satiric commentaries upon modernity in the 1920s with a Victorian literary tradition.

The Hogarth Press' publications on Victorian literature and culture during the 1930s included Virginia Woolf's own *Flush* (1933), her fictional portrait of both Elizabeth Barrett Browning's spaniel and the life of the Victorian poet; a two-volume edited edition of the letters and diaries of Bertrand Russell's parents, *The Amberley Papers* (1937);[12] *The Authorship of Wuthering Heights* by Irene Cooper Willis (1936);[13] and E. M. Delafield's *The Brontës, Their Lives Recorded by Their Contemporaries* (1935) and *Ladies and Gentlemen in Victorian Literature* (1937). This range of publications – from the family papers of Leonard and Virginia Woolf's friend, Russell, to a study by the established academic Willis to the popular Delafield's work in a genre outside of fiction and journalism – indicates that the Hogarth Press was networked into the mainstream 'public culture', to borrow a phrase from Lawrence Rainey (56). More than acting as 'democratic highbrows' who sought to introduce the reading public to modernist literature and art or past works of 'genius', Leonard and Virginia Woolf used the Hogarth Press to publish academic and intellectual discussions on middlebrow culture, and were thus arguing against maintaining strict cultural hierarchies in literature. There is, however, a key difference between the work of E. M. Delafield and that of the Russells or Willis. Middlebrow literature was often denigrated for being traditional and pleasurable, rather than modern and intellectually stimulating. E. M. Delafield, as Powell emphasises, took great pleasure in reading Victorian literature (140). And when writing for the Hogarth Press, Delafield sought to convey the enjoyment she experienced when reading the Brontës, Charlotte M. Yonge and others, and clearly encourages her readers to do the same.

The decision to publish two texts by E. M. Delafield was far more radical than working with Rose Macaulay, a writer with many of the same friends as Leonard and Virginia Woolf and with whom they shared similar familial, political, aesthetic and academic views and experiences. Unlike Macaulay, Delafield did not move in elite intellectual circles regularly, nor was she the beneficiary of a university education or a highbrow heritage. As the author of the *Provincial Lady* series, she could merely make biting comments about women's positions in Britain to a women's league or explore nineteenth-century fiction by making a much-publicised (but little-enjoyed) visit to Louisa May Alcott's home. Her views on politics, class and gender were relegated to satiric articles in *Time and Tide*, the popular and intellectual feminist weekly review on politics, literature, current events and the arts edited by Lady Rhondda. While *Time and Tide* allowed Delafield to work alongside leading women writers of her day (including Woolf), her fascination with nineteenth-century fiction was used as an endearing but sentimental trait of the 'provincial lady' through much of her career.

The Diary of a Provincial Lady (1931), *The Provincial Lady Goes Further* (or *The Provincial Lady in London*) (1933), *The Provincial Lady in America* (1934), *The Provincial Lady in Russia* (1937) and *The Provincial Lady in Wartime* (1940) depict the life of a middle-class wife and mother who writes for *Time and Tide* reader-competitions and in her diary – when she is not running her household, raising her children, attempting to hire new servants and stretching her budget. The Provincial Lady is a struggling amateur writer at the start of the series; she achieves fame when her diary is published, but rarely considers herself a professional writer. For Delafield, the *Provincial Lady* series brought success but also marked a break from her literary heritage and her work to portray professional women in the literary public sphere.

The Hogarth Press, however, offered her an opportunity to 'flex her literary muscles' as Violet Powell puts it, at a time when Delafield was increasingly frustrated by her limited opportunities in the middlebrow publishing sphere. Powell claims that the owners of the Hogarth Press 'would obviously have been pleased to add the successful E. M. Delafield to their list' (141), but in actuality, as Virginia Woolf's comments on Compton-Burnett above show, Delafield was especially fortunate to be publishing with the Hogarth Press. Delafield, like Macaulay, was aware of this privilege. She used her work with the Hogarth Press to argue for the recognition of middlebrow literature as modern and pleasurable 'legitimate culture'.

E. M. Delafield's and Virginia Woolf's relationship is perhaps remembered best by Delafield's depiction of the 'very, very distinguished lady novelist', presumed to be Woolf, in *The Diary of a Provincial Lady*

(78). The Provincial Lady finds the 'lady novelist' to be a terrible bore who discusses nothing but sales, her own books and literary scandals. When this was written, Virginia Woolf was the esteemed author of *Mrs. Dalloway* (1925) and *To the Lighthouse* (1927), while Delafield was a respected but fairly traditional writer who worked outside of high literary modernism. In a February 1935 diary entry, Virginia Woolf quickly dismissed Delafield as 'the [Winifred] Holtby type' – a reference that most likely refers to Delafield's active role in *Time and Tide* and her immensely popular women's novels, rather than her sexuality (*D4* 279). But just eight months later, in a letter to Angelica Bell, Virginia Woolf has clearly gained sympathy and respect for Delafield. She writes 'I've been seeing E. M. Delafield, who writes the Provincial Lady; she is called Dashwood really; Elizabeth Dashwood; and lives in an old house like a character in Jane Austen; whom she adores. But she has to scribble and scribble to pay for it and her children' (*L5* 445). In this portrait, Delafield is the struggling woman writer who must produce novels and journalism at a stunning rate to support her family, and is thus incapable of pursuing her own more intellectual or scholarly interests. Delafield began working with the Hogarth Press between Woolf's two descriptions: *The Brontës, Their Lives Recorded by their Contemporaries* was published in May 1935 and *Ladies and Gentlemen in Victorian Fiction* was published in June 1937.

Delafield's first project with the Hogarth Press was one of many contributions to the middlebrow Brontë 'obsession' during the 1930s (Humble 176). Virginia Woolf claimed in a letter to Lady Cecil in July 1932 that she could not 'follow the Brontë enthusiasts', although Woolf did read E. F. Benson's biography of Charlotte Brontë and quickly dismissed Alice Law as a 'lunatic' for daring to presume that Branwell Brontë wrote *Wuthering Heights* (*L5* 80). Delafield's reading public would presumably also be familiar with Rachel Ferguson's *The Brontës Went to Woolworths* (1931), Clemence Dane's *Wild Decembers: A Play in Three Acts* (1932) and E. Thornton Cook's *They Lived* (1935), to name just a few of the Brontë novels, plays, collections and studies published throughout the 1930s. For Humble, Delafield's *The Brontës* 'serves as a useful indication of the range of the Brontës' appeal at this time—from the middlebrow whimsy . . . to the high cultural seriousness' (Humble 177). Yet for Delafield, her work on the Brontës and the later *Ladies and Gentlemen in Victorian Fiction* showed not merely a range, but hybridity; both her mainstream and Hogarth publications addressed women in literature, reading practices, cultural hierarchies and the Victorian period.

Delafield introduced and edited over two hundred entries that describe the lives of the Brontës, from their childhood through their critical reception, for *The Brontës, Their Lives Recorded by Their Contemporaries*. In this text, Delafield guides her readers through a historical study of the Brontës and to her new role as a literary critic working for the Hogarth Press. *Ladies and Gentlemen in Victorian Fiction* is a far bolder study than *The Brontës*, for the former seeks to renew interest in forgotten nineteenth-century women writers whose careers closely resemble that of Delafield. As with her work on the Brontës, Delafield insists upon recognising the literary value of Victorian fiction. In *Ladies and Gentlemen*, however, she focuses primarily on popular Victorian women writers, particularly Charlotte M. Yonge (1823–1901), a writer who, like Delafield, produced an enormous quantity of literature on everyday life but was not considered to be an elite or high author. Delafield used this opportunity with the Hogarth Press to emphasise the importance of studying everyday life in the Victorian period and in modernity, for the introduction calls for research on the impact of the wireless within domestic spaces, changing roles within family life and the rise in suburban middle-class life.

Delafield's work in *Ladies and Gentlemen* parallels the feminist principles that Virginia Woolf outlines in *A Room of One's Own*; both Delafield and Woolf seek to recognise the work of women writers and create a history of women's literature. Yet rather than uphold the mythical 'Shakespeare's Sister' or women of 'genius', Delafield endorses the literature most like her own, and that of her middlebrow contemporaries. In the introduction of *Ladies and Gentlemen*, she explains that

> the true lovers of the Victorian domestic traditions are born rather than made—and not all born in the reign of Good Queen Victoria, either. To such, the minor aspects of the social and domestic scene of those days are even more fascinating than are its major or public implications. Of these, many official records exist, and many descriptions can be found in the pages of classical fiction. The present volume attempts no more than to present certain less well-known extracts from minor novelists, writing of the contemporary outlook in the mid- and late-Victorian English middle-class home. (9)

Ladies and Gentlemen in Victorian Fiction recovered lost documents of women's history and culture that were not found in the 'official records', just as Virginia Woolf encouraged scholars to do in *A Room of One's Own*. Many of the excerpts which Delafield provided and discussed revolve around the everyday lives of fictional middle-class Victorian women, as described by 'minor' middle-class Victorian women writers. And, as a literary descendent of Charlotte M. Yonge and other popular Victorian writers, Delafield was also arguing for her own literature to be recognised for its literary and historical value.

This contribution for the Hogarth Press aligns Delafield's work in fiction – on women's lives, domestic spaces and the everyday – and the Bloomsbury world of this supposedly highbrow publishing house and its 'very very distinguished novelist'. The Hogarth Press offered Delafield a method of reaching a new audience and working in new genres. At the same time, Delafield served as a liaison between the Press and a broader spectrum of the British reading public and women's literary history. Delafield's ardent support for Victorian and modern middlebrow literature in a Hogarth Press publication indicates an important shift within cultural hierarchies in the mid 1930s, and a significant change in Virginia and Leonard Woolf's relationships with middlebrow women writers. While Rose Macaulay struggled to discuss the challenges of middlebrow authorship in *Catchwords and Claptrap*, E. M. Delafield openly endorses a history of women's middlebrow culture and calls for the recognition of contemporary middlebrow texts as legitimate culture in her Hogarth Press publication. Through this work, then, the Woolfs and Delafield sought to 'recognize that a multiplicity of cultural agendas for the arts were still available . . . not all of which positioned artists and intellectuals comfortably in allegiance with difficulty, highbrow culture, and the academy' (Ardis 427).

By publishing the work of E. M. Delafield, Rose Macaulay and other middlebrow women writers alongside their established highbrow contributors, Leonard and Virginia Woolf created an alternative social forum for women writers free from the pressures of the editors and publishers of the mainstream literary establishment. Virginia Woolf, in particular, became a great champion for women writers at the Press, an endeavour which positions Leonard and Virginia Woolf as 'outsiders' to the elitist aims of some of their highbrow contemporaries, such as John Lehmann or F. R. and Q. D. Leavis. In a May 1938 diary entry, for example, Virginia Woolf records that she 'suspect[s] [their] first breach with John [Lehmann]. It'll be over his fashion complex. HP must be in the movement' (*D5* 138). Virginia Woolf had endorsed Kathleen Nott's *Mile End*, a novel about Jewish garment factory workers in London's East End. According to Woolf, it was 'a powerful Arnold Bennett novel', but John Lehmann[14] found it too 'old fashioned' and thus not an acceptable representative of the Hogarth Press (138). As Leonard Woolf explains, he and Virginia Woolf hoped that John Lehmann would help them 'keep in touch with the younger generation or generations', so that they could remain connected to the latest progressive and experimental literature; this sort of friction was thus predictable and Lehmann aligned them with emerging highbrows of the day (*Downhill* 174).

The case of *Mile End*, however, illustrates Leonard and Virginia

Woolf's dual positions within the literary field during the late 1930s. On the one hand, they supported avant-garde, modernist and progressive writers, including the poets who published with *New Writing*, the periodical that Lehmann edited for the Hogarth Press. But Leonard and Virginia Woolf published *Mile End* because they came to appreciate a wider range of literary styles, which included those middlebrow women who wrote in the realist fashion and were often delimited within the mainstream literary public sphere. Rather than focus upon the 'hunting' of the highbrow or the taint of the middlebrow, they sought to encourage new research and discussions on women's culture, which included middlebrow literature. They thus helped establish a dynamic and fluid interwar literary field by arguing that a heterogeneous modernism and hybrid middlebrow could overlap and work alongside each other.

Notes

1. The title of Margaret Cole's study is, perhaps intentionally, remarkably similar to the Hogarth Press *Books and the Public* (1927). As Melba Cuddy-Keane succinctly puts it, 'the argument of [*Books and the Public*] is that people need to buy more books, but the underlying concern is the survival of the highbrow press' (Cuddy-Keane 63). The Hogarth Press also published the work of Margaret Cole's husband, G. D. H. Cole, including *Politics and Literature* (1929) and *The Machinery of Socialist Planning* (1938). The Coles also co-authored detective fiction and poetry.
2. While the 'battle of the brows' is a hyperbolic descriptor invoking mythic struggles between high-, middle- and lowbrows, there were increased interests in defining, categorising and upholding boundaries between cultural hierarchies throughout much of the interwar period.
3. University-educated middlebrow women writers included Rose Macaulay, Winifred Holtby, Vera Brittain, Dorothy Sayers, Margaret Kennedy (all at Somerville, Oxford) and Storm Jameson (Leeds).
4. Throughout the 1930s Rose Macaulay, Vera Brittain, Rosamond Lehmann, Storm Jameson and Winifred Holtby were engaged in many of the same political activities as the Woolfs. The Hogarth Press' increase in political publications in the 1930s, according to Willis, was predominantly inspired by Leonard Woolf and provided an 'almost . . . new identity for Hogarth' (Willis 213). Since, however, Virginia Woolf's female contemporaries often figure prominently in her diaries and letters – either as friends or as competition – their work at the Hogarth Press indicates that both Leonard and Virginia Woolf's roles as public intellectuals, editors and writers influenced their decision to use the Hogarth Press to encourage the interests of middlebrow women writers.
5. In the foreword to Vita Sackville-West's book on Joan of Arc, for example, readers are told that '[n]othing vital has been omitted, but an attempt has

been made to present the facts of history as vividly as possible for the interest of young readers.'

6. Vita Sackville-West's novels, such as *The Edwardians* (1930) and *All Passion Spent* (1931), offered the Press substantial financial gains and public recognition; the former was so successful that it became one of the first Penguin Books selections in 1935. For a discussion of Vita Sackville-West's influence upon the work of Virginia Woolf (and Woolf's influence upon Sackville-West) see Karyn Z. Sproles' *Desiring Women: The Partnership of Virginia Woolf and Vita Sackville-West*.

7. Ironically, Compton-Burnett would have been an ideal choice for the Hogarth Press, for as her career progressed she was increasingly respected as a great realist woman writer with 'highbrow difficulty' and 'middlebrow pleasures' (Humble 26). And as Humble explains, Woolf's opinion on Compton-Burnett changed over time: 'Virginia Woolf took her seriously as a highbrow rival, recording in her diary in 1937 the sleepless nights produced by the contrast of the favourable reviews received by Compton-Burnett's *Daughters and Sons* and those for her own *The Years*' (Humble 26).

8. This jealousy was, in part, because Macaulay was only one year Woolf's senior, yet she attended university; began publishing novels nine years earlier than Woolf, and received nearly immediate acclaim; attained commercial success nearly a decade before Woolf; and was the recipient of the Prix Femina-Vie Heureuse six years earlier than Woolf.

9. In *Hunting the Highbrow*, Leonard Woolf confronted issues of anti-intellectualism, the posthumous popularity of most 'great' authors and the roles of 'pseudo highbrows', ostensibly middlebrows who pretend to enjoy high culture for the sake of appearances.

10. Novels advertised on the dust jacket of *Keeping Up Appearances* include Katherine Tynan's *Lover of Women*, J. D. Beresford's *All or Nothing*, Phyllis Bottome's *Strange Fruit*, W. C. Tuttle's *Hashknife of the Canyon Trail*, Agatha Christie's *The Mystery of the Blue Train* and, interestingly, G. D. H. and Margaret Cole's *The Man From the River*, one of their detective fiction tales.

11. Neither Leonard nor Virginia Woolf discusses *Catchwords* in detail in any of their papers and any possible drafts of the essay Macaulay possessed would have been destroy in the WWII bombing of her flat. It is thus impossible to know if the omissions in her Hogarth essay are due to self-censorship or a suggestion by the Woolfs.

12. Bertrand and Patricia Russell edited the collection of letters and diaries of Lord and Lady Amberley. The handsome *Amberley Papers* includes numerous illustrations that depict Victorian life as humorous or enchanting.

13. Irene Cooper Willis' *The Authorship of Wuthering Heights* (Hogarth, 1936) is a carefully researched and well-developed argument that rejects Branwell Brontë as the author of *Wuthering Heights*. Willis' text is a formal, academic and feminist attack upon critics who fail to believe that a woman could write a novel with the power and genius of *Wuthering Heights*, but she does so in a way that is easily accessible for the average reader.

14. In 1938 John Lehmann worked for Leonard and Virginia Woolf; he did not take over Virginia Woolf's partnership in the Hogarth Press until 1939. An earlier plan to redistribute the ownership of the Hogarth Press called for a board of editors, one of whom was to have been John Lehmann's older sister, the esteemed and popular middlebrow writer Rosamond Lehmann (Lee 705). If this transition had instead occurred, Rosamond Lehmann would have had to contend with the other young poets, such as Stephen Spender, who would have joined the Press. But she most likely would have also supported the Hogarth Press' work in recruiting and publishing other middlebrow woman writers more often, including her close friends Rose Macaulay and Ivy Compton-Burnett.

Works cited

Ardis, Ann. 'The Dialogics of Modernism(s) in the *New Age*'. *Modernism/modernity* 14.3, 2007: 407–34.

Bourdieu, Pierre. *Distinction: A Social Critique of the Judgment of Taste*. Trans. Richard Nice. Cambridge: Harvard University Press, 1984.

—. *The Field of Cultural Production: Essays on Art and Literature*. Ed. Randal Johnson. New York: Columbia University Press, 1993.

—. *The Rules of Art*. 1992. Trans. Susan Emanuel. Cambridge: Polity Press, 1996.

Cole, Margaret. *Books and the People*. London: Hogarth Press, 1938.

Crawford, Alice. *Paradise Pursued: The Novels of Rose Macaulay*. Madison: Fairleigh Dickinson University Press, 1995.

Cucullu, Lois. *Expert Modernists, Matricide, and Modern Culture: Woolf, Forster, Joyce*. Basingstoke: Palgrave MacMillan, 2004.

Cuddy-Keane, Melba. *Virginia Woolf, The Intellectual, and the Public Sphere*. New York: Cambridge University Press, 2003.

Delafield, E. M., ed. and Introduction. *The Brontës, Their Live Recorded by Their Contemporaries*. London: Hogarth Press, 1935.

—. *The Diary of a Provincial Lady*. Chicago: Academy Chicago Publishers, [1931] 2002.

—. *Ladies and Gentlemen in Victorian Fiction*. London: Hogarth Press, 1937.

Emery, Jane. *Rose Macaulay: A Writer's Life*. London: John Murray, 1991.

Gambrell, Alice. *Women Intellectuals, Modernism, and Difference: Transatlantic Culture 1919–1945*. Cultural Margins 4. New York: Cambridge University Press, 1997.

Humble, Nicola. *The Feminine Middlebrow Novel, 1920s to 1950s: Class, Domesticity and Bohemianism*. New York: Oxford University Press, 2001.

Jaffe, Aaron. *Modernism and the Culture of Celebrity*. Cambridge: Cambridge University Press, 2005.

Lee, Hermione. *Virginia Woolf*. New York: Alfred A. Knopf, 1997.

LeFanu, Sarah. *Rose Macaulay*. London: Virago Press, 2003.

Levine, Lawrence. *Highbrow/Lowbrow: The Emergence of Cultural Hierarchy in America*. Cambridge: Harvard University Press, 1988.

Macaulay, Rose. *Catchwords and Claptrap*. London: Hogarth Press, 1926.

—. *Keeping Up Appearances*. London: William Collins, 1928.

—. 'Problems of a Writer's Life'. *A Casual Commentary*. London: Methuen, 1925.

Marcus, Laura. 'Virginia Woolf and the Hogarth Press'. In Ian Willison, Warwick Gould and Warren Chernaik, eds. *Modernist Writers and the Marketplace*. New York: St. Martin's Press, 1996: 124–50.

Mather, Rachel R. *The Heirs of Jane Austen: Twentieth Century Writers of the Comedy of Manners*. New York: Peter Lang, 1997.

Powell, Violet. *The Life of a Provincial Lady: A Study of E.M. Delafield and her Works*. London: Heinemann, 1988.

Rainey, Lawrence. *Institutions of Modernism: Literary Elites and Public Culture*. New Haven: Yale University Press, 1998.

Russell, Bertrand and Patricia Russell, eds. *The Amberley Papers: The Letters and Diaries of Lord and Lady Amberley*. London: Hogarth Press, 1937.

Sackville-West, Vita. *Joan of Arc*. London: Hogarth Press, 1937.

Sproles, Karyn Z. *Desiring Women: The Partnership of Virginia Woolf and Vita Sackville-West*. Buffalo: University of Toronto Press, 2006.

Willis, Irene Cooper. *The Authorship of Wuthering Heights*. London: Hogarth Press, 1936.

Willis, J. H. *Leonard and Virginia Woolf as Publishers: The Hogarth Press 1917–41*. Charlottesville: University Press of Virginia, 1992.

Woolf, Leonard. *Downhill All the Way: An Autobiography of the Years 1919 to 1939*. New York: Harcourt Brace Jovanovich, 1967.

—. *Hunting the Highbrow*. London: Hogarth Press, 1927.

Woolf, Virginia. *The Diary of Virginia Woolf*. Ed. Anne Olivier Bell and Andrew McNeillie. 5 vols. New York: Harcourt Brace, 1977–84.

—. *Letters of Virginia Woolf*. Eds Nigel Nicolson and Joanne Trautmann. 6 vols. New York: Harcourt, 1975–80.

—. *A Room of One's Own*. 1929. New York: Harcourt Brace, 1989.

Chapter 3

'Woolfs' in Sheep's Clothing: The Hogarth Press and 'Religion'

Diane F. Gillespie

'Beware of false prophets, which come to you in sheep's clothing, but inwardly they are ravening wolves'

(Matthew 7:15)

In the 1920s and 30s, Leonard and Virginia Woolf's avant-garde Hogarth Press published several books in a category labelled, belatedly and conventionally, 'Religion'. To the Woolfs and their liberal audience, however, neither the 'Religion' category nor the authors and titles within it were conventional. An era that challenged literal interpretations of scriptural texts with critical and historical readings and replaced institutional religious dogma with New Testament ethics influenced modernist poetry and novels (Lewis, 'Religion' 20–1; 'Churchgoing' 671) as well as other kinds of Hogarth Press publications. The Woolfs, interested themselves in discussions of material and spiritual, scientific and religious, institutional and individual values, produced several direct interrogations of entrenched religious concepts and institutions.[1]

Publications under the 'Religion' heading in the Complete Catalogues (up to 1934) were relatively few (Fig. 3.1). Anticipating the category, but published under 'New Publications' or 'General Literature', then listed by spring 1925 as out of print, was Logan Pearsall Smith's *Stories from the Old Testament* (1920). Included later under 'Religion', were R. [Richard] B. [Bevan] Braithwaite's *The State of Religious Belief* (1927), Sigmund Freud's *The Future of an Illusion* (1928), Rose Macaulay's *Some Religious Elements in English Literature* (1931), and J. [John] C. [Charleton] Hardwick's *A Letter to an Archbishop* (1932). Added to the list in 1939 was Freud's *Moses and Monotheism*. Since Freud's contributions are well known,[2] this chapter looks at lesser-known books and pamphlets and outlines the social and intellectual networks they reflected.

29

RELIGION

Braithwaite. THE STATE OF RELIGIOUS BELIEF. By R. B. BRAITHWAITE, Fellow of King's College, Cambridge. (1927.) Cr. 8vo. 4s. 6d.

Freud. THE FUTURE OF AN ILLUSION. By SIGMUND FREUD. (1928.) International Psycho-Analytical Library, No. 15. Royal 8vo. 6s.

Hardwick. A LETTER TO AN ARCHBISHOP. By J. C. HARDWICK. (1932.) Hogarth Letters, No. 10. Cr. 8vo. 1s.

Macaulay. SOME RELIGIOUS ELEMENTS IN ENGLISH LITER-ATURE. By ROSE MACAULAY. (1931.) Hogarth Lectures on Literature, 1st Series, No. 14. Cr. 8vo. 3s. 6d.

Figure 3.1 'Religion' list in the Hogarth Press Complete Catalogue of Publications, arranged under subjects, to the end of 1934. Courtesy of Manuscripts, Archives and Special Collections, Washington State University. Used by permission of The Random House Group Ltd.

Although few in number, these publications evidence the Press' increasingly professional engagement in the 1920s and 30s with a larger world of letters and serious cultural debate. Logan Pearsall Smith, R. B. Braithwaite, J. C. Hardwick and Rose Macaulay, who all had early religious affiliations, developed preoccupations with religious history and spiritual change as well as aesthetic and/or rationalist biases. Yet Pearsall Smith's playful, anachronistic rewriting of Old Testament stories appeared prior to the establishment of the 'Religion' category, in part because of his interest in the Hogarth Press (Willis 54), but largely because of a close social tie with the Woolfs, especially Virginia. The Press evolved into a more commercial and professional enterprise, however, as Leonard Woolf's work with periodicals, especially *The Nation and Athenaeum*, created broader intellectual networks. Thus he drew in R. B. Braithwaite, moral philosopher and methodologist of science at King's College, Cambridge, to analyse the questionnaire data on changing religious beliefs that had raised such a storm of controversy in *The Nation*. Increased engagement with the issues of the day also enabled the Press to call upon an expert like J. C. Hardwick, who, interested in the history of the Anglican Church, tried to reform it from within and open it to manifestations of spirituality compatible with new directions in the visual arts and scientific research. University-educated Rose Macaulay maintained, as another woman novelist, an uneasy friendship with Virginia Woolf, but she also was part of a larger set of scholarly people drawn in professionally by the Woolfs' publishing enterprise. In her historical survey biased towards rationalism and tolerance, Macaulay retained her fascination with religious controversy as she followed the evolution of English literature through the centuries.

'The desire to create gone slightly crooked'

Neither Leonard nor Virginia Woolf, it is generally agreed, was 'religious' in any dogmatic or institutionalised sense. Leonard, born of 'respectably religious' Jewish parents, declared at fourteen that he 'was an unbeliever' (Leonard Woolf, *Sowing* 42).[3] He did not think disbelief unusual among intelligent people or that it affected him 'morally either for good or for bad' (*Sowing* 43). Inspired by G. E. Moore, his ethics included a 'right and wrong and a good and bad in the nature of things' rather than in any religion (Spotts 7). When he read and reviewed books on religious subjects, he consistently condemned propaganda and intolerance and exposed contradictions and inconsistencies.[4] Ultimately, what amazed him 'about . . . religious people' was their 'extraordinary arrogance, rudeness, and uncharitableness' and their too frequent violations of all that Christ most valued (*Letters* 555).

Those who look at Virginia Woolf's attitudes towards religion most often label her 'mystic' or 'atheist'.[5] In 1969, Leonard Woolf suggested support for both terms: 'There was, I daresay, a streak of what people call mysticism in Virginia, but not, I think, of religion. She had no more sense of a God than I have' (*Letters* 573). It is worth citing what she wrote to her sister Vanessa Bell in 1927 (the year Braithwaite's book appeared). If religion has a value, she said, having watched a Roman Catholic procession in Sicily, it is only because 'it is an attempt at art . . . the desire to create gone slightly crooked, and no God in it at all' (*L3* 360–1). Virginia was especially outspoken on such creative misfires in her arguments with Ethel Smyth during the 1930s, when 'Religion' emerged as a Hogarth Press publication category. Like Leonard, she denounced the 'arrogance and monopoly' of a 'protestant orthodoxy' (*L4* 83; *L5* 59) that justifies suffering and appropriates 'the prime human virtues' to itself (*L5* 320, 322; cf. *L4* 375). Yet she maintained a general and 'devout belief in the human soul' (*L4* 208), a 'living belief . . . in human beings' (*L6* 50) and their intense responses to the quotidian world. Thus the Press' publications on 'Religion' suggest a cultural context for certain aspects of Virginia Woolf's own desire to create, satisfied by fiction rather than by gods, dogmas or rituals. She is among those who, in the 1920s, treat modern fiction as 'the sacredness of the everyday' (Lewis, 'Churchgoing' 670–1) or – in essays like 'Modern Fiction', 'Mr. Bennett and Mrs. Brown' and 'Character in Fiction' – as a rejection of Edwardian materialism in favour of the reality of people's inner lives, unified by larger patterns. As she famously concluded in 'A Sketch of the Past' (begun in 1939), 'The whole world is a work of art', and 'we are parts of the work of art'. Although a play or a musical composition is 'the truth about this vast mass that we call the world . . . there is no Shakespeare, there is no Beethoven; certainly and emphatically there is no God; we are the words; we are the music; we are the thing itself' (*Moments* 72).

Lack of conventional religious belief clearly did not negate the Woolfs' interest in an important aspect of human psychology, culture and history. Leonard Woolf admired the Book of Job and considered it among 'the great books of all time', just as he numbered Christ among the 'great people who changed the world' (Glendinning 40, 47). Virginia Woolf planned to read the Bible already in 1903 (*Passionate Apprentice* 178). Yet, in 1935, after all but one of the books advertised on the 'Religion' list had appeared, she recorded she was finally 'illuminating that dark spot' in her education (*D4* 271), dipping into a Bible she had purchased,[6] as well as Ernest Renan on St Paul and the New Testament (*L5* 362; cf. *L5* 366),[7] research soon to emerge in *Three Guineas*.[8] Until the 1930s, however, much of Virginia Woolf's knowledge of religious beliefs came indirectly through her reading of literature, biographies, essays and historical accounts. She wrote already in 1917 that it didn't matter whether she, or even writers like Sir Thomas Browne (*E3* 369) or 'Milton and Dante believed the truth of the doctrines of which they sang' since 'it is possible to enjoy them to the utmost without agreeing with them' (*E2* 145; cf. *L6* 67).

'States of consciousness'

The Woolfs' awareness of the Judeo-Christian religion as part of human history and literature explains, in part, their curiosity about Logan Pearsall Smith's Old Testament stories when he first showed them to Virginia in May of 1919 (*L6* 496–7). The Woolfs clearly liked the retellings well enough to publish them in April of 1920. By then, Pearsall Smith (1865–1946) had published a collection of short prose sketches and, in 1918, had combined some of them with others written for Desmond MacCarthy, literary editor of *The New Statesman*, under the title *Trivia*. MacCarthy later recalled that Pearsall Smith's audience had greeted the book with 'angry contempt', and found his 'self-conscious preciosity . . . irritating' (147). Virginia Woolf, in a review, had been kinder. David Porter thinks she damns with faint praise *Trivia*'s 'lack of substance' (12). She does describe it as 'a bunch of variously coloured air balloons' designed for 'pleasure alone' (*E2* 250). Yet she considers Pearsall Smith's 'purpose . . . as serious as' that of books that appear 'more ambitious'. He wants 'to catch and enclose certain moments which break off from the mass, in which without bidding things come together in combination of inexplicable significance.' Woolf calls these essentially spiritual experiences 'moments of vision' (*E2* 250–1), a phrase that titled her review and became a central tenet of her own creative process.

Early in their relationship and in her career as a writer and publisher, therefore, Virginia Woolf felt some affinity with Logan Pearsall Smith. Porter thinks they primarily saw each other as mutually beneficial, in part as reviewers.[9] Logan was also a man whose reputation, connections and advice could benefit the Press which, in turn, could publish him (Porter 13). His *Stories from the Old Testament* was one of nine books printed during the Press' first four years and one of three appearing in 1920.[10] In length (53 pages) and unconventional treatment, it fit the Press' goal to 'produce . . . short works which commercial publishers could not or would not publish' (Leonard Woolf, *Downhill* 66). Its cover is also typical of the 'gay, striking, and beautiful papers' the Woolfs initially favoured (*Downhill* 74). The copy remaining in the Woolfs' library (WSU) sports a geometric design of tan, criss-crossing diagonal lines forming diamonds, each with a tan dot in the centre, against a background of horizontal tan and orange stripes (Fig. 3.2).

A month after the publication of this small, visually attractive book, however, Virginia Woolf noted in her diary that *Stories from the Old Testament* 'flags & we run the risk of losing money by it. A bad review in the Times, another in Athenaeum; no rush of orders' (*D2* 39–40). In June, Virginia confided to a friend that 'we don't altogether think Stories from the O. T. up to the very very highest standards of prose composition' (*L2* 433). Yet, of those original publications, *Stories from the Old Testament* had the third-highest net profit (after Maxim Gorky's *Reminiscences* and Virginia Woolf's *Kew Gardens*) (Leonard Woolf, *Beginning* 253).

The reviews were also less damning than Virginia Woolf made out, although they did hint at something sophomoric about Pearsall Smith's tone and superficial about his method. In a short note in *The Athenaeum*, an anonymous reviewer dismissed the Biblical subject: 'The Old Testament is such an easy prey that we are surprised that so witty

Figure 3.2   Cover of Logan Pearsall Smith's *Stories from the Old Testament* (1920). Courtesy of Manuscripts, Archives and Special Collections, Washington State University. Used by permission of The Random House Group Ltd.

a writer as Mr. Pearsall Smith should waste his time in sniping at it.' Ironically, this reviewer prefers the minutiae of 'sentimental, "psychological" ' Biblical commentators like those Pearsall Smith parodies. One example is a 'note . . . on wolves in sheep's clothing' in which, according to the reviewer, ' "Dean Stanley remarks that the wolves in Palestine are larger and of a greyer colour than those found elsewhere" ' ('List' 653). Perhaps Virginia read 'wolves in sheep's clothing' as a pun on 'Woolfs' and an indirect criticism of a relatively insignificant book.

The unidentified reviewer in the *Times Literary Supplement* looked at Pearsall Smith's 'Humour of Anachronism'. When anachronisms make us feel superior to an earlier age or show up our own as inferior, the reviewer says, they can be funny. The 'real fun', however, is when anachronisms show 'men as alike always with the . . . same little undignified problems' ('New' 298). Although Pearsall Smith achieves some of that fun, and his method requires educated readers, the reviewer thinks he could have done more to make the stories 'cumulative', to link them as indications of 'the rationalizing process'. To be 'a little disappointed' ('New' 298), however, is not to dismiss the book.[11]

Logan Pearsall Smith was prepared to rewrite Old Testament stories by his religious background. Born in America to Quaker parents, business people who became revivalist preachers and tract writers, Logan was converted at an early age and taken on a revivalist tour of England (Basu 242, Porter 4–6). He lost his faith but turned to literature and fine writing with equal zeal. Virginia may have shared his devotion to art but she criticised his habit of quoting bits of Charles Lamb and Thomas Browne, having 'several of these sentences always on his person, and read[ing] them aloud in a high nasal chant, which again suggested the priest, and the eunuch' (*L2* 359).[12] Pearsall Smith is an exaggeration of Pericles Lewis' conclusion that 'the most important substitute for religion that the modernists found was literature itself' ('Religion' 20).

Pearsall Smith certainly treated literary texts far more reverently than traditionally sacred ones. In his ironic and misleading introduction, he says his audience is churchgoers and his debt is to Biblical scholars like 'A. Bugg and F. Pott' (*Stories* 5). Crafting a 'modern and psychological portrayal' of the 'Old Testament worthies' (*Stories* 5), again he emphasises 'moments of vision' in ways that, however light-hearted, would have caught Virginia Woolf's attention. An initial example is Joshua's making sun and moon stand still: 'a miracle of psychology and imagination', according to Pearsall Smith, 'rather than . . . a so-called supernatural occurrence' (10). His poetic and artistic David, remembering the amazing day when he slew Goliath (1 Sam. 17:49), is aware that 'action in itself was nothing' compared with 'states of consciousness' (*Stories*

13). When Pearsall Smith describes how two she-bears tear apart forty-two children who have mocked the prophet Elisha's bald head (2 Kings 2:23–4), he alludes to Freud's work. Perhaps, he speculates coyly, they had 'little anti-baldness complexes in their little insides, Oedipus complexes, quite beyond their control, against bald fathers' (39–40).[13]

Stories from the Old Testament also highlights women's roles and perspectives. Pearsall Smith, recreating the viewpoint of Michal, David's wife, uses anachronisms to emphasise her intellectual curiosity. Wondering about the Ark David wants returned to Jerusalem, she consults an encyclopedia and reads not only 'Ark', but also 'Alkali, Arctic Exploration, Arbitration, and Arizona' as well as a list of biographies from 'Arius' to 'William Archer' (*Stories* 18). Michal, the Old Testament does indicate (2 Sam. 6: 16), is horrified to see how David celebrates the Ark's return. In Pearsall Smith's version, David 'had thrown off his royal garments, and was leaping and gyrating in public with practically nothing on but a pair of white spats'! (19). Contemporary Anglican clergymen, Logan adds wryly, denounce Michal for lack of 'wifely sympathy', but these same clergymen, making excuses for David as 'an Oriental', inconsistently excuse themselves from following his example (20–1).

The best instance of Pearsall Smith's focus on women, however, is his reinterpretation of Jezebel of 1 Kings. Even the *TLS* reviewer thinks this apology is not only amusing but also serious and that she is 'the only person we can admire in the story' ('New' 298). From 'a cosmopolitan and highly-cultured society' at Tyre, where she served tea to 'Plotinus and William James', sang in a Bach choir, conversed with Schliemann about his discoveries, with Renan about 'Saint Paul and with Holman Hunt about Pre-Raphaelitism', Pearsall Smith's learned Jezebel suddenly finds herself in 'little provincial' Samaria. What could she do, he asks, but investigate the local religion with its picturesque 'temples of the rustic Baals or fertility gods'? How could she not sympathise with the 'kindly old clergymen' cast out by 'a fanatical monotheistic cult'? Finally, how could a 'strong feminist' like Jezebel not appreciate a religion that included Astoreth, a goddess? (*Stories* 28–30). Pearsall Smith admits that some of her acts were brutal, but certainly we can understand her making 'away with a party of evangelical missionaries' who hated her, denounced her to her husband and slaughtered the elderly clergymen she had befriended. What were her sins compared 'to Elijah's record of bloodshed and unprovoked slaughter' and with the horrible 'slaughter of Jezebel' herself by the Jahvists? One cannot help but wish, he concludes, 'to revise that cruel verdict of history under which, for three thousand years, Jezebel has so unjustly suffered' (*Stories* 30–1).

Stories like this one must have diverted both Woolfs, especially

Virginia, with their playful psychology, learned references and irreverent revisions. They must have appreciated the humanising treatments of Old Testament characters, not only women but also other minor ones like Ammiel whose little-known story concludes the book. Mentioned only once in the book of Numbers (13:12) as one of twelve spies sent ahead into the Promised Land to report back to Moses, Pearsall Smith's Ammiel is a writer who records his findings in a personal, now fragmentary journal (47). Pearsall Smith's use of this historical artefact, including Ammiel's complaints about his 'wretched stylographic pen' (47), anticipates the elliptical quotations from surviving diary and letter fragments in Chapter Three of Woolf's *Orlando* (126–9).

Pearsall Smith's Ammiel and fellow spies infiltrate Palestine disguised as 'Cook's tourists', each wearing a 'check suit of large pattern . . . and weeping whiskers of the English milord' (47). Visiting tourist sites, Ammiel feels alienated. He fears his costume is turning him into an English gentleman, contemptuous of the natives (*Stories* 52), an insight that anticipates Woolf's more complex questions about clothes and their relation to identity in *Orlando*. Do they 'change our view of the world and the world's view of us', Orlando asks; do they also define or reflect sexual differences, or mask androgyny? (*Orlando* 187–9).[14]

The Old Testament Ammiel is one of ten who die of plague for bringing back an 'evil report upon the land' (Num. 14:37–8), a fact Pearsall Smith does not mention. It may explain, however, why the book ends with Ammiel pondering the monotheistic 'Omnipotence, . . . His whims and freaks and fancies, His frenzied megalomaniac boastings' (53). In his introduction, Pearsall Smith describes his treatment of Old Testament characters and events as reverent, but his irony masks a serious acknowledgement that every individual, major or minor, male or female, has a unique perspective, one often critical of cultural expectations.

Virginia Woolf's deteriorating relationship, over the years, with Logan Pearsall Smith is documented in her diaries, both their letters and in critical and biographical treatments. Although Leonard Woolf remembered Pearsall Smith as one of the 'good writers . . . whom we published during the first five years of the Hogarth Press' (*The Journey* 125), both Woolfs increasingly found his personal affectations and literary rituals off-putting (cf. *Downhill* 99–100). Problems between Virginia and Logan surfaced in July 1924 over his response to her article 'Character in Fiction'. He agreed that 'the whole tendency of the time . . . [is] the discovery and exploration of our consciousness', but not that 'we are . . . "trembling on the verge of one of the great ages of English literature"' (*Chime* 20–1). Then, in 1925, Logan criticised Virginia for stooping to write, for money, articles for popular women's magazines like *Vogue,* a disagreement most everyone who considers Woolf and *Vogue* notes.[15] Finally, in 1932, reports of Logan's mocking comments about Bloomsbury and Virginia's similar remarks about Chelsea triggered a series of superficially conciliatory and ironic, but also tense and hurtful letters (*L5* 115, 118, 131, 133–4 and n1; and *Chime* 61–4). The resulting social rift was never repaired (e.g., *D4* 145, 162).[16]

Still, in 1932, Logan wrote to compliment Virginia on her *Common Reader: Second Series* essays and to say that he would like to republish his out-of-print *Stories from the Old Testament*. 'I find', he boasted ironically, 'they have helped many to find salvation, and I have thus been carrying on my family trade of saving souls, and hope to wear these diamonds in my heavenly crown.' He has some jewels already due to his father's popular tract, *How Little Logan Was Brought to Jesus*, and its 'especially powerful effect on the Red Indians of the West' (*Chime* 61). Virginia's response to this tract when Logan sent it is equally ironic. It is amusing, she wrote, and 'edifying in the extreme; and the portrait is delightful'. If Logan would write an introduction, she'd even hand print it, 'if only to carry on the work of conversion and find a shorter way to Heaven myself' (*L5* 131 and n1, 290 and n1). When the tract appeared elsewhere (*L5* 290 n1), Virginia initialled a copy and, writing to thank him, said she would put it 'on my shelves in the hope, as you suggest, that I may profit by it' (*L5* 420).[17]

Stories from the Old Testament was not reprinted. It constitutes a small, curious chapter in the early history of the Hogarth Press. None of the later books and pamphlets in the 'Religion' category was satirical in tone or playful in method. Possibly, however, Virginia learned from the reviewer's criticism of Logan's anachronisms as lacking in cumulative structure. In *Orlando*, she shows individuals of different historical periods 'as alike always with . . . the same little undignified problems', as the reviewer says Logan does ('New' 298). Instead of proliferating anachronisms, however, she creates an individual character whose life bridges centuries and sexes, who piles one facet of her personality on top of another 'as plates are piled on a waiter's hand' (*Orlando* 308). Woolf retains the fun of playing with historical figures and texts. At the same time, she finds a way to create a more complex view of human psychology and personality than Pearsall Smith ever did.

'Cold, indifferent, and meaningless'

The Hogarth Press' later forays into the field of religion probed institutionalised beliefs and moralities in a more serious way, and plain title–author covers replaced gaily papered ones. This shift occurred as the Press expanded its professional engagement with the larger world of letters and serious cultural debate. Press contributions to this wider range of discussion occurred in part because Leonard Woolf became increasingly involved with periodical networks, and also because he and others like John Lehmann assumed larger roles than Virginia. The first product of these wider connections, so far as the 'Religion' category was concerned, was R[ichard]. B[evan]. Braithwaite's *The State of Religious Belief: An Inquiry Based on 'The Nation and Athenaeum' Questionnaire* (1927).

Braithwaite's slender book grew out of a controversy over Leonard Woolf's review in *The Nation and Athenaeum* (12 June 1926) of several books on religion. Leonard declared himself a 'rationalist' like the authors of two of them (a new edition of J[ohn]. M[ackinnon]. Robertson's *The Dynamics of Religion* and John Collier's *The Religion of an Artist*) but confessed his incomprehension of Arthur Clutton-Brock's 'state of mind' in *Essays on Religion* ('Rationalism' 279). An angry letter to the editor (3 July 1926) called false Leonard's claim that 'the Universe is "obviously" cold, indifferent, and meaningless' to us (Alder 381). Leonard responded immediately that, while he had been quoted out of context, he congratulated the writer if he could see any life in today's Church or meaning in the universe (381). H[erbert]. G[eorge]. Wood (17 July 1926) then challenged Leonard to support his generalisations and suggested '*The Nation* canvass its readers' (440).[18] Leonard replied that he had spoken from personal experience, but that canvassing was a possibility (441). The argument over rationalism versus religion continued sporadically until 14 August when an unsigned editorial summed up the debate and announced that a questionnaire would appear in the next issue: 'We are convinced that many of our readers will find it an absorbing task to answer candidly the searching questions' ('Religious' 547).

Crafted by Leonard Woolf with suggestions from several others,[19] the questionnaire duly appeared as an insert on 21 August 1926 (Fig. 3.3), then again in two subsequent issues. Some publishers saw the debate as an opportunity to advertise. In the 28 August issue, for instance, a heading that reads 'HAS THE QUESTIONNAIRE MADE YOU THINK?' lists titles that 'will help you to solve the many problems raised by these questions' (619). Then another editorial summarised criticisms of the questionnaire (4 September 1926). To charges that several questions were imprecise, that yes/no formats were too limiting and that questionnaires were inappropriate for such a complex subject, the editor agreed, yet insisted on the value of the exercise, especially since the

Supplement to *The Nation.*

Questionnaire on Religious Belief

Question	Answer ("Yes" or "No")
1. Do you believe in a personal God ?	
2. Do you believe in an impersonal, purposive, and creative power of which living beings are the vehicle, corresponding to the Life Force, the *élan vital*, the Evolutionary Appetite, &c. ?	
3. Do you believe that the basis of reality is matter ?	
4. Do you believe in personal immortality ?	
5. Do you believe that Jesus Christ was divine in a sense in which all living men could not be said to be divine ?	
6. Do you believe in any form of Christianity ?	
7. Do you believe in the Apostles' Creed ?	
8. Do you believe in the formulated tenets of any Church ?..	
9. Are you an active member of any Church ?	
10. Do you voluntarily attend any religious service regularly ?	
11. Do you accept the first chapter of Genesis as historical ?	
12. Do you regard the Bible as inspired in a sense in which the literature of your own country could not be said to be inspired ?	
13. Do you believe in transubstantiation ?	
14. Do you believe that Nature is indifferent to our ideals ?	

Signature _____

 Address _____   *Date* _____

This questionnaire should, when completed, be returned to THE EDITOR, "THE NATION," 38, Great James Street, London, W.C.1.

Signatures are required as a guarantee of good faith ; but **all answers and the names of all persons answering will, of course, be kept strictly confidential**. The results will be published in "The Nation" in the form of aggregate figures of those answering "Yes" and "No" respectively to each question ; but no names will be published or otherwise divulged.

Figure 3.3   'Questionnaire on Religious Belief'. Supplement to *The Nation* (21 August 1926). Used by permission of the University of Sussex and the Society of Authors for the Estate of Leonard Woolf.

survey would now also appear in *The Daily News* ('The Questionnaire' 630–1).

As answers came in, the *Nation* published first and further results on 11 and 18 September 1926. Final results from both periodicals, published on 26 October, now became the topic of ongoing discussion in *The Nation*. H. G. Wood, who had suggested the canvass and been among those who had given Leonard Woolf suggestions, not only defended the exercise but advised that it be repeated periodically. He declared that the results validated 'Woolf's generalisation that a majority of educated people now regard the Universe as cold and meaningless' ('The Questionnaire' 82). Wood further concluded that 'more readers believe in some form of Christianity than believe in personal immortality, more believe in personal immortality than believe in a personal God, more believe in a personal God than accept the divinity of Jesus Christ.' Further, 'more readers believe in some form of Christianity than attend public worship regularly, more attend services than are active members of any church, and there are more active members than there are believers in their formulated tenets' ('The Questionnaire' 82). J. M. Robertson, responding to a request for comments from others who had assisted in framing the questions, also decided that the results suggested a pervasive agnosticism and a decline of orthodoxy (174–5).[20] Discussion of the results and of Wood's and Robertson's responses continued for several more issues.

Leonard Woolf seized the opportunity for the Hogarth Press to contribute to the discussion. He thought R. B. Braithwaite qualified 'to interpret the results of the questionnaire', as the cover says. Braithwaite (1900–90) grew up in a Quaker family, was a pacifist who served in the Friends' Ambulance Unit during the Great War, and retained his interest in religious issues by becoming a university lecturer and then professor of moral philosophy at King's College, Cambridge (Mellor 309).[21] As a fellow, he had been a member of the intellectually elite Apostles as well as one 'of Maynard Keynes' inner . . . circle' (*D2* n4; Harrod 321).[22] Virginia Woolf mentioned Braithwaite after she and Leonard visited Cambridge in May 1925 (*D3* 16–17). He also was known to the Woolfs through present Cambridge connections: their nephew Julian Bell who, an Apostle himself, went up to read history in 1927.

In his small book, Braithwaite reiterates the object of the questionnaire, to define 'educated opinion' on 'the main dogmas of religion (and especially of the Christian religion)' (26). His interest was primarily statistical: 1,849 people responded to *The Nation* questionnaire and many more – 15,168 – replied when *The Daily News* published the same questions (41). Although both journals were primarily liberal,

The Daily News 'got surprisingly religious results', Braithwaite writes (16). For instance, 40% of *The Nation* responders claimed belief in a personal God, versus 72% of *The Daily News* responders; 6% of *The Nation* responders accepted Genesis 1 (creation in seven days) as historical versus 38% of *The Daily News* responders (7–8). Braithwaite tries to figure out who might have responded in each case and if that group was representative. Having examined the language of the questionnaire and analysed all the data in statistical terms, he concludes that the sample probably 'was biased, but not too biased, against religion' (62).

Like Wood, Robertson and some of the other contributors to the discussion in the *Nation*, Braithwaite decides that 'the Christianity in which many people believe is of an exceedingly strange character' based neither on Scripture, nor the Apostles Creed, nor the divinity of Christ, nor even, in many cases, on a personal god (62). Responders seem to accept Christian ethics and thus to regard 'some of Christ's moral teaching as very important' (63); however, 'the Christian God' and 'His associated dogmas' have lost popularity, and even church attendance, which has declined, is no guarantee of belief (66). Braithwaite considers science largely responsible, since it has rendered 'ultimate explanations of the universe . . . impossible' (68). Although we may continue to have individual emotional or mystical experiences, he writes, they cast no light upon 'the riddle of the universe' (73). Leonard Woolf, still mulling over the issue as late as 1960, concludes that 'in less than a century' God's 'position had suffered a change almost exactly like that of the British monarchy. He had become a constitutional instead of an absolute God' (*Sowing* 43).

The Woolfs' immediate reaction to Braithwaite's book, however, was in their role as commercial publishers. Virginia noted in October 1927 that Press financial 'prospects seem flourishing' if books like Braithwaite's don't 'eat up all profits' (*D3* 162). Although an unlikely best-seller, there is no evidence that the Woolfs held this fact against him personally, and their occasional amicable encounters continued. In 1929 Virginia described Braithwaite, widowed the year before, roaring 'like a bull' at the ribaldry of their dinner conversation (*L4* 43 and n2). She mentioned seeing him in December of that year (*L4* 119 and n2); going to visit him in January of 1930 (*D3* 281–2); and seeing Julian Bell, along with Braithwaite 'full of argument about the universe', in Cambridge in February 1931 (*L4* 292). That Braithwaite favoured degrees for women at Cambridge University (Mellor 302) certainly would have impressed Virginia, whatever her opinions of Oxbridge in general.

These engagements with Braithwaite, however infrequent, influenced an unpublished fragment from a satirical play S. P. Rosenbaum thinks

Virginia Woolf wrote around 1931 (*Platform* 8). In the manner of Mrs Ramsay's mockery of Charles Tansley's academic and philosophical language in *To the Lighthouse* (1927), Woolf has Julian Bell, trying to write a poem, plan to 'ring up Richard Braithwaite and ask what a thing is when it is a thing and not another thing and put that into poetry'. Then she imagines Julian, irritated that the Stephen side of his heritage demands writing instead of shooting game, consider 'a summing up' to his poem 'in the manner of Richard Braithwaite, George Moore' (*Platform* 34–5).[23] Braithwaite continued to appear occasionally in Virginia Woolf's letters (*L5* 18, 155, 172; *L6* 19–20). In a memoir of Julian she wrote after his death in Spain in July 1937, Braithwaite made a final appearance, reduced from his dignified role as a moral philosopher and statistician at Cambridge to that of a terrified passenger in a car Julian once drove so recklessly (*Platform* 31).

'Old opinions' versus 'new manifestations'

H. G. Wood, when defending Leonard Woolf's questionnaire as a useful exercise, also speculated on evolution in religious thinking. The greater number of believers among the middle-class and artisan readers of *The Daily News*, he wrote, actually may represent 'a more advanced type of Christian thought' than the dismissals of intellectuals who read *The Nation and Athenaeum*. The latter, he said, still under the influence of Renan's *Vie de Jesus*, have not kept up with ideas that reject 'the old antithesis between the divine and the human' ('The Questionnaire' 82–3). A large number of such 'more advanced' believers accept 'some form of Christianity' although they 'doubt . . . all formulations of Christianity, and perhaps . . . all definite creeds' (83).

John Charlton Hardwick (1885–1953), author of another lesser-known Hogarth publication in the category of 'Religion', looks at change and advocates what H. G. Wood called 'a more advanced type of Christian thought'. Hardwick's *A Letter to an Archbishop* (1932), part of the Hogarth Letters series, politely addresses 'Your Grace' and signs himself 'J. C. Hardwick, Priest'. Thus he wrote from the perspective of an insider, an Anglican churchman, formerly a chaplain at Ripon Hall, Oxford, then a Vicar (Partington, Cheshire). By 1932 Hardwick, already a Vicar for eleven years, had published books on *Religion and Science from Galileo to Bergson* (1920) and *Institutional Religion* (1929) as well as a pamphlet on *Religion and Science* (1925). His *Freedom and Authority in Religion* and *A Professional Christian* appeared in the same year as his Hogarth piece (1932).[24] Perhaps Leonard Woolf knew of Hardwick's books, but more likely John Lehmann did. Although Lehmann called the Hogarth Letters 'our joint enterprise' (*In My Own Time* 121) and 'one of the "swarm of new ideas"' he, Leonard and Virginia had 'planned so eagerly in the first few weeks of my apprenticeship' (*Thrown* 29), Lehmann also considered himself 'Papa of the Series' (Lee xiv). The one letter to Hardwick (7 April 1932) remaining in the Press archives at the University of Reading, is catalogued as Lehmann's. Using the editorial 'we', he accepts Hardwick's manuscript for the series, states financial terms and asks for minor editing.

Sharing with other Hogarth Letter writers what Hermione Lee defines as a 'language of rational humanism, deployed on behalf of intellectual tolerance and in opposition to various forms of tyranny and reaction' (xiv), Hardwick tactfully but firmly blames the Church itself for causing responses much like those already documented in Braithwaite's book. The Church, Hardwick thinks, is too busy keeping traditional institutional machinery running to react with anything but evasive platitudes to the intellectual, 'theological and ethical' realities of a changing world (283). He sides with those who wish to change the Church from merely 'a society for the preservation of old opinions and customs out of which the life has departed' into one ready to experiment with new ideas and 'better modes of behaviour' (294).

Hardwick contrasts the larger role of the prosperous, turn-of-the-century Church with its current, more narrowly focused, internal proceedings. The government has stepped in, for example, to oversee outreach activities like charity and education, formerly provinces of the Church. Although the questionnaire Braithwaite analyses requests neither the respondent's age nor sex, Hardwick considers both. Various youth movements, he says, like scouting, have drawn young people away, while the cinema and other entertainments threaten to usurp 'the lighter sorts of parochial activity' (274–5). Feminism drew thinking women from the Church 'with a vengeance', he adds (276–7), reminding us of Pearsall Smith's blue-stockinged Jezebel and anticipating Virginia Woolf's objection in *Three Guineas* to St Paul's silencing of women. Recent historical scholarship applied to Biblical texts also has challenged traditional theology, Hardwick says, but the Great War really accelerated the Church's decline. Then, refusing to question and think altogether, many clergymen dispensed what Hardwick calls 'the most distressing sentimentalities of a pseudo-religious, hundred per cent patriotism' and buried themselves in routine church business (281).

After the war, idealists did try to revive the Church's spirituality as well as its viability in the larger society. They tried to make the organisation more efficient and democratic and, by restricting 'doctrinal latitude', tried to stem what they considered 'the dangerous and rapid growth of Modernism' (*Letter* 285). This effort failed, Hardwick writes, because the problem with the Church is not organisational, 'or even moral . . . but intellectual' (287). Hardwick, whose own publications mark him as an exception, criticises clerics for scholarly evasions, cowardice and weakness in the face of challenges to Anglican theology (291). Although 'the thinker', like Hardwick, 'not the doer, is the hero' for the Hogarth Letter writers, generally 'doers outnumber thinkers' in England (Lee xvii).

One of Hardwick's primary descriptors of thoughtful, vitalising change is the visual arts, connecting him with Bloomsbury aesthetic values. Hardwick's comments also agree with other Hogarth Letter writers who debate the role of art in society. Raymond Mortimer, for example, in another of the Letters (*The French Pictures: A Letter to Harriet*), calls painting 'the healthiest' contemporary art (98). 'Experience teaches', Hardwick similarly writes, that living religious traditions, like artistic traditions, 'will continually produce new manifestations . . . as the generations pass' (291). He quotes sculptor Jacob Epstein, insisting that innovators work from within to preserve and enrich a tradition, even if they are ' "considered rebels by their contemporaries" ' (292). Although efforts of younger church members to turn their minds and creativity to new embodiments of the religious spirit 'might be as startling . . . as futurism in art' (293–4), Hardwick concludes, the Church badly needs this kind of energy. One of his own potentially startling interests – a variation on Pearsall Smith's playful use of psychology – was the difficulty for both religion and science of explaining miracles. By the time Hardwick wrote his letter for the Hogarth Press Letters series, he was moving towards incorporating the findings of the Society for Psychical Research to explain miracles as 'products of psychic energy emanating from within the personality' (Bowler 252). He envisioned a future in which scientific research would not oppose religion, but would illuminate both the natural world and human spirituality.

'Clash or conflict'

For another Hogarth series, Lectures on Literature, Rose Macaulay (1881–1958) wrote *Some Religious Elements in English Literature* (1931), also advertised in the 'Religion' category. Macaulay's contribution began, according to the correspondence in the Hogarth Archives, with a request from Leonard Woolf (23 July 1929), who suggested she pen a lecture on the art of letter writing. She proposed, and Leonard accepted, supernatural or religious effects on literature (24 July 1929), then agreed to focus on religion and the literature of England (12 September 1929).

Macaulay's lecture added a literary historian's perspective on religious change to what Braithwaite had analysed statistically and Hardwick, a year later, would consider from a progressive theologian's point of view. She admits that *Some Religious Elements in English Literature* is a tiny foray into an 'enormous subject' (5) that includes all peoples, times and places. Whether one worships nature, ancestors, the sun, 'the Father of heaven, the Mother of earth, the Son who minds human destinies, his human mother who bends to earth an even more attentive ear, . . . the same emotions' arise. These she calls, in a version of Virginia Woolf's 'moments of vision', 'that tremendous leaping spring in man, the religious sense' (14–15).

Macaulay arranges her book according to a theory 'that most religious literature was the outcome of . . . a clash or conflict' (5). She titles her chapters accordingly: 'English and Latin', 'English and Norman', 'Humanism and the Churches', 'Anglican and Puritan' and 'Reason and Passion'. She notes, however, that actual works of English literature challenge her convenient theory and that neatly demarcated literary periods break down. Great writers like Shakespeare, for instance, have always transcended dualisms and sects and appealed to readers of many faiths (71–2). 'We herd literature together in masses, like dumb driven cattle', Macaulay concludes, 'and possibly we have to, in self-defence, carrying on our pathetic task of seeking to co-ordinate and understand the history' of humankind (127).

A summary of Macaulay's name-filled literary history would be a fruitless exercise. It is worth noting, however, that her overview shares the rationalist bias of the other books and pamphlets discussed here. Macaulay traces the early, comfortable blending of 'Christian and heathen thought' in medieval life and literature (16) through 'the controversial note' that emerged when Wycliffe and his helpers translated the Bible into English (57). With the Renaissance came the clash between secular and religious interests. The Reformation and Puritans, however, prevented Renaissance Anglicanism and literature reflecting it from developing, as Macaulay puts it, 'into a wider, more rational, more intellectual, tolerant, humane, and spiritual body, than it yet has' (112), a theme Hardwick's *A Letter to an Archbishop* a year later carries into the late-nineteenth and early-twentieth centuries.

Macaulay's final chapter, documenting the 'widespread piety', 'general literary interest in religious questions' (141), combined with the 'scientific spirit' (143) expressed by eighteenth-century writers, nevertheless voices frustration. Although E. S. Hertell, in a *Bookman* review, compliments Macaulay not only for writing 'with charm and urbanity, and frequently with sly wit', but also for including every 'author of any note' (219), she finds herself overwhelmed by abundance (*Some* 127).[25] Invoking Leslie Stephen on eighteenth-century Wesleyism, she returns, as will Hardwick, to the loss of the rational and intellectual in religion: Wesleyism 'represents heat without light—a blind protest of the masses, and a vague feeling after some satisfaction to the instincts which ends only in a recrudescence of obsolete ideas' (151). Macaulay finds she cannot take her survey into the present, or even the immediate past. There is too much of both 'literature and religion' (154), and the necessary distance is increasingly difficult to achieve.

Rose Macaulay, like Logan Pearsall Smith, came from a religious background. When the Woolfs had first met her in 1921, Virginia speculated that Rose 'might be religious . . .: mystical perhaps' (*D2* 93). Woolf apparently did not know that Macaulay had been attracted to the Anglican Church following her brother's death, but that a discreet 'love affair' with the married novelist Gerald O'Donovan had resulted in a 'lengthy exile' from that institution. Although Macaulay found church dogma incompatible with her feminism, she, like many writers of this period, remained preoccupied with religious controversies and practices (Squier 255, 253; cf. Emery ch. 10).[26]

Like her relationship with Pearsall Smith, Virginia Woolf's with Rose Macaulay was conflicted, but for different reasons. Woolf identified Macaulay not with literary rituals and affectations but, more like Braithwaite, with masculine academic discourse. Her reaction to Macaulay's novel, *Potterism*, which she read in 1920, was that it was 'a don's book' or a book by 'the daughter of a don', which of course Macaulay was. Woolf dubbed the book 'hard-headed, masculine, atmosphere of lecture room, not interesting to me' (*D2* 57). When, in 1926, Macaulay's *Catchwords and Claptrap* appeared as one of the second series of Hogarth Essays, Woolf must have thought it another 'donnish' piece of writing (Emery 213–14). Macaulay, it is true, had specialised in seventeenth-century history at Somerville College, Oxford, and by the time she wrote *Some Religious Elements in English Literature*, she had returned to earlier scholarly interests to write a biography of Milton, published in 1930.

Virginia Woolf recognised the importance to life as reflected in literature of a 'pageant of the world' that is, on the one hand, 'marvellous' and, on the other, a 'vanity' to escape in death (*E4* 68). Rose Macaulay, however, as the traditionally trained scholar, was the more appropriate person to trace this evolving pageant in the Press' lecture format.

Although the two women may have had their differences as scholarly versus common readers of literature, Virginia's diary shows that they saw each other several times during the 1920s. In spite of a formal dinner hosted by Macaulay in 1926 at which both Woolfs embarrassed themselves (*L3* 251), the two writers were friends by the 1930s, and they met and corresponded until Virginia Woolf's death. As in the case of Pearsall Smith, it is true, her comments in diaries and letters on Macaulay often seem more malicious than empathetic. Jane Emery suggests that Woolf faulted Macaulay for concerns she had about herself – spitefulness, sexual identity, sensitivity to reviews, a 'dowdy' appearance and a tendency to overwork (211–12; cf. *D4* 249–50, *L* 3 501). Yet, when Macaulay praised E. M. Forster in *The Writings of E. M. Forster*, Woolf admitted her jealousy of her contemporaries (*D5* 130), especially those so much liked by people whose good opinion she valued (Emery 213).

Virginia Woolf and Rose Macaulay maintained a friendship based on their 'talent for fantasy and imaginative exaggeration and the interest in gender identity' (Emery 214).[27] I would add their common desire to prevent war and suggest that Macaulay's Peace Pledge Union pamphlet, *An Open Letter to a Non-Pacifist* (1937), is her small prelude to Woolf's *Three Guineas* (1938). Also, by the time Macaulay wrote *Some Religious Elements in English Literature*, she wisely had accepted the fact that 'it amused' Woolf 'to embellish, fantasticate and ironise her friends, as she embellished, fantasticated and ironised all she wrote of' (Emery 215).

'Modern scholarship'

Another indication of the Hogarth Press' growth from a coterie press into one also fully integrated into the larger professional, commercial, periodical, intellectual and aesthetic networks of the twenties and thirties is its brief involvement with a quarterly publication called *The Search*. From January to October 1931, the Press published and marketed the research of the Search Society whose ambitious aim was to investigate, summarise and examine relationships among aspects of 'modern scholarship in religion, philosophy, science, literature, and art' (Willis 368). Religious discussion in the first four issues, for instance, includes commentaries on the translation, interpretation and history of scriptural writings; descriptions of religious beliefs of other cultures; interrogations of astrology, magic and mysticism; examinations of science in relation to religion; and several treatments of related themes in verse. Unlike Virginia Woolf's 1921 story, 'A Society', where the all-female 'society for asking questions' mocks both men's accomplishments in all fields and their own group's inconclusive search for truth ('A Society' 125), the Search Society, a decade later, clearly is co-educational. The first issue of *The Search*, for example, contains an essay by novelist Margaret Legge,[28] who, anticipating Virginia Woolf's 'A Sketch of the Past', dismisses professional, institutionalised religion and searches for spiritual truth in the human creative spirit that perceives patterns, unifies and makes 'of life a work of art' (53–4).

The Search Society, in some ways, began to do in microcosm what the Hogarth Press had been doing on a larger scale, aiming to draw together contributions by different writers to the study of controversial subjects, one of which was the nature and status of religion in modern culture.[29] The four Hogarth Press writers discussed in this chapter had developed, from traditional religious backgrounds, the aesthetic and/or rationalist biases reflected in their books and pamphlets. Like the multiple points of view in a Virginia Woolf novel, however, each interacted with the Press in a different way and brought a unique perspective and method to the topic. Logan Pearsall-Smith, while linked socially to the Woolfs, especially Virginia, amused a relatively small, educated audience with playful anachronisms and irony in his psychological treatments of Old Testament stories. As the Hogarth Press, largely through Leonard Woolf's work for and with periodicals, tapped wider cultural networks, its treatment of religion became more serious, and its authors were intellectuals like R. B. Braithwaite, who marshalled statistics to sum up the findings of *The Nation and Athenaeum* questionnaire; J. C. Hardwick, who drew upon his knowledge of theology and church history to advocate, from within the established church, change as radical as that in the visual arts and the sciences; and Rose Macaulay, whose university training in literary scholarship enabled her to trace through the centuries the reflection in English literature of different manifestations of the human religious spirit. Their publications, reflecting avant-garde and iconoclastic impulses in a changing society, helped to encourage the Press' ever-widening circles of writers and readers not so much to move warily with heretical Woolfs about, but to join them in creative thinking and cultural debate.

Notes

1. I would like to thank Trevor Bond of Manuscripts, Archives and Special Collections at the Washington State University Libraries; Verity Andrews of Special Collections at the University of Reading; the British Library, and

Helen Southworth, editor of this volume, for assistance with the research and/or drafting of this essay.

2. On the Hogarth Press as Freud's English publisher see Leonard Woolf (*The Journey* and *Downhill*); Willis; Meisel & Kenddrick; and (in connection with Virginia Woolf's work) Abel.

3. Leonard kept an 1833 *Holy Bible* signed on the title page, 'Leonard Sidney Woolf, Oct. 1900'; an Oxford edition of the *Holy Bible* (1893?) inscribed to him by his mother; and a Greek New Testament signed 'Leonard Sidney Woolf 1900'. These are in Manuscripts, Archives and Special Collections (hereafter MASC) at the Washington State University (hereafter WSU) Libraries.

4. See 'Religion (LW on)' in the index of Luedeking (295) for a list of such reviews.

5. On 'mystic' see, for example, Kane, Marcus and Moore. On 'atheist' see Lackey and Oldfield.

6. Why Virginia needed to buy any biblical text is puzzling. Among the Woolfs' books (MASC, WSU) are an old, authorised version of the Old and New Testaments signed by 'Virginia Stephen' in 1901; a Bible given her by Violet Dickinson in 1907; and another inscribed, 'To my dear wife Virginia Woolf'.

7. Ernest Renan (1823–92) wrote from a philological and historical perspective. Virginia inherited Leslie Stephen's copies of *L'Antechrist* (1873) and *Vie de Jesus* (1867?). Among the Woolfs' books (MASC, WSU) are also an unsigned *The Life of Jesus* (1927) and *Souvenirs d'enfance et de jeunesse* (1930), annotated by Leonard and signed by Virginia. In *The Years* (1937), Eleanor is somewhat embarrassed to be found reading Renan (150).

8. In her efforts to explain the increasing withdrawal from the Church of educated men's daughters, Woolf went further and included, for instance, the Report of the Archbishops' Commission on the Ministry of Women (*TG* 117–27 and notes).

9. Logan reviewed Virginia's *Kew Gardens* in 1919 and praised *Jacob's Room* in 1922. Virginia reviewed Logan's *A Treasury of English Prose* in 1920 (*E3* 171–6).

10. The other eight were Leonard and Virginia Woolf's *Two Stories* (1917), Katherine Mansfield's *Prelude* (1918), Virginia Woolf's *Kew Gardens* (1919), T. S. Eliot's *Poems* (1919), J. Middleton Murry's *The Critic in Judgment* (1919), Hope Mirrlees' *Paris* (1919), E. M. Forster's *Story of the Siren* (1920) and Maxim Gorky's *Reminiscences of Tolstoi* (1920).

11. Knowing who reviewed for what periodicals, and reviewers themselves, the Woolfs may have detected more negativity.

12. Similarly, Wilson says Pearsall Smith 'consecrated his life to writing' and refers to his 'worship of literature' (100, 105).

13. Freud defined the 'Oedipus complex' in *Totem and Taboo* which appeared in English translation in 1918.

14. Also detecting echoes in Woolf's writing, Whitworth links Nick Green in *Orlando* with some of Pearsall Smith's theories of literature.

15. Virginia's reaction to Logan was 'Bunkum' (*L3* 154). Logan ironically congratulates Bloomsbury for performing a 'noble, if lucrative duty to culture' (*Chime* 58). See, for example, Luckhurst, Garrity and Brosnan.

16. Virginia aired her dislike of Logan to a receptive Ottoline Morrell (*L5*

139) and in her diary (*D4* 26, 130, 162). Logan too had grievances against Virginia (Gathorne-Hardy 20).

17. The pamphlet is no longer among the Woolfs' books at WSU.
18. Wood (1879–1963) had published *Living Issues in Religious Thought, from George Fox to Bertrand Russell* in 1924.
19. H. G. Wood, J. M. Robertson, Bernard Shaw and Augustine Birrell 'offered suggestions merely' to Leonard Woolf and did not give final approval to the questionnaire (Braithwaite 26).
20. Robertson (1856–1933) published on a wide variety of literary and religious topics. His two-volume *A History of Free Thought in the Nineteenth Century* (1929) is among the Woolfs' books (MASC, WSU) with Leonard's annotations.
21. Braithwaite joined the Church of England in 1948 (Mellor 302).
22. Braithwaite (1900–90) also was a defender of 'Keynes' achievement as a "humane Utilitarian"' (Skidelsky 145). He is best known for 'his explication of the concept of probability', and his *Scientific Explanation* (1953) is 'a classic work' in the methodology of science (Mellor 302).
23. Braithwaite's later book, *George Edward Moore, 1873–1958* (1962) remains among the Woolfs' books (MASC, WSU) inscribed to Leonard by the author.
24. Hardwick continued to publish, including a biography of Samuel Wilberforce (1933), *The Light that Failed* (1933), *What to Believe* (1935) and *No Casual Creed* (1937).
25. Macaulay's frustrations with masses of material were obvious to early readers. Dobrée noticed a decline of skill in the latter part of the book (147). A reviewer in *The Times* compliments her for 'the freshness of her comments' but notes 'breathlessness' after 1700 ('*Some*' 607). A letter to the Hogarth Press at the University of Reading (7 March 1936) suggests the Press lost money on *Some Religious Elements*.
26. Macaulay published 'Church-Going' in *Personal Pleasures* (1936). Comparing Anglican, Roman Catholic, Quaker and Unitarian services, she opts for those with beautiful ceremonies and without 'hell-fire sermons' (125).
27. Fromm thinks Macaulay influenced Virginia Woolf more than scholars have detected (295), especially the prose style of *Orlando* and portraits of women in *The Years*.
28. Legge published seven novels (1912–29) dealing with modern issues including the women's movement (Blain 645).
29. Like *The Search*, the Hogarth Press published creative work on religious themes. Under 'Poetry' or 'Politics', examples are Herbert Palmer's *Songs of Salvation, Sin and Satire* (1925), Dorothy Wellesley's *Jupiter and the Nun* (1932) and C. Day Lewis' *Noah and the Waters* (1936), a political parable of revolution.

Works cited

Abel, Elizabeth. *Virginia Woolf and the Fictions of Psychoanalysis*. Chicago: University of Chicago Press, 1989.

Alder, J. 'Rationalism and Religion'. *The Nation and Athenaeum* 39, 1926: 381.

Basu, Sayoni. 'Smith, (Lloyd) Logan Pearsall'. In H. C. G. Matthew and Brian Harrison, eds. *Oxford Dictionary of National Biography*. Oxford: Oxford University Press, 2004.

Blain, Virginia, Patricia Clements and Isobel Grundy, eds. *The Feminist Companion to Literature in English: Women Writers from the Middle Ages to the Present*. New Haven: Yale University Press, 1990.

Bowler, Peter J. *Reconciling Science and Religion: The Debate in Early-Twentieth-Century Britain*. Chicago: University of Chicago Press, 2001.

Braithwaite, R. B. *The State of Religious Belief: An Inquiry Based on 'The Nation And Athenaeum' Questionnaire*. London: Hogarth Press, 1927.

Brosnan, Leila. ' "Whoring after Todd": *Vogue* and the Question of Value'. *Reading Virginia Woolf's Essays and Journalism: Breaking the Surface of Silence*. Edinburgh: Edinburgh University Press, 1997: 49–58.

Dobree, Bonamy. Review of *Some Religious Elements in English Literature*. *The Spectator* 147, 1931: 360.

Emery, Jane. *Rose Macaulay: A Writer's Life*. London: John Murray, 1991.

Fromm, Gloria G. 'Re-Inscribing *The Years*: Virginia Woolf, Rose Macaulay, and The Critics'. *Journal of Modern Literature* 13.2, 1986: 289–306.

Garrity, Jane. 'Virginia Woolf, Intellectual Harlotry, and 1920s British *Vogue*'. In Pamela L. Caughie, ed. *Virginia Woolf in the Age of Mechanical Reproduction*. New York: Garland, 2000: 185–218.

Gathorne-Hardy, Robert, ed. *Ottoline at Garsington: Memoirs of Lady Ottoline Morrell 1915–1918*. New York: Alfred A. Knopf, 1975.

Glendinning, Victoria. *Leonard Woolf: A Biography*. New York: Free Press, 2006.

Hardwick, J. C. 'A Letter to an Archbishop'. *The Hogarth Letters*. Athens: University of Georgia Press, 1986: 267–97.

Harrod, Roy. *The Life of John Maynard Keynes*. New York: W. W. Norton, 1951.

Hertell, E. S. 'Review of *Some Religious Elements in English Literature*'. *Bookman* 74, 1931: 219.

Kane, Julie. 'Varieties of Mystical Experience in the Writings of Virginia Woolf'. *Twentieth Century Literature* 41.4, 1995: 328–49.

Lackey, Michael. 'Virginia Woolf and T. S. Eliot: An Atheist's Commentary on the Epistemology of Belief'. *Woolf Studies Annual*. Vol. 8. New York: Pace University Press, 2002: 63–91.

Lee, Hermione. 'Introduction'. *The Hogarth Letters*. Athens: University of Georgia Press, 1986: vii–xxviii.

Legge, Margaret. 'Creative Religion'. *The Search* 1, 1931: 43–55.

Lehmann, John. *In My Own Time: Memoirs of a Literary Life*. Boston: Little, Brown, 1969.

—. *Thrown to the Woolfs*. London: Weidenfeld and Nicolson, 1978.

Lewis, Pericles. 'Churchgoing in the Modern Novel'. *Modernism/modernity* 11.4, 2004: 669–94.

—. 'Religion'. In David Bradshaw and Kevin J. H. Dettmar, eds. *A Companion to Modernist Literature and Culture*. London: Blackwell, 2006: 19–27.

'List of New Books': *Stories from the Old Testament* by Logan Pearsall Smith. *The Athenaeum* 14 May 1920: 653.

Luckhurst, Nicola. *Bloomsbury in Vogue.* London: Cecil Woolf, 1998.

Luedeking, Leila. 'Leonard Woolf and the Book Review'. Appendix 3 in Leila Luedeking and Michael Edwards, eds. *Leonard Woolf: A Bibliography.* Winchester: St. Paul's Bibliographies, 1992: 284–90.

Macaulay, Rose. 'Church-Going'. *Personal Pleasures.* Freeport: Books for Libraries Press, [1936] 1971: 119–32.

—. *An Open Letter [to a Non-Pacifist].* London: William Collins for the Peace Pledge Union, 1937.

—. *Some Religious Elements in English Literature.* London: Hogarth Press, 1931.

—. *The Writings of E. M. Forster.* London: Hogarth Press, 1938.

MacCarthy, Desmond. 'Logan Pearsall Smith'. *Memories.* London: MacGibbon & Kee, 1953: 145–8.

Marcus, Jane. 'The Niece of a Nun: Virginia Woolf, Caroline Stephen, and the Cloistered Imagination'. *Virginia Woolf and the Languages of Patriarchy.* Bloomington: Indiana University Press, 1987: 115–35.

Meisel, Perry and Walter Kendrick, eds. *Bloomsbury/Freud: The Letters of James and Alix Strachey: 1924–1925.* New York: Basic Books, 1985.

Mellor, D. H. 'Braithwaite, Richard Bevan (1900–1990)'. In H. C. G. Matthew and Brian Harrison, eds. *Oxford Dictionary of National Biography.* Vol. 7. Oxford: Oxford University Press, 2004: 302.

Moore, Madeline. *The Short Season Between Two Silences: The Mystical and the Political in the Novels of Virginia Woolf.* Boston: George Allen & Unwin, 1984.

Mortimer, Raymond. ‚The French Pictures: A Letter to Harriet'. In Hermione Lee, ed. *The Hogarth Letters.* Athens: University of Georgia Press, 1986: 79–107.

'New Books and Reprints'. *Stories from the Old Testament* by Logan Pearsall Smith. *Times Literary Supplement* 13 May 1920: 306.

Oldfield, Sybil. *The Child of Two Atheists: Virginia Woolf's Humanism.* London: Virginia Woolf Society of Great Britain, 2006.

Porter, David. *Virginia Woolf and Logan Pearsall Smith: 'an exquisitely flattering Duet'.* London: Cecil Woolf, 2002.

'The Questionnaire: A Reply to Critics'. *The Nation and Athenaeum* 39, 1926: 630–1.

'Religious Belief: An Inquiry'. *The Nation and Athenaeum* 39, 1926: 547.

Robertson, J. M. 'That Questionnaire'. *The Nation and Athenaeum* 40, 1926: 174.

Skidelsky, Robert. *John Maynard Keynes: Hopes Betrayed 1883–1920.* New York: Viking, 1986.

Smith, Logan Pearsall. *A Chime of Words: The Letters of Logan Pearsall Smith.* Ed. Edwin Tribble. New York: Ticknor & Fields, 1984.

—. *Stories from the Old Testament.* Richmond: Hogarth Press, 1920.

'*Some Religious Elements in English Literature*'. *Times Literary Supplement* 6 August 1931: 607.

Spotts, Frederic. 'Cambridge'. *Letters of Leonard Woolf.* San Diego: Harcourt Brace Jovanovich, 1989: 3–12.

Squier, Susan M. 'Rose Macaulay (1881–1958)'. In Bonnie Kime Scott, ed. *The Gender of Modernism: A Critical Anthology*. Bloomington: Indiana University Press, 1990: 252–9.

Whitworth, Michael. 'Logan Pearsall Smith and *Orlando*'. *Review of English Studies* 55, 2004: 598–604.

Willis, J. H. *Leonard and Virginia Woolf as Publishers: The Hogarth Press, 1917–41*. Charlottesville: University Press of Virginia, 1992.

Wilson, Edmund. 'Books: Virginia Woolf and Logan Pearsall Smith'. *The New Yorker* 26, 1950: 99–105.

Wood, H. G. 'Rationalism and Religion'. *The Nation and Athenaeum* 39, 1926: 440.

—. 'The Questionnaire: Some Reflections on the Answers'. *The Nation and Athenaeum* 40, 1926: 82–3.

Woolf, Leonard. *Beginning Again: An Autobiography of the Years 1911–1918*. New York: Harcourt Brace Jovanovich, 1963.

—. *Downhill All the Way: An Autobiography of the Years 1919 to 1939*. New York: Harcourt Brace Jovanovich, 1967.

—. *The Journey Not the Arrival Matters: An Autobiography of the Years 1939 to 1969*. New York: Harcourt Brace Jovanovich, 1969.

—. *Letters of Leonard Woolf*. Ed. Frederic Spotts. San Diego: Harcourt Brace Jovanovich, 1989.

—. 'Rationalism and Religion'. *The Nation and Athenaeum* 39, 1926: 279.

—. *Sowing: An Autobiography of the Years 1880 to 1904*. New York: Harcourt Brace Jovanovich, 1960.

Woolf, Virginia. 'A Society'. In *The Complete Shorter Fiction of Virginia Woolf*. Ed. Susan Dick. 2nd edn. San Diego: Harcourt Brace Jovanovich, 1989.

—. *The Diary of Virginia Woolf*. Ed. Anne Olivier Bell. 5 vols. New York: Harcourt Brace Jovanovich, 1974–84.

—. *The Essays of Virginia Woolf*. Ed. Andrew McNeillie. 4 vols. London: Hogarth Press and San Diego: Harcourt Brace Jovanovich, 1986–94.

—. *Letters of Virginia Woolf*. Ed. Nigel Nicolson and Joanne Trautmann. 6 vols. New York: Harcourt Brace Jovanovich, 1975–80.

—. *Moments of Being*. Ed. Jeanne Schulkind. 2nd edn. San Diego: Harcourt Brace Jovanovich, 1985.

—. *Orlando: A Biography*. New York: Harcourt Brace Jovanovich, [1928] 1956.

—. *A Passionate Apprentice: The Early Journals 1897–1909*. Ed. Mitchell A. Leaska. San Diego: Harcourt Brace Jovanovich, 1990.

—. *The Platform of Time: Memoirs of Family and Friends*. Ed. S. P. Rosenbaum. London: Hesperus Press, 2007.

—. *The Years*. New York: Harcourt, Brace & World, [1937] 1965.

—. *Three Guineas*. New York: Harcourt, Brace & World, [1938] 1966.

Part Two

Global Bloomsbury

Chapter 4

The Hogarth Press and Networks of Anti-Colonialism

Anna Snaith

In *Hearts of Darkness: White Women Write Race*, Jane Marcus calls for the Indian writer Mulk Raj Anand (1905–2004) to be brought 'back to Bloomsbury' (5), where he lived and worked from the mid 1920s to the mid 1940s. Recently, critics have begun to investigate Anand's position in the leftist circles of interwar London (see Bluemel and Innes), but not specifically his interactions with the Woolfs and the Hogarth Press. Anand was one of several colonial writers involved with the Press; the Trinidadian, Marxist, historian and cultural critic Cyril Lionel Robert James (1901–89), when he made his 'voyage in', first stop Bloomsbury, published with the Hogarth Press, and arrived keen to participate in the intellectual debate synonymous with the area's artistic communities. The position of these two colonial intellectuals in London – both polymaths and radicals – emphasises the metropolis' role as a crucible of anti-colonial politics. In particular, the Hogarth Press was a key disseminator of anti-colonial thought in the interwar period, suggesting an alternative take on its role as a facilitator of international modernism. The Press' publication list reinforces Leonard Woolf's position as one of the foremost theorists of anti-imperialism in the 1920s and 30s, and its general function as a nodal point for networks of colonial and metropolitan intellectuals committed to the dissolution of empire. James' and Anand's collaborations with the Woolfs typify the conflicted yet transformative exchanges which occurred between colonial and British writers in modernist London. These interactions also question the stability implied in Marcus' statement, and point to the transnational signification of 'Bloomsbury', an identification formed not only via identifiable geographical markers, but as a set of values whose reach extends far beyond the squares, bedsits, bookshops and drawing rooms. The slippage evoked in the term between geographical location and the cultural capital signified by the area's artistic intelligentsia – the Bloomsbury Group – is marked in the work of many colonial writers making the voyage in. Both Anand and James saw negotiations with Bloomsbury as essential to their 'arrival' in London; Bloomsbury clearly circulated in colonial sites, signifying not the canonical versions of British literary tradition central to cultural imperialism, but a Britishness to do with bohemian modernity and intellectual freedoms (see James, *Letters* 21). The Press, located in the heart of Bloomsbury at this point, becomes a symbolic sign of those freedoms and the cultural geography that accompanied them. Anand's proofing work at the Tavistock Square office, for instance, was an entry point into networks which led him to T. S. Eliot, D. H. Lawrence and E. M. Forster amongst others.[1]

The impact of colonialism on British metropolitan modernism is not simply about spatial disruption, the influx of artefacts into the metropolis, or artistic sampling (although these are of course pertinent), but also about the physical presence of colonial intellectuals, interacting in a wide variety of literary and political networks which invariably altered the trajectory of their activism as well as their fictional and non-fictional writing. In this period of transitional imperial relations, it is often those encounters with metropolitan individuals, and their political and artistic attitudes, which galvanise the anti-imperialism of intellectuals such as James and Anand. These conjunctions can be simultaneously sustaining and inhibiting, in that their creative fuel derives from antagonism. British modernist art's implication in cultural imperialism, and those definitions of modernity founded on various kinds of racial hierarchies, complicate intersections between British and colonial writers. As Simon Gikandi has written, 'modernism sought energies in the strangeness and distance of the other but it could only bring this other back in the terms that seemed to fit into its essentially Eurocentric framework' (49). More specifically, the 'conversations in Bloomsbury' had by Anand and James, both Marxists and anti-imperialists, demonstrate the multifariousness of anti-colonial resistance in the 1920s and 30s.

Work on the Woolfs and empire has been late coming. As Jeanette McVicker has written,

> as a white, English, middle-class, feminist, bi-sexual, socialist, pacifist, anti-fascist, anti-imperialist writer she [Virginia Woolf], sometimes by default and sometimes by choice, was *also* a proud inheritor of the English literary tradition, a beneficiary of the British Empire's imperialist practices, and an enabler of its *civilizing mission*, however unevenly. (211)

For this reason critics have varied in the extent of their indictment of Woolf. Early postcolonial readings found a thoroughgoing anti-imperialism in Woolf's oeuvre (see Marcus and Phillips), while later work has been more insistent on qualifying her anti-colonial politics.

She came at the topic of empire via anti-patriarchal and anti-fascist concerns, therefore her anti-imperialism focuses on the systems and discourses (educational, sexual, familial, cultural) through which imperialism is constructed and perpetuated. 'Woolf always challenges the master narratives of patriarchy and British imperialism, but she does not additionally trouble England's representations of the world outside itself. And because her anti-imperialism does not manifest itself through claims about racial or cultural equality, Woolf's novels often reproduce a wide range of assumptions about nonwhite otherness as well as inscribe tropes of racial differences onto white English identity' (Seshagiri 60). Her treatment of empire is undoubtedly subtle and sustained, as seen for example in her representation of imperial trade networks and the erasure of labour in 'The Docks of London', the links she makes between colonial and familial rebellion in the case of Ireland in *The Years*, the deconstruction of the spectacle of empire in 'Thunder at Wembley', but the voices of those being oppressed by these systems are rarely heard (see Snaith). So, too, Leonard's constant advocacy of colonial independence, both in print and in his capacity as an advisor for the Labour Party on its Imperial Committee during the interwar period, has not received the attention it deserves. Victoria Glendinning's recent biography of Leonard Woolf fails to illuminate this aspect of his political career, or the involvement of his wife in these projects and publications.[2] The origin of his political position in his work as a colonial administrator in Ceylon – a taint on the 'purity' of his later support for decolonisation – is symptomatic of the reasons behind the slow emergence of work on modernism and empire more generally. As Anuradha Dingwaney Needham has recently argued, our desire for 'resistance to occupy an absolutely autonomous, uncontaminated space from which to launch the "truth" of its "pure" opposition to the West' overlooks or dismisses 'those articulations of resistance that emphasize the multilayered, mixed, or hybrid cultural and historical formations' (28), such as James' essentially British public-school education or Anand's experience as a doctoral student at University College London working on British empiricist philosophy. Both James and Anand were as keen to sample and prove themselves within the literary culture of Bloomsbury as they were to resist it. Neither was that ambivalence lasting; it was a catalyst for radicalisation, paralleled by concurrent changes in colonial power relations. The complexities of Woolf's own position in class and gender terms, as outlined in *Three Guineas*, mirror the ways in which Anand and James conceived of their outsider-insider status in their early years in Britain, something Anand was quick to recognise in his encounters with her. The Press must play a crucial role in emergent scholarship on postcolonial Woolf, or modernism and colonialism more generally. It acts as a hub, not only in terms of personal contact with colonial writers, but in terms of the circulation of ideas and political discourses.

Both Anand and James were prolific intellectuals, engaged in a wide range of political and publishing endeavours, but after setting up pertinent contexts for their early years in Britain, I want to focus on James' *Letters from London* (1932, 2003) and Anand's *Conversations in Bloomsbury* (1981). In these autobiographical essays they write about their position as newcomers in London, and specifically their engagement with Bloomsbury and its highbrow literary culture. I will then turn to their involvement with the Hogarth Press, and its place at the shifting intersections of anti-colonial thought, modernity and literary culture in the modernist period.

Cultural and Political Contexts for the 'Voyage in'

C. L. R. James came to London in March 1932 from Trinidad. He spent several weeks living in Heathcote Street, Bloomsbury, before travelling north to Lancashire to stay with the black cricketer, Learie Constantine. While in Bloomsbury he wrote six articles for the *Port of Spain Gazette*, re-published as *Letters from London*. Two of these essays are about Bloomsbury, originally published untitled in Trinidad on 21 and 22 June 1932.[3] James travelled to Britain with two manuscripts, one for a novel, *Minty Alley*, published by Secker and Warburg in 1936, and the other a political biography of the Trinidadian Labour leader and Mayor of Port of Spain, Captain André Cipriani, engaged, as James puts it, 'in a series of struggles against the bad manners, the injustice, the tyranny, and the treachery of Crown Colony Government' (1). This was published as *The Life of Captain Cipriani: An Account of British Government in the West Indies* in 1932 by Coulton & Co. Ltd, a small northern press in Nelson, Lancashire. Leonard Woolf then asked James to abridge it for publication by the Hogarth Press (Dhondy 41). It is likely that James' contact with the Leonard Woolf came, not by chance as Farrukh Dhondy suggests, but through the Fabian and campaigner for colonial self-government, Lord Sydney Haldane Olivier, governor of Jamaica from 1907 to 1913, and a friend of the Woolfs, particularly in the early 1930s.[4] James quotes Olivier in *The Case for West Indian Self-Government* (49–50; see also Howe, *Anticolonialism* 100), and the Press published Olivier's *The Myth of Governor Eyre*, about Eyre's brutal tactics in suppressing the 1865 uprising in Jamaica, alongside *The Case* in 1933 (Woolmer 114). In 1933 1,200 copies of *The Case for West Indian Self-Government* were published as No. 16 in the Woolfs' Day to Day political pamphlet series started in 1930 (Woolmer 113). James had in effect separated the polemic from the biography to suit a British readership.

James' Marxism and anti-colonialism became steadily more radical as a result of his time with Constantine in the Lancashire mill town of Nelson, his involvement with the Independent Labour Party and Trotskyism in the mid 1930s (see Bogues), and his collaborations with Trinidadian George Padmore in London in the mid 1930s. But it was the invasion of Abyssinia by Mussolini in 1935 which consolidated his pan-Africanism and developed his ideas on the relationship between revolutionary politics and anti-colonialism: this just as the Comintern were speaking out against anti-colonial activity (see Bogues 39–40). James was chairman of the International African Friends of Abyssinia (later to become the International African Service Bureau), formed to support Ethiopia in the fight against imperialism (see Innes 176). James continued to support organisations ranged across the political spectrum, however. He served, for example, on the executive committee of the fairly moderate League of Coloured Peoples led by Jamaican doctor Harold Moody, and contributed to their journal, *The Keys*, writing specifically on the invasion of Abyssinia.[5]

Mulk Raj Anand came to London in 1925, living initially in Burton Street and then Little Russell Street, Bloomsbury, as a voluntary exile after his arrest for nationalist agitation in India (see Innes 218 and Fisher 24). He quickly became involved in a wide variety of leftist literary networks. While a PhD student in philosophy at University College London he opposed the students involved in strike-breaking during the 1926 General Strike (Anand, *Apology* 58–9). He was to write later: 'the Strike of 1926 had shown me categorically that Britain was organised and run in the interests of a small minority which could suppress the majority as violently at home as it did in the Empire' (*Apology* 64). Associated with the 'Leaning Tower' scene in the 1930s, Anand represented India at the International Writer's Conference Against Fascism in 1935 and volunteered briefly for the International Brigade until he was given a post reporting for the Communist Party from Madrid (Bluemel 82).[6] Both Anand and James contributed to Nancy Cunard's *Authors Take Sides*.[7] Like James, his experiences in London fused a closer relationship between his socialism and his anti-imperialism.

Ideological conflict caused him to refuse a job at the BBC's Indian Section in 1939 and indicates the divided position he occupied in London, split between his anti-fascism and his Indian nationalism (see Orwell, *Orwell* 14–15 and Bluemel 18–19).[8] Later, however, his friendship with Orwell, and Russia entering the war on the Allied side, led him

to do a substantial amount of freelance BBC work. This included drafting programmes for and participating in five instalments of Orwell's
wartime, six-part, radio poetry magazine, *Voice*, in particular a broadcast on the 'Oriental Influence on English Literature' with T. S. Eliot,
Venu Chitale, M. J. Tambimuttu, Una Marson and William Empson
(see Orwell, *Orwell* 37, 200 and *Complete Works* 141, 210–11).[9]
This programme, with readings by young poets from their own work,
was a radical departure for the BBC.[10] Anand read 'First Jasmines' by
Tagore for 'Voice 3'; and it is likely that he read passages from 'The
Secrets of the Self' by his mentor Sheikh Muhammed Iqbal on 'Voice
5', although the script has not survived (Orwell, *Complete Works* 211).
The series sought to expose young writers, but its home in the Eastern
Service meant that many of the contributors were colonial writers.[11]
Broadcasts on the Eastern Service, such as E. M. Forster's on modern
Indian writing, were instrumental in publicising writing by Anand and
other English-language Indian writers (Orwell, *Orwell* 187–8). While
colonial contributors often felt compromised by their complicity with
wartime propaganda, the BBC nevertheless provided essential political
and social networks for Indian and West Indian artists and intellectuals
in London.[12]

Anand reviewed for *The Criterion* between 1928 and 1930, and
worked as a proof-corrector at the Hogarth Press (probably in 1927)
two afternoons a week (Marler 135). It seems as though Anand was
working unpaid at the Hogarth Press as there is no record of him in the
Hogarth Press archives.[13] He later published with the Hogarth Press
via John Lehmann; his stories 'The Barber's Trade Union' and 'Duty'
appeared in Lehmann's *New Writing* series in 1936 and 1938.[14] In 1928
he started his first novel, *Untouchable*, about the life of Bakha, an Indian
sweeper and latrine cleaner, eventually published in 1935 by Wishart
with an introduction by his friend E. M. Forster, after rejections from
nineteen publishers.[15] Anand recalls an early impetus for the novel: a
comment made by Edward Sackville-West during a party at Virginia
Woolf's that 'there can be no tragic writing about the poor. You can
only laugh at them.' Anand continues:

> at that time I was writing the story of an untouchable boy. But I was so
> shocked by this dictum that I left my studies and went back to Gandhi's
> Ashram, to learn to be myself. Well, fortunately for me, Gandhi disrobed me
> of my corduroy suits and necktie and suede shoes. ('Talking of Tambi' 197;
> see also Berman 469)

That disrobing occurred as much in Bloomsbury as in India.
Untouchable ends with 'Simla – ss Viceroy of India – Bloomsbury'

(1933), indicating Anand's investment in and identification with this particular area of London, as well as the lines of geographical and metaphorical movement which symbolise the connections and conflicts that fuelled his writing in this period (see Innes 218).[16]

In comparing these two intellectuals, it is important to make distinctions between the place of Indians and West Indians in interwar London. Indian nationalism clearly had a much higher profile in Britain than, for example, the late 1930s riots in the West Indies, and the population of Indians in London was significantly higher than that of West Indians. Also Anand's self-proclaimed, Marxist humanism is very different from James' 'pan-African socialist nationalism' (Howe, *Anticolonialism* 85). Certainly, then, Anand's politics and cultural background allowed him easier access to the networks of modernist London, but both clearly felt that to conduct literal and textual conversations with Bloomsbury was part of their initiation process in the metropolis.

James, *Letters from London* and Bloomsbury

C. L. R. James' essay 'The Bloomsbury Atmosphere' documents his 'own impression' of a lecture by Edith Sitwell at the Student Movement House in Russell Square, which he describes as 'a club for London students, white and coloured, but with its chief aim giving coloured students in London an opportunity to meet together' (*Letters* 44). The incident is heavy with signification: Sitwell represents the 'modern school' (44); the occasion typifies Bloomsbury and its atmosphere. Bill Schwarz has talked of James occupying a 'low Bloomsbury' (2003), geographically proximate yet symbolically distant from the drawing rooms of Gordon Square, yet James' account of the evening suggests that his contributions are made in the name of highbrow literary culture. For example, Sitwell refers enigmatically at one point to a young American writer whose work rivals Lawrence, and James supplies the audience with Faulkner's name. He has what he calls an 'argument' with Sitwell about the relationship between talent and experimentation and after the talk surprises her with the name of an obscure composer to whom she referred. As he writes in *Beyond a Boundary*, 'in March 1932 I boarded the boat for Plymouth. I was about to enter the arena where I was to play the role for which I had prepared myself. The British intellectual was going to Britain' (111). Britain was 'the source of all light and leading' (30), Bloomsbury was the prime site of literary modernity, and James showed himself up to the job. The essay ends by celebrating the values of intellectualism and open debate found so readily in Bloomsbury (*Letters*

47), but James' urgency to prove himself implicitly suggests his fear that his West Indian identity might preclude him from such debate. His racial and national identity goes unmentioned, but his emphasis on Sitwell's surprise at his contributions belies a suspicion that her shock stems from a perceived mismatch between his blackness and his cultural capital. The essay segues between James' gratitude to various scholars who correspond with him and great confidence in his own intelligence, education and Britishness ('I had educated myself into a member of the British middle class with literary gifts' (32)). As Schwarz has argued: 'he came to Britain already convinced of his own cultural superiority . . . He imagined himself not black, but British' (6).

In the second of his essays for the *Gazette*, 'Bloomsbury Again', a fast-paced account of the 'intellectual ferment' of the area, James presents a cosmopolitan site of political and cultural interaction (54). He meets Indian nationalists, a West African student who 'reads a volume of Proust at a sitting' (42), and discusses fascism, Tagore and Pirandello. The text is peppered with references to high art and topical political debate. Of course, James is writing for a Trinidadian audience, and having to prove himself back home, but he depicts a 'natural' alliance with this admittedly 'highly artificial' lifestyle (52): 'both by instinct and by training I belong to it and have fit into it as naturally as a pencil fits into a sharpener' (54).

But these essays must be placed in the context of the manuscript he had in his suitcase and which would be published by the Hogarth Press the next year: *The Case for West Indian Self-Government*. While seemingly incongruous – the desire for cultural assimilation in his Bloomsbury essay and this document of cultural nationalism – James' performance in Bloomsbury underlines his argument in the *Case for West Indian Self-Government*: 'cut off from all contact with Africa . . . they present today the extraordinary spectacle of a people who . . . are essentially Western and, indeed, far more advanced in Western culture than many a European community' (49). Later in the decade, in *The Black Jacobins*, James developed his thesis about the modernity of African slaves in the New World: 'James sees the unique history of Africans in the diaspora as not only determining a modern essence *avant la lettre* but as the very condition of possibility of Occidental development and the emergence of a world system' (Nielsen 20). In *The Case*, after an analysis of the social and political structure of West Indian society, James argues that there is no place for a system 'based on assumptions of superiority which have no foundation in fact' (61). Crown Colony government allows 'a privileged few to work their will on hundreds of thousands of defenceless people', people whose natural development and ambition is stifled (61). By juxtaposing these early essays, then, we can see the conflicted nature of James' position and the beginnings of his later radicalism: through Bloomsbury he celebrates cultural modernity and his own participation within it, but this necessarily points to the political, cultural and economic dependence of the West Indies. While he may be confident in his own abilities and entitlements, the essay contains an underlying suspicion about the metropolis' reaction to this 'black European', as he called himself (Needham 29), and the 'openness' he ends the essay by evoking.[17]

Melba Cuddy-Keane has used the term 'democratic highbrow' to investigate the importance Virginia Woolf placed on the availability of highbrow cultural values to the common reader. So too with James and Anand: their socialism does not preclude a celebration of the cultural activity that they encountered in Bloomsbury, but both are concerned with identifying non-conventional sites of 'highbrowism' and resisting a definition which connotes elitism and excludes the vernacular. For James, as for Anand and *Untouchable*, *The Case for West Indian Self-Government* is right behind, a reminder of the various ways in which colonialism denies, or complicates, this kind of interchange. In addition, reading James' Bloomsbury essays alongside *The Case* implies another critique of metropolitan enlightenment: the text, when published by the Hogarth Press, assumed a high degree of ignorance about the West Indies: as he wrote later, 'most people were hazy about both the islands and the people. The majority . . . thought the West Indies had to do with India' (*Beyond* 117).

In his last essay for the *Port of Spain Gazette*, 'The Nucleus of a Great Civilisation' (August 1932), James makes a crucial displacement act. He moves the reader from London, 'the peak, the centre, the nucleus of a great branch of western civilisation' (111), to the northern, working-class community of Nelson. He cites the townspeople's support of striking cinema operators as evidence of the spirit of freedom and equality on which British civilisation is premised. By resituating values associated with Britishness in a 'marginal' location, James produces a nuanced account, attuned to his own inheritance, as well as the brutality and oppression also a constituent part of the term. He deflates the myth of the centre, decrying the emptiness of metropolitan public life and the intellectual bankruptcy of the inhabitants who have enjoyed 'sixty years of compulsory education and all the advantages of a great modern city' (111). James moves the locus of centrality, not only north of London but also to the Caribbean ('Far better the *Port of Spain Gazette* than any of these products of a great civilisation' [120]), placing the residual benefits of modern civilisation in those groups who have also been oppressed by such a concept.

Anand, *Conversations in Bloomsbury* and the Woolfs

Anand wrote about his encounters in Bloomsbury throughout his life (*Apology for Heroism, The Bubble*), but it is his memoir *Conversations in Bloomsbury* (1981) that interests me here.[18] His time in Bloomsbury was not merely a contained phase in his political development; it was a long-lasting, if uneven, engagement. *Conversations* charts a topographical, as well as an intellectual and political, initiation, characterised by a conflicted position similar to that of James: he is 'a naïve poet – just arrived from India' (2), eager to learn from the eminences of Bloomsbury, and a political outsider, keen to express his Marxist and anti-colonial views. His opposition to British ignorance and prejudice about India is much more vociferous than James', but of course Anand is writing half a century after the fact; indeed he makes reference to Edward Said's *Orientalism* in the preface to the second edition (1995).

While the topography of Bloomsbury in the 1920s and 30s was certainly characterised by racial and cultural difference – one reason it was a favoured destination for many colonial travellers – Anand found in those intellectuals loosely aligned with the Bloomsbury Group a disappointing adherence to the status quo. Their refusal to move from aesthetic to political commitment or to translate ideas of freedom to anti-colonial contexts was a betrayal of their position as 'custodians of European culture' (*Apology* 54), the emptied intelligentsia noted by James. *Conversation*'s preface argues that with the exception of E. M. Forster and Leonard Woolf, 'they remained enclosed in their precious worlds, without guilts about their status as aristocrats having been achieved by the labour of generations of industrial workers in Midlands and the colonies' (viii). In one sense the situation is simple – Anand viewed himself as a politicised writer, a social realist, suspicious of Bloomsbury aestheticism, and he mixed later more fully with Orwell, Lehmann and Stephen Spender – but what is interesting is that he still found those conversations/arguments worth having and worth writing about, even years later. *Conversations* allows insight into the developing political consciousness of a colonial intellectual in the metropolis; the metropolitan environment, and Bloomsbury more specifically, acted as a galvanising arena in which multiform desires and allegiances were played out.

The essays document his discussions with not only the Woolfs, to whom one edition of the text is dedicated, but Clive Bell, Nancy Cunard, T. S. Eliot, Aldous Huxley, Lytton Strachey, Eric Gill, Arthur Waley and D. H. Lawrence amongst others. He talks to Nancy Cunard about the *Negro* anthology and D. H. Lawrence's primitivism, to Eliot about

Hinduism, to Leonard Woolf and E. M. Forster about the links between public-school ethos and imperialism, to Clive Bell about 'significant form' and the erroneous distinction between craft and art, to John Middleton Murry, Lawrence, Aldous Huxley and others about Indian nationalism, art and poetry.

The memoir's form contributes to the text's critique and the unevenness of Anand's self-construction.[19] The Bloomsbury Group defined itself, in part, via freedom of speech, conversation and fellowship. The uncensored and rigorous debate crystallised in private gatherings in Bloomsbury rooms (the Thursday evening gatherings and later the Memoir Club) created a model of exchange which moved outwards into the public arena in terms of commitment to an internationalist vision of human rights and democratic self-government (see Froula). Anand's memoir is unusual in the way it literally 'gives voice' – a series of verbal exchanges presented in direct speech – so as to emphasise the role of debate, gossip and dialogue in cross-cultural interaction, as well as the anecdotal and ephemeral nature of knowledge exchange (simultaneously undercut by the half-century time lag). By enacting conversation, Anand questions the very premise or possibility of a free exchange of ideas given the wider, geopolitical context of unequal colonial relationships: 'I felt that there was an uncanny gap between me and people, as though I was inferior and others were superior' (*Conversations* 18). Like James, he seizes on another concept by which the Group identified itself – that of friendship, or 'fraternity':

> I feel that the sharing of these values . . . the experimentation with ideas – all this was part of living together as an international fraternity. I think, frankly, if I hadn't gone to this school of creativeness, which I call the friendship of people, I may not have written novels. (qtd in Fisher 36)

The concept of friendship is simultaneously evoked and undercut – moments of contact punctured by anger at the ignorance and condescension he faced – the 'lurking prejudice'. *Conversations* interrogates the cross-cultural signification of the values central to Bloomsbury's self-definition. It simultaneously performs open debate, or verbal exchange, while marking its impossibility in the context of colonial violence. As Anand writes in *Apology*: 'there can be no dignity in the personal relations of British and Indian intellectuals unless British writers realize that the freedom of speech and opinion which they take for granted is denied to their Indian friends' (52).

Anand's self-assertion happens not only through his demonstration of his intellectual credentials, but also through the text's spatial politics. He situates himself in key Bloomsbury sites (the Poetry Bookshop, the British

Museum, Tavistock Square). He claims the space, charting its topography. As Sara Blair writes: 'the cluster of venues is a generative cultural landscape: a space in which diasporic, exilic, and colonial figures, like Anand, could create themselves as players on a local yet transnational cultural field' (833). But despite the careful localising of each encounter, images of gaps, remoteness and distance recur. Out of these gaps, not only a politicised aesthetics, but a selfhood constituted via national struggle arises. The period's transitional colonial power relations are paralleled in the forms of post/colonial life-writing. Bloomsbury, here, is a testing ground, site of the performance of multiple selves: 'The dominant metaphor was my various selves, flying off in different directions', 'going through various incarnations . . . Hegelian rationalist . . . sceptic . . . would-be revolutionist, Surrealist, anti-bourgeois, murderous egotist . . . unable to reconcile all those selves' (*Conversations* 35, 77).

Much as he acts the neophyte, many of the literary 'giants' are portrayed as buffoonish at best. The encounters are often charged, Anand suppressing his anger more or less successfully:

> I was too overwhelmed by the presence of these legendary literary men. I felt that they did not know very much about my country, and what they knew was through Kipling, or through superficial impressions, except for Leonard Woolf, who had lived and worked in Ceylon and even resigned from the Civil Service because he did not want to be part of Imperialist rule. I, who had been to jail in the Gandhi movement, was fuming inside . . . I decided . . . I would fight for the freedom of my country forever, though I may admire these English writers for their literary skills . . . the thing that disturbed me was that I . . . would be a hypocrite, hating British rule in India and living on its dole. (23–4)

The text is riven with oscillating responses; he is at once overwhelmed at his position at the heart of literary London ('I felt stupid and gauche and naïve' (26)), yet furious at the racist attitudes he encounters ('I had come to learn from not to teach Eliot, I reminded myself, though I had the irrepressible urge in me out of my own disillusionment with Europe, to show the concave mirror to the Western intellectuals, however eminent they may be' (169)). This conflict between intellectualism and politics finds some resolution in the novels, *Untouchable* and *Coolie*, which result from these encounters: 'I am going to rewrite Kipling's Kim . . . from the opposite point of view' (50).

Anand's essay on Virginia Woolf, 'Tea and Empathy From Virginia Woolf', is anomalous in the collection for his depiction of her interest in Hindu mysticism and his sense of her as an outsider to Bloomsbury, the latter accounting for the former. The encounter starts with reference to Kipling, cynosure for British ignorance about India, and his own expressions of inadequacy – 'shy and tentative, I entered the Woolfs' drawing room', 'I was afraid of her verdict on my amateurish writing' (102). Quickly the conversation turns to Hinduism, Woolf asking Anand about the androgynous union of Shiva and Shakti, and the rediscovery of the worship of women by the Tantra cults. 'I have a feeling that we are male-female-male, perhaps more female than male. I am writing a novel, *Orlando*, to suggest this' (111), she says, and asks him to introduce her to a Yogi friend of his, Dr Ramji. As narrated by Anand, his literal voyage in is met with a metaphorical voyage out on Woolf's part, a desire to see beyond her own cultural boundaries and create points of transcultural understanding. Her feminism and ambivalence about Bloomsbury's thoroughgoing rationalism create a situation of empathy, and not merely the empathy 'from' Virginia Woolf of the essay's title: Anand feels her to be 'crazed by her loneliness in the midst of cynics like her husband and Lytton Strachey, Roger Fry, Clive Bell and John Maynard Keynes' (107).[20] He sees in her his own frustration at the rationalism of Bloomsbury intellectuals, constructing the meeting as mutually revelatory.

Anand was to have further dealings with Leonard, who wrote an introduction to his *Letters on India*, published by the Labour Book Service in 1942. Although the introduction is epistolary, addressed 'Dear Anand', it takes issue with what he sees as Anand's presentation of the 'extreme' Congress [Indian Congress Party] case (vii). Woolf repudiates Anand's nationalism, comparing it with Irish nationalism, and arguing that it distorts British involvement in India and marginalises the Muslim position. Woolf declares that he agrees with Anand's 'socialist interpretation' of the history of India, has for years been in favour of Indian independence and shares Anand's criticisms of the 1935 Government of India Act (viii), but that 'imperialism produces an extreme nationalist psychology in its victims and its nationalism is just as ugly and dangerous in Indians as in Britons' (viii). After two examples of Anand's 'misrepresentation' of facts relating to British involvement in India, Woolf comes to his main point, Anand's allusions to the Muslim minority:

> Your references to the problem and to the Muslim League are – you speak plainly in your book, and you won't mind my doing the same in the introduction – fantastic. The nationalism of the Irish – largely due to British imperialism – has started an insoluble Ulster problem in which religion and nationalism have intertwined to produce incalculable harm. You and the Congress Party are beginning to treat the Muslims and Mr. Jinnah as Mr. de Valera treated Ulster. (ix)[21]

Anand's measured response, addressed 'Dear Woolf', is also printed in the edition.

Leonard had, in the 1920s, been secretary to the Labour Party's Advisory Committee on International and Imperial Questions, and in this capacity had pressed the government to move forward on Indian self-government. He was the Committee's expert on African affairs, but he identified Indian self-government (and its repercussions in Burma and Ceylon), and economic exploitation in Africa as the two key political issues of the 1920s and 30s (*Autobiography* 352–3). The Committee was instrumental in the period after Anand's arrival in London in advising government on Indian issues, from the Simon Commission (1927) on the progress of devolution in India, to the Round Table Conferences (1930–3) and the formation of the Government of India Act (1934–5).[22] He also chaired the New Fabian Research Committee for International Affairs and helped to found the Fabian Colonial Bureau in 1940 (Peter Wilson 116). As Leonard was to write in his autobiography,

> at each stage the demands of Congress for self-government, and Dominion status were met by such grudging and contemptible dollops of self-government that any politically conscious Indian could only conclude that once more the tragedy of freedom would have to be acted out in India – the alien rulers would release their hold on the subject people only if forced to do so by bloody violence . . . if British government had been prepared in India to grant in 1900 what they refused in 1900 but granted in 1920; or to grant in 1920 what they refused in 1920 but granted in 1940; or to grant in 1940 what they refused in 1940 but granted in 1947 – then nine-tenths of the misery, hatred and violence, the imprisonings and terrorism, the murders, floggings, shootings, assassinations, even the racial massacres would have been avoided; the transference of power might well have been accomplished peacefully, even possibly without partition. (355)[23]

While he was certainly in agreement with Anand's driving political motivations – anti-imperialism and socialism – his hatred of nationalism's effects on minority peoples, along with some residual defensive patriotism, caused him to introduce the text with what reads as a serious indictment, defending himself by stating that his views are in line with those of the Selection Committee of the Labour Book Service. The book should be published, but readers need the caveat that this is one view on the logistics of Indian independence so they 'won't uncritically swallow it whole' (vii). The gesture is one of cultural imperialism: Woolf the rationalist acting to correct the bias of colonial extremism. The text cannot be self-sufficient, just as Wishart demanded that *Untouchable* be published only with Forster's endorsement, in effect a cleansing of its faecal subject matter, as Anand put it, to 'protect the book against being called "dirty" because it dealt with dung' ('Talking of Tambi' 99). Kirsten Bluemel has discussed Anand's gradual dissociation from London leftists, as 'he tested the limits of their revolutionary commitments', particularly in relation to Indian independence (87), but these collaborations and conversations, however fraught or antagonistic, are a constituent part of later articulations or artistic representations of the postcolonial.

The Hogarth Press

One of the main reasons that colonial writers made the journey to London was to increase their publishing and readership opportunities. That Anand and James wished to work for and publish with the Hogarth Press, and that the Woolfs wished to publish them, underlines the Press' internationalism and its role in the context of anti-imperial politics, one often superseded by its influence on psychoanalysis or high modernism. As Christine Froula has argued, 'one way that Leonard and Virginia Woolf publicly deployed their freedom of speech in the struggle for civilization was by creating the Hogarth Press' (10). The publication list 'reflects its owners' internationalist vision', as well as 'a cross-section of multidisciplinary thought toward "a new life praxis"' (11). The conjunction of avant-garde aesthetics and anti-imperial polemic is not contradictory, but rather evidence of the interrelationships between revolutions in form and social and political systems found particularly in the work of Virginia Woolf. Modernism meant a revolution in living, on both global and domestic levels.

John Lehmann's part in the internationalism of the Press must also be acknowledged, given that he was apprentice manager in 1931–2 and then part owner and general manager from 1938 until 1946 when Leonard bought him out (Gaither xxviii). Lehmann was deeply committed to exposing the British reading public to non-European writers such as Anand: 'we had welcomed Mulk Raj Anand and Ahmed Ali as young Indian writers who held the same ideals as ourselves' (Lehmann, *Whispering* 263). Ahmed Ali was one of the founders, along with Anand, in 1936 of the All-India Progressive Writers Association. Priyamvada Gopal has traced the genesis of the PWA to London Bloomsbury circles, the intellectuals gathered by Anand in 1935 at the Nanking Restaurant to form the Progressive Writers' Group prior to the official founding of the PWA in Lucknow the following year (Gopal 23, 25).[24] Ali's novel *Twilight in Delhi* was published by the Hogarth Press in 1940. It was the first novel written by a Muslim to be published in English and its route to publication speaks to the Press' and the Woolfs' insistence on freedom of speech.[25] When the printers ordered deletions of certain 'subversive' depictions of the 1857 'mutiny', Forster and Desmond MacCarthy suggested that Virginia Woolf send the book to Harold Nicolson, the official censor. He passed the novel and it was published intact (Ali xvi–xvii).[26]

The Press' list of titles on anti-imperialism is extensive. This is testament particularly to Leonard's contributions to anti-colonial thought in this period. In the 1920s and 30s 'he assumed Hobson's mantle as Britain's foremost anti-imperialist theorist' (Wilson 83). For Elleke Boehmer, Leonard is the most politically radical member of the Bloomsbury Group; after his experience in Ceylon he 'spent the rest of his career as a publisher, journalist and political adviser translating his opposition to imperialism both into committee action on decolonization and into unprecedentedly far-sighted political analyses of imperialism-as-violence and the benefits of international government' (Boehmer 183, 181). While the Press' publications on colonial matters bear Leonard's imprint more than his wife's, the division between political and literary publications does not divide neatly down the husband–wife axis. Leonard's own writings feature prominently, but they themselves are evidence of the collaborations between the Woolfs.[27] In 1917 Virginia was closely involved in researching and indexing for *Empire and Commerce in Africa* (1920), written for the Fabian Society (Leonard Woolf 350), and she read the finished text twice (Phillips viii and Chapman 210). She used a phrase from one of Leonard's epigraphs to the book in *A Room of One's Own* (Black 177).

The many publications on African affairs in late 1920s and early 30s reflect Leonard's personal interests in African politics, as well as the Press' response to topical issues. One of its key authors on Africa was Norman Leys: *Kenya* (1924), *Last Chance in Kenya* (1931) and *The Colour Bar in Africa* (1941). Leys had worked in the British colonial medical service in Nyasaland and in British East Africa, before he became an ardent anti-imperialist and spent the rest of his life writing about the atrocities he had witnessed (Willis 214–15). Lord Olivier, too, was another prominent Press author: *The Anatomy of African Misery* (1927) and *White Capital and Coloured Labour* (1929). Both Leys and Olivier were involved with the Labour Party's Imperial Advisory Committee (Leonard Woolf 360), and they frequently put newer writers, such as James, in touch with the Press. One such writer was Githendu Parmenas Mockerie, whose text *An African Speaks for His People* (1934), with a foreword by Julian Huxley, was the first book in English by a Kikuyu (Willis 231). Mockerie had come to London in 1931 on behalf of the Kikuyu Central Association to contribute, alongside Jomo Kenyatta, to a Joint Select Committee on East African affairs. While he was refused a hearing at the Select Committee (although he gave evidence the following year for the Carter commission on Kenyan land issues), he found an audience instead via the Hogarth Press (Calder 128–30). Press publications on India include Edward Thompson's *The Other Side of the Medal* (1925), Graham Pole's *India in Transition* (1932) and K. M. Panikkar's *Caste and Democracy* (1933) (Willis 232). All three were anti-imperialist in subject matter. While a focus on the Press' publication of anti-colonial theory complicates accounts of its coterie constituency, Leonard's position and network of contacts within the Labour Party is certainly reflected in the Press' titles. The decision to develop the Press' profile as a publisher of political theory is deeply entwined with Leonard's government work, and of course his own writings.

The political force of the Press had much to do with its pamphlet series. The Day to Day Pamphlets, which included James' essay, were one of a number of series, such as the Hogarth Essays, the Hogarth Sixpenny Pamphlets, and the Hogarth Letters. The forty Day to Day essays were published between 1930 and 1939, and dealt exclusively with contemporary political, social and economic issues (Gaither xxxii). The majority of the early Day to Day Pamphlets were on Russia (Maurice Dobb, *Russia To-Day and To-morrow* (1930); C. M. Lloyd, *Russian Notes* (1932); Aneurin Bevan et al., *What We Saw in Russia* (1931)) (Woolmer 197), but James inaugurated a series of titles on anti-imperialism (W. G. Ballinger, *Race and Economics in South Africa* (1934); Leonard Woolf, *The League and Abyssinia* (1936); Leonard Barnes, *The Future of the Colonies* (1936)) (Woolmer 199). James' pamphlet was followed swiftly by Benito Mussolini's *The Political and Social Doctrine of Fascism* (1933); part of Leonard's anti-fascism was a dissemination of the opposing position. He later commissioned *The Political and Social Doctrine of Communism* (1938), by R. Palme Dutt (Willis 251–2).[28] In contrast to the censorship imposed on Anand's writing at the BBC (see Note 8), the Hogarth Press represents the freedom of speech ironically sought in the capital by many colonial intellectuals (see Robinson 372). It is interesting to speculate, then, why *Untouchable* was not one of the Press' titles. Perhaps the Woolfs rejected it but, if so, it is curious that there is no mention of Anand in the archive or in Virginia Woolf's diaries. Another clue may lie in Anand's essay, 'In Conversation with H. G. Wells' (1983). Anand tells Wells, whom he has met at a talk by Krishna Menon, that *Untouchable* has been rejected by thirteen publishers, and this triggers a tirade against Virginia Woolf from Wells: ' "Never you mind – it will get published. But not by Hogarth Press. They are snobs – only publish Lady Virginia. She has messed up the novel form" ' (88–9). But Anand knew first hand the falsity of this charge. The range of progressive political and philosophical thought disseminated by the Press make it, not a reflection of the interests and friendships of its main author–publishers, but central to accounts of transnational modernism, and those contact zones which generate cultural thought and praxis.

Bloomsbury was a crucible for identities fractured by colonialism. Anand wrote in his autobiographical novel that he had taken home from England 'the freedom to dissent . . . against the police rule of the White Sahibs' (*The Bubble* 81).[29] For Anand and James, Bloomsbury was part of the process of definition of emergent vocabularies of nationalism, and transnational manifestations such as pan-Africanism. As Said has described it: 'the voyage in constitutes a specially interesting variety of hybrid cultural work. And that it exists at all is a sign of adversarial internationalization in an age of continued imperial structures' (31). Furthermore, British metropolitan modernists did not remain unchanged as the geographical boundaries of empire ruptured. Both thinkers rail against and seek to reverse metropolitan ignorance about the colonies amongst supposedly 'enlightened' intellectuals. As Orwell wrote in a review of Anand's *The Sword and the Sickle*: '[he is] interpreting Asia to the west' and a 'westernizing influence among [his] own countrymen' (*Collected Essays* 253).[30]

Virginia Woolf's interest in learning from Anand might be seen in relation to *Orlando* or the importance of India in *The Waves*, but James and Anand's shifting positions are also useful for thinking about Woolf's own ambivalence about the Bloomsbury Group but also about British culture generally. Like these two colonial intellectuals, keen to participate in a subsection of British culture that they in part resisted, Woolf's position does not divide neatly along insider-outsider lines. The outsider position she delineates in *Three Guineas* is not one of complete withdrawal, but one in which women might 'inform themselves of the practice' of whatever aspect of the culture they are objecting to. 'Thus they would be creative in their activities, not merely critical' (*A Room* 319). Anand's novel *Untouchable* and James' *The Black Jacobins* (originally performed in London in 1936 with Paul Robeson in the starring role) emerged out of their metropolitan experiences, suggesting the creative and critical conjunctions of modernism and empire.[31] This is not to suggest that London was the only catalyst for either thinker. American culture features prominently in James' oeuvre, of course, as does Dublin in Anand's.[32] Anand, like James, came to learn about European civilisation, 'to reside for a time in a world where ideas of social and human equality could at least be discussed freely' (*Apology* 87), but, like James, he finds only a partial commitment to these values.

Recent work on the contextualisation and hybridity of resistance has meant a subtler appreciation of anti-colonial thinkers in the modernist period. Grant Farred has written about the impossibility of seeing political allegiance as a 'binarized choice' in James' case despite his origins within a black educated middle class in Trinidad (105). James 'created an intellectual vantage point that was neither distinctly British nor Caribbean ... always informed by his brand of radical politics, his love for high culture, his growing appreciation for the popular, and his conflicted, dialectical movement toward the vernacular' (106). This ambivalence has been seen to undermine his 'revolutionary credentials as a theorist of (and actor, in some cases, in) decolonisation movements in the Caribbean and Africa' (Needham 2). Kirsten Bluemel has written about precisely this problem in relation to Anand's critical reception:

> discredited by the very words that distinguish him, 'Indo-Anglian,' 'radical,' 'eccentric,' Anand's peculiarly English context and language of dissent becomes a liability, the sign of the tainted legacy and continuing dominance of English language and liberalism for members of India's cultural elite. This taint, easy to spot, promotes the agendas of postcolonial critics who can quickly apply their theoretical tools, master, and then dispatch with Anand's writing. (Bluemel 100)

This desire for 'pure resistance' lies behind the relative silence surrounding the interrelationships between empire and modernism, and applies equally to the Woolfs, as to James and Anand, part of the reason why their conjunction is pertinent. Both Woolf's feminism and her anti-imperialism have faced the same charge: disqualification due to her privileged class position; however, many of her novels explore the impossibility of pure or all-pervasive resistance, as seen for example in Sara's anti-Semitism in *The Years*. In that novel, Woolf represents the plethora of motivating and interdependent forces – familial, sexual, political – that determine the individual, class or society's capacity for change. Particularly in periods of embryonic social change, as nationalist movements form and relations with imperial masters morph and rupture, resistance is a modulating force, always implicated in the discourse it opposes. 'The meaning of a resistant act, or practice, or event, is not transparent or simply "given" ... "it is socially constructed" a product of interpretation in which historical moment and milieu interact with the purposes and interests of those assigning meaning' (Needham 6). Re-interpreting those multifarious acts of resistance, part of a revaluation of modernism in the context of empire, means altering our vantage point on figures like the Woolfs, or the Hogarth Press, or Bloomsbury itself. The Press is a key site for assessing the conjunction of colonial and metropolitan individuals, texts and ideas. The Woolfs took risks via the Press, publishing new colonial writers like James and Anand, and bringing together a heterogeneous collection of writers, suggesting the inseparability of their political and aesthetic endeavours.

Notes

1. A version of this essay was published as '*Conversations in Bloomsbury*: Colonial Writers and the Hogarth Press'. In Lisa Shahriari and Gina Potts, eds. *Virginia Woolf's Bloomsbury*. Vol. 2. New York: Palgrave Macmillan, 2010: 138–57. I am very grateful to Palgrave Macmillan for granting me permission to reproduce my essay.
2. Duncan Wilson's political biography of Leonard Woolf includes two chapters on his anti-imperialism, but does not treat the Hogarth Press in any detail or link these two aspects of his career.
3. The first essay was originally reprinted in *The C. L. R. James* Reader (edited by Anna Grimshaw) as 'Bloomsbury: An Encounter with Edith Sitwell', and recently appeared in *Letters from London* renamed 'The Bloomsbury Atmosphere' by editor Nicholas Laughlin, who named the second untitled essay 'Bloomsbury Again'.
4. See Virginia Woolf, *D4* 149. Olivier was also Anne Olivier Bell's grandfather (Willis 227–8).
5. James wrote for the journal in 1933, 1934 and 1936. See issues 1.1, 1933; 1.4, 1934: 72; and 4.1, 1936: 4. The last is a provocative article entitled 'Abyssinia and the Imperialists' in which James discusses the ways in which the invasion demonstrated the 'savagery and duplicity of European imperialism in its quest for markets and raw materials' (*C. L. R. James Reader* 63).
6. John Lehmann describes the way in which Anand, despite his cultural difference, shared the concerns of British writers of the 1930s: 'that a writer like Mulk Raj Anand, for instance, author of *The Coolie* [*sic*] and other novels, should take as his world not the feudal splendours and feudal mysticism of traditional Indian literature, but the hard and suffering lives of the millions of his country's poor' (Lehmann, *New Writing in Europe* 79). Anand's plays, including *Famine*, which was produced to raise money for famine relief work in India, were staged at Unity Theatre, a venue for revolutionary American and Russian plays (Packham 54). Packham also demonstrates how Anand's blend of Marxism and humanism differed from other British radicals in the 1930s.
7. Anand writes, 'in this tragic hour of Spain's destiny, in the moment of her utmost suffering, it is the duty of all of us to look into our consciences and inquire whether we can sit still and see the flower of Spain's manhood sacrificed before the greed of a few who dream of power and feed their insatiable lust for glory and wealth on the blood of men, women and children.' James: 'Against Fascism, against Franco, but against bourgeois democracy too. For the independent action of the workers in the struggle for a Soviet Spain, the defence of the U.S.S.R., and international Socialism' (Cunard).
8. In his refusal letter to Malcolm Darling, Anand writes, 'since the breakdown of negotiations between the Viceroy and Gandhiji, the position of

Indians in this war has become very invidious. Particularly this is so with regard to Indians resident in England at the moment. Because, even those who have the most distant affiliations with the Congress, are bound to feel a certain sense of national humiliation if, with full awareness of the internment of hundreds of their compatriots and the savage sentence on Pandit Nehru, they do anything to help the war effort' (Orwell, *Orwell* 15).

9. Anand also did talks on Wells and Shaw in 1942 for a series called 'These Names Will Live', one on *War and Peace* for 'Books That Changed the World', and his talk about the Spanish Civil War for Orwell's series, 'The History of Fascism', was banned by the MOI (see Bluemel 19, 24–5; Orwell, *Orwell* 287, 44; and Orwell, *Complete Works* 70, 85). Anand also ran a series called 'Meet My Friend' (Orwell, *Orwell* 194, 199–200) and 'A Day in My Life', interviewing ordinary people involved in war work (Orwell, *Orwell* 216).

10. Each programme focused around a topic such as 'childhood', 'war poetry' and 'American poetry' and interspersed discussion with readings.

11. Orwell defended the programme against claims of dilettantism given the wartime conditions, by arguing that 'there are some of us who feel that it is exactly at times like the present that literature ought not to be forgotten' (Orwell, *Orwell* 80).

12. This is particularly true of the BBC's 'Caribbean Voices' programme founded by Una Marson and continued by Henry Swanzy.

13. The dating of his work at the Tavistock Square office is also uncertain. Given that *Conversations in Bloomsbury* was written nearly sixty years after the events it describes, critics have questioned its accuracy (see Marler 134–5). Anand writes, for example, in 'Tea and Empathy from Virginia Woolf', 'I am sorry I could not finish reading the proofs of *Henry James at Work*. I'll do them tomorrow' (106) and in 'A Wordy Quarrel with Clive Bell', 'You may remember Mr Woolf talking to you about the little book on Henry James at Work. Here are the galleys' (115). This essay by Theodora Bosanquet, the only book in the Hogarth Essays series to be hand-printed by the Woolfs, was published in 1924 before Anand arrived in Britain. A second impression was printed by the Garden City Press in 1927, but would not have required proof correction (Woolmer 25–6).

14. *New Writing* 2: 8–15 and *New Writing* 1: 208–12.

15. See Ruvani Ranasinha for a discussion of Anand's publishing history in Britain in the context of other South Asian contemporaries such as R. K. Narayan and Raja Rao.

16. See also Susheila Nasta. Not only does Nasta provide further contextual material about the publication of the novel by Wishart, but also usefully complicates the polarised geographical, political and artistic contexts of production and reception in which the novel (and Anand's oeuvre more generally) has been read.

17. See Laura Winkiel for further discussion of James' arguments about Caribbean modernity in *The Case*, a 1933 BBC broadcast, and in *The Black Jacobins*.

18. I am grateful to Anouk Lang for alerting me to the possible allusion to George Moore's *Conversations in Ebury Street*.

19. See Bluemel 189, n1 for a discussion of 'fictional autobiography' in relation to *Conversations*.
20. See also Jane Marcus' recent discussion of Anand's *Coolie*, in terms of the connections he makes between Indian men and European women (*Hearts of Darkness* 173).
21. Victoria Glendinning, countering George Orwell's review of *Letters on India* in the *Tribune* in which he notes that Leonard had written 'a rather angry letter this time which is printed as a foreword', misrepresents Leonard's introduction, stating that 'his only disagreement with Anand in the fore-word, in fact, had been with Anand's attitude to the Muslim minority' (356).
22. See Peter Wilson for the specifics of Leonard's views on anti-imperialism (including his theories of economic imperialism, mandates and education) (83–142).
23. See Duncan Wilson for details of Committee's involvement on Indian self-government (165–71).
24. See also Innes 219–20.
25. See Amin Malak.
26. See also Ahmed Ali's contribution to *E. M. Forster: A Tribute*.
27. Leonard's Hogarth publications on imperialism include *Empire and Commerce in Africa* (1925; previously published in 1920 by the Labour Research Department), *Imperialism and Civilization* (1928) and *The League and Abyssinia* (1936).
28. Leonard originally asked John Strachey and Maurice Dobb to write the book, but both refused, Strachey suggesting Dutt as a possible author (Willis 251–2).
29. *The Bubble* contains versions of several scenes from *Conversations in Bloomsbury*, including 'Tea and Empathy from Virginia Woolf'.
30. Interestingly, in this review Orwell discusses not only the importance of the English language, as a transnational weapon against fascism, but also the emergence of an Anglo-Indian dialect in Anand's writing (Orwell, *Collected Essays* 253).
31. The play, about the eighteenth-century revolution in San Domingo, was called *Toussaint L'Ouverture* and was performed at the Westminster Theatre before James rewrote it as non-fiction.
32. See Part Six of *The Bubble*, entitled 'Dublin Diary' (467–534). See Jessica Berman for a comparative account of Joyce and Anand, as well as a reading that complicates his label as 'social realist' writer.

Works cited

Ali, Ahmed. Chapter III. In K. Natwar-Singh, ed. *E. M. Forster: A Tribute*. 2nd edn. New Delhi: Rupa, 2002: 33–40.
—. *Twilight in Delhi*. New York: New Directions, 1994.
Anand, Mulk Raj. *Apology for Heroism: A Brief Autobiography of Ideas*. New Delhi: Arnold-Heinemann, [1946] 1975.
—. *The Bubble*. New Delhi: Arnold-Heinemann, 1984.
—. 'In Conversation with H. G. Wells'. *The Journal of Commonwealth Literature* 18.1, 1983: 84–90.

—. *Conversations in Bloomsbury*. New Delhi: Oxford University Press, [1981] 1995.

—. *Letters on India*. London: The Labour Book Service, 1942.

—. 'Talking of Tambi: The Dilemma of the Asian Intellectual'. In Jane Williams, ed. *Tambimuttu: The Bridge Between Two Worlds*. London: Peter Owen, 1989: 191–201.

Berman, Jessica. 'Comparative Colonialisms: Joyce, Anand, and the Question of Engagement'. *Modernism/modernity* 13.3, 2006: 465–85.

Black, Naomi. *Virginia Woolf as Feminist*. Cornell: Cornell University Press, 2004.

Blair, Sara. 'Local Modernity, Global Modernism: Bloomsbury and the Places of the Literary'. *ELH* 71.3, 2004: 813–38.

Bluemel, Kirsten. *George Orwell and the Radical Eccentrics: Intermodernism in Literary London*. New York: Palgrave Macmillan, 2004.

Boehmer, Elleke. *Empire, the National and the Postcolonial 1890–1920*. Oxford: Oxford University Press, 2002.

Bogues, Anthony. *Caliban's Freedom: The Early Political Thought of C. L. R. James*. London: Pluto, 1997.

Calder, Angus. 'A Note on Parmenas Mockerie'. *The Journal of Commonwealth Literature* 18.1, 1983: 128–30.

Chapman, Wayne. 'Leonard and Virginia Working Together'. *Virginia Woolf Miscellanies: Proceedings of the First Annual Conference on Virginia Woolf*. Ed. Mark Hussey and Vara Neverow-Turk. New York: Pace University Press, 1992: 209–10.

Cuddy-Keane, Melba. *Virginia Woolf, the Intellectual and the Public Sphere*. Cambridge: Cambridge University Press, 2003.

Cunard, Nancy, ed. *Authors Take Sides on the Spanish War*. London: Left Review, 1937.

Dhondy, Farrukh. *CLR James*. London: Weidenfeld and Nicolson, 2001.

Farred, Grant. *What's My Name?: Black Vernacular Intellectuals*. Minneapolis: University of Minnesota Press, 2005.

Fisher, Marlene. *The Wisdom of the Heart: A Study of the Works of Mulk Raj Anand*. New Delhi: Sterling Publishers, 1985.

Froula, Christine. *Virginia Woolf and the Bloomsbury Avant-Garde*. New York: Columbia University Press, 2005.

Gaither, Mary E. 'The Hogarth Press 1917–1946'. In J. Howard Woolmer, ed. *A Checklist of the Hogarth Press 1917–1946*. Revere: Woolmer/Brotherson, 1986.

Gikandi, Simon. 'Africa and the Epiphany of Modernism'. In Laura Doyle and Laura Winkiel, eds. *Geomodernisms: Race, Modernism, Modernity*. Bloomington: Indiana University Press, 2005: 31–50.

Glendinning, Victoria. *Leonard Woolf: A Biography*. New York: Free Press, 2006.

Gopal, Priyamvada. *Literary Radicalism in India: Gender, Nation and the Transition to Independence*. London: Routledge, 2005.

Howe, Stephen. *Anticolonialism in British Politics*. Oxford: Clarendon, 1993.

Innes, C. L. *A History of Black and Asian Writing in Britain, 1700–2000*. Cambridge: Cambridge University Press, 2002.

James, C. L. R. *Beyond a Boundary*. London: Serpent's Tail, 1994.

—. 'Bloomsbury: An Encounter with Edith Sitwell'. *The C. L. R. James Reader*. Ed. Anna Grimshaw. Oxford: Blackwell, 1992: 43–8.

—. 'The Bloomsbury Atmosphere'. In *Letters from London*.

—. 'The Case for West Indian Self-Government'. *The C. L. R. James Reader*. Ed. Anna Grimshaw. Oxford: Blackwell, 1992: 49–62.

—. *Letters from London*. Ed. Nicholas Laughlin. Oxford: Signal Books, [1932] 2003.

—. *The Life of Captain Cipriani: An Account of British Government in the West Indies*. Nelson: Coulton, 1932.

Lehmann, John, ed. *New Writing*. Vol. 1. London: Hogarth Press, 1938.

—, ed. *New Writing*. Vol. 2. London: Hogarth Press, 1936

—. *New Writing in Europe*. Harmondsworth: Penguin, 1940.

—. *The Whispering Gallery*. London: Longmans, 1955.

McVicker, Jeanette. 'Postcolonial Approaches'. In Anna Snaith, ed. *Palgrave Advances in Virginia Woolf Studies*. Basingstoke: Palgrave Macmillan, 2007: 209–26.

Malak, Amin. *Muslim Narratives and the Discourse of English*. New York: SUNY Press, 2005.

Marcus, Jane. 'Britannia Rules *The Waves*'. In Karen R. Lawrence, ed. *Decolonizing Tradition: New Views of Twentieth-Century 'British' Literary Canons*. Urbana and Chicago: University of Illinois Press, 1992: 136–82.

—. *Hearts of Darkness: White Women Write Race*. New Brunswick: Rutgers University Press, 2004.

Marler, Regina. *Bloomsbury Pie: The Making of the Bloomsbury Boom*. London: Virago, 1997.

Nasta, Susheila. 'Between Bloomsbury and Gandhi? The Background to the Publication and Reception of Mulk Raj Anand's *Untouchable*'. In Robert Fraser and Mary Hammond, eds. *Books Without Borders*. Vol. 2. Basingstoke: Palgrave Macmillan, 2008: 151–69.

Needham, Anuradha Dingwaney. *Using the Master's Tools: Resistance and the Literature of the African and South-Asian Diasporas*. New York: St. Martin's Press, 2000.

Nielsen, Aldon Lynn. 'The Future of An Allusion: The Colour of Modernity'. In Laura Doyle and Laura Winkiel, eds. *Geomodernisms: Race, Modernism, Modernity*. Bloomington: Indiana University Press, 2005: 17–30.

Orwell, George. *The Collected Essays, Journalism and Letters of George Orwell: My Country Right or Left 1940–1943*. Vol. 2. Ed. Sonia Orwell and Ian Angus. Harmondsworth: Penguin, 1970.

—. *The Complete Works of George Orwell*. Vol. 14. Ed. Peter Davison. London: Secker and Warburg, 1998.

—. *Orwell: The War Broadcasts*. Ed. W. J. West. London: Duckworth, 1985.

Packham, Gillian. 'Mulk Raj Anand and the Thirties Movement in England'. In K. K. Sharma, ed. *Perspectives on Mulk Raj Anand*. Ghaziabad: Vimal Prakashan, 1978: 52–63.

Phillips, Kathy. *Virginia Woolf Against Empire*. Knoxville: University of Tennessee Press, 1994.

Ranasinha, Ruvani. *South Asian Writers in Twentieth-Century Britain: Culture in Translation*. Oxford: Oxford University Press, 2007: 17–23.

Robinson, Cedric J. *Black Marxism*. London: Zed Press, 1983.

Said, Edward. 'Third World Intellectuals and Metropolitan Culture'. *Raritan* 9.3, 1990: 27–50.

Schwarz, Bill. 'Modernism & Cultural Studies: Black Bloomsbury?' Transcript of talk given at the MSA Conference, Birmingham, 2003.

Seshagiri, Urmila. 'Orienting Virginia Woolf: Race, Aesthetics, and Politics in *To the Lighthouse*'. *Modern Fiction Studies* 50.1, 2004: 58–83.

Snaith, Anna. *'The Exhibition in is Ruins': Virginia Woolf and Empire*. Sixth Annual Virginia Woolf Birthday Lecture. Southport: Virginia Woolf Society of Great Britain, 2005.

Willis, J. H. *Leonard and Virginia Woolf as Publishers: The Hogarth Press, 1917–41*. Charlottesville: University Press of Virginia, 1992.

Wilson, Duncan. *Leonard Woolf: A Political Biography*. London: Hogarth Press, 1978.

Wilson, Peter. *The International Theory of Leonard Woolf: A Study in Twentieth-Century Idealism*. Basingstoke: Palgrave Macmillan, 2003.

Winkiel, Laura. *Modernism, Race and Manifestos*. Cambridge: Cambridge University Press, 2008: 211–26.

Woolf, Leonard. *An Autobiography*. Vol. 2. Oxford: Oxford University Press, 1980.

Woolf, Virginia. *The Diary of Virginia Woolf*. Vol. 4. Ed. Anne Olivier Bell. London: Hogarth Press, 1982.

—. *A Room of One's Own and Three Guineas*. Ed. Morag Shiach. Oxford: Oxford University Press, 1992.

Woolmer, J. Howard, ed. *A Checklist of the Hogarth Press 1917–1946*. Revere: Woolmer/Brotherson, 1986.

Chapter 5

William Plomer, Transnational Modernism and the Hogarth Press

John K. Young

William Plomer (1903–73), a self-described 'Anglo-Afro-Asian' novelist, poet, editor and librettist, spent only the early years of his lengthy career as a Hogarth Press author but still ranks as one of the Woolfs' most prolific writers, with a total of nine titles issued during his seven years with the Press. Like Katherine Mansfield, Plomer made his mark with Hogarth before signing with a more established firm, but the depth and breadth of Plomer's career with the Woolfs is significantly greater: his five volumes of fiction presented Hogarth's readers with groundbreaking portraits of South African, Japanese and (British) working-class cultures. In 1933 Plomer moved to Jonathan Cape, though he continued publishing poetry with Hogarth, both in his own volumes and in John Lehmann's collections, into the 1940s. Beginning in 1937, Plomer replaced the famed Edward Garnett as Cape's editorial adviser, serving in that capacity for the remainder of his career.[1] Though perhaps now best known, especially in Britain, for the finely crafted verse of his later years, Plomer is a noteworthy figure in new histories of modernism for his role in the international scope of that movement. In this essay I focus primarily on Plomer's South African fiction, especially *Turbott Wolfe* (1926) and 'Ula Masondo' (1927), two incisive portraits of racialisation's effects on both black and white subjects, aimed at a British reading public. While his later Hogarth novels, *Sado* (1931) and *The Case Is Altered* (1932), may seem to lack the experimental dynamism of *Turbott Wolfe*, I locate their underlying social subversiveness through queer narratological readings. Finally, I relate Plomer's career with the Woolfs to their own transition from a coterie Bloomsbury hand press to a 'proper publishing business' by the 1930s, in Leonard's words (*Downhill* 68).

Because Plomer's works are so various – and I mean here only his Hogarth fictions, much less his later libretti and poetry – they may seem to resist critical categorisation, thus adding to his relative obscurity within accounts of modernism. But what is most striking about Plomer's career, especially in its earlier phases, is precisely his works' refusal to situate themselves within easily recognisable patterns. The highly charged experimental style with which *Turbott Wolfe* illuminates the corrosive effects of interracial taboos in South Africa, or the attempt to inhabit the narrative perspective of a black subject in 'Ula Masondo', seem nowhere to be found in the almost glacial description of British–Japanese interactions in *Sado*. Even if we read this stylistic change as expressive of *Sado*'s (sub)textual portrait of homosexuality, that narrative tendency then seems to disappear in *The Case Is Altered*, a crime drama based on a sensational London murder. Given Plomer's consistent interest in his own situatedness – as his cultural and geographical contexts were moving from Zululand to Tokyo to London – his contributions to modernism may best be understood within the rubric of geomodernism, a term advanced by Laura Doyle and Laura Winkiel to express a '*geocultural* consciousness—a sense of speaking from outside or inside or both at once, of orienting toward and away from the metropole, of existing somewhere between belonging and dispersion' (4). These are certainly the terms in which Plomer saw his own career, especially in its Hogarth Press phase; as he wrote to Leonard Woolf in 1927, 'Since I was 16 I have lived in daily contact with non-Europeans, & sometimes before that, so you can see why my view of Europe is not like that of a European: & I defy anybody to say that it is distorted' (Archives).

Plomer produced his early fictions from a position between London and the 'savage' colony: as the son of English emigrants to South Africa who spent his formative years in that country, Plomer operates as both a guide to South African culture, for his British metropolitan readers, and as a fierce critic of that culture, for his local audiences, many of whom reacted with outrage at both *Turbott Wolfe* and *Voorslag*, a short-lived journal founded by Plomer, Roy Campbell and Laurens van der Post (later a Hogarth author himself, with the 1934 novel *In a Province*). Plomer's debut novel appeared in the midst of European modernism's complex negotiations with the necessary alterity of the African other; as Simon Gikandi concludes, 'modernism sought energies in the strangeness and distance of the other but it could only bring this other back in the terms that seemed to fit into its essentially Eurocentric framework' (49). In his early fictions, then, Plomer functions as a (white) representative of colonial exchanges with the (black) African other, as the narrator of *Turbott Wolfe* is a character named 'William Plomer', and as suggested by the very title of *I Speak of Africa* (1927), the volume of stories that followed *Turbott Wolfe*. While *Turbott Wolfe* is unique in its advocacy of interracial sexuality 'as a possible *solution* to the colour question' (Rabkin 78), the novel also shies away from any consistent engagement with the points of view of its black characters, as part of a modernist tendency 'to separate the body of the savage from its aesthetic objects so that the latter could be valued even in the face of hostility toward the former' (Gikandi 42). The critiques of South African racialisation in *Turbott Wolfe* come almost invariably from its white characters, as in the following declaration: ' "You take away the black man's country, and, shirking the future consequences of your action, you blindly affix a label to what you know (and fear) the black man is thinking of you— "the native question." Native question, indeed! My good man, there is no native question. It isn't a question. It's an answer" ' (71). The speaker here is neither 'William Plomer' (the character) nor a 'native' African, but Mabel van der Horst, a Dutch settler who helps to found the Young Africa movement advocating 'miscegenation' and marries Zachary Msomi, a black African. Mabel effectively serves as her husband's spokesperson, as the novel does not occupy Zachary's perspective itself, focusing on his symbolic value in lieu of actual subjectivity, and thus signalling the limits of *Turbott Wolfe*'s capacity for operating outside of its own racialised circumstances of production.

After briefly outlining Plomer's biography, the remainder of this chapter seeks to examine such complexities in the bulk of his Hogarth fiction, not only in the early interventions into what was still commonly referred to in South Africa as 'the colour question' in the 1970s (as in the quotation from David Rabkin above), but also in his later entries into other zones of alterity for his Hogarth readers: Japan, the British working class and, at least implicitly, a range of queer subcultures. To (re)inscribe William Plomer into histories of the Hogarth Press, and of transnational modernism more broadly, I conclude, means not only restoring a significant historical figure, but also revising still commonly held conceptions of literary modernism itself, in relation to colonialism/ imperialism and to contemporary methods of historicising the period.[2]

'A displaced person': Plomer's Biography

Reflecting on his life for the 1967 article 'Anglo-Afro-Asian', Plomer concluded that, almost forty years after his return to England, 'I am critical of England and the English and although at home among them I do not wholly belong to them' (11). Plomer's sense of himself as a 'displaced person', as he puts it elsewhere in the same essay (10), was rooted primarily in the travels of his childhood and youth, as he moved back to England in 1929 and largely remained there until his death in 1973. Plomer was born in the Transvaal region of modern South Africa in December 1903, when the effects of the recently concluded Boer War were still visible in the garrison that was central to his village (Alexander 1). His father, Charles Plomer, was sent by his parents from England to South Africa at nineteen, and eventually landed a position with the colonial civil service, in the Department of Native Affairs at Pietersburg, not quite two hundred miles removed from Johannesburg. Plomer's mother, Edythe Browne, moved back to England with her infant son shortly after his birth, returning to Pietersburg in the summer of 1905, before moving back to England again with Charles later that year, after he had contracted malaria (8). Following the birth of Plomer's brother, John, in 1907, the family moved to Louis Trichardt, a destination that Plomer's biographer describes as 'a still hotter, more fever-stricken town than Pietersburg' (8). From there the Plomers continued to shift back and forth between England and South Africa, until settling, apparently for good, in South Africa in 1918. Four years later, following a possible nervous breakdown (68), Plomer's father left the civil service and relocated to Entumeni, to run a trading station in the Zululand outpost. It was here that Plomer would begin writing *Turbott Wolfe*, at the rather remarkable age of twenty-one. Plomer maintained a conflicted relationship with his father throughout his life, going so far in 1929 as to insist that his last name be pronounced to rhyme with 'rumour', in contrast to the family tradition (maintained by Plomer's brother) of pronouncing it to rhyme with 'Homer' (155).

Of his early years, Plomer writes, 'We never had a settled home, and "at home" meant "in England," so I could hardly think of myself as a South African' ('Anglo-' 6). This sense of dislocatedness led Plomer to an outsider's perspective on the racialised structures of South African society. 'It occurred to me quite early in life that the terms "black" and "white" were too arbitrary', he writes in his late autobiographical essay. 'One thing was constant and rigidly clear—that the presumed line between so-called white and so-called black must never be crossed—at least openly' (6). The writing of *Turbott Wolfe* represented one way of attacking such arbitrary systems; another was the short-lived magazine *Voorslag*, an Afrikaans word for 'whip', with both title and content intended 'to sting with satire the mental hindquarters, so to speak, of the bovine citizenry' of South Africa (*Double Lives* 43). Plomer worked as an editor and major contributor on the magazine's first three issues in 1926 with two other key figures of South African literature from this period, Campbell and van der Post, before Campbell resigned in August of that year following what he viewed as unacceptable editorial control imposed by *Voorslag*'s financial backer. The third issue included a truncated conclusion of Plomer's story 'Portraits in the Nude', which he later published in its original form in *I Speak of Africa*. (The edited version of the story cut several lines from the closing description of Lily Du Toit, the family governess, regarding her naked body by candlelight before the desired entrance of Cormorant, a visiting Englishman. As Plomer noted in his preface for the Hogarth Press version in *I Speak of Africa*, the story 'is here printed for the first time as it was written' (vii). Like Virginia Woolf herself, then, who famously considered the Press to have made her 'the only woman in England free to write what I like' (*D3* 43), Plomer enjoyed an editorial liberty with Hogarth that had proved impossible in South Africa.)

Voorslag featured contributions in both English and Afrikaans, and Campbell had hoped to include material in Zulu as well (Gardner & Chapman 1). Beyond this cosmopolitan content, the journal also expressed its editors' interest in what they viewed as the superior aesthetic and moral standards of European culture. While *Voorslag* has acquired a significant reputation in histories of twentieth-century South African literature, it remains, as Colin Gardner and Michael Chapman note in their introduction to its facsimile reprint, 'for many people a legend rather than a concrete reality; it seems likely that the journal was not actually read or even seen by many of the writers who responded in a general way to its appeal and challenge' (13).[3]

Following the magazine's dissolution, at least in its original scope, in 1926, Plomer and van der Post took advantage of an unexpected opportunity to leave South Africa, sailing for Japan at the invitation of two sailors van der Post had befriended, with Plomer now installed as a special correspondent for the *Natal Witness*, a local newspaper. The ship's captain, Katsue Mori, in turn hoped to employ Plomer, who had acquired a reputation as the author of *Turbott Wolfe*, as part of his company mission to erode barriers against Japanese trade by securing the imprimatur of established cultural figures in Africa (Alexander 113). Plomer remained in Japan until 1929, completing work on *I Speak of Africa* and composing another volume of stories, *Paper Houses*, as well as a collection of poems. At this point Leonard Woolf also invited Plomer to serve as Hogarth's book traveller in Japan, offering the 'usual commission of 10% of the net order' but Plomer declined (Archives).[4]

The immersion in an entirely different society seems to have freed Plomer, relatively, to pursue a more openly homosexual life. Unlike his later friend E. M. Forster, Plomer portrayed a range of gay relationships in his fiction, most notably in *Sado*, *The Case Is Altered* and

The Invaders (1934). Generally, Plomer viewed his formative Japanese experience as 'my university':

> I was being changed from a spasmodic improviser into a shaper, I was learn-
> ing to think as well as to feel, and was acquiring a viewpoint which would
> enable me to see distant England and English civilization through Japanese
> eyes, as well as in a new perspective through my own. (I say nothing of South
> Africa, which was by then out of sight and almost out of mind.) In short, I
> was being educated. ('Anglo-' 9–10)

Plomer settled in England in 1929, publishing *Sado* with the Woolfs in 1931 and *The Case Is Altered* the following year. While *Sado* lost £64 in its first year (Willis 196), *The Case Is Altered* became Plomer's most commercially successful novel, and one of Hogarth's best-sellers during the period in which Virginia Woolf worked actively as an editor and publisher. Indeed, Plomer's third novel was the August selection for the Book Society, leading to a £150 advance (rather than the usual £10) and helping Plomer earn more than £1,000 in 1932, easily the highest profits of his career to that point (Alexander 182). Hogarth reissued a cheaper edition in 1935, part of a series called Hogarth 2/6 Fiction, which also included Vita Sackville-West's *Family History* and F. M. Mayor's *The Rector's Daughter*. Despite discussions of a film adapta-tion in both Britain and the USA, no such version materialised: Warner Bros. found the novel 'interesting but lacking a strong enough plot for film purposes', while a British version seems to have foundered over the question of rights fees (Archives).

Plomer left Hogarth amicably in 1933, publishing *The Child of Queen Victoria and Other Stories* with Jonathan Cape, though the Woolfs issued his *Selected Poems* in 1940 as well as reprints of *Sado* and *The Case Is Altered*.[5] As Leonard explained in a letter to Vita Sackville-West (after she had received a competing offer to publish with Heinemann), Hogarth had lost money on all of Plomer's books after *Turbott Wolfe*, until the commercial explosion of *The Case Is Altered* (*Letters* 318). The remaining decades of his varied and remarkable career included editing the diary of the Victorian clergyman Francis Kilvert; serving as a civil-ian naval intelligence analyst during World War II; collaborating with Benjamin Britten on the opera *Gloriana*, produced for Queen Elizabeth II's coronation in 1953; writing a final novel, *Museum Pieces*, about his long-time companion, Anthony Butts, who had committed suicide in 1941; producing several acclaimed volumes of verse and three memoirs (including his posthumously published autobiography); being named a Commander of the British Empire; and winning the Whitbread award for a book of illustrated children's verse in the year of his death. Like many other illustrious authors, who either began their careers with the Hogarth Press before departing for larger firms, or who could offer it more ephemeral publications while under contract elsewhere for their major works, William Plomer helped to make the Hogarth Press more than the publisher of Virginia Woolf's works, or indeed even of Woolf's, Vita Sackville-West's and Sigmund Freud's works, as it is often still regarded. The remainder of this chapter returns first to Entumeni to cover that territory in greater detail.

'Nearer the heart of things than any other publisher in London': Publishing South African Fiction in Britain

In June 1924 the Woolfs received a letter from a twenty-one-year-old aspiring novelist in Zululand, announcing that he wished to send them the manuscript of his first book because 'I suspect you are nearer the heart of things than any other publisher in London' (qtd in Willis 128). That Plomer, a young man living in a fairly remote section of Africa, should have been familiar with Hogarth when the firm was still in its early stages of development seems rather surprising.[6] But Plomer's interest in the Woolfs may have derived from their previous forays into colonial works, such as Katherine Mansfield's *Prelude* (1918), and because their Bloomsbury sensibility was willing to question the racial and sexual foundations of empire, as in Leonard Woolf's novel, *The Village in the Jungle*, published in 1913 by Edward Arnold and written to reflect Woolf's uncomfortable experiences as a colonial administrator in Ceylon.[7] Leonard wrote twice to Plomer in early 1925, expressing his own interest but wishing to wait until Virginia had also reviewed the manuscript before issuing a contract. Leonard's letter of 1 February reports, 'The MS. of your novel has arrived and I have read sufficient of it already to see that it is very interesting. I should like to take some time to read it carefully and I should also like my wife, who is at the moment ill, to read it before we come to any definite decision. . . .' (Archives). Two months later, there had still been no 'definite decision' – a fairly short interval by many publishers' standards but no doubt a vexing one for Leonard. He wrote to Plomer again on 3 April:

> I am really ashamed at not having yet made a definite decision about your book. I have read it myself & think very highly of it, but I am most anxious that my wife should also read it. She is much better & so we have come here [Rome] for a short holiday. As soon as we get back to London after Easter, she will read it & I will let you know our decision at once. The book could

not in any case be published until the autumn. But I must really apologise to you for this delay.

Personally I think the book in many ways remarkable, & should like if it is possible to publish it (Archives).

From there work proceeded quickly, as by the following month both Virginia and Donald Brace (as Plomer's prospective American publisher) had reviewed the manuscript, and both agreed with Leonard that a lengthy speech from the missionary Friston should be cut, as he suggested in a letter to Plomer on 21 May (Archives). A month later, Plomer replied, 'I suffer very much from having no local criticism of my work, and I am obliged to admit that Friston's speech is tedious—but if you only knew the conditions under which I write! I am immediately considering how I can shorten this speech, and directly I get home I will re-draft and forward it to you' (Archives). True to his word, Plomer had completed this revision by 28 June, but the planned autumn publication was delayed until 1926 by a printers' strike.

The procedures employed to approve of *Turbott Wolfe* as a Hogarth Press title are noteworthy within the Woolfs' history as publishers, as they constitute one of the few surviving examples of Virginia's work as a publisher. Woolf apparently read every fiction manuscript submitted to the Press before selling her share to John Lehmann in 1938, but few records of her actual editorial work have survived. Hermione Lee takes this lack of evidence to conclude that Hogarth's 'editorial acumen [was] mostly, but not entirely, Leonard's' (367), but the Hogarth historian J. H. Willis makes a convincing case for 'Virginia's essential role as a reader of fiction manuscripts', with Leonard's insistence on receiving her input on *Turbott Wolfe* as his primary example (129). Virginia's diaries include occasional mentions of manuscripts the Press rejected – as in her note of rejecting submissions by Mary Butts and two other writers because 'Novels are the great blood-suckers . . . I fancy that we don't do as well as we should with novels' (150) – but actual editorial advice seems almost always to come from Leonard. This evidence may suggest that Virginia served more as a reader for the Press than as an actual editor, but, if we consider the Woolfs as a collaborative entity, as suggested by Catherine Hollis' important essay on Hogarth's 'double signature', we might easily imagine that Virginia expressed her editorial judgements about incoming manuscripts with Leonard in conversation, and that he then conveyed these criticisms and suggestions within his own correspondence with Hogarth authors. Indeed, Leonard's letter to Plomer about revising *Turbott Wolfe* indicates precisely such a dynamic: 'Mr. Brace said with regard to the MS that he enjoyed it very much up to the speech of Friston which he thought much too long. As a matter of fact both my wife and I had independently thought the same. We think that you rather spoilt the effect of your book by "preaching" the moral at too great length, which really comes through, and should be allowed to come through, in the remainder of the book' (Archives). Rather than viewing Hogarth's editorial 'acumen' as largely Leonard's, then, the much more likely scenario seems to me to be that which we see in evidence with *Turbott Wolfe* and in later correspondence from Leonard about *Sado* and *The Case Is Altered*: Leonard's letters reflect both his and Virginia's editorial opinions, and the process of sorting out from which spouse and co-publisher a particular idea originated is likely impossible at this point in history, if it even would have been at the time.

Aside from their usual publishing habits, the Woolfs would no doubt have been especially concerned to arrive at a joint opinion about the manuscript of *Turbott Wolfe*, given both the novel's experimental design and, more importantly, its culturally explosive content. The latter was especially an issue in South Africa, though Britain was hardly immune to anxieties about sexuality and race, as demonstrated, for example, by the reactions to Nancy Cunard's relationship with Henry Crowder, the African American pianist.[8] Throughout the publication process, Leonard remained highly concerned that Plomer's novel would resemble too closely actual people and events in Zululand. Plomer assured him several times that the events and characters were fictional, and the published novel carried the following note: 'None of the characters in this book refers to any living person, nor are their opinions necessarily those of the author.' Nevertheless, Plomer's copy of the book, now housed among his papers at the Durham University Library, includes more than fifty of Plomer's handwritten notes connecting characters and events to historical incidents.[9]

Despite Nadine Gordimer's lament in her introduction to *Turbott Wolfe*'s Modern Library reissue in 2003 – 'It is an inexplicable lapse on the part of literary scholars and critics that *Turbott Wolfe* is not recognised as a pyrotechnic presence in the canon of renegade colonialist literature along with Conrad' (xix) – Plomer's debut novel has remained decidedly on the margins of modernist literary histories, so a brief summary is likely in order. A Conradian narrative in which the title character relates his experiences as a white trader in Zululand to the narrator, himself named William Plomer, *Turbott Wolfe* is probably most notable today for its advocacy of so-called miscegenation as the way to promote a 'Eurafrican' society, a transition the novel's main characters imagine will occur as part of their conviction that 'the white man's day is over. Anybody can plainly see that the world is quickly and inevitably becoming a coloured world' (59). This is part of a manifesto for a group that calls itself Young Africa, insisting that 'All this Empire-building's a blooming blind alley' (72). After becoming powerfully attracted to Nhliziyombi, a servant girl whom he finds 'aboriginal, perfectly clean and perfectly beautiful' (30), Turbott Wolfe joins Young Africa, along with the romantic triangle of Friston, a missionary; Mabel van der Horst, a Dutch settler; and Zachary Msomi, a 'native' (as the novel calls him) who eventually marries Mabel. Although Wolfe identifies his desire for Nhliziyombi at first to be 'not only against my conscience, but against my reason; against my intellect; against my plans; *against myself*' (33), it leads to his political support for the Young Africa movement, and in turn to his trading licence being revoked by the watchful local government.

Plomer's debut novel is also noteworthy for its experimental style and structure. While most of the narrative consists of Wolfe's recollections for his occasionally intrusive interlocutor, the book ends with two appendices, ostensibly consisting of papers found by Wolfe following Friston's suicide. These include notes about a new type of man called the 'politico-aesthete', who 'staggers . . . under the weight of the past; and struggles . . . under the load of the future' (135), along with three poems (originally written, like the notes, by Plomer himself). These appendices have the distinctly modernist effect of destabilising the narrative's conclusion, which now shifts from Wolfe's dying voice to Friston's writings and to the editorial intervention of Plomer the narrator. As Stephen Gray observes, 'The real shock of *Turbott Wolfe* is that, while satirizing the society around him, as all agree, Plomer is also sabotaging its most reliable form, realist fiction' (197). In its seemingly disjointed structure, shifting among Wolfe's oral recollections, diary entries, letters, and newspaper articles, before finally settling on a set of documents that transfer attention away from the apparent narrative centre, Plomer's novel is again evocative of Conrad's representational techniques, which, as Michael Valdez Moses notes, 'are *the concrete manifestations of the systems of social organization and communication that prevail at the peripheries of empire*' (62, original emphasis). As Moses explains, 'the peculiarly dispersed, mobile, heterogeneous, decentralized, and unorganized European community on the fringes of empire was unusually dependent on and particularly challenged (even disadvantaged) by the unevenly developed and distributed system of communication that prevailed' (62). Plomer himself was both inside and outside that kind of 'European community'; as he notes in his essay 'Anglo-Afro-Asian', the words 'at home' for his family signified 'in England', so 'I could hardly think of myself as a South African' (6), but after living in England for forty years he still found himself feeling of the English 'although at home among them I do not wholly belong to them' (11).

As a narrative seeking to represent black subjectivity for white South African and British audiences, *Turbott Wolfe* positions its author/ narrator within a customary colonialist dialectic of desire, even as it seeks to unsettle such structures. As Jacqueline Rose asks, 'given that in the colonial setting, to act in the other's interests was the problem rather than the solution (acting on behalf of blacks has been one of colonialism's strongest rationales), whose desire or fantasy are we dealing with here?' (334). *Turbott Wolfe* does not fit precisely into this kind of framework, most notably in its refusal of the usual anxieties about desires between European women and 'coloured' men (as in *A Passage to India*, say). At the same time, Plomer's novel is consistently presented from within the narrative perspectives of Turbott Wolfe, who finds himself 'intestinally sick' at the 'catastrophe' of Mabel van der Horst's relationship with Zachary Msomi (76); and Friston, who imagines himself as the 'father of a half-caste nation' (107). The narrative occupies Mabel's consciousness only through her dialogue with other characters, and offers even less entry into the mind of Zachary, focusing on his physical appearance through other characters' perceptions. Such hesitancy is no doubt complicated by Plomer's efforts to conceal the homosexual origins in his own desire to cross racial boundaries, but the novel as a whole, for all the reactionary controversy it aroused in South Africa, remains finally in the colonialist mode of representing the African 'experience' to white metropolitan readers; as Peter Blair notes, Wolfe in joining the Young Africa movement 'attempts not to confront but to circumvent the entire problem of otherness by eradicating distinctions of race' (591). As Turbott Wolfe tells Plomer (as the narrator) early in the novel, ' "I don't want you to think that I had ever really been out of sympathy with the natives: it was simply that their existence, their *blackness*, if you see what I mean, had seemed too much for me" ' (27). While Plomer and his novel clearly distance themselves from this estrangement with the fact of blackness, they also remain, perhaps inevitably within this historical moment, implicated in a fundamentally racialised epistemology. I would not go so far as Peter Blair's claim that, because Wolfe's support for interracial sexuality is rooted in his own vexed desire for Nhliziyombi, the novel 'risks undoing its own indictment of antimiscegenation prejudice' (592); rather, I see that indictment proceeding from the racialised structure of early twentieth-century Zululand society, so that *Turbott Wolfe* critiques the South African race/sex system while also retaining a textual self-awareness of its situatedness within that system.

While *Turbott Wolfe*'s narrative structure operates entirely within a racialist epistemology, 'Ula Masondo', the most noteworthy story in Plomer's next volume of Hogarth fiction, gestures towards different narrative possibilities by virtue of its focalisation through the title character's perspective. Just as Plomer's later Hogarth novels will implicitly question the heterosexual normativity of their heterodiegetic narrators, 'Ula Masondo' compels a readerly self-awareness of its narrator's presumed whiteness. In its portrayal of a young man's life-changing journey to Johannesburg and life in the diamond mines before returning to his small town with his pregnant lover, 'Ula Masondo' is an early example of a common narrative motif in twentieth-century South African fiction, and thus of a narrative structure that implies a white audience desiring a transient identification with an archetypal black character. More so than most such fictions, I would argue, Plomer's text remains aware of the readerly dynamics around which it is structured. The story begins:

> The white storekeeper who sold Ula Masondo a blanket was a jovial-looking man. The morning had begun well, he thought, counting the money into the till: twenty-five shillings before breakfast.
>
> 'Goodbye,' he said cordially when the native turned to go.
>
> '*Ja, baas*, stay in peace.'
>
> The white man wondered 'what that boy wanted with such an expensive blanket,' for he fancied himself a little as a psychologist. He could not find a satisfactory reason, so he consoled himself with the thought that 'those Masondos are all alike, extravagant, improvident, but you can't help liking them all the same'. (51)

After opening with a standard white perspective on the 'native' customer, who receives not even a pronominal referent in his line of dialogue, the story shifts to Ula Masondo's point of view for the next seventeen of its nineteen sections, returning to the storekeeper only in the final, framing paragraphs. But even in its seemingly normative introduction, 'Ula Masondo' gestures toward a different narrative economy, by making explicit mention of the storekeeper's racial identity in the second word. Whereas modern American literature, in Toni Morrison's famous insight, signals a character's whiteness precisely through the absence of any racial reference, Plomer's story reverses that dynamic with its opening description of the shopkeeper, implying a reader who identifies characters in racialised terms, but who does not necessarily proceed from whiteness as an unmarked norm.

This is not to suggest that traces of racialised cultural norms are not still at work within 'Ula Masondo'. After a mining accident has left Ula severely injured, for example, the narrator reports: 'Although he moved with something of the natural style of his race, and although he was trying now to walk jauntily in the style he most admired, an injury still obliged him to limp' (77). This reference to a black African 'natural style' combines with such features as the story's title to construct an implied reader outside of Ula Masondo's frame of narrative reference, a reader who can approach the story's title character only on this external basis, even while entering into the shared fiction of the story's restricted focalisation along the way. The necessity for the framing device of the shopkeeper's conversations, first with Ula himself and then with the storekeeper's wife, implies a reader who can gain access to Ula's story only through such points of white entry, an effect heightened by the limited access to Ula's consciousness even in those sections narrated through his point of view. Derek Attridge observes of a later white South African novelist's portrait of a black focalised subject, J. M. Coetzee's Michael K, that the narrative's frequent use of such phrases as 'he thought' has the effect of 'continually reminding us that we are outside Michael K's consciousness', so that 'although we learn in moving detail of his thought processes and emotions, we never feel that we have assimilated them to our own' (50). For Attridge, the use of the construction 'he thought' in this context conveys 'the authorial voice's inability or reluctance to speak for the character by means of free indirect discourse' (50 n32). A similar distancing is at work in 'Ula Masondo', though perhaps without the full carefulness and complexity evident in Coetzee's *The Life and Times of Michael K*; in the case of Plomer's story, the framing device in conjunction with the limits of Ula's focalisation produce a self-conscious limitation of the narrative's capacity for inhabiting the subject positions it imagines. As in the title of the volume itself, *I Speak of Africa*, Ula Masondo remains an object described rather than a speaking subject. Further, just as the title's 'of' implies Plomer's own distance from Africa in relation to his metropolitan British readers, the narrative mechanics at work in 'Ula Masondo' invite a readerly self-awareness of modernism's vexed engagement with and representation of African alterity.

Queer Narratives in Plomer's Later Hogarth Fictions

Aside from some selections in *The Child of Queen Victoria and Other Stories*, published in 1933 with Jonathan Cape, Plomer's fiction did not return to South African terrain once he had settled in England. His last two Hogarth Press novels, *Sado* and *The Case Is Altered*, differ substantially from each other and from *Turbott Wolfe* and *I Speak of Africa*, both in their focus on English subjects and in their shift towards more conventional narrative techniques than the disruptions and ambiguities of *Turbott Wolfe*. Plomer was living in England when *Sado* and *The Case Is Altered* were published, and in both novels a young wandering Englishman returns to his roots: Vincent Lucas, a painter travelling in Japan who comes to feel that 'All his youth and strength pointed him towards Europe' (*Sado* 236); and Eric Alston, who drives away from London and 'into the country' (*Case* 339) following a sensational murder at his boarding house. In these respects Plomer seems to retreat from the transnational modernism of his early years, transitioning from a novel set in Japan but largely focalised through an English protagonist to a novel set almost entirely in London. Such shifts may reflect Plomer's gradual integration into English literary circles of the day, especially through his friendship with Forster; along these lines *The Case Is Altered* participates in a broader movement in 1930s British fiction toward proletarian subjects, as in John Hampson's *Saturday Night at the Greyhound* (1931) or Edward Upward's *Journey to the Border* (1938), to cite two Hogarth Press examples.

Simultaneously, though, *Sado* and *The Case Is Altered* unsettle readerly expectations along the lines of sexuality, in each case queering narrative structures through their often subtextual portrayals of gay male relationships. As Ruth Page notes in her discussion of how sex/gender systems relate to narrative structures, 'readers may bring gendered assumptions with them that influence their interpretation of narrators, even when the heterodiegetic narrator is unmarked for sex' (197). The narrators in both *Sado* and *The Case Is Altered* are so unmarked, but, as I will argue in this section, these narrators' relationships to their narratives compels Plomer's readers to unsettle their own sexed assumptions.

Sado, based in part on Plomer's own experiences in Japan, moves slowly through the story of Lucas, a young English painter journeying through Japan, and his relationships with the title character and Iris Komatsu, an Englishwoman who has married into Japanese society. The romantic attachments between Lucas and Sado, a perpetually depressed undergraduate, are hinted at and gestured toward as the narrative develops but never quite depicted overtly. When Lucas finally departs to begin his artistic career in earnest in England, he obliquely informs Iris of his sexual relationship with Sado. In response, she exclaims, ' "Don't you see that I've been waiting and waiting for a word, a sign, a hint from you of some kind of pretence of sympathy or affection" ' (249), but Vincent responds only, ' "But I thought you realised—" '(250) and then offers a kiss as a parting "'mark of good faith'" (252). This material, and the novel's representation of the Lucas–Sado relationship, was surely not *too* oblique for its original readers, however, as it is hinted at even in the book's title. *Sado* appeared three years after the famous obscenity trial for Radclyffe Hall's *The Well of Loneliness*, at which the Woolfs and many of their Bloomsbury associates were barred from testifying. In its handling of its central gay relationship, *Sado* falls somewhere between the directness of Hall and the opaqueness of Forster in his published fiction (and is also more circumspect than Plomer's own later fiction, especially *Museum Pieces*).[10] As they had with *Turbott Wolfe*, the Woolfs included on later book jackets (in this case for a 1946 reissue of *The Case Is Altered*) excerpts from original reviews, including the following from Sackville-West's (gay) husband Harold Nicolson: 'If I started out to write a book on inversion I should be more plucky about it from the start.'

If not 'plucky' in its content, *Sado* is more so in its narrative style and structure. As Susan Lanser suggests in her essay 'Queering Narratology', 'heterosexual presumptions operate as designators for a narrator's or character's *sexuality* unless an alternative sexuality is explicitly marked' (253–4, original emphasis). *Sado* gestures toward its protagonist's sexuality, for instance in the report that while visiting Japanese courtesans 'the emotions strongest in Lucas were those of the painter' (130–1), but also consistently distances the novel's presumed heterosexual readers, and indeed doubles that distance through its descriptions of a Japanese culture that would have been available in largely stereotypical terms for British readers in 1932. More broadly, *Sado*'s narrative architecture undercuts its readers' tacit assumptions about the sexuality of its narrator. As Lanser observes, perceptions of narratorial reliability are 'perilously tautological' (256), as readers' judgements about the 'norms' by which a narrator and implied author operate are inevitably influenced by the cultural norms in the background of such readerly observations. In the case of *Sado*, the portrayal of Lucas' sexuality constitutes less a classic instance of unreliability than what James Phelan terms 'reliable *elliptical narration*, that is, telling that leaves a gap that the narrator and the implied author expect their respective audiences to be able to fill' (52). The disembodied narrator of *Sado* and its implied author, that is, do not deliberately mislead the reader (just as Lucas does not intentionally deceive Iris) about Lucas' sexuality. Rather, by gesturing towards that aspect of Lucas' character, which has not been evident in the novel's long opening sections describing his experiences in Japan, *Sado* yields a reconsideration of its apparently 'straightforward' narrative once Lucas' homosexuality is evident, thus queering ostensibly standard reading practices.

The Case Is Altered, for the first time in Plomer's career, tells a strictly British story, focusing on a London boarding house and the landlady's murder at the hands of her crazed husband. While *Sado* builds slowly through its young protagonist's formative relationship with the title character, culminating in Lucas' return home to England, *Case* reads much like a novel of manners in its detailed descriptions of the social life surrounding Beryl Fernandez and her tenants, before veering into the violent conclusion. Obviously in the latter case the novel's slow pace adds dramatic effect to the final scenes, though (as with *Sado*) the underlying narrative is apparent all along, in this case because the story was based on a sensational episode at Plomer's own boarding house. Plomer's landlady, known as Sybil Starr, was herself killed by her husband in November 1929; Plomer escaped likely death himself thanks to a vacation at the time.[11]

The narrative shifts among various tenants and their eventual responses to the murder, but focuses primarily on Eric Alston and his uneasy relationship with Amy and Willy Pascall, siblings who serve as Eric's fiancée and source of true desire, respectively. That Eric finds a greater pleasure in the faintly erotic relationship with Will, a romanticised figure who sails the globe and returns home only when the whim strikes him, is only slightly submerged in the narrative's focalisations through Eric. As Willis notes, this relationship 'was Plomer's most overt statement of his sexual identity in fiction' (204). In its representations of British working-class culture in the early 1930s, *The Cased Is Altered* is most notable for its assembly of a variety of classes and backgrounds among the population of the boarding house that serves as the narrative's geographical and social centre. In addition, as one scholar notes, the book's 'unconscious anti-Semitism and sexism [are] typical of liberal British writing of the 1930s' (Boxwell 261). The narrator describes Beryl Fernandez, for example, as 'in her Jewishness . . . typical of the spirit of modern life, which is Jewish, feminine, and paradoxical' (110). While the narrator's tone is lightly ironised throughout, the discussion here of the 'spirit of modern life' continues to describe the modern world as one that 'thinks of everything in terms of capitalism and communism' and 'seeks negation instead of the godlike, desires death, perhaps, rather than life' (111). This world is also implicitly a heteronormative society, as becomes clear in the closing descriptions of Alston and Pascall together with Amy:

> Imagine these two, a few days after the murder, driving off with Amy into the country in a little old two-seater car which Alston had borrowed from somebody, the three of them wedged in together, Amy in her little red hat with the swallow ornament, Pascall at the wheel with his curls blowing about, and Alston between them, enjoying some of the best moments of his life, while the leafless woods flew past and the speedometer needle, pointing to the highest figure it could reach, trembled as if it were pointing to the magnetic pole of joy. (339)

Thus the novel takes the sensational murder as its ostensible climax, while framing that event with the more significant story of the erotic triangle. As with *Sado*, this narrative structure compels a reconsideration of the narrative as a whole, with an eye towards the ways in which readers' sexed assumptions about the novel's disembodied (and thus presumed heterosexual) narrator have in fact operated precisely according to such assumptions, without having made room for the queer subplot within the novel's depiction of 'ordinary' events in the lives of Londoners.

Commercial Horizons: Plomer's Career With and Beyond the Woolfs

The Case Is Altered propelled both Plomer's career and Hogarth's fiction list further toward a mainstream market. As I noted above, *Case* was easily Plomer's most commercially successful novel with Hogarth, and helped generate net profits of nearly £1,700 for the Woolfs in 1932 (Willis, Appendix B). As I will suggest here by way of conclusion, Plomer's movement toward a more commercially oriented style in *Case* mirrors Hogarth's similar shifts in that direction, as the Woolfs' list in the 1930s increasingly includes both experimental and more conventional titles. (Even Virginia Woolf's own publications in this period transitioned from *The Waves*, which appeared the year before *The Case Is Altered*, to *Flush*, which was published the year after.) On this level *The Case Is Altered* hints as well at the delicate negotiations the Woolfs maintained with the British literary marketplace in the 1920s and 30s; in transforming themselves from a hand press designed for their own and their friends' short work to, in Leonard's words, 'a proper publishing business' (*Downhill* 68) in the late 1920s and early 30s, the Woolfs increasingly located themselves inside the mainstream of the literary market. This is not to suggest that the Hogarth Press became a mainstream firm as such during this period, but it is important to recognise that the Woolfs profited handsomely from such titles as C. H. B. Kitchin's murder mystery *Death of My Aunt* (1929) and Sackville-West's *The Edwardians* (1930) and *Family History* (1932), in addition to *Case* and *Flush*.[12] (Interestingly, Forster includes *The Case Is Altered*, *Saturday Night at the Greyhound* and *The Memorial* among his recommended novels for a December 1932 BBC radio talk.) As I have argued elsewhere, such revenues importantly financed the 'intellectual freedom' that depends upon 'money', as Woolf writes in the manuscript version of *A Room of One's Own* (179), and that continued to make possible the more challenging texts published by Hogarth in the 1930s, such as *Three Guineas* (1938), Christopher Isherwood's *The Memorial* (1932) or Yuri Olesha's *Envy* (1936). We might then read Plomer's decision to leave the Woolfs for the larger and more established firm of Jonathan Cape through this lens as well. And like Virginia Woolf herself, who, as Hogarth's de facto fiction editor, could set the list within which her own novels appeared, Plomer in his capacity as reader for Cape was in the position of at least influencing the field in which his own later works were published.

Finally, reassessments of both the Hogarth Press and the transnational modernist movement in which it participated should view Plomer's early career as part of a productive exchange between the metropolitan literary market and the challenging representations of coloniality in a novel like *Turbott Wolfe*. As Michael Valdez Moses remarks of Conrad's influence on T. S. Eliot, Woolf and other English modernists, 'our theory of the origins of the aesthetic form of modernist literature must take account of the decisive contribution made by the peculiarly disorienting experiences of the modern European consciousness at the imperial periphery' (46). Along these lines we can see a similar, if more local, intellectual exchange between the Woolfs as publishers and Virginia Woolf as author. The experience of reading and publishing works like *Turbott Wolfe* and *I Speak of Africa*, for example, surely informs the representations of coloniality in Woolf's later texts, such as the famous Anglo-Indian aunt in *A Room of One's Own* or Percival's Indian death in *The Waves*, just as the representations of class systems in *The Case Is Altered* or *Saturday Night at the Greyhound* register in the background of *The Years*' narrative approach to social history.

Plomer's tenure as a Hogarth Press author also coincided with the Woolfs' development into international publishers. Willis notes that by 1929 the Woolfs had made arrangements for distribution in Canada, and by 1936 had retained agents in Australia, New Zealand and South Africa (392) – not to mention, of course, Virginia's American publications through Harcourt Brace from 1921 on. While locally metropolitan in its origins, then, the Hogarth Press was international in its reach, part of what Sara Blair identifies as Bloomsbury's ability to become 'global in its resonances, a site of cultural contact and contestation where both canonical high modernisms and an emergent anticolonial modernism take shape' (814). Plomer's particular contribution to such resonant contestation comes through his work's liminal position on the borders of both nationality and sexuality, a queer geomodernism that eventually reflects the 'sense of speaking from outside or inside or both at once' (Doyle & Winkiel 4) in *Turbott Wolfe*'s South Africa back onto the London boarding house of *The Case Is Altered*. Similarly, the Hogarth fiction list for the 1920s and 30s revises conventional notions of gender and nationality: colonial fiction from Laurens van der Post (*In a Province*, 1934) and Anna Whyte (*Lights Are Bright*, 1936, in addition to the new edition of Leonard's *The Village in the Jungle* in 1931) appears alongside queered narratives of postwar Europe (Christopher Isherwood's Sally Bowles series), which in turn are juxtaposed with feminist satires (Sackville-West's *Seducers in Ecuador*, 1924, or Julia Strachey's *Cheerful Weather for the Wedding*, 1932). Coupled with the Continental and Russian fiction Hogarth issued in translation – such as Italo Svevo's *The Hoax* (1929), I. A. Bunin's *The Gentleman from San Francisco* (1922) and Yuri Olesha's *Envy* (1936) – the diverse array of fiction from the 'Anglo-Afro-Asian' Plomer and the other works listed above provide a glimpse into the depth of the Woolfs' transnational status, especially during the politically turbulent decade of the 1930s. Plomer's publishing history with the Woolfs thus exposes the cultural networks that intersected the Press, and, by extension, the important ways in which Hogarth titles delivered a diverse array of cultural contexts to their ostensibly local Bloomsbury readership. Leonard and Virginia's growth from a coterie publisher into a commercial firm overlapped with Hogarth's development as a kind of cultural conduit between its broad range of authors and its British, and increasingly international, audiences, rendering the Hogarth Press as precisely the kind of economic and cultural network which now seems quintessentially modernist. A fuller investigation of such connections lies outside the scope of this chapter, but in order to raise such questions we first need a broader sense of the various dimensions in which Woolf's activities as author, editor and publisher intersected with the business and the art of the Hogarth Press, and thus of the specific circuits through which modernist fiction was produced.

Notes

1. In that capacity Plomer recommended such diverse new writers as Derek Walcott, Stevie Smith and Ian Fleming, among others, while also failing to convince his firm of Vladimir Nabokov's marketability and rejecting Malcolm Lowry's *Under the Volcano* (only to be overruled by Cape). I would like to thank Duff Hart-Davis, executor of the Plomer estate, for permission to use items from the Plomer collection at Durham, and Random House for use of Hogarth Press related material.
2. For important expressions of the changing conceptual dynamics of modernist studies in relation to colonialism and periodisation, see especially the

September 2006 special issue of *Modernism/modernity* on 'Modernism and Transnationalism', as well as the collections edited by Booth and Rigby, and Begam and Moses.

3. For more detailed discussions of *Voorslag*, see Hallett and Oxley.

4. On Plomer's representations of Japan in *Sado* as well as the stories set there in *Paper Houses* and in later poems, see Allen.

5. 'I cannot pretend that I was not sorry to get your letter', Leonard Woolf wrote in April of 1933, after Plomer had announced his decision to switch to Cape; 'I do not like to think of the publishing ties between us being broken, but it will not, I hope, make any difference to our other ties' (*Letters* 315).

6. By the end of 1923 the Woolfs had published a total of thirty-three volumes since the inception of the Press in 1917, with 1923 the first year in which the annual total reached two figures (and just barely that, with eleven). The total reached twenty-eight volumes in 1925, and remained between twenty and thirty-eight all but one year thereafter until 1939 (Willis, Appendix A).

7. The Woolfs did not make formal distribution arrangements in South Africa until 1936 (Willis 392), so Plomer presumably acquired Hogarth publications through his English relatives. Hogarth issued a reprint of *The Village in the Jungle* in 1931 alongside *The Waves*, among other notable titles for that year.

8. See Jane Marcus' chapter on Cunard in her *Hearts of Darkness: White Women Write Race*.

9. As Alexander observes, these annotations omit Teddy Wolfe, a Johannesburg painter who, like Plomer, struggled with the means of representing his homosexuality, especially the doubly proscribed attraction to African men (80). Plomer's manuscript included several of his own drawings as well, which the Woolfs advised him not to publish. Stephen Gray's '*Turbott Wolfe* in Context' includes selected reproductions of the drawings.

10. On the Hall trial in relation to the Woolfs as publishers and Woolf as author, see Marshik; on the absence of published gay fiction in Forster's career, see Matz.

11. For further details, see Plomer's *Double Lives* 241–3, and Alexander 162. Woolf relates Plomer's grisly description of the episode at a dinner party in her diary for 30 November 1929 (268).

12. As Gillespie notes, the Woolfs' publication of Kitchin's two detective novels indicates another respect in which they 'challenged traditional literary categories': they 'marketed Kitchin's novels in ways that emphasized their hybrid intellectual and psychological nature' (36, 37). Gillespie reads Kitchin's mysteries in relation to Woolf's own interests in crimes against women, children and animals.

Works cited

Alexander, Peter F. *William Plomer: A Biography*. Oxford: Oxford University Press, 1991.

Allen, Louis. 'William Plomer (1905–1974) and Japan'. In Sir Hugh Cortazzi and Gordon Daniels, eds. *Britain and Japan 1859–1991: Themes and Personalities*. London: Routledge, 1991.

Archives of the Hogarth Press. Special Collections Department. University of Reading Library.

Attridge, Derek. *J. M. Coetzee and the Ethics of Reading: Literature in the Event*. Chicago: University of Chicago Press, 2004.

Begam, Richard and Michael Valdez Moses, eds. *Modernism and Colonialism: British and Irish Literature, 1899–1939*. Durham: Duke University Press, 2007.

Blair, Peter J. 'That "Ugly Word": Miscegenation and the Novel in Preapartheid South Africa'. *Modern Fiction Studies* 49, 2003: 581–613.

Blair, Sara. 'Local Modernity, Global Modernism: Bloomsbury and the Places of the Literary'. *ELH* 71.3, 2004: 813–38.

Booth, Howard J. and Nigel Rigby. *Modernism and Empire*. Manchester: Manchester University Press, 2000.

Boxwell, D. A. 'William Plomer'. In George M. Johnson, Richard Layman and C. E. Clark, eds. *Dictionary of Literary Biography*. Vol. 191. Detroit: Gale, 1998.

Doyle, Laura and Laura Winkiel. 'Introduction: The Global Horizons of Modernism'. In Doyle & Winkiel.

Doyle, Laura and Laura Winkiel, eds. *Geomodernisms: Race, Modernism, Modernity*. Bloomington: Indiana University Press, 2005.

Forster, E. M. *The BBC Talks of E.M. Forster 1929–1960: A Selected Edition*. Eds. Mary Lago, Linda K. Hughes and Elizabeth MacLeod Walls. Columbia: University of Missouri Press, 2008.

Hallett, Robin. 'The Importance of *Voorslag*: Roy Campbell, William Plomer, and the Development of South African Literature'. *Theoria* 50, 1978: 29–39.

Gardner, Colin, and Michael Chapman. Introduction to *Voorslag: A Magazine of South African Life and Art. Facsimile Reprint of Numbers 1, 2 and 3 (1926)*. Pietermaritzburg: University of Natal Press, 1985.

Gikandi, Simon. 'Africa and the Epiphany of Modernism'. In Doyle and Winkiel.

Gillespie, Diane F. 'Virginia Woolf, The Hogarth Press, and the Detective Novel'. *South Carolina Review* 35.2, 2003: 36–48.

Gray, Stephen. '*Turbott Wolfe* in Context'. In William Plomer. *Turbott Wolfe*. Ed. Stephen Gray. Johannesburg: A. D. Donker, 1978.

Hollis, Catherine W. 'Virginia Woolf's Double Signature'. In Karen V. Kukil, ed. *Woolf in the Real World*. Northampton: Clemson University Press, 2005.

Lanser, Susan S. 'Queering Narratology'. In Kathy Mezei, ed. *Ambiguous Discourse: Feminist Narratology & British Women Writers*. Chapel Hill: University of North Carolina Press, 1996.

Lee, Hermione. *Virginia Woolf*. New York: Alfred A. Knopf, 1997.

Marcus, Jane. *Hearts of Darkness: White Women Write Race*. New Brunswick: Rutgers University Press, 2004.

Marshik, Celia. 'Publication and "Public Women": Prostitution and Censorship in Three Novels by Virginia Woolf'. *Modern Fiction Studies* 45, 1999: 853–86.

Matz, Jesse. '"You Must Join My Dead": E. M. Forster and the Death of the Novel'. *Modernism/modernity* 9, 2002: 303–17.

Morrison, Toni. *Playing in the Dark: Whiteness and the Literary Imagination*. New York: Vintage Books, 1993.

Moses, Michael Valdez. 'Disorientalism: Conrad and the Imperial Origins of Modernist Aesthetics'. In Begam and Moses.

Oxley, William. 'Two Gentlemen of *Voorslag*: Roy Campbell and William Plomer'. In: James Hogg, ed. *Poetic Drama and Poetic Theory*. Salzburg: Institut fur Anglistik & Amerikanistik, 1982.

Page, Ruth. 'Gender'. In David Herman, ed. *The Cambridge Companion to Narrative*. Cambridge: Cambridge University Press, 2007.

Phelan, James. *Living To Tell About It: A Rhetoric and Ethics of Character Narration*. Ithaca: Cornell University Press, 2005.

Plomer Collection. Archives & Special Collections Department. University of Durham Library.

Plomer, William. 'Anglo-Afro-Asian'. *The Malahat Review* 1, 1967: 5–11.

—. *The Case Is Altered*. London: Hogarth Press, 1932.

—. *Double Lives: An Autobiography*. London: Cape, 1943.

—. *I Speak of Africa*. London: Hogarth Press, 1927.

—. *Sado*. London: Hogarth Press, 1931.

—. *Turbott Wolfe*. London: Hogarth Press, 1926.

—. *Turbott Wolfe*. New York: Modern Library, [1926] 2003.

—. 'Ula Masondo'. In William Plomer. *Selected Stories*. Ed. Stephen Gray. Cape Town: Africasouth Paperbacks, 1984.

Rabkin, David. 'Race and Fiction: *God's Stepchildren* and *Turbott Wolfe*'. In Kenneth Parker, ed. *The South African Novel in English: Essays in Criticism and Society*. New York: Africana Publishing, 1978.

Rose, Jacqueline. 'Wulf Sach's *Black Hamlet*'. In Christopher Lane, ed. *The Psychoanalysis of Race*. New York: Columbia University Press, 1998.

Willis, J. H. *Leonard and Virginia Woolf as Publishers: The Hogarth Press, 1917–41*. Charlottesville: University Press of Virginia, 1992.

Woolf, Leonard. *Downhill All the Way: An Autobiography of the Years 1919 to 1939*. New York: Harcourt Brace Jovanovich, 1967.

—. *Letters of Leonard Woolf*. Ed. Frederic Spotts. New York: Harcourt Brace Jovanovich, 1989.

Woolf, Virginia. *The Diary of Virginia Woolf*. Vol. 3. Ed. Anne Olivier Bell. London: Hogarth Press, 1980.

—. *Women & Fiction: The Manuscript Versions of* A Room of One's Own. Ed. S. P. Rosenbaum. Oxford: Shakespeare Head Press, 1992.

Chapter 6

The Writer, the Prince and the Scholar: Virginia Woolf, D. S. Mirsky, and Jane Harrison's Translation from Russian of *The Life of the Archpriest Avvakum, by Himself* – a Revaluation of the Radical Politics of the Hogarth Press

Jean Mills

In January 1924 the leader of the 1917 Bolshevik Revolution, Vladimir Ilyich Ulyanov Lenin, died of a stroke at the age of fifty-four and Leonard and Virginia Woolf, both in their 30s, decided to move their tiny Hogarth Press from Richmond to a new home at 52 Tavistock Square, London. At first blush (?), it may seem untoward to connect two wildly disparate historical events in terms of significance with the conjunction 'and', but part of my objective in doing so is to provoke an understanding of the ways in which the dailiness of life can have unexpected and far-reaching relevance to large-scale historical and political realities. Also in that month, St Petersburg was quickly renamed Leningrad, Lenin's body was publicly placed in a Mausoleum in Red Square, and despite the ordeal and vagaries of finding, negotiating and securing a lease (tasks mostly accomplished by Virginia), the Woolfs published fourteen new titles that year, including *The Life of the Archpriest Avvakum, by Himself*.[1]

Avvakum, a slim little volume bound in boards with a blue and black mottled cloth, came to the Press by way of the great 'J—H—', of Virginia Woolf's *A Room of One's Own*, the Classical anthropologist, Jane Ellen Harrison (1850–1928). She was Virginia Woolf's intellectual mentor, an ardent socialist and Russophile in her own right and, by 1924, a leading figure in the networks of Russian émigrés scattered throughout London and Paris. Harrison's companion, at this point of fourteen years, the poet, Hope Mirrlees,[2] acted as co-translator, and Harrison's friend and, in many ways, linguistic protégé, the Russian literary historian and critic, Prince D. S. Mirsky, who was living in exile, shuttling between London and Paris in 1924, wrote the preface. The book, itself, considered by Dostoevsky to be untranslatable (Brostrom vii), was the first English translation of the earliest autobiography ever written in the Russian language, and recounts, in a colloquial, personal voice, the archpriest's adventures and the abuses he suffered at the hands of his religious persecutors.

My aim, here, is to use the publication of *The Life of the Archpriest Avvakum, by Himself* as a nexus uniting Harrison, Mirsky and Woolf, and as a catalyst for rethinking the ways in which the Hogarth Press was engaged in international cultural and political networks, for I read the text as representative of the very public, left-wing, radical activities of Leonard and Virginia Woolf and their burgeoning small press. In addition to problematising prevailing views on Russian Primitivism and forcing a more nuanced understanding of Harrison's involvement with the Hogarth Press and Virginia Woolf's own literary method, *Avvakum* represents an early example of Prince Mirsky's controversial political engagement with Russian nationalism, Bolshevism and his proto-Communist views. Furthermore, I explore *Avvakum*'s curious erasure from J. H. Willis' otherwise detailed 1992 history of the Press, as indicative of a Cold War sensibility among critics that unconsciously, perhaps, strove to 'protect' the Woolfs and the reputation of their press from associations with Russian Communism, for the internationalism, so precious to us now, was then seen to be speciously socialist.[3]

Now that the last brick of the Berlin Wall has crumbled into the dust, and the Soviet Union has completed its collapse into independent nations, *Avvakum* gives us an opportunity to revaluate the Woolfs' political values and especially to remark upon the role the Hogarth Press and its choice of publications played internationally in the intellectual life of the twentieth century. Certainly the publication, also in 1924, of the Austrian Jewish Sigmund Freud's Psychoanalytic Library is notable among the Press' publications that encouraged an internationalist outlook. Choosing the American T. S. Eliot as their first poet also points to the Woolfs' readiness to take risks, while establishing international connections at the same time. The full range of the Hogarth Press' Russian translations, along with the Woolfs' cultivation of a kind of political salon in the 1917 Club made clear the Woolfs' support of the Russian Revolution and its ideas. The thrill of learning the Russian language, however incompletely, in support of the literature brought to the Press by its exiles, introduced them to what at first appeared to be a brave new world. Trying to translate was a bridge to that world and its importance to the Woolfs, as well as for Britain, is part of my argument about the connections between the Woolfs, the Russians and Harrison that I find embodied in *Avvakum*'s publication. With the exception of Marilyn Schwinn-Smith's important essay 'Bears in Bloomsbury: Jane Ellen Harrison and Russia', which was the first to seriously discuss *Avvakum* (together with Harrison and Mirrlees' other Russian translation *The Book of the Bear*, a collection of folktales [Nonesuch 1926]) and Jane Harrison's role 'in facilitating a connection' between Bloomsbury and Russia, *Avvakum* has been largely overlooked. Its publication and its neglect from the history of the Press and throughout decades of criticism written under the aegis of the Cold War, distinguish it from the rest of the Press' Russian list. It also demonstrates that Virginia and Leonard Woolf were not only interested in language and aesthetics, but in revolutionary politics, as well. Harrison and Mirsky's involvement in bringing *Avvakum* to the Woolfs ultimately casts the Press as a combination not only of the personal and professional, as is often proclaimed, but of the politically highly charged.

The Importance of Being 'Earnest'

In his account of the Press, Willis writes 'In the three years after the appearance of *Reminiscences of Tolstoi*, the Hogarth Press published seven more translations from Russian literature, all but one brought to the Woolfs by the earnest émigré S. S. Koteliansky' (80). Willis' use of the word 'earnest' to characterise 'Kot', as he was familiarly known, was a euphemism for left-wing politics and a descriptive Virginia Woolf personally despised. Koteliansky's contact with the Hogarth Press is well documented and his translations with Leonard and Virginia Woolf are discussed in detail by Laura Marcus and Stuart N. Clarke (2006). Unlike the aristocratic and well-educated Prince Mirsky, whose life was completely upended by the catastrophic changes brought about by World War I and the 1917 Bolshevik Revolution, Kot was a Ukrainian Jew, who arrived in England as a political refugee from Ostropol in 1911. He translated Russian legal documents before befriending John Middleton Murry, Katherine Mansfield, with whom he was unrequitedly in love, and D. H. Lawrence in 1914. He first met the Woolfs in 1917 and became their Russian consultant and translator, collaborating with both Leonard and Virginia in their early translations and connecting them with Maxim Gorky and other Russian authors both in exile and inside Russia.

Mirsky arrived in London and Paris in 1921, with the help and support of Russian scholar, Bernard Pares, who gave him a position as Russian Lecturer at the School of Slavonic Studies in London, and the Hon. Maurice Baring, who promoted Mirsky's journalism and literary criticism as early as October 1920, with Mirsky writing en route from Athens, in the *London Mercury* and other publications. Because they travelled in the same literary and social circles in Bloomsbury, it is likely that Koteliansky and Mirsky met, but there is no evidence to support such a meeting. Mirsky's biographer, G. S. Smith, writes that, 'although Mirsky never seems to have recorded anything negative about Koteliansky in public print, as someone who had recently emerged from the thick of the Petersburg literary scene he must inevitably have regarded "Kot" as a provincial amateur—which is essentially what he was' (*D. S. Mirsky* 99). Also in contrast to Mirsky, whose political views and post-Revolutionary response to his native land were complex, controversial and in a constant state of revision as he navigated his relationship to the changes taking place in Russia, Kot's politics were quite clear and more in step with Leonard Woolf's socialist views.

Mirsky, on the other hand, who initially fought against the Bolsheviks as a member of the Imperial Army in 1917, and was still referring to himself as 'anti-Communist' as late as 1925 (Smith *D. S. Mirsky* 126), ultimately became radicalised by yet another political sea-change in Soviet Russia after Lenin's death and Stalin's rise to power. In 1929, one year after Harrison's death, Mirsky wrote a biography of Lenin, a copy of which Koteliansky gave to Esther Salaman, telling her that its author was 'rotten . . . he was prepared to tell any number of lies, to humiliate himself to any extent, just to be allowed to return to Russia: he needed not anger but our prayers' (qtd in Smith *D. S. Mirsky* 99). Mirsky himself credited his research and biography of Lenin for fuelling his desire to return to Russia. In his preface to *Lenin*, Mirsky downplays his connection to the aristocracy (which he calls the 'squirearchy') and explains his revised political position:

> It has been pointed out to me that, coming as it does from a member of the class that was most effectively eliminated by the great Russian Revolution, and adopting at the same time a pro-revolutionary standpoint, the present book [on Lenin] calls for some explanation *pro domo sua*. . . . it must not be forgotten that by the eve of the Revolution the Russian squirearchy had reached such a state of cultural degeneracy that the mere fact of possessing a certain amount of intellectual culture 'unclassed' those of its members who

possessed any, and dissociated them from their mother class, which had become incapable of having its own intelligentsia. (v)

Mirsky claimed that this shedding of class identity brought about by the 1917 Revolution was 'fortuitous' and that '[i]n so far as they were intellectuals they were no longer members of the class they were born into' (v). Mirsky was also said to resemble Lenin, a fact of which he was said to be 'very proud' (qtd in Smith, *D. S. Mirsky* 209). The differences between Kot and Mirsky accentuate the complicated political terrain the Hogarth Press actively sought to participate in and *Avvakum*'s publication helps to elucidate not only Mirsky's progressive radicalisation, but also the Woolfs' ongoing and influential pro-Soviet revolutionary sentiments that were nonetheless critical of Stalinism. Furthermore, *Avvakum*'s erasure and neglect prevent readers from seeing the Hogarth Press' key role in the networks of the European intellectual left.

Avvakum and Russian 'Aspects': Complicating the Slav Soul

It does seem odd at first that a couple of atheists and pacifists like Virginia Woolf and Jane Harrison[4] would join a pre-Revolutionary St Petersburg aristocrat with family ties, through two great-great aunts,[5] to the Russian Orthodox Old Believers, to translate and publish the experiences and martyrdom of the sect's seventeenth-century extremist leader, the Archpriest Avvakum. Its publication and their seemingly unlikely collaboration can be explained in part by a long-standing impulse in British literary circles to romanticise and mythologise Russia. The Woolfs also deeply respected Harrison's reputation, scholarship and politics. Mirsky's need for support, financially and linguistically, as a 'temporary' Russian exile in London would have also appealed to Leonard and Virginia Woolf and to Harrison, who were all known for their support of refugees. Lastly, all three parties shared a profound and mutual love of language, and Harrison's translation of *Avvakum* to this day captures a unique vernacular voice that she, Mirsky and Virginia Woolf highly valued.

Avvakum also marked a significant point of transition for all the parties involved. For the Woolfs, it stood at the outer edge of the Hogarth Press' Russian list, and in 1924 helped characterise the Press' political left-wing presence. For Mirsky, *Avvakum* marked yet another point of political transition, as he struggled to articulate his response to post-Revolutionary Russia, and the text exemplifies many of the tenets of the Russian nationalist Eurasian Movement, in which Mirsky played an active role between 1922 and 1926, before his conversion to Marxism in 1929 and his membership of the Communist Party of Great Britain, which he publicly declared in 'Why I became a Marxist' on 30 June 1931 in *The Daily Worker*. *Avvakum* also initiated an intimate and intellectually and financially productive relationship for Mirsky with Harrison. She became his 'linguistic mentor', a first investor in his Russian language literary journal *Vyorsts* ('Milestones', 1926–8) (Smith, 'Letters' 86–7) and an effective editor of his masterworks, *Contemporary Russian Literature: 1881–1925* (1926) and *A History of Russian Literature: From the Earliest Times to the Death of Dostoyevsky (1881)* (1927), both of which he dedicated to Harrison. In 1949 these two volumes were combined, becoming 'a work that has been acclaimed as the best one-volume, single-author history of Russian literature' today (Smith, *DLB* 235) and 'put[ting] Mirsky incontestably in the position he has never subsequently lost, as the principal intermediary between Russian literature and the English-speaking world' (Smith, *D. S. Mirsky* 114). It is a work which Harrison shepherded into existence, a fact that is often lost, when subsequent editions of the text frequently relegated his dedications to her to an 'editor's note'. Harrison, also, along with Hope Mirrlees, introduced Mirsky to French literary circles in Paris and it was through Harrison's contacts that Mirsky joined the prestigious Pontigny seminars begun by the Humanist, Paul Desjardins, during the interwar years. The group was a gathering of the intellectual elite of Europe who came together to discuss philosophical questions, but it was also politically linked to reformed socialism. For Harrison, the renowned, 'forever young' scholar of the matrifocal origins of Greek religion, the intellectual leader of the Cambridge Group of Cultural Anthropologists (later the Cambridge Ritualists), the gifted linguist and vocal pacifist during World War I, *Avvakum* marked the fulfilment of a life-long dream to study Russian, as well as the beginning of the end of her life. After *Avvakum*, she translated a second book with Mirrlees, and in 1925, at Virginia Woolf's insistence, she wrote for the Hogarth Press her memoir, *Reminiscences of a Student's Life*, at the age of 75. Harrison died in April 1928 and is most frequently remembered in relation to Virginia Woolf's work as the acclaimed and revolutionary female scholar, 'J—H—' haunting the grounds of Woolf's fictional Fernham College in Woolf's tribute to Harrison, *A Room of One's Own*.

Schwinn-Smith has outlined *Avvakum*'s significance as an example of Modernism's embrace of Russian exoticism, but I also see *Avvakum* as a text, ironically, aimed at dismantling that stereotype, a romanticised view of Russia often fostered and promoted by British and European writers, their reading publics and by post-Revolutionary Russian émigrés themselves. *Avvakum* is indeed a product of a modernist attraction to a mythologised Russia. It was a kind of Russian Primitivism, and Harrison, Woolf and Mirsky certainly knew it. But I also see *Avvakum* as an exception, or as striving to be an exception, to that discourse. For this translation is a serious attempt by Mirsky and Harrison to complicate and redefine that stereotypical view. Furthermore, Virginia Woolf's agreement to publish *Avvakum* in 1924 after nearly a decade of critical reviews praising Russian novelists in translation, suggests to me her own embrace of a more multidimensional response to Russian literature and her own literary methods. I read *Avvakum* as being in step with Woolf's fascination with biography and autobiography. Would the Russians write completely different 'lives' than the Europeans, she wondered?

Virginia Woolf's high regard for Russian literature is well known. She often used the writings of Tolstoy, Dostoevsky and Chekhov, for example, as well as many other more obscure authors like Saltikov and Elena Militsina, as standards by which to measure English literature in her own reviews, essays, letters and diary entries. In her 1919 essay, 'The Russian Point of View', published in *The Common Reader* in 1925, Woolf, as was not unusual in British criticism of Russian writers, identifies an abiding spirituality and understanding of 'the soul' she finds lacking or culturally unacceptable, if not unattainable, in English literature.

Woolf's understanding of Russian literature as 'more soulful' and exotic was not uncommon during the early decades of the twentieth century, but it is a perspective informed, and also complicated, by Harrison's passion for Russia. As Schwinn-Smith notes, 'Harrison took up the study of Russian to get at the literature, to read Tolstoy, Dostoevsky and Chekhov in the original' (123), which reminds us that Woolf first learned Greek to read and translate the Classics denied her as a woman. Woolf later took up Russian, in order to bypass what she characterised as the obstacles of translation:

> When you have changed every word in a sentence from Russian to English, have thereby altered the sense a little, the sound, weight, and accent of the words in relation to each other completely, nothing remains except a crude and coarsened version of the sense. (*Common Reader* 174)

The challenges of reading works in translation, of the inability to 'trust ourselves not to impute, to distort, to read into them an emphasis which is false' were central themes in Harrison's *Aspects, Aorists, & the Classical Tripos*, a copy of which Virginia Woolf owned and which was published in 1919 at the same time as Woolf's 'The Russian Point of View'. *Aspects* was an expansion of an earlier piece, 'Russia and the Russian Verb: A Contribution to the Psychology of the Russian People' from 1915, and one with which Woolf was familiar. Woolf had met Harrison as a young Virginia Stephen in 1904 through her Greek tutor, Janet Case. She became aware of Harrison's example and reputation through her lectures, publications and research on pre-Olympian Greek art and ritual, and maintained contact with her until her death in 1928. A closer reading of Harrison's *Aspects*, however, reveals a more nuanced picture of her love of 'all things Russian', other than the oft-cited remark that 'the Russian stands for the complexity and concreteness of life—felt whole, unanalysed, unjudged, lived into' (*Aspects* 35). It also complicates our understanding of Virginia Woolf's knowledge of Russian letters.

For if we read Woolf's reading of the Russians through Harrison, and add to that Hogarth's acquisition of *Avvakum*, then we mark a shift away from the 'Slav soul', and away from what was essentially a French construction and a view based on reviews of French translations of mostly nineteenth-century Russian texts, in particular Tolstoy's and Dostoevsky's novels.[6] European reaction to Russian literature at this time became known as The Dostoevsky Cult, which was 'at its height between 1912 and the early 1920's' (Laura Marcus, 'Introduction' ix). Harrison's *Aspects* has very little to do with European audiences' popular response to Russian letters, and *Avvakum* with its eloquent simplicity could be said stylistically to be devoid of 'soul'.

Aspects is a treatise on linguistics and Russian parts of speech, not Russian 'soulfulness' and exoticism, but the relationship between language and psychology. *Aspects* turns, as does much of her best scholarship and prose 'on the imaginative art' of research, putting forth 'a reality seen through a temperament' and has 'a fleet-footed subtlety and elegance of logic that is characteristic of her scholarly demonstrations', as Mirsky wrote in the second Jane Harrison Memorial Lecture, *Jane Ellen Harrison and Russia* (15, 16). Rather than advocating for the 'Slav soul', the essay ostensibly argues for the inclusion of Russian in the curriculum at Cambridge, proposing that Russian should be equally weighted alongside ancient Greek in the Classical Tripos and that 'an accurate knowledge of the Russian and Greek languages together with an intimate understanding of the two civilizations should furnish a humanistic education at once broad and thorough' (Harrison, *Aspects* 36). Harrison, who, with the acquisition of Russian, knew sixteen languages, returned to teach Russian at Newnham College shortly before she retired in 1922.[7]

Aspects is an example of Harrison's linguistic gifts, and a bid for an appreciation of the simplicity of the structure of the Russian language at its core. The essay becomes a philosophical discussion of Russian, but at its heart explores the significance of the 'dominance of "aspect" over tense and of "imperfective" over "perfective"', an idea she links to Bergson's concept of *durée*, but which has more of a dialectical relationship to Hegel and Marx (Mirsky, *J. H. and Russia* 17). Harrison writes:

> The imperfective has internal time but no time order; it may be past, present or future . . . The perfective is of the accomplished act . . . standing on its apex or vertex; the imperfective is of *non*-accomplishment, of process. (Mirsky, *J. H. and Russia* 17)

Harrison begins *Aspects* by pointing out that she is interested in 'getting at the literature', but that this motivation masks her true desire, which is the language itself, for 'to fall in love with a language is not to fall in love with a literature. It is well to note – a fact too often forgotten – that a rich language does not necessarily mean a rich literature' (5). For Harrison, 'Language is the *un*conscious or at least subconscious product of the group, the herd, the race, the nation. Literature is the product more or less conscious of the individual genius, using of course the tools made by the blind herd, but, after the manner of live organisms, shaping these tools even as he uses them.' Harrison, as she often does, begins with a seedling of an idea, which she carefully unfolds, as she 'proceeds to lay bare these roots', increasingly and incrementally widening her scope onto 'even larger vistas' of thought (Mirsky, *J. H. and Russia* 16). *Aspects* begins with literature, moves into language, discovers philosophy, reveals cultural psychology, explores morality, turns back to literature, re-emphasises language, all the while arguing a practical proposal for policy change within the curriculum of an academic department. What lies behind 'the ideas of completion or non-completion' in the aspects of Russian verbs is the psychology of a people and a philosophy and science of human existence. Mirsky explains:

> The perfective is the contemplation of action from outside, the affirmation of the abstract and analyzing attitude. The imperfective is life seen from the inside, felt as a complete and continuous unity. In Russian the past and the future may be either perfective or imperfective, that is to say may be considered as abstracted points of time severed from their relation to the continuing stream of life, or as organical parts of the same continuity of which the present is merely the focus. But the present can only be imperfective, can be only lived and felt, not seen from without. (*J. H. and Russia* 15)

As Harrison writes, 'We can live *into* the future and the past. Only for the perfective the present tense is taboo.' She uses an example of popular Russian fiction, Ivan Goncharov's *Oblomov*, the quintessential slacker, endearing, but a hopelessly indolent everyman, as a model of 'the Imperfective in Literature', at which point *Aspects* becomes a hilarious but insightful and provocative review of what Mirsky, who highly praised *Aspects* for 'the truth in it' (Smith, 'Letters' 67), called 'the most pregnant and brilliant criticism of the Russian novel' he had encountered (*J. H. and Russia* 17). Harrison's choice of the commoner, Oblomov, also resonates with her later choice in translating the vernacular voice of *Avvakum*.

Although *Aspects* complicates Harrison's response to Russia, as does her highly regarded explication of Tolstoy's theory of art in 1913's *Ancient Art and Ritual*, in her personal correspondence she often does indeed reinforce Russian primitivist views.[8] G. S. Smith sees Harrison's role as significant amidst 'like-minded intellectuals' in shaping British literary attitudes towards Russia as 'other' that had been 'theorised before the Great War' (*D. S. Mirsky* 98). He cites the familiar line from *Aspects* of the Russian standing for the 'concreteness' of life, as well as personal postcards and notes. While I believe he misses the point of *Aspects*, and its contribution to a wide range of disciplines, he makes good use of Harrison's personal correspondence, which sometimes reveals a romanticised Russia. In a postcard, one of hundreds she wrote to her colleague and friend, Cambridge classicist and ritualist, Gilbert Murray,[9] Harrison writes 'Yes, that is what I longed to have said—that whatever sort of a wild beast Russia makes of herself she still cares more than any other nation for the things of the spirit, and that is priceless (though as you say dangerous)' (J. H. Papers). Harrison's passion for, one might even say 'fetishization' of, Russia began long before she met Mirsky, sometime in the winter of 1923–4, and even before she met the young Virginia Stephen in 1904. She opens her 1926 memoir, *Reminiscences of a Student's Life*, with the following recollection: 'In view of my present cult for Russia and things Russian, I like to think that my first childish memory is of the word "Moscow"' (9). When Harrison was at Newnham, she was thrilled to have the opportunity to give Turgenev a tour. Harrison, already an accomplished and devoted linguist wondered, 'Dare I ask him to speak just a word or two of Russian? He looked such a kind old snow-white Lion' but 'alas! He spoke fluent English' (44).

The 1917 Club and the Left-Wing 'Spirit of the Age'

Russian 'soul', in other words, to Harrison, to Virginia Woolf and to other Western Europeans, was a version of primitivism. Just as Harrison exoticised and foregrounded pre-classical Greek rituals of violence, sex, war and sacrifice, in her three ground-breaking works on pre-Olympian religious cults a decade earlier, *Prolegomena to the Study of Greek Religion* (1903), *Themis* (1912) and *Ancient Art and Ritual* (1913), most of the writers, thinkers and artists of the post-Revolutionary period were Primitivists, including the Russians themselves. The 'primitive' past of Russia's folk traditions and peasant crafts, songs, fables and dances was valorised by exiled Russians, many of whom were aristocrats, like Prince Mirsky, to counter the effects of the profound changes brought about by the atheist Communists who made the Revolution in 1917.

For the Woolfs, the Russian Revolution meant freedom and an extraordinary release from tyranny. Leonard wrote in his autobiography that 'the outbreak of the Russian Revolution of 1917 produced the same feeling of liberation and exhilaration' as he imagined the French Revolution of 1789 produced in young people in the early stages of that cataclysmic historic event: 'In the long, grim history of despotisms the Tsarist regime of the 19th century must take a high place for savage, corrupt, and incompetent government' (*Beginning Again* 208–9). On 3 June 1917 Leonard was involved in the 'Great Labour, Socialist *and* Democratic Convention *to hail the* Russian Revolution *and* to Organise *the* British Democracy *To follow Russia*' a convention he described as 'one of the most enthusiastic and emotional that I have ever attended.' He reminds us that 'All Labour people—indeed nearly all people in England—hated the Tsarist regime; they felt extremely uneasy when they remembered that they were fighting the war with that regime on their side, a war which we were fighting, according to President Wilson, because "the world must be made safe for democracy"' (211). Leonard, who was Jewish, claimed that even in hindsight, looking back at the Russian Revolution of 1917 from the vantage point of 1963, 'I would again welcome the Russian Revolution [because] it destroyed an ancient, malignant growth in European society, and this was essential for the future of European civilization' (215). He does not dismiss or condone the violence and horror that ensued, but confides that 'if I could return to 1789 and 1917, I would still be on the side of the revolution—though I have no doubt that I should have been guillotined by Marat and liquidated by Stalin' (215).

In a move that captures 'the spirit of the age', Leonard, together with Oliver Strachey, founded the left-wing 1917 Club, taking out a lease on Gerrard Street in Soho, which was 'in those days a rather melancholy haunt of prostitutes daily from 2:30 p.m. onwards' (216). Their first general meeting was 19 December, but the club, while intended as political, quickly embraced 'an element of unadulterated culture, literary and artistic' (217). Although Rebecca Beasley argues that 'it would be difficult to claim a coherent shared project' in the establishment of the 1917 Club, she admits that 'in the last years of the war, the left-wing literary groupings of pre-war Britain were propelled, by their opposition to the government, to the war, and by their support for the Russian Revolution, into something like an intelligentsia' (28). Leonard lists several Labour Party activists and socialists, such as Ramsay MacDonald, J. A. Hobson, H. N. Brailsford, Mary Agnes (Molly) Hamilton, a Labour Party politician who later became an MP, and Emile Burns, who later became a communist, but also notes that on any given afternoon, 'Virginia was often there and there was a strong contingent of Stracheys, including Lytton and a retinue of young women and young men who often accompanied him' (*Beginning Again* 217). He claims that the club in later years became the haunt of stage actors and performers, but that during his tenure there the 1917 Club counted the stage and screen star Elsa Lanchester and the musician Cyril Scott as members. In any case, the Woolfs frequently met at the club and stayed connected to it for over a decade.

An ardent pacifist who vigorously opposed, but sought to understand, Britain's rush to war in 1914, Harrison, like the Woolfs and most of England, experienced a strong sense of 'good riddance' to the Tsarist regime in 1917.[10] The Russia she envisions in *Aspects*, as Mirsky tells us, 'is not the Russian civilization of to-morrow . . . it is the civilization of nineteenth-century Russia minus Tsarism—the civilization of the intelligentsia and intelligentsiafied gentry, of the peasants, and to a certain extent of the Orthodox Church' (*J. H. and Russia* 14), but she was cautiously optimistic about Russia's future. As a 'philosophical radical' Harrison helped to dismantle and rethink much of the narrowness and injustice of the Victorian Age, as she lived into the early decades of the modern twentieth century, but she also retained much of her Victorian love of order, reason and practical common sense that came from her Northern Yorkshire roots, a 'Little Englander' quality that gave her the perspective Mirsky believed separated her from the English Dostoevskyites. Further complicating any facile assessment of Harrison's relationship to Russia as 'other', unlike much of Britain and Europe, Harrison was not flocking to Dostoevsky (nor to Freud), drunk or sober, but she sincerely tried to understand the whole of their work. Mirsky writes in 1930:

> The least attractive and most repulsive expressions of the process of dissolution of nineteenth-century English culture are connected with the English Dostoevskyians, and with the whole world of ideas that centered round him. (It is only within the last few years that the younger generation is beginning

to discover in Dostoyevsky other elements than the brutal throwing down of emotional inhibitions; they have not as far as I know yet discovered the stable, inhibitive and social elements of the teaching of Freud.) (*J. H. and Russia* 8)

Harrison, however, had. Although critics often use her comments on Dostoevsky as examples of her 'othering' of Russia, I would argue, in agreement with Mirsky, that in these particular instances Harrison is advocating a more informed understanding of Russian literature and Russian language. She personally admitted to having a 'dash of the Bolshevik' in her political make-up, and she never spoke publicly against the Russian Revolution, leading Mirsky to believe she held 'more than a lurking sympathy' (14) for it, despite the fact that '[t]he Russians have since become themselves a "governing people," and the "tabulation of results" [which Harrison did not associate with her view of Russia minus Tsarism] has almost absorbed the whole life of the country' (16). Harrison was a pacifist, who loathed violence and the oppression that came with war. She was appalled when Mirsky sent *Avvakum* to the Russian press to be reviewed and the book was returned marked 'Non-admis' or 'forbidden'. 'Oh dear!' she wrote 'will intolerance never cease to breed intolerance?' In another letter from December 1920 Harrison entertained by chance a Bolshevik who had just married the daughter of Newnham's College nurse. She was thrilled to have the chance to prac-tise her Russian and horrified by the bias against Communist Russians. 'What is the use of a League of Nations' she wrote, 'without Russia, without Germany? I get disheartened, don't you? Civilised women say they "wouldn't sit down to tea with a Bolshevik." Well, thank goodness I never asked them' (qtd in Stewart 174–5). And Harrison cultivated this 'dash of the Bolshevik' in her in Paris and the social networks she established there. She wrote to her friend and colleague, Gilbert Murray, in 1920 that she must return to Paris where she met 'your socialist friend Sembat' who was a pacifist member of the Revolutionary Socialist Party and had been head of the Socialist Party of France in 1902. Harrison reports that according to Sembat, he and Juares, a radical leftist politi-cian who advocated for the working classes and who was assassinated in 1914 by a right-wing extremist, 'nurtured their souls' on her book *Themis* and Murray's *Rise of the Epic*. She bears his response as a point of pride and admits that her 'head was rather turned by his admiration' and it encourages her to continue writing and advocating for 'all the new thinking' she has been discovering in Paris (J. H. Papers). Murray, at the time, had been working along with Leonard Woolf and others on the League of Nations.

To a certain degree similar to the Woolfs' 1917 Club and in many ways akin to the legendary Paris-based salons of Natalie Barney and Gertrude Stein, Harrison and Mirrlees' various residences in hotels and apartments, also in Paris, were active, vital meeting places for leading intellectuals, authors and philosophers between 1915 and 1926 when they returned to Mecklenburgh Square in Bloomsbury. In addition to entertaining Leonard and Virginia Woolf, Harrison and Mirrlees set up meetings, made introductions and discussed literature, politics and art with such notables as Murray, David Garnett, Logan Pearsall Smith, Jacques Rivière, Jean Schlumberger, Charles du Bos, Paul Valéry, the philosopher Lev Shestov, Aleksey Remizov, whom Mirsky had met in Berlin in 1922, and the poet Marina Tsvetaeva (Smith, *DLB* 234). And during these years, Mirrlees was connected to the avant-garde poetry scene in Paris. She published the highly experimental poem *Paris* with the Hogarth Press in 1920.

At what I am characterising as the Harrison–Mirrlees Paris Salon or 'Women of the Left Bank, II', Mirsky and Harrison developed an intense correspondence and productive relationship out of their shared intellectual and political interests and by way of their mutual friends. Harrison and Mirrlees had lived together in the Hotel de L'Elysée at 3 Rue de Beaune since 1914 when both of them enrolled in a Russian language class in October at the nearby Ecole des Langues Orientales. By 1922 Harrison left Cambridge, bitterly disappointed that the university continued to deny women degrees and deeply troubled by the attack at Newnham that followed the vote (Briggs 89). She and Hope moved into an apartment at the American Women's Club, where they continued to foster their intellectual and political connections.

This is the political and intellectual climate Harrison had established and cultivated when she met Mirsky and decided to translate *Avvakum*. Pinpointing the date of that meeting and when the Woolfs met Mirsky is difficult and often clouded by mistakes and inconsistencies in the public record. G. S. Smith records that Mirsky met the Woolfs in Spring 1924 in Harrison's apartment in Paris. He uses Leonard Woolf's recollection that he had met Mirsky at Harrison's flat as evidence, but Leonard does not date this meeting, and indeed Leonard and Virginia Woolf were not in Paris at all in the spring of 1924. The Woolfs had visited the flat in the spring of the previous year. Stewart dates Harrison and Mirsky's acquaintance to the Pontigny colloquia in 1923, but, as G. S. Smith points out, Mirsky did not attend Pontigny until summer 1924. G. S. Smith suggests that Harrison and Mirrlees decided to translate *Avvakum* at Mirsky's suggestion, and that through Mirsky, they met the Russian writer and artist, Aleksey Mikhailovich Remizov and his wife, Serafima Pavlovna Dovgello, who would help, along with Mirsky, with the translation. But Schwinn-Smith suggests that Harrison and Mirrlees met the Remizovs through the Russian philosopher Lev Shestov, and next met Mirsky, 'the second Russian to collaborate on the translations' (125), through the Remizovs. Harrison's first correspondence with Remizov, in Russian, is dated 1 March 1924, but they are new correspondents, because Harrison does not yet know Remizov's patronymic, Mikhailovich. She writes:

> Deeply respected Alexei Remizov, (I'm sorry I don't know your patronymic name!) What an unfortunate incident. We were very sad without you on Sunday but we are very happy that you are well. If you are free next Sunday, the 9th we will be very happy if you come and see us. Please forgive my poor handwriting and language.
>
> Jane Harrison

In her next letter, dated 7 April, she invites the Remizovs to tea on 9 April, and writes in a postscript in French 'Ce sera un grand plaisir – de recevoir Madame aussi. Nous attendons le prince Mirsky qui vous adore!' [This will be a great pleasure – to receive Madame also. We expect Prince Mirsky, who adores you] (Remizov Papers). Turning to Mirsky's publishing record up until the first mention of his name in the letter to Remizov on 7 April 1924 helps us construct the likelihood that Harrison must have at the very least been aware of his work. Although we have no hard evidence of their meeting until April 1924 and most likely through Harrison's Pontigny connection Lev Shestov, as a Russophile, Harrison would have been familiar with Mirsky's publications on Russian letters in the English press as early as 1920. She would have also likely heard about his work through her contact with Shestov at Pontigny during the summer of 1923. And certainly by January 1924, if, according to G. S. Smith, we learn that Mirsky 'made his debut' (*D. S. Mirsky* 132) in the émigré press in Paris with articles in the Russian language literary supplement *The Link* (*Zveno*), Harrison would have been aware of Mirsky before she made contact with the Remizovs in March 1924. In any case, we gain a sense of the extent and complexity of the networks with which Harrison, Mirrlees, Mirsky and the Woolfs were engaged, and the political climate in which the idea for translating and publishing *Avvakum* came about.

By April 1924 the subject of *Avvakum* had been broached in Harrison's correspondence with both Remizov and Mirsky. She writes on 19 April 1924 of Mirsky's attempt to secure a Russian-language copy of *Avvakum*: 'How kind of you to try and get me the Avvakum text! But I hear it is difficult' (Smith, 'Letters' 67) and on 14 May 1924, 'How kind of you to go on hunting for Avvakum. If you can get a copy

from Russia I shall be more than glad to have it.—but—for the immediate need, Mr. Shestov tells me that Mr Remizov has a copy and will
gladly lend it me' (67). But by 26 May 1924, although they have begun
to work with the Remizovs on the introduction, and to talk about the
tone she is trying to adopt, according to Mirrlees, 'a mixed Jeremy
Taylor + Old Testament style' (68), 'the difficulty still remains of getting
the text' (Smith, 'Letters' 68). By 16 June 1924 she writes a postcard to
inform Mirsky that 'to my great joy I have been able to secure the loan
of another copy of Avvakum' and that the translation is going well and
will be finished by the time she meets him at Pontigny in August.

As Harrison's correspondence continued with Mirsky, their relationship grew more intimate. By August 1924 in a letter to Murray (misdated
1923 by Stewart) Harrison writes 'I lost my heart to a Bear Prince—why
did I not meet him fifty years ago when I could have claimed to be his
Princess? As it is I have compelled him to write a preface to my next
book' (qtd in Stewart 192). She tells Mirsky about Jean Schlumberger's
reception of *Avvakum*: 'he only cares for the quite first rate & he could
talk of nothing all this lunch but the strength and beauty of Avvakum'
(Smith, 'Letters' 75). *Avvakum* may have initiated Harrison's relationship with Mirsky but their work together on the project cemented their
bond, furthered their shared literary objectives and expanded their
social and political network.

Avvakum's 'True' Russian Voice and the Russian Nationalist Eurasian Movement

Mirsky, who consistently 'denigrated his aristocratic origins' (Smith,
D. S. Mirsky 210), objected to the reductive and limited view of Russia
and Russian culture he found in England and throughout Western
Europe. His interest in *Avvakum* represented his desire to return to a
'true' Russian voice. *Avvakum* can also be seen as related politically to
his earlier interest in Russian nationalism and his involvement in the
Eurasian Movement, leading up to the book's publication in October
[November] 1924, and carrying on throughout his relationship with
Harrison until her death in 1928. Schwinn-Smith notes that 'on points
of language and style, the aesthetics of Mirsky and Remizov coincided:
live, colloquial speech was the *sine qua non* for both' (127), qualities
he found in *Avvakum* and that were appreciated by both Harrison and
Woolf. After the lessons and challenges of translating *Avvakum,* on 3
April 1925 Harrison is attentive to Mirsky's position on language, when
she writes 'What you say about "ornamental prose" is a real help to me'

(Smith, 'Letters' 82). Later, on 23 May 1925 in response to Mirsky's essay 'O moskovskoi literature I protopope Avvakume', she confesses 'the part about Avvakum's style made me feel how rash we had been to attempt translating him—however I cannot repent—it's all so pleasant' (Smith, 'Letters' 83).

Mirsky, for his own part, vigorously sought both publicly and privately to change, enlighten and inform British and European audiences of the complexities of the Russian character, and to promote Russian writers who adhered to his standards. Although he would have advocated for a translation of *Avvakum* because Avvakum was a spiritual and political leader, representative of a 'native' Russian as opposed to the educated new men of 1917, *Avvakum* is also an attempt by Mirsky to revise this notion of Russian 'soul', which, he consistently points out to Harrison and his readers in the *London Mercury* and elsewhere, is a French invention.

Mirsky's 'return' to a native language is intimately linked to his desire to 'return' to his native land, and complicated by his own personal history. Before World War I he was already connected to Russian literary circles through St Petersburg University. However, his early ambivalence towards his class combined with the later pressures and unmanageability of his position in exile confronted him with a series of difficult and ultimately disastrous decisions, and he eventually returned to Stalinist Russia in September 1932. Writing in 1930, two years after Harrison's death, Mirsky compared Harrison's own conflict, straddling the Victorian and Modern ages, to that of the Russian émigré, Peter Kropotkin, but he could very well have applied the comparison to himself:

> This combination of a Radical intellect with Conservative tastes and manners cannot fail to remind one of those Russian revolutionaries born in aristocratic families who espoused and developed with the greatest sincerity the boldest revolutionary doctrines, but were never able to throw off the habit of behaviour, the tone, and the sensibility of the class into which they had been born. Their hatred of their past and of their social roots was thorough-going and sincere, but their every word and movement betrayed their antecedents. (Mirsky, *J. H. and Russia* 7)

Mirsky never escaped his past and was forced to continually revise his politics and beliefs in a constantly shifting and volatile historical and political climate, which resulted in an ongoing crisis of identity. Harrison, on the other hand, was much more at ease with intellectual and political contradictions. The pioneering, visionary scholar could co-exist with her own 'Aunt Glegg' ways, for example – the provincialism of George Eliot's character with whom Harrison identifies in

Reminiscences. And one wonders to what extent Mirsky's position also resonates with the position of Virginia Woolf as a class traitor, who is unable to completely rid herself of racism. G. S. Smith also makes an analogy between Mirsky and Virginia Woolf, comparing Mirsky's inability or lack of desire to begin his own family, despite his loyalty to his 'parental family for as long as it lasted', and his preference for 'boarding houses' to a home to Virginia Woolf's 'childless and asexual arrangement' with Leonard Woolf (*D. S. Mirsky* 210).

By 1922 Mirsky, who was still struggling to form a response to post-Revolutionary Russia, became involved in the Eurasian Movement after meeting with musicologist Petr Suvchinsky in Berlin. The Eurasian Movement's 'members accepted the Bolshevik Revolution but rejected Communist power and ideology and argued for a future Russia based on Orthodoxy and on what they saw as the nation's true cultural identity as neither European nor Asian' (Smith, *DLB* 234). The Eurasian Movement's principles embracing Russian Orthodoxy as a foundational premise reflect Mirsky's interests in the Russian Orthodox *Avvakum*. Furthermore, Mirsky was involved in the group's activities and governance throughout the production of Harrison's translation and its publication in October 1924 by the Hogarth Press. The movement eventually broke apart, however, when he, Suvchinsky and poet Marina Tsvetaeva's husband, Sergei Efron, became increasingly more pro-Soviet or left-wing (Smith, *DLB* 234).

When Mirsky began researching his biography of Lenin in 1929, a year after Harrison's death, he made a formal break with the Eurasian Movement 'and as a result of his preparatory reading for it he placed himself irrevocably on the side of the Soviets', even casting off his admiration for and love of the Orthodox Church, which *Avvakum* had represented. When he returned to Moscow in 1932 under the patronage of Maxim Gorky, he was marginalised and gradually censored, banned and persecuted by the Soviet government, despite his new-found political beliefs and adherence to Marxist ideology, views that in Stalinist Russia were seen as dated and dangerous. Mirsky was also considered a risk due to his connections to British and European literary circles. When Gorky died in 1936 Mirsky, without patronage, was denounced, arrested and deported to a labour camp where he died on 6 June 1939. This was a fate that Virginia Woolf felt sure of when she confided in her diary with a telling description of the physical and psychological toll on the exile's life, after seeing Mirsky for the last time:

Mirsky was trap-mouthed; opened & bit his remark to pieces: has yellow misplaced teeth; wrinkles his forehead; despair, suffering, very marked on his face. Has been in England, in boarding houses for 12 years; now returns to Russia 'for ever'. I thought as I watched his eye brighten & fade—soon there'll be a bullet through your head. That's one of the results of war: this trapped cabin'd man. (*D4* 113)

In *Downhill All the Way* Leonard remembered Mirsky as an intellectual, a lover of arts and letters, who had an 'air of profound pessimism' about him. To Leonard, Harrison was 'one of the most civilised persons I have ever known. She was also the most charming, humorous, witty, individual human beings' – and he mourned the fact that 'from that environment [Mirsky] should have been drawn into the spider web of Soviet Russia to be destroyed there . . .' (26–7).

In one of the last pieces he wrote, in a scathing and bitter example of the extremes of his political conversion, Mirsky denounced many of the Bloomsbury writers, including Virginia Woolf. Willis called Mirsky's attack 'an unexpected Marxist assault' (46). In a chapter entitled 'The Highbrows' in *The Intelligentsia of Great Britain*, Mirsky characterised Bloomsbury radicalism as 'definitely bourgeois' and as a 'thin-skinned humanism for enlightened and sensitive members of the capitalist class' (qtd in Majumdar 347–9). He singled out members of Bloomsbury, many of whom he had met via Harrison – Virginia Woolf, E. M. Forster, Lytton Strachey and John Maynard Keynes, among others – as examples of psychological hair-splitters and experts in 'the sufferings of the parasitic cream of the bourgeois'. He mocked the premises of Woolf's *Mrs. Dalloway* and *A Room of One's Own* and characterised her style as 'a fine example of the narcotic function which art takes on in the hands of liberal esthetes, who turn it into a new and more perfect form of dope' (350). The rebuke and stinging remarks hurt Virginia Woolf and she writes about the difficulties creative people face in exposing themselves to the criticism and, in this case, attacks that are unwarranted, politically motivated, nasty and unfair. Mirsky's remarks made her feel that 'I'm hated & despised & ridiculed' (*D4* 289).

Before his departure for Soviet Russia, however, and before that fateful research in 1929 on Lenin, and during his tenure as an active member of the Eurasian Movement, Mirsky uncompromisingly argued for the destruction of the stereotype of the Russian character and against one-dimensional thinking in reviews of Russian literature. *Avvakum* is an example of that struggle. Once he met Harrison and began corresponding with her, he was often trying to convince her to see a more complete picture of Russia. Harrison was resistant at first to at least one of his pleas, when she wrote on 14 May 1924 'o yes I know full well there is another side to the Russian character but then that is a side that we English & the Germans & French possess too so it does not interest me. It gives me nothing fresh to live by' (J. H. Papers). But their high regard and respect for one another is also clear from their letters and from his 1930 tribute to Harrison. He does not place her with the English Dostoevskyites, as he makes clear when he comments '[a]nd indeed can one imagine the unerring taste of Jane Harrison being drawn by that cheapest and vulgarest of French inventions—"the Slav soul"'! (*J. H. and Russia* 11). Harrison remains his exception, until his conversion to hard-line Stalinism.

Harrison herself worked to clarify her position in relation to Russian Primitivism. When she was in the midst of her study of Greek vases, she travelled to St Petersburg to work on the Kertsch Antiquities, but was so all-consumed with her focus on Greece that she missed the opportunity to learn more about Russia, an experience that leads her years later to recount in *Reminiscences* the following dream:

> One night soon after the Russian revolution I dreamt I was in a great, ancient forest—what in Russian would be called a 'dreaming wood'. In it was cleared a round space, and the space was crowded with huge bears softly dancing. (78)

Harrison, ironically, uses the dream to illustrate and articulate 'what Russia has meant to me', and to distance herself from any one-dimensional or exotic view of 'Russianness'. She writes:

> And let there be no misunderstanding. It is not 'the Slav soul' that drew me. Not even, indeed, Russian literature. Of course, years before I had read and admired Turgenev and Tolstoy and Dostoevsky, but at least by the last two I was more frightened than allured . . . No, it was not these portentous things that laid a spell upon me. It was just the Russian language. If I could have my life over again, I would devote it not to art or literature, but to language. Life itself may hit one hard, but always, always one can take sanctuary in language. Language is as much an art and as sure a refuge as painting or music or literature. It reflects and interprets and makes bearable life. (*Reminiscences* 79)

And, indeed, it is the Russian language, I would argue, that convinced Harrison, who characterised her upbringing in the 'narrow school of Evangelicalism—reared with sin always present, with death and judgment before you', (80) to take on the translation of the Orthodox religious zealot *Avvakum*. As Mirsky explained to her and went on to write in his brilliant preface to *Avvakum*, 'In the Eastern Church the Writ and the Liturgies were translated into the vernacular of every newly converted nation . . . Old Slavonic, and not Greek, was the language of Civilization', and Moscow, after the fall of Rome and Constantinople, was considered 'the Third Rome, and there would never be a Fourth' (7).

In unpacking many of the aspects of Avvakum's extremism, he explains 'it is very important to realise that Avvakum's fanaticism, though historically conditioned by patriotic and nationalistic arguments, was primarily and fundamentally religious and not patriotic. Russia was holy to him because it was the vessel of orthodoxy, not orthodoxy because it was Russian' ('Preface' 17).

Mirsky brings up *Avvakum* in nearly every preface he writes, whether in his social histories or literary histories of Russia, and, at the time of *Avvakum*'s publication is dedicated to promoting this 'native' Russian voice. It is a voice Harrison was in love with and Virginia Woolf wanted to capture in terms of finding a new aesthetic for her own work. As Mirsky reminds us in the preface to *Avvakum*:

> Avvakum is startlingly unlike his predecessors and contemporaries. Taken in historical perspective, he is one of the most purely and unexpectedly original writers that ever wrote. He entirely broke with the rhetorical tradition . . . and created a literary language of his own. His groundwork is the spoken language of his time, that is, a language essentially the same as the spoken language of to-day. . . . It is a matter of historical fact that Avvakum's enormous influence was largely due to this familiarity of his language. . . . Avvakum's Russian, archaic in detail, is essentially the same as the spoken Russian of to-day—which knows (or at least ten years ago knew) no slang. (26–7)

He emphasises *Avvakum*'s relevance to contemporary times and appeals to writers of his day to look to *Avvakum*'s language as a model for their art. The authenticity of *Avvakum*'s colloquial Russian is a quality Mirsky finds lacking in a contemporary literature he too often judged derivative or overladen with political and sociological accessories. Mirsky's own prose style is crisp, clear and free of adornment, and, to my mind, often very much like reading the 'eloquent logic' of Harrison, who often helped edit his manuscripts. Mirsky's position that the most important Russian writers were still in Soviet Russia, in particular, Moscow, and not found nearly so frequently among members of 'Russia Abroad', provoked criticism of his work but also resonated with his desire for contemporary Russian writers to reclaim *Avvakum*'s voice. He writes:

> For all that Avvakum's style is very literary, but literary in a different way from the common run of Muscovite literature. This is almost a miracle. The use of the language of everyday is a thing unknown to the unsophisticated stages of civilization. This is what makes Avvakum so astonishingly modern. It is hardly an exaggeration to say that the Russian literary craftsman of to-day has more to learn from Avvakum than from any writer of the nineteenth century. Turgenev and Tolstoy, whose Russian seemed so colloquial and fresh that foreigners have even asserted that there is in Russian no dif-

ference between the spoken and the written language, seem as academic as *Rasselas* in the presence of Avvakum's daring modernity. (27–8)

This is the voice Mirsky brings to Harrison and Mirrlees to translate and Harrison and Mirrlees bring to Leonard and Virginia Woolf to publish. According to Mirsky, in his *Russia: A Social History*, Avvakum 'was one of the greatest writers ever produced by Russia; he began his career as a preacher and introduced into his written works the spirit of popular preaching and the language of the street. He was the first to use colloquial Russian for literary purposes', an idea that appealed to Harrison, who spent a good deal of her professional life battling the strict grammarians and philologists of Oxbridge's Classical departments, who would, according to her, rather 'parse' a sentence than understand the meaning behind it. Harrison and Mirrlees' translation continues to capture the modern imagination and to accomplish Mirsky's claim in the preface that 'It would be superfluous in the presence of his *Life* to multiply words as to the personality of Avvakum. He has given expression to it with a fierceness and sincerity that will go home to the most superficial reader even if he fails to find anything else in the book' (17). The simplicity, sincerity and vitality were qualities Mirsky longed for in contemporary Russian writers, a desire expressed by both Harrison and Virginia Woolf in their own work.

Avvakum is a master storyteller who keeps his listeners involved and entertained with the cogency of his prose. Brostrom's translation and others that came later leave out the rhythm and much of the personality of the Harrison–Mirrlees translation.[11] As Schwinn-Smith writes, Brostrom's version appealed more to the eye, while Mirsky and Harrison's version placed an 'emphasis on ear over eye' (128). Harrison was proud of her translation, which was for her at 74 years of age linguistically 'a phenomenal achievement' (Robinson 296). She wrote to Murray that 'As a prize for goodness of heart I send you the Archpriest Avvakum. If you don't think he is a loveable old bear our acquaintance ceases automatically' (qtd in Stewart 193). One of her former students, Jessie Stewart, writes that 'the erudition and skill of [*Avvakum*] caused Jane's friends in Paris to rank her Russian work on a level with her early books' (174).

Political *Avvakum*

Avvakum remains an example of the complicated left-wing political engagement of the Hogarth Press as well as an important part of any discussion of the Press' Russian translations and the activism of Leonard and Virginia Woolf. The text also suggests the changing views of Virginia Woolf, Harrison and Mirsky on language, Russian Primitivism and Russian politics. After the publication of *Avvakum*, Harrison's death in 1928, Mirsky's departure and the shifting political winds of Stalinism in the 1930s, Russian literature brought conflicting associations for Virginia Woolf. Laura Marcus writes that for Virginia Woolf 'Dostoevsky . . . became unreadable, or unreadable for her in the 1930s' ('Dimensions' 354). She tries Turgenev, but her ambivalence towards Dostoevsky and her early remonstrations of 'soul' in his work and other Russian writers fade, as she writes in 'Phases of Fiction' about Dostoevsky that 'the violence also lays bare regions deep down in the mind where contradictions prevail' (Woolf, 'Phases of Fiction' 126). The publication of *Avakkum* in 1924, and Harrison's key role in the leftist social and political networks between Bloomsbury and the Russian émigré press, informed Woolf's revision of her views on Russian literature and marked yet another political transition for Mirsky as well.

Although Mirsky defected and perished in the labour camps of Siberia, Harrison's example continued to maintain a presence in Virginia Woolf's intellectual life and, indeed, in the literary lives of a generation. 'While her co-translator, Hope Mirrlees, was the same generation as "New" Bloomsbury, Harrison had known most of "New" Bloomsbury since they were children' (Schwinn-Smith 121), and yet her ability to stay current resonated in Mirsky's tribute to her in 1930. He writes that:

> the ideas of Jane Harrison, inseparable from her personality and from her time, will live as part of a more human history, for they are an unremovable part of her age, which she expressed in a way that was unmistakenly hers and no one else's but which enters as one of the brightest threads into its living texture. The way walked by her from the study of Greek vases through that of primitive religion to Freud and to Tolstoy will be recognised as one of the most illuminating expressions of the intellectual evolution of the English mind at the turn of two historical epochs. . . . as a historical influence Jane Harrison belonged to a younger generation than she did by birth. Her personality reached its full development in the last decades of her life. (4–5)

Or, as Jessie Stewart once wrote, 'she was the Lady Themis. She liked to be Potnia Keron, the Lady of the Sprites [but] of that tradition', tellingly illustrating Harrison's importance to our reading of Woolf and the Hogarth Press, she says, 'let Virginia Woolf speak' (187). *Avvakum* ultimately fell into obscurity tainted by Mirsky's complicated response to the 1917 Russian Revolution, Harrison's own 'dash of the Bolshevik' and the Woolfs' interest in leftist politics. It seems a long-overdue critical moment to look again at the political values and at the literature from a more radical perspective, for the seventieth anniversary of the Hogarth Press passed by nearly twenty-five years ago, in 1987, with *Avvakum* and Jane Harrison barely warranting a footnote. And while Lenin may still be on view in Red Square, by 1991, after the disintegration of Soviet Russia and the fall of the Berlin Wall, Leningrad was once again renamed St Petersburg.

Notes

1. I would like to thank the archivists Anne Thomson and Pat Ackerman of the Jane Ellen Harrison Papers at Newnham College Cambridge for their efforts, support and expertise. The use of Jane Harrison's papers is by permission of The Principal and Fellows, Newnham College Cambridge. With special thanks to archivist Stanley Rabinowitz and his assistant Isabel Duarte-Gray at the Amherst Center for Russian Culture, and to Evgenia Karolyova of The Graduate Center, City University of New York, for her translations. I would also like to acknowledge the late Julia Briggs, Jane Marcus and Marilyn Schwinn-Smith for their support of this project.
2. Hope Mirrlees had been Jane Harrison's student at Newnham College. Virginia Woolf met Jane Harrison 'and all the other learned ladies at Newnham' (*L1* 145) in 1904 and Hope Mirrlees in 1914. Woolf published Mirrlees' poem *Paris* between 1919 and 1920. See Briggs 2006 and 2007.
3. Willis does not mention *Avvakum* in his history of the Press but Laura Marcus includes a brief discussion in her 'The European Dimensions of the Hogarth Press'. For discussion of Harrison's influence on Woolf's novels, see Jane Marcus 1987, Carpentier 1999 and my 2007 dissertation, *Goddesses and Ghosts: Virginia Woolf and Jane Ellen Harrison*.
4. For examples of Jane Harrison's atheism, see repeated references in her essay collection *Alpha and Omega* (1915), in particular 'Alpha and Omega' given in 1910 for the Sunday Essay Society of Trinity College, Cambridge. See also, 'Heresy and Humanity', the inaugural address she gave to The Heretics Society on 7 December 1909, and her memoir recounting her experiences being raised in an evangelical household in *Reminiscences of a Student's Life* (1925); for Virginia Woolf, see several references to her ambivalence towards organised religion throughout her diaries and letters.
5. Mirsky's two great-great aunts supported Avvakum's beliefs and were exiled as a result. In a letter to Gilbert Murray, Harrison writes that 'the ladies Morozova [Russian martyrs, painted by Sutiakim, 1886] whom Avvakum sentimentalises over (113) are his [Prince Mirsky's] great great aunts. Wouldn't you like to have aunts like that?' (Stewart 193).
6. Laura Marcus writes 'While there were scattered English translations of his [Dostoevsky's] work in the late-nineteenth century, these came much later than the translations in France and Germany, and were frequently out of print' ('Introduction' vii).
7. Although G. S. Smith argues that Harrison could not be said to have

'mastered' Russian, by all accounts at Newnham, her method of teaching the language was effective. As early as 1915 we learn that Harrison's instruction enabled Professor Elsie Butler to join the Scottish Women's Hospital Unit in Russia, and in two weeks she was able to read Turgenev with Harrison's help (*D. S. Mirsky* 206; Stewart 173).

8. *Ancient Art and Ritual* was given to Virginia Woolf as a Christmas gift in 1923, inscribed by the author (Jane Marcus 195).
9. Gilbert Murray, though an Oxford scholar, was a key member of Harrison's group, later dubbed The Cambridge Ritualists. Murray, Regis Professor of Greek at Oxford, was best known for his *The Rise of the Greek Epic* (1907); *The Four Stages of Greek Religion* (1912) later expanded to *The Five Stages of Greek Religion* (1925); and for his work and translations of Euripides' *The Bacchae*. He also contributed an 'Excursis on the Ritual Forms Preserved in Greek Tragedy' for Harrison's *Themis* (1912), and his correspondence with Harrison comprises the majority of Harrison's surviving letters housed in Newnham College's Jane Harrison papers.
10. See Harrison's brilliant 'Epilogue on War: Peace with Patriotism' collected in *Alpha and Omega*, and which serves as a model, in my view, for Virginia Woolf's *Three Guineas*.
11. See Schwinn-Smith for a good close reading and comparison between translations.

Works cited

Avvakum. *The Life of the Archpriest Avvakum by Himself. Translated from the Seventeenth Century Russian by Jane Harrison and Hope Mirrlees, with a preface by Prince D. S. Mirsky*. London: Hogarth Press, 1924.
Beasley, Rebecca. 'Russia and the Invention of the Modernist Intelligentsia'. In Peter Brooker and Andrew Thacker, eds. *Geographies of Modernism*. Routledge, 2005: 19–28.
Briggs, Julia. 'Modernism's Lost Hope: Virginia Woolf, Hope Mirrlees and the Printing of *Paris*'. *Reading Virginia Woolf*. Edinburgh: Edinburgh University Press, 2006.
—. 'Commentary on *Paris*'. In Bonnie Kime Scott, ed. *Gender in Modernism*. Champaign: University of Illinois Press, 2007: 287–303.
Brostrom, Kenneth N. 'Translations, Annotations, Commentary, and a Historical Introduction'. *Archpriest Avvakum, the Life written by himself: with the study of V.V. Vinogradov*. Ann Arbor: Michigan Slavic Publications, University of Michigan, 1979.
Carpentier, Martha C. *Ritual, Myth, and the Modernist Text: The Influence of Jane Ellen Harrison on Joyce, Eliot, and Woolf*. Library of Anthropology Series, Amsterdam: Gordon and Breach, 1998.
Harrison, Jane Ellen. *Alpha and Omega*. New York: AMS Press, [1915] 1973.
—. *Aspects, Aorists, and the Classical Tripos*. Cambridge: Cambridge University Press, 1919.
—. 'Heresy and Humanity' in *Alpha and Omega*.
—. *Reminiscences of a Student's Life*. London: Hogarth Press, 1925.

The Jane Ellen Harrison Papers. Newnham College Archives. Newnham College. Cambridge University.

Majumdar, Robin, ed. *Virginia Woolf: An Annotated Bibliography of Criticism, 1915–1974.* New York: Garland, 1976.

Marcus, Jane. *Virginia Woolf and the Languages of Patriarchy.* Bloomington: Indiana University Press, 1987.

Marcus, Laura. 'The European Dimensions of the Hogarth Press'. In Mary Ann Caws and Nicola Luckhurst, eds. *The Reception of Virginia Woolf in Europe.* London and New York: Continuum, 2002: 328–56.

—. 'Introduction'. In Stuart N. Clarke, ed. *Translations from the Russian: Virginia Woolf and S.S. Koteliansky.* Southport: The Virginia Woolf Society of Great Britain, 2006.

Mirsky, D. S. *Jane Ellen Harrison and Russia.* Cambridge: W. Heffer, 1930.

—. *Lenin.* Boston: Little, Brown, 1931.

—. 'Preface'. *The Life of the Archpriest Avvakum by Himself.* Trans. Jane Harrison and Hope Mirrlees. London: Hogarth Press, 1924.

The Remizov Papers. The Amherst Center for Russian Culture. Amherst, Massachusetts.

Robinson, Anabel. *The Life and Work of Jane Ellen Harrison.* Oxford: Oxford University Press, 2002.

Schwinn-Smith, Marilyn. 'Bears in Bloomsbury: Jane Ellen Harrison and Russia'. In Maria Candida Zamith and Luisa Flora, eds. *Virginia Woolf: Three Centenary Celebrations.* Porto: Faculdade de Letras da Universidade de Porto, 2007: 119–44.

Smith, G. S. *D.S. Mirsky: A Russian-English Life, 1890–1939.* Oxford: Oxford University Press, 2000.

—. 'Jane Ellen Harrison: Forty-seven Letters to D. S. Mirsky, 1924–1926'. *Oxford Slavonic Papers.* New Series. Vol. 28. 1995: 62–97.

—. 'Prince D.S. Mirsky'. In Maria Rubins, ed. *Dictionary of Literary Biography: Volume 317 Twentieth-Century Russian Émigré Writers.* New York: Thomson Gale, 2005: 230–6.

Stewart, Jessie. *Jane Ellen Harrison: A Portrait in Letters.* London: Merlin Press, 1959.

Willis, J. H. *Leonard and Virginia Woolf as Publishers: The Hogarth Press, 1917–41.* Charlottesville: University Press of Virginia, 1992.

Woolf, Leonard. *Beginning Again: An Autobiography of the Years 1911 to 1918.* New York: Harcourt Brace Jovanovich, 1963, 1964.

—. *Downhill All the Way: An Autobiography of the Years 1919 to 1939.* New York: Harcourt Brace Jovanovich, 1967.

Woolf, Virginia. *The Diary of Virginia Woolf, 1931–1935.* Vol. 4. Ed. Anne Olivier Bell. New York: Harcourt, 1982.

—. *The Letters of Virginia Woolf.* Eds Nigel Nicolson and Joanne Trautmann. 6 vols. New York: Harcourt Brace Jovanovich, 1975–1980.

—. 'Phases of Fiction' in *Granite and Rainbow.* New York: Harcourt, 1975: 126.

—. 'The Russian Point of View' in *The Common Reader.* Ed. Andrew McNeillie. New York: Harcourt, 1925.

Part Three

Marketing Other Modernisms

On or About December 1928 the Hogarth Press Changed: E. McKnight Kauffer, Art, Markets and the Hogarth Press 1928–39

Elizabeth Willson Gordon

The Hogarth Press was innovative not only in its literary productions but also in its relations to the marketplace. In 1928 the complex aesthetics of Hogarth Press books, typified visually by the designs of Vanessa Bell and Duncan Grant, intersected with the American designer E. McKnight Kauffer. Kauffer's contributions to the Press, little studied to date, include a number of dust jackets and, perhaps most importantly, a new wolf's head logo. This chapter traces the relations of Kauffer with the Press and examines his contribution to Press aesthetics and marketing. The focus will therefore be on the networks of people and texts that connected Kauffer to the Press and his connections to other Bloomsbury figures and presses, focusing particularly on his interactions with the Woolfs and the Press between 1928 and 1939. His visual presence at the Press also connected Hogarth to other figures and movements, both commercial and elite. The larger context for the relationship is the debates about art, advertising and the market in which both Kauffer and the Hogarth Press were involved. Kauffer's new logo was accompanied by new distribution and advertising practices at the Press; his involvement signalled a shift of relations between the Press and the market. As with many aspects of the Hogarth Press, Kauffer's contributions were usefully ambivalent: productively engaged with art and commerce, books and markets. In including Kauffer's work and name, the Press added a different and yet compatible discourse about artistic purpose and productions.

The primary monograph on Kauffer, *E. McKnight Kauffer: a designer and his public*, does not specifically mention the Hogarth Press and includes only one illustration of a dust jacket for the Press, without comment. More surprisingly, work on the Hogarth Press only briefly mentions the presence of Kauffer's work at the Press, if at all. He, like the Press, is difficult to categorise, highlighting the problem of simple distinctions or oppositions between art and commerce or 'serious' and mass-produced art; he crosses categories and fields of study with his work as a painter, a poster artist, a graphic designer, a book illustrator and a dust jacket designer. A study of Kauffer, therefore, contributes to the 'new modernist studies', as outlined by Mao and Walkowitz in *Bad Modernisms*, that pays 'heightened attention to continuities and intersections across the boundaries of artistic media' (2). In England Kauffer and his work became famous and instantly recognisable. He was a 'dominant design influence in England of the inter-war period' (Haworth-Booth 32). In Evelyn Waugh's *Brideshead Revisited* (1945), for example, the protagonist, Charles Ryder, decorates his rooms at Oxford in a youthful, too-popular style with 'a poster by McKnight Kauffer[1] and Rhyme Sheets from the Poetry Bookshop, and most painful to remember, a porcelain figure of Polly Peachum' (29). Kauffer's work signals poor-taste, commonplace art, for which the artist Ryder is enthusiastic, until he embarks on his aesthetic education and redecorates his rooms. Kauffer, a complex figure, evokes productive debates about value and the relation of art to the marketplace as he was an artist producing in the tension-filled field of commercial art. His fame, commercial success and artistic recognition were all part of the reputation he brought to the Hogarth Press and parallel some of the tensions the Press itself was negotiating.

A book illustrator or dust jacket designer is like a publisher in that he/she adds a layer of signification to the authorial creation of a book. Kauffer's name and reputation had weight, but not in the same way as a 'pure' painter or a literary author. As Pierre Bourdieu notes, 'the sociology of art and literature has to take as its object not only the material production but also the symbolic production of the work' and therefore to consider 'not only the direct producers of the work in its materiality (artist, writer, etc.) but also the producers of the meaning and value of the work—critics, publishers, gallery directors' (37). Publishers and designers participate in what Aaron Jaffe terms necessary and 'illegitimate literary work, based on the punitively collaborative work of promotion', work used to 'fix "masterpieces"' and distinguished from 'legitimate literary work, based on exclusionary standards of literary reputation and originality' (177). A publisher 'proclaim[s] the value of the author he defends (cf. the fiction of the catalogue or blurb) and above all "invests his prestige" in the author's cause, acting as a "symbolic banker" who offers as security all the symbolic capital he has accumulated' (Bourdieu 77). An illustrator or designer, too, is part of the network of names, reputations and imprimaturs that transfers some of his/her symbolic capital to the book, and conversely receives symbolic capital through association with a work of value. Some names – not associated with 'masterpieces' – have more commercial significations. A book is created by more than the author.

I argue that 1928 was a turning point for the Press and that Kauffer's contributions were central in signalling, and accomplishing, the shift. In this year the Hogarth Press altered its relation to the market, increased its scope of distribution and added a dedicated traveller. It also changed its logo and adopted new advertising practices. The Press published thirty-six titles in 1928 including ones by Sigmund Freud, Herbert Read, Viscountess Rhondda and Vita Sackville-West. The most important title, however, was, not surprisingly, Virginia Woolf's *Orlando*. Leonard asserts, 'The turning-point in Virginia's career as a successful novelist came in 1928 with the publication of *Orlando*' (*Downhill* 143). The success of the novel's sales resulted from, and spurred changes at, the Press. What may surprise is Kauffer's role in designing the Press' new 1928 logo that marked the shift in advertising.

The Hogarth Press was advertising in newspapers by 1920, putting print ads in *The Times*, *Nation*, *Manchester Guardian* and *New Statesman*. The early print ads were fairly simple. Willis notes that the 'style used in the early Hogarth Press ads was visually unsophisticated, the type heavy and black, the copy cramped, this list of titles and prices assaulting and dulling the eye' (375). These ads did not differ greatly from other publishers' advertisements at the time. Where they placed ads was also an important consideration and they tended to only use the 'serious' publications. Hogarth Press advertisements did not remain static, however. Kauffer's modern wolf's head announced a more sophisticated and commercially savvy style of promotion. The new logo was first used in 'a half-page ad for the pre-Christmas sale in the December 8, 1928 issue of the *Nation and Athenaeum*' (Willis 376). Willis remarks, 'Suddenly in December 1928 . . . the Hogarth Press found a style of its own', and the new ad 'communicated a new degree of stylishness, efficiency, and crisp intellectuality' (376–7). The copy of the advertisements became more sparse, including fewer titles and varying the size of the type. After 1928 'all Hogarth ads carried McKnight Kauffer's single or double wolf's-head device, becoming as instantly recognizable and distinctive as the best publishing house ads' (Willis 377). The double wolf's heads, facing inwards, often flank the Press' name at the top of the advertisements, both drawing in the eye and reinforcing the brand. Kauffer's device is both a cause of changes at the Press and a reflection of changes originating elsewhere.

Kauffer's Early Career

Kauffer's contributions to the Hogarth Press begin largely in 1928, but it is important to have a sense of the career and reputation that Kauffer had prior to the point of intersection. An American, born in 1890 in Great Falls, Montana, he worked as a young man for 'the San Francisco bookseller and art dealer Paul Elder' where he developed 'a life-long passion for books' (Haworth-Booth 10). Kauffer studied painting in the evenings and later spent a number of months at the Art Institute of Chicago. He then moved to Europe to study painting in 1913 and it was there, primarily in England, that he produced most of his work. In 1915 Kauffer met Frank Pick, the Publicity Manager of the London Underground Electric Railways, and he gave Kauffer a commission for a poster: 'Over the next 25 years the company became [Kauffer's] major client and he their major poster artist. The company gave Kauffer an audience of millions—in return he gave the company a succession of designs of sparkling originality and widespread influence' (Haworth-Booth 14). Pick was interested in raising the quality of advertising and heeded the recommendations of the Society for Checking the Abuses of Public Advertising (SCAPA), improving the posters themselves as well as their display, creating, as Kauffer noted, 'goodwill for the company by respecting the public' (Haworth-Booth 15). Pick commissioned Edward Johnston 'to design an exclusive sans serif typeface and logo for the Underground (both are still in use), as well as hire a number of England's best artists to design beautiful posters for its stations' (Heller 3). Artists of note were brought into the realm of advertising to elevate the work produced. Wyndham Lewis indicated the social impact of advertising when superior designs might be used: 'the Public taste could thus be educated in a popular way to appreciate the essentials of design better than picture galleries have ever done' (qtd in Haworth-Booth 16).

Kauffer's early paintings and posters were part of a number of networks. His work, influenced by Van Gogh, and then increasingly by Japanese colour woodcuts (Haworth-Booth 16), participated in English Vorticism. He was a figure of the avant-garde. As a painter, Kauffer was associated with the London Group, 'a society of adventuresome painters who embraced Cubism', and exhibited with this group (Heller 3). As secretary for the group he also 'designed exhibition posters, invitations and abstract symbols for catalogue covers' (Haworth-Booth 22). Roger Fry wrote an introduction to an exhibition of Kauffer's work in 1917 and Fry 'kept a portfolio of Kauffer's drawing on sale at his Omega Workshops' (Haworth-Booth 22). In 1920 Kauffer became a member of the X Group, painters organised by Wyndham Lewis who left the London Group. The April exhibition of the X Group was 'the last flourish of Vorticism' (Haworth-Booth 26), and Kauffer stopped painting in 1921. As Haworth-Booth remarks, 'Kauffer now found a hypocrisy in maintaining distinctions between "pure" and commissioned work' (28) and focused on his design work. His style continued to change. After 1923 he entered 'his so-called "Jazz style," in which he created colorful, art moderne interpretations of traditional form' (Heller 4). The relation and debate surrounding advertising and art and what they reveal about the purpose of art is a central concern of this chapter.

As we have seen, Kauffer was 'almost a national figure in England by the early 1920s' (Haworth-Booth 31). His status and reputation make him an interesting collaborator with the Hogarth Press, but he was also part of more exclusive and artistically sanctioned circles. His relations to Bloomsbury figures and friends of the Woolfs are numerous. In 1925 'a Retrospective Exhibition of posters' was held, including, in addition to examples of ten years of poster work, 'original drawings, first drafts, colour schemes, a selection of calendars, show-cards, labels, book-jackets, [and] drawings for newspaper advertisements' (Haworth-Booth 44). The show was held in Bloomsbury, and Fry wrote the introduction to the catalogue. Fry also reviewed the exhibition in *The Nation*. When 'the exhibition was afterwards shown at the Ashmolean Museum, Oxford, [Fry] gave a lecture on Commerce and Art' (Haworth-Booth 44). This talk was then revised and published in 1926 as a pamphlet by the Hogarth Press as part of the Hogarth Essays series.

Kauffer's work at the Hogarth Press was also preceded by his work at Gerard Meynell's Westminster Press, where for a time he was 'Director of Pictorial and Poster Advertising' (Haworth-Booth 33). He also designed advertisements with Francis Meynell of the Pelican Press (which printed some Hogarth Press books), and the designs 'bristled with new, newly imported or newly revived typefaces, set off by Kauffer's hand-drawn ornaments' (Haworth-Booth 33). Kauffer designed the dust jacket for Lytton Strachey's *Eminent Victorians* (a 1921 reprint for Chatto and Windus of their 1918 title). In addition to his relationship with Roger Fry and Wyndham Lewis, Kauffer became good friends with T. S. Eliot and also with the publisher Harold Monro of the London-based Poetry Bookshop. The Poetry Bookshop sold Hogarth Press books from at least 1918. It was Kauffer who designed the new 'painted sign-board for the Poetry Bookshop when it moved to new premises at 38 Great Russell Street' (Haworth-Booth 38) across from the British Museum and in Bloomsbury in 1926. Kauffer was multiply visible in select spaces in Bloomsbury as well as in London, and its underground, much more generally.

Connections to Bloomsbury and London's literary world occurred as well through book illustrations. The variety of Kauffer's work meant that it appealed to many different people, for conflicting reasons, creating an ambivalent reputation. Book illustrations have a conflicted status as artistic works, being both more conventionally recognised as art and supplementary to another, more primary, work of art: the book being illustrated. Kauffer's illustrations were often done for important works and authors with significant symbolic capital; his associations with these projects gave him a different kind of credibility than did his work in designing posters. Often the books he illustrated were done in small press runs, and the limited editions were valuable and collectible as art objects. The restricted circulation and alternate relation to the market conferred prestige on these books and those associated with them. In 1925 Kauffer illustrated Robert Burton's *The Anatomy of Melancholy* for Francis Meynell's Nonesuch Press, produced in two volumes. Fry reviewed Kauffer's illustrations and notes:

> It seems to me that real illustration in the sense of reinforcing the author's verbal expression is quite impossible. But it may be possible to embroider the author's ideas, or rather to execute variations on the author's theme which will not pretend to be one with the text but are rather, as it were, a running commentary, like marginal notes written by a reader. ('The Author' 10)

Kauffer understood the supplemental, powerful role of the illustrations and his contributions do not attempt to replicate the linguistic component of the text. Anthony Blunt, in a review of a 1935 exhibition of Kauffer's work including illustrations, book-jackets and posters, compared his achievement to 'that of a very good translator of literature' as he

> has not himself invented any of the important styles such as Cubism or Superrealism . . . nor has he even taken a direct part in their inception. What he has done is rather to take from these styles as soon as they appeared exactly those elements which were relevant to his particular purposes and has translated these elements into terms of illustration or poster art. (qtd in Haworth-Booth 70)

He is not the author or originator in any conventional sense, and therefore 'since he is not a pure painter or sculptor or architect, but an illustrator and a designer of book-covers and posters, he must, technically, be classed as minor' (Blunt qtd in Haworth-Booth 70). The medium places limits on assessments of artistic achievement, though the quality of Kauffer's work was such that he made Blunt 'resent the division of the arts into major and minor' (Haworth-Booth 68). The discussion of Kauffer's ability to cross and trouble boundaries will be discussed in greater depth below.

One important element in addition to his use of new artistic styles was his adoption of innovative illustrative techniques. Kauffer illustrated Herman Melville's *Benito Cereno* (1926) (Fig. 7.1) published by the Nonesuch and printed at the Curwen Press. The book notes that the 'pictures are hand-coloured through stencils' and the copies, 'for sale in England and America' (n.p.), are numbered. The seven full-page illustrations used the pochoir process, in which watercolour is added to line drawings using stencils, that became 'popular in Paris in the early twenties and was very successfully transplanted to England by the Curwen Press' (Haworth-Booth 53). Historian Desmond Flower described the frontispiece for Melville's book as 'one of the most brilliant designs he ever conceived' (qtd in Haworth Booth 53).

Kauffer also illustrated the two-volume *Don Quixote* (1930) for Nonesuch, drawing twenty-one illustrations in total. In 1929 he illustrated *Robinson Crusoe* for Etchells and Macdonald. The illustrations for Arnold Bennett's *Elsie and the Child*, also of 1929 (Fig. 7.2), were 'stencilled gouache applied as colour solids' and produced an image of 'unparalleled richness' (Gilmour 77). The print run for this book was 750 numbered copies, published by Cassell.

Kauffer illustrated a second book of Bennett's, *Venus Rising from the Sea* (1931), also for Cassell. The print run of 350 copies contained twelve of Kauffer's drawings. These books were beautifully produced, desirable and collectible. The Hogarth Press sought and achieved these elements in a number of its volumes, often illustrated by Grant, Bell or Fry.

Another important element of Kauffer's artistic production as an illustrator was the drawings he made for the series of T. S. Eliot's *Ariel* poems printed at the Curwen Press for Faber and Gwyer. Each finely produced little folder contained 'one poem, with a line or colour woodcut frontispiece, and a design on the cover' (Haworth-Booth 55). Kauffer illustrated and provided the cover design for Eliot's *The Journey of the Magi* (1927) (Fig. 7.3). This book was limited to 350 copies on handmade paper. He also illustrated other poems by Eliot in the series: *A Song for Simeon* (1928), *Mariana* (1930) and *Triumphal March* (1931). Eliot, who published multiple works with the Hogarth Press, remarked on Kauffer's 'great gifts, . . .

Figure 7.1   Frontispiece for *Benito Cereno* (1926).

Figure 7.2   Illustration from *Elsie and the Child* (1929).

Figure 7.3 Illustration from *Journey of the Magi* (1927).

not only of his powers as an artist, but of the gift of sympathy and understanding which made him a good illustrator. I am grateful for his illustrations to my own "Ariel" poems' (qtd in Haworth-Booth 56). Thus Kauffer's work blended technical skill, artistic feeling and a genius for his own media.

The Fraught Relationship Between Art and Advertising

To better understand the significance of Kauffer's work and of his contributions to the Hogarth Press in particular, we must establish a fuller sense of the contemporary debates about advertising and its relation to art, as well as Kauffer's own complex reputation. In the early 1920s Kauffer 'questioned the growing schism between fine and applied art' and 'could see no reason for conflict between good art work and good salesmanship' (Heller 3). One productive way to think of Kauffer's position is that of bridging or combining art and commerce. The competing discourses outlined below also provide a context for the complex negotiations of positions in which the Hogarth Press was engaged, though the Press' position differed from Kauffer's in a number of key ways.

In some discourses of the 1920s 'art was integrated with advertising, producing a distinctive visual practice whose effectiveness was measured in commercial terms. It was art with a purpose—commercial art' (Hewitt 32). Art was not distinct or antithetical to advertising. Such a definition is problematic for an understanding of art that insists on its disinterestedness or even its lack of effect. Commercial art, then, is not true art. Bourdieu notes, industrial art 'is doubly suspect, being both mercantile and "popular"' (50). Another view bases the distinction between types of commercial art on a number of factors, including the relationship between viewer and advertisement. In his article 'Posters of Distinction' John Hewitt discusses the discourse surrounding advertising, and posters in particular, taking place in journals, newspapers and in organisations such as SCAPA and the Campaign for the Preservation of Rural England (CPRE). He argues that many texts written at the time sought to 'establish aesthetic, not commercial, criteria by which to judge posters' (Hewitt 21). In order to foster the focus on determining aesthetic qualities and promote the poster as art, it was made to resemble a painting: 'the more the poster looked like a painting, an object whose aesthetic quality had been validated elsewhere, in other sites and discourses, the more it was able to activate tasteful consumption' (Hewitt 22). Rather than simply being consumed as advertising or 'painted cant', posters with this kind of artistic value encouraged 'disinterested contemplation, . . . tasteful discernment' and would 'wait passively for their meaning to be exposed by the sensitive gaze of the connoisseur' (Hewitt 22). Tasteful consumption indicates 'aesthetic pleasure' and 'is seen as an end in itself. It is disinterested, contained, and does not prompt action', but the problem of the poster is that it 'addresses the viewer not as connoisseur but as consumer' (Hewitt 23). The answer for many advertising campaigns was to work to have the poster fulfil a double function: 'it must give information as well as aesthetic pleasure' (Hewitt 24). Railways created posters 'as close to paintings as reprographic technique would allow. They awaited the connoisseurial gaze. They informed the viewer about the company and its services in a discrete and unemphatic way' (Hewitt 26). This altered relationship between viewer and poster meant that 'posters could persuade without appearing to hustle. They could appeal as art, while operating as advertising' (Hewitt 29). Further, these paintings were done by eminent Royal Academicians and so doubly referred to recognised art in both product and producer. A similar argument for elevated status accompanied by a changed relation between viewer and poster could be made for the Underground campaign of which Kauffer was a central part. Though not a member of the Royal Academy, Kauffer had been a 'pure' painter, and, as previously discussed, was recognised as an important artist by critics, galleries and other authorising institutions. He edited and arranged the book *The Art of the Poster* in 1924. His posters and other work brought aesthetic pleasure, were exhibited, reviewed and praised in catalogues, thus accumulating their own symbolic capital, if still on a different register from 'pure' painting.

Unlike the railway campaigns discussed by Hewitt, Kauffer's posters looked like modern art; they were innovative in form and technique rather than emulating traditional landscape paintings. Fry argues in *Art and Commerce* (1926) that 'a really creative design has a certain violence and insistence, a spiritual energy, which is disquieting to people at first sight' (19). The number of Kauffer's advertising designs that ended up unused, even at times by the Hogarth Press, attests to the fact that his work pushed against boundaries and that he continued to explore rather than replicate successful designs and styles. One can read in his career a deep concern for his work and an independence that also helps to align him as an artist. In a 1920 issue of *Arts and Decoration* magazine Robert Parker included an article entitled 'E. McKnight Kauffer—A Commercial Artist with Ideals'. Ideals, artistic integrity and seriousness combined in Kauffer with what was often referred to as genius. These characteristics were read in his work, which not only revealed his 'mastery of synthesis—wedding abstract, dynamic form to everyday products' but also that 'His posters and advertisements were not motivated by the common tactic of deceiving a customer into believing false claims, nor by appealing to their base instinct; rather he wanted to encourage people to simply be aware of a product or message by piquing their aesthetic sensitivities' (Heller 4). His work encouraged a connoisseurial gaze and was motivated by ideals above base consumerism and advertising tricks.

Fry did not assert the impossibility of posters being works of art. In part because posters were inexpensive it is 'possible here for the industrialist to take risks' and though 'posters will very rarely be works of art', there is 'a chance here and there that a work of art might pass muster both with the employer and the public' (Fry, *Art* 21). Kauffer is quite possibly that exception, a man Fry thought of as an artist. An artist is 'an intolerant individualist claiming a kind of divine right to the convictions of his peculiar sensibility' (Fry, *Art* 9). Kauffer was able to produce what would be recognised as art within commercial realms and genres such as the poster because his work demonstrated, and was read as demonstrating, a commitment to more than money or sales in both his practice and product. Kauffer struggled to 'meet his creative needs, his clients' commercial interests and his viewers' aesthetic preferences' (Heller 5). First mentioned is Kauffer's attention to his obligations as a creator, and he combined this with other requirements. His productions were also able to fit within the category of art as defined by Fry: an object that has a 'quite particular quality, the quality of expressing a particular emotion which we call the esthetic emotion' (*Art* 7). Another element that distinguished Kauffer's design for advertisements was artistic philosophy, echoing that of people like Fry with the emphasis on form: '[Kauffer] did not want to attach to a product a spurious symbol—lending it the frisson of sex or the piety of religion—but to find a form to express the essence of whatever it was he advertised' (Gilmour 75). Aldous Huxley praised Kauffer's work as it 'reveals his affinity with all artists who have ever aimed at expressiveness through simplification, distortion and transportation' (qtd in Heller 5). The priority of form and the adherence to a higher design standard than the usual put Kauffer's work, at least for some, into a different category, a hybrid category that was useful for the Hogarth Press.

Steven Heller writes that 'Kauffer was hailed for elevating advertising to high art' (1). The assertions and justifications of Kauffer's status as artist point to a key barrier: the media in which he worked. Commercial art is problematic for artistic discourse in terms of artistic purpose, autonomy and originality. Johanna Drucker highlights the ongoing problems of simplistic distinctions between high art and commercial art and the evaluation of commercial art using the criteria of high art. She writes, 'the complex nature of the relation of fine art to mass-media imagery requires a more subtle characterization of the interlinked identity of the two domains' rather than casting 'the relation as one in which fine art is the privileged term in any opposition—high/low, elite/popular, authorial/industrial' (46). The importance of Kauffer's work has been undermined or simply ignored because of divisive categories over proper objects of study.

The Hogarth Press on Art and the Market

While one could characterise Kauffer's position as one of artistic production within commerce and advertising, a relationship of compat-
ibility within certain parameters, the official position of the Hogarth
Press, while containing elements of art and commerce, established the
two as antagonistic. Practices and rhetoric at the Press were, however,
both contradictory and useful. The Press had already established, by
the 1920s, a certain reputation and niche as small and non-commercial
through early practices and products. The continuation of hand printing, until 1932, was one way that the Press reminded people of its origin
as a letterpress operated by Leonard and Virginia Woolf and its early
characterisation as amateur. Such decisions also continued to emphasise
their market niche and positioning. The official rhetoric of the Hogarth
Press is very aware of the discourses of art and disinterestedness, and
it goes to some pains to define the Press both by what it is and what it
is not. On the occasion of the fifth anniversary of the Press, in 1922,
the Press sent out a circular to 'lay before you a few facts about the
Hogarth Press and its future prospects' (LWP). The announcement
reviews the original aims of the Press, using the more personal first
person plural rather than 'the Press': 'We aimed in the first place at
producing works of genuine merit' that 'could scarcely hope to secure
publication through the ordinary channels' (LWP). They attended to the
marginal work of artistic value shunned by mainstream channels and
were in that sense non-commercial. The announcement goes on to say,
'In the second place we were resolved to produce no book merely with
a view to pecuniary profit. We meant to satisfy ourselves to the best of
our ability that the work had literary or artistic merit before we under-
took to produce it' (LWP). The Press is explicitly not a money-making
venture, though there is not a complete disavowal of economics, and the
first priority and privileged element is merit. Such a statement reveals
a sense of mission. There is also an explanation for the Press' expansion that categorises the changes as reactions: the announcement goes
on to assert that 'It had been our original intention to print every book
with our own hands, but the sales much exceeded our expectation' and
therefore they found themselves 'compelled to issue' (LWP) larger editions. In this construction they are only responding to an audience and
a market; they are not creating the demand. The official rhetoric of the
Press continued to emphasise this characterisation as merit first, reminding people of its origins as time went on. Even as the Press became
more economically successful, both practices and rhetoric continued to
maintain a multiplicity that made it difficult to pin down a characterisa-

tion. Bridget Elliott and Jo-Ann Wallace argue that Woolf herself was in tension as a modernist woman 'between, on the one hand, a "feminist" ideology of professionalism which demanded the right to a fair, living wage for one's cultural labour and, on the other hand, an individualist and "modernist" ideology of artistic (and financial) disinterestedness' (70). Over time there was a shift towards a more public and commercial business, but the oscillation between more and less obviously commercial practices continued.

The relations of Kauffer's reputation and work to art and the market are not the same as the relations of the Hogarth Press. The designer and the Press are part of two differing discourses as well as differing media; however, they are not contradictory. Kauffer elevates the explicitly commercial to art and the Press produces art and then sells it. Both are mixtures, hybrids, placing importance on art, however it is defined, as well as on the concepts of integrity and merit. Both have multiple types of appeal: Kauffer did paintings and the Hogarth Press published bestsellers. The multiplicity was useful and productive for both and made them good partners. The Press entrusted Kauffer with redesigning its logo in 1928.

Logos

During his career Kauffer designed a number of trademarks and logos, also known as devices, for businesses and groups other than the Hogarth Press. He designed, for example, in 1916, 'a set of bale labels for use on cotton goods' exported by the textile company Stenthan & Co. to South America (Haworth-Booth 21). He designed the symbol for the Arts League of Service in 1919 and his 'Vorticist-derived symbols' were used 'for the important quarterly *Art and Letters*' (Haworth-Booth 26). In 1925 Kauffer developed the monogram for the Film Society in London (Haworth-Booth 47), which he helped found. He also designed, for the Empire Marketing Board, a ' "National Mark" which identified British goods on packaging and in advertising' (Haworth-Booth 51). In 1930 he designed 'a silver phoenix among bronze flames' as a symbol for the Phoenix Theatre (Haworth-Booth 53). In the same year, Kauffer designed the 'letter-headings, brand-labels and dress-boxes' for Cresta Silk, using Eric Gill's 'newly available Sans Serif letter' and giving the firm 'an abstract, witty and memorable trademark' (Haworth-Booth 64). Kauffer had experience designing logos with a variety of purposes and messages by 1928.

A publisher's logo is a key visual component of the brand[2] and shapes its relation to the market. As S. H. Steinberg notes, the purpose of a device is 'to serve as a hall-mark of quality, and to safeguard what later became known as copyright' (132). A mark of this nature indicates merit, authorisation, the symbolic capital the publisher confers on the book, and it is also a matter of legality and financial considerations. The logo is both a sign of ownership and a legitimation of the book. Similar to the logo is the trademark, which acts as a 'pledge of good faith to [the] customer' (Preston & Arch 26). The 'Mark is [present] as undisputable evidence of the origin and merits of the article in question' (Preston & Arch 27) and must be transferable, a unifying element among various objects. In the case of a publisher's logo on a book, the merits are not so much an issue of the physical quality of production, although that can be part of the appeal, as of the characterisation of the content of the book. Much discussion about book advertising in the 1920s and 1930s focused on the idea that books were unlike other consumer products. Stanley Unwin asserts that the 'ordinary advertising expert is of little assistance to the book publisher' (242). Since books are unique there is a relatively small budget for each title, and 'the demand for publishers' wares is seldom repetitive, like the demand which successful advertising can secure for, let us say, soap or cigarettes' (Unwin 243). While each title is unique, creating a publisher as an identifiable brand, in large part through its logo, creates the possibility of ongoing demand. People would buy Penguins or Hogarth Press books as they liked and trusted those publishers. In this way Press' books worked on a similar logic to that of the series, encouraging the collection of all elements in a list. The Hogarth Press brand, communicated through the logo (Fig. 7.4), makes books not totally unique: a characterisation and an incitement to buy based on reputation. The logo, in the case of the Hogarth Press, confers some symbolic capital onto the new publication by means of the publisher's device: the wolf's head.

The logo has a material component, an image and a visual signifier. It is a bibliographic code though not a frequent topic of study in works on the Hogarth Press beyond a brief mention. There are two versions of the Hogarth Press logo. The first appeared in 1925 and was designed by Vanessa Bell. It is a depiction of a wolf's head, enclosed in a medallion. Kauffer's logo is 'a strong, nearly abstract animal head more like a wolfhound than a wolf but unmistakably bold and modern' (Willis 376). Though still a wolf's head, the new logo is sleek and signals changes at the Press while still associating it with its past. The Hogarth Press logos have a very condensed meaning. The choice of device invites a close association with the people involved, as does the choice of the name Hogarth. Part of the logo's reference is to who the Woolfs are, to

Figure 7.4 Kauffer's Hogarth Press logo. Used by permission of The Random House Group Ltd.

their reputations and imprimatur. Mary Gaither argues the 'fame [the Press] has achieved has been the result of its very close identification with its owners' (xvii), and the choice of device invites the pun 'Woolf's head'.

The Changes of 1928

There is a temporal aspect to advertising. If a large amount of money is spent on advertising, the results often occur after a delay: 'it is the following books by the same author that derive the maximum benefit from any extensive advertising' (Unwin 247). The example of Woolf's novels bears this out. The Press published *To the Lighthouse* in 1927 and it won the Femina Vie Heureuse prize, as well as the Northcliffe prize in 1928. *To the Lighthouse* sold well, but as is often the case after awards and critical acclaim, the next work by the same author sells even better. *Orlando: A Biography* met with major sales success and greatly increased Press profits. The first Hogarth Press print run in October was 5,080 copies, the second impression was 3,000 copies, also in October, and a third impression of 3,000 copies was produced in January (Woolmer 69), far outstripping initial sales of *To the Lighthouse*.

In 1928 the 'success of *Orlando* ha[d] persuaded LW that it might be worthwhile sending [Press employee Richard Kennedy] out into

the wilderness—in other words, the provinces, to sell the Press' books'
(Kennedy 54). The scope of distribution widened in part because
of the success of Woolf's novel. Kennedy travelled to Manchester,
Nottingham, Liverpool, Edinburgh and Glasgow. He notes, 'Sold only
two sets of *Hogarth Lectures on Literature*. These are practically the
only books you can sell here and, of course, *Orlando*: twenty-five copies
of *Orlando*' (Kennedy 57–9). By the mid 1920s Woolf's novels were
generally well received by booksellers.

Significantly, Kauffer's device first appeared in December advertisements in 1928, and it continued to be used for advertising purposes.
This logo was for more commercial purposes, coming from a commercial artist. It was used on the title pages of some books, including Virginia Woolf's posthumously published *The Death of the Moth*
(1942), and it was the central element of the cover design for the Day
to Day Pamphlet series, started in 1930. The series, focusing on current
issues, was a good match for the new-look logo, publishing works such
as Maurice Dobb's *Russia To-Day and To-Morrow* (1930), Henry
Noel Brailsford's *If We Want Peace* (1932) and W. F. Watson's *The
Worker and Wage Incentives* (1934) among the forty titles. Yet where
the logo proliferated was in Press advertisements. Kauffer's device did
not replace Vanessa Bell's device. Bell's logo remained common on
title pages of books. Virginia Woolf's novels, for example, continued
to feature Bell's logo on their title pages in the 1930s. The presence of
dual Press devices emphasises a key element of Hogarth Press aesthetics and practice, that of multiplicity. The Press embraced variation in
book covers within editions, a wide range of print runs (from fewer than
one hundred to tens of thousands) and a broad scope of authors, just
to name a few examples. Like its logo, the Press was multiple and used
more than one symbolic signification: encompassing past and future,
symbolic and economic capital.

It was also in 1928 that the Press first had, according to Leonard, 'a
representative who traveled our books: Alice Ritchie was, I think, the
first woman to travel for a publisher and some booksellers did not like
the innovation' (*Downhill* 169). She was the 'first salaried traveler' and
worked 'on a part-time basis' (Willis 392). Ritchie was also the author
of two Hogarth Press novels, *The Peacemakers* (1928) and *Occupied
Territory* (1930). Acting as the 'publisher's representative', she 'proved
to be a good, if unconventional, commercial traveler, and on the whole
she enjoyed taking [t]he Hogarth Press books round the booksellers and
getting orders from them' (Woolf, *Journey* 173).

Some of the books travelled in 1928 and later had McKnight Kauffer
dust jackets.

Dust Jackets and Book Design

By the mid 1920s many Hogarth Press books came to be bound in cloth, a practice common in British publishing. As Michael Sadleir explains in the Hogarth publication *Books and the Public*,[3] the prevalence of cloth bindings was influenced by the popularity of lending libraries that could not 'for obvious reasons accept wrappered books for continuous circulation'; thus 'the convention of cloth binding' became 'firmly established, and an insistence on cloth-bound books is by now [1927] as characteristic of the bookseller as of the librarian' (43). With cloth binding comes the dust jacket. The dust jacket, 'which began simply as a protective cover for the book and the elegant decorative binding beneath it, has evolved into a vital instrument in publicizing and selling the book, so much so that collectors of modern books attach as much importance to its condition as to that of the rest of the book' (Adams & Barker 21). The first dust jacket dates from 1833, but it 'was not until the 1880s that the provision of jackets became at all common. In the late 1890s the front inner flaps were used for blurbs . . ., relative to the book they enclosed' (Glaister 259). James Beechey notes that before the 1920s '[d]ust-jackets were not commonplace' and 'until then, illustrated covers involved the laborious process of mounting four-colour prints on cloth cases' (16). Because dust jackets are detachable, Gerard Genette considers them 'as appendages to the cover', and 'as if they were constitutively ephemeral, almost inviting the reader to get rid of them after they have fulfilled their function as poster and possibly as protection' (27). In part because the dust jacket is detachable and ephemeral it often becomes rare and therefore valuable. Dust jackets now exponentially increase the cost of books for book collectors.

The dust jacket has 'a dual message: advertising for the book itself and a signal of recognition for the publishing house' (Greengard 97). It is analogous to a logo in a number of ways. Though there was not a house style, Vanessa Bell 'was the most prolific designer to work for the Hogarth Press, and she created what became almost its house style' (Beechey 18). She designed covers for series publications as well as individual authors – including Henry Green, Edward Upward and Susan Buchan – and of course she designed the first and much-used wolf's head logo. Her work became part of a triangular cross-referencing association linked to both Virginia Woolf and to the Hogarth Press. The production of covers was a collaborative process between the Woolfs, Press employees and outside artists; quite a few different artists were involved in their production and many have received little attention. Cover designers include Duncan Grant, John Banting,[4] Richard Kennedy, Trekkie Ritchie, John

Armstrong, Dora Carrington, Ronald Grierson, Quentin Bell, Eugene McCown, Enid Marx and Robert Medley, as well as Kauffer. The people involved in Press design were often both friends of the Woolfs and noted professionals, a combination that suited the Press well.

The first dust jacket done by the Press was Bell's design for Woolf's *Jacob's Room* in 1922. It was famously 'almost universally condemned by the booksellers, and several of the buyers laughed at it' because it was what 'in 1923 many people would have called reproachfully post-impressionist' (Woolf, *Downhill* 76). Hogarth Press dust jackets drew on a mixture of styles and they too were difficult to pin down and categorise. Some books were more akin to fine printing, some moved towards convention, and others, like much of the material contained in them, looked, and were, experimental and even avant-garde. Kennedy notes that when travelling Hogarth Press books in 1928, there was still resistance to the unconventional dust jackets. He records, the buyers 'don't like our covers and say the public don't like them' (Kennedy 60).

Looking at dust jackets collectively can also reveal concerns with trends and issues of the day in a way that only the titles of works may not. David Porter notes that a number of Hogarth Press dust jackets from the 1930s 'respond—as do so many Hogarth Press books of the time—to the Woolfs' keen awareness of the growing threat of fascism' (8). He specifically cites Kauffer's jacket for Leonard Woolf's *Quack, Quack!* (1935) (Fig. 7.5) that depicts an image of Adolf Hitler saluting (more on this below).

The cover for Libby Benedict's *The Refugees* (1938) features swastikas; the cover of Wilfred Benson's 1930 novel *As You Were* depicts men in army uniforms. Kauffer himself was increasingly concerned with the social implications of his work in the 1930s. He 'saw his work as a healing art, the more effective as it was part and parcel of ordinary business transactions. He even saw the enlightening commerce between artist and public as obstructed only by conscience-less, badly directed, commerce' (Haworth-Booth 84). He saw his work performing an important social function, grounded and connected in ways that 'pure' painters were not.

For Kauffer the 'poster (or the book jacket, which for him was a mini-poster) was designed to be interpreted rather than accepted at face value' (Heller 5). Kauffer helped to pioneer 'the essential Modern poster with its symbolic imagery and sparse selling copy' (Heller 2) and this aesthetic is also applicable to his book design. The first dust jacket he designed for the Hogarth Press was for George Rylands *Words and Poetry* in 1928 (Fig. 7.6).

In 1935 he designed the striking cover for Leonard Woolf's *Quack,*

Figure 7.5   Dust jacket for *Quack, Quack!* (1935). Used by permission of The Random House Group Ltd.

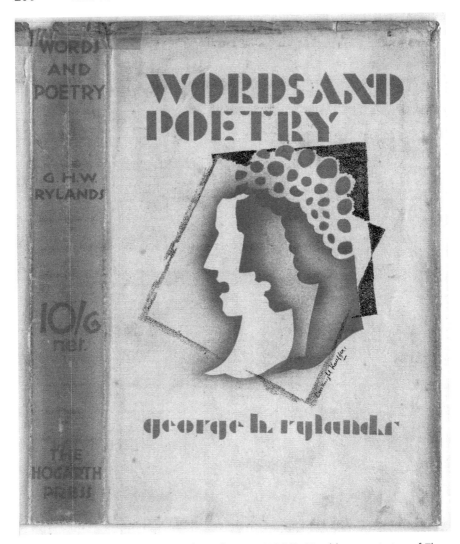

Figure 7.6   Dust jacket for *Words and Poetry* (1928). Used by permission of The Random House Group Ltd.

Quack![5] In this same year Kauffer also designed the jacket for H. G. Wells' *Things to Come*, the design for which 'draws on Sir Alexander Korda's film version of H. G. Wells' futuristic text, *The Shape of Things to Come*' (Haworth-Booth 68). Kauffer's jackets continued to be innovative and striking. In subsequent years Kauffer designed two more dust jackets for the Hogarth Press: R. M. Fox's *Smoky Crusade* (1937) and H. T. Hopkinson's *The Man Below* (1939) (Fig. 7.7). His designs are abstract, using bright colours to create an image recognisable as his own. Sabrina Abid and Pearl McHaney note, 'the design features contributing to the successful signature "McKnight Kauffer" style are evident in Kauffer's dust jackets: bold color blocks, contrast, geometric shapes, slanted lines, silhouettes, distinctive but not distracting lettering' (Abid & McHaney 4). Kauffer's other dust jacket designs of the 1930s and later include those for John Betjeman's *Continental Dew* (1937), Herbert Read's *Art Now* and many titles for Modern Library including Hemingway's *The Sun Also Rises*, Faulkner's *Light in August*, Huxley's *Point Counter Point* and D. H. Lawrence's *Women in Love*. In addition to the Hogarth Press, Kauffer designed dust jackets for 'Alfred Knopf, Harcourt Brace, Harper Brothers, Random House and Pantheon Books' (Abid & McHaney 4). Thus, Kauffer visually draws the Hogarth Press into connection with other publishers and authors.

By 1931 Kauffer was painting again and work for a 1931 show was done during 'a stay at Clive Bell's villa behind Cassis' (Haworth-Booth 78). He continued looking for new techniques and artists, introducing the 'German graphic designer Hans Schleger, professionally known as Zero, to British design circles' (Haworth-Booth 68). Kauffer also continued his commercial designs, working for Jack Beddington the 'director responsible for publicity' (Haworth-Booth 76) at Shell-Mex BP Ltd. He produced 'a whole series of 'lorry bills' (Haworth-Booth 80), posters displayed on the sides of Shell trucks. Kauffer continued to produce across a range of genres and in an array of media, but as his career progressed he became increasingly praised, recognised by official organisations. In the 1930s he became an Honorary Fellow of the Society of Industrial Artists, a Council member for the Council for Art and Industry, joined the Advisory Council of the Victoria and Albert Museum and became in 1936 'the first Honorary Designer for Industry, chosen by the Royal Society of Arts. This title was intended to provide designers with professional recognition comparable to the Royal Academicians. The faculty soon received permission to add Royal to the title' (Haworth-Booth 74). In some circles he had reached the peak of recognition, imbuing credibility to the whole field of graphic design and industrial art. *The Scotsman*, in 1935, labelled Kauffer 'the Picasso of advertising design' (qtd in Haworth-Booth 68), and yet the amount of recognition, discussion and critical attention that Kauffer receives continues to assert the difference in valuation of commercial and 'pure' artists. Similarly, we can see a disproportionate focus on the hand-printed books and famous titles published by the Hogarth Press over the popular, political and more obscure publications.

Figure 7.7   Dust jacket for *The Man Below* (1939). Used by permission of The Random House Group Ltd.

Looking at the Hogarth Press together with E. McKnight Kauffer reciprocally illuminates the designer and the publishing institution. Present in Kauffer's wolf's head logo are contrasts and points of convergence within a number of the debates surrounding commerce and art at the time. In adding his aesthetic presence Kauffer connects the Press to a new network of associations and foregrounds porous boundaries. His contributions signalled a shift, but it was not a break with the past. The Hogarth Press changed in 1928: Kauffer's work was both cause and effect, a new element and what the Press had always done.

Notes

1. In the iconic 1981 mini-series *Brideshead Revisited*, starring Jeremy Irons, Ryder's rooms include a poster depicting one of Kauffer's advertisements for the London Underground. The poster would be contemporary with the 1923 setting.
2. For a discussion of modernist brands and the use of letterheads see Jaffe 90–3.
3. In addition to *Books and the Public*, which features chapters by J. M. Keynes, Stanley Unwin, Basil Blackwell and Leonard Woolf, as well as Sadleir and others, the Press published a number of books and pamphlets on the topics of art, commerce and the book industry. One of the earlier titles was Fry's *Art and Commerce* (1926). Other titles include Hubert Waley's *The Revival of Aesthetics* (1926), E. E. Kellett's *The Whirligig of Taste* (1929) and Graham Bell's *The Artist and His Public* (1939).
4. For further discussion of Banting's contributions to the Press see Buck.
5. Correspondence between Kauffer and Leonard Woolf regarding the cover design for the book reveals a tension between striking artistic design that Kauffer called 'different and to the point' (5 April 1935) and what Leonard stated was the 'too serious' nature of the book's content (8 April 1935). Kauffer's first design, based on the mask illustration from the book, was found to be 'unsuitable', though 'simply superb'; Leonard instead asks for a photo-montage, stating it would 'be the most suitable form, although it will not be half as effective as your design' (8 April 1935). In a subsequent letter Leonard mentions he has suggested the first jacket design to Donald Brace for use in the Harcourt Brace edition of *Quack, Quack!* published in America. Leonard claims that Kauffer's more avant-garde design is more to his taste (17 April 1935), yet it is not suitable for a British audience. In this case, the commercial artist's design was too avant-garde for the Press.

Works cited

Abid, Sabrina and Pearl McHaney. 'Author and Artist: Welty and Edward McKnight Kauffer'. *Eurdora Welty Newsletter* 31.2, [2007], 10 February 2008 <http:www2.gsu.edu/~wwwewn.htm>.

Adams, Thomas R. and Nicolas Barker. 'A New Model for the Study of the Book'. In Nicolas Barker, ed. *A Potencie of Life: Books in Society*. London: British Library, 2001: 5–43.

Beechey, James. 'Introduction'. In Tony Bradshaw. *The Bloomsbury Artists: Prints and Book Design*. Aldershot: Scolar Press, 1999: 2–24.

Bennett, Arnold. *Elsie and the Child*. London: Cassell, 1929.

Bourdieu, Pierre. *The Field of Cultural Production: Essays on Art and Literature*. Ed. Randal Johnson. New York: Columbia University Press, 1993.

Buck, Louisa. 'John Banting's Designs for The Hogarth Press'. *The Burlington Magazine* 127.983, 1985: 88–92.

Drucker, Johanna. 'Who's Afraid of Visual Culture?' *Art Journal* 58.4, 1999: 36–47.

Eliot, T. S. *Journey of the Magi*. London: Faber and Faber, 1927.

Elliott, Bridget and Jo-Ann Wallace. *Women Artists and Writers: Modernist (im)positionings*. New York: Routledge, 1994.

Fry, Roger. *Art and Commerce*. London: Hogarth Press, 1926.

—. 'The Author and the Artist'. *The Burlington Magazine for Connoisseurs* 49.280, 1926: 9–12.

Gaither, Mary. 'Introduction'. In Woolmer: xvii-xxxiv.

Genette, Gerard. *Paratexts: Thresholds of Interpretation*. Trans. Jane E. Lewin. Cambridge: Cambridge University Press, 1997.

Gilmour, Pat. *Artists at Curwen*. London: Tate Gallery, 1977.

Glaister, Geoffrey Ashall. *Encyclopedia of the Book*. 2nd edn. New Castle: Oak Knoll Press, 1996.

Greengard, Steven. 'Cover Story'. *The Journal of Decorative and Propaganda Arts* 7, 1988: 96–109.

Haworth-Booth, Mark. *E. McKnight Kauffer: a designer and his public*. London: V & A publications, [1979] 2005.

Heller, Steven. 'The Essential Modernist'. *The American Institute of Graphic Arts* (AIGA), 20 January 2008. <http://www.aiga.org/content.cfm/medalist-emcknightkauffer>.

Hewitt, John. 'Posters of Distinction: Art, Advertising and the London, Midland, and Scottish Railways'. *Design Issues* 16.1, 2000: 16–35.

Jaffe, Aaron. *Modernism and the Culture of Celebrity*. Cambridge: Cambridge University Press, 2005.

Kauffer, E. McKnight. Letter to Leonard Woolf. 5 April 1935. Hogarth Press Files. University of Reading Library, Reading.

Kennedy, Richard. *A Boy at the Hogarth Press*. London: Heinemann Educational Books, 1972.

Mao, Douglas and Rebecca Walkowitz, eds. 'Introduction "Modernisms Bad and New"'. In *Bad Modernisms*. Durham: Duke University Press, 2006: 1–18.

Melville, Herman. *Benito Cereno*. London: Nonesuch Press, 1926.

Porter, David H. *Virginia Woolf and the Hogarth Press: 'riding a great horse'*. London: Cecil Woolf, 2004.

Preston, John and Eric Arch. *Advertising, Printing and Art in Commerce*. London: Chapman & Hall, 1927.

Sadleir, Michael. 'Ambiguities of the Book Trade: The Literary Agent, The

Circulating Library'. In *Books and the Public*. London: Hogarth Press, 1927: 31–44.

Steinberg, S. H. *Five Hundred Years of Printing*. Harmondsworth: Penguin, [1955] 1974.

Unwin, Stanley. *The Truth About Publishing*. London: Allen & Unwin, [1926] 1960.

Waugh, Evelyn. *Brideshead Revisited*. London: Penguin, [1945] 2003.

Willis, J. H. *Leonard and Virginia Woolf as Publishers: The Hogarth Press, 1917–41*. Charlottesville: University Press of Virginia, 1992.

Woolf, Leonard. *Downhill All the Way: An Autobiography of the Years 1919 to 1939*. London: Hogarth Press, 1967.

—. *The Journey not the Arrival Matters: An Autobiography of the Years 1939 to 1969*. London: Hogarth Press, 1969.

—. Letter to E. McKnight Kauffer. 8 April 1935. Hogarth Press Files. University of Reading Library, Reading.

—. Letter to E. McKnight Kauffer. 17 April 1935. Hogarth Press Files. University of Reading Library, Reading.

—. (LWP) Leonard Woolf Papers, University of Sussex Library, Brighton.

Woolmer, J. Howard. *A Checklist of the Hogarth Press 1917–1946*. Revere: Woolmer/Brotherson, 1986.

Chapter 8

'Going Over': The Woolfs, the Hogarth Press and Working-Class Voices

Helen Southworth

In his study of the Hogarth Press, J. H. Willis distinguishes between the 'worldly affairs' associated with Leonard Woolf and the 'fields of literature, art, and biography associated with Virginia Woolf' (212). Separate chapters examine 'Pamphlets and Politics' and 'Freud and Freudians' in a study otherwise focused on the literary output of the Press, this despite the fact that close to half of the approximately 450 works published between 1917 and 1941 were not literary. In this chapter I question the line drawn by Willis, and argue for a connection between the socio-political work and the literature published by the Press and, by extension, between the editing work and the ideologies of Leonard and Virginia Woolf. With a focus on the British worker, whose presence in Hogarth Press publications is revealed to be substantial in his or her capacity as subject, as author and as reader, this chapter explores the efforts of both Leonard and Virginia Woolf to 'go over'. I borrow Valentine Cunningham's metaphor for 'the sense [in the 1930s] of being in transit or transition . . . particularly into new poetic and political country' (211).[1] Although Leonard Woolf's commitment to the welfare of the working man and woman is clear, most obviously in terms of his work with the British Labour Party, but neglected by critics, Virginia Woolf's relationship to working-class authors and audiences is complicated by an avowed reluctance on her part to speak for a segment of the population to which she had little access and of which she had limited knowledge. That the Hogarth Press provided Leonard and Virginia Woolf an opportunity to bridge 'the gulf' separating an old world 'divided by hedges' from a new 'world without classes and towers' represents the focus of this study (Virginia Woolf, 'The Leaning Tower' 30–1). I argue further that it offers a fascinating context in terms of which to re-examine questions about the Woolfs', and more generally the early-twentieth-century London publishing establishment's relationship with and marketing of working-class authors.

An omission from books about the reading and writing of the British working class is discussion of Leonard Woolf's political career and his work at the Hogarth Press to promote the cause of working people, work that to some degree cost him his career as a novelist.[2] In his *British Writers of the Thirties*, Cunningham does not mention Leonard Woolf in his capacity as Hogarth Press editor, in part because his subject is literature. Explicit reference to the Press and Leonard Woolf is similarly missing from Jonathan Rose's book about the 'intellectual lives' of the British working classes and Christopher Hilliard's book about how working-class and lower-middle class writers came to writing, this despite the fact that Hilliard identifies John Lehmann, Hogarth Press apprentice (1931–2) and later co-editor, as 'the most successful supporter of working-class fiction' in the 1930s (130). Rose accuses Leonard Woolf of 'shar[ing] his wife's snobberies', citing a single passage about the class of a co-worker in Ceylon from the first volume of Leonard Woolf's autobiography (401–2). In both Cunningham and Hilliard, Virginia Woolf is quoted repeatedly, but in neither case is a clear assessment made of her contribution; she receives negative treatment in Rose in this regard (see 431–3).

When the Woolfs launched the Hogarth Press in 1917 with the mandate to publish writers of merit who might not otherwise find a publisher, it seems clear that they intended to include those whose working-class origins or whose distance from London meant that they did not have the credentials or the networks available to their middle-class, metropolitan counterparts. Close scrutiny of the list reveals that the Woolfs were quite successful in this regard. Leonard Woolf was involved, beginning in 1912, with the Cooperative Movement and Margaret Llewelyn Davies, and in this context produced his book *Cooperation and the Future of Industry* (Allen & Unwin, 1919). Later he took up with the Fabians and the British Labour Party, and worked on publications such as the *New Statesman*, *Political Quarterly* and the *Nation*. In this way he was ideally placed to access new writing talent. Indeed, in his autobiography, Woolf explains how he used his literary editorship at the *Nation* as a means of providing financial support to potential Hogarth Press writers via book review assignments, allowing him to 'try . . . out [an unknown writer] with articles and reviews before encouraging him to write a book' (*Downhill* 130).

Among these new writers was Orcadian poet and literary critic Edwin Muir (1887–1959) whom Leonard Woolf describes as doing the kind of writing for which the Hogarth Press existed (*Downhill* 131). Woolf singles out Muir's long poem 'Chorus of the Newly Dead' (1926), although the Press also published his *First Poems* in 1925. Muir was the son of a farmer and later a socialist, whose work Woolf likely discovered in the *New Age*, to where he was 'recruited first in 1913 [by *New Age* editor A. R. Orage], when working as a wretchedly paid clerk in a Glasgow beer-bottling plant' (Carswell 122). For Woolf, Muir was 'a real, a natural poet; he did not just "write poetry," the sap of poetry was in his bones and veins, in his heart and brain' (*Downhill* 131). Muir and his wife Willa Muir, whose *Women: An Inquiry* (1925) the Hogarth Press also published, were 'real' people, according to Leonard Woolf: 'They both came from Orkney. An aura of gentleness, soft sea air, the melancholy of the remote islands set in turbulent seas surrounded them' (*Downhill* 132).[3] Muir stayed exclusively with the Press between 1925 and 1928 and in so doing contributed to the Woolfs' efforts to aid up-and-coming writers with which they began their work as publishers.[4] Muir also provided the Hogarth Press with an opportunity to move outside of what Lehmann has called 'the magic (and tyrannical) triangle of London-Oxford-Cambridge' in terms of his own efforts in the late 1930s with projects such as the literary journal *New Writing*, published in the late 1930s and early 40s by the Hogarth Press (*In My Own Time* 170).

'The Other Chap's Point of View'

Beginning in the mid 1920s, at about the same time as Muir embarked on his relationship with the Woolfs, the Hogarth Press published a series of works on domestic issues, and specifically the British mining and manufacturing industries. In this cluster of books a desire for authenticity, a wish to hear from those 'writing from the inside' emerges, similar to that voiced by Leonard Woolf in terms of Muir, as works become less academic and more autobiographical and their authors more diverse and from further afield (Lehmann, *IMOT* 167). This shift can be explained by the fact that, over the course of the 1920s, the Hogarth Press was becoming better known and, therefore, was receiving and publishing a higher volume of submissions; however, the selection of these texts also reflects the Woolfs' efforts, which I will show reached across categories at the Press, to bring different voices to readers and to create a dialogue between the impoverished north of England and the more affluent south, which was comparable to their attempts to bring colonial voices to the metropolitan centre. These titles also demonstrate that the Hogarth Press had become known as a viable entry point onto the London scene for provincial and working-class writers.

One of the earliest socio-political pieces focused on a domestic subject to appear at the Hogarth Press was Kingsley Martin's *The British Public*

and the General Strike in 1926.[5] This was the first of a number of publications concerned with the coal industry and the 1926 General Strike,
including in part Leonard Woolf's own 1931 study of communal psychology, *After the Deluge*, in which he reveals his support for the miners
in a section on how patriotism was used during the strike to rally support
for the mine owners (298–320).[6] Significantly, in her recent book on
modernism, labour and selfhood (which ends with an analysis in terms
of the General Strike of the 'Time Passes' section of Virginia Woolf's
1927 novel *To the Lighthouse*, composed as the strike was taking place)
Morag Shiach identifies the General Strike as 'integral' to 'the imagination and the experience of human labour in the early years of the twentieth century' (200). The Hogarth Press' treatment of the General Strike
in particular, and questions of labour in general, support Shiach's claim.

The General Strike is a scholarly assessment of the 'social philosophy'
surrounding the strike and of the newspapers' treatment of the strike
and the strikers. The 'aim' of Martin's short book is 'to discover what
issues were really involved in the strike and offer[] some suggestions as
to its significance in the mental history of the nation' (10). In his ironic
introduction, Martin condemns the cowardice of the British middle
classes in terms of their failure to orchestrate change in the wake of
the General Strike. 'English people prefer to face a problem rather in
terms of power than in terms of philosophy' (12), he suggests, and the
English 'instinctive[ly] avoid[] . . . actions involving unnecessary pain to
[themselves]' (15). Strongly critical of the celebration of the strike's end
as a victory for all, Martin warns that the British public's conception of
themselves as a 'common-sense sporting people' is no longer appropriate
to the crisis at hand (16).

Martin was a Cambridge graduate and a part-time lecturer at the
London School of Economics when he published *The General Strike*.
He subsequently wrote for the *Manchester Guardian* (1927–30) and
was editor at the *New Statesman* (1930–60). He became an ally of
John Maynard Keynes and Leonard Woolf and also George Bernard
Shaw and Harold Laski; however, despite his status as an insider to
Bloomsbury and an outsider to the British Midlands, Martin's sympathy
for the miners and his strong condemnation of England as a 'pietistic
middle-class country' suggest a keen sense of the dangers of a divided
nation (16). In his 1966 autobiography, Martin makes clear the anti-
establishment quality of what he admits 'was a youthful [but nonetheless heartfelt] production', when he describes the reprimand he received
for it from LSE director William Beveridge, himself a member of the
Samuel Coal Commission (*Father Figures* 163).

Coal: A Challenge to the National Conscience followed Martin's book a year later in 1927. Alan Porter was a poet and psychologist, contributor to the *New Age* as well as other periodicals, as were his co-authors, V. A. Demant, Philippe Mairet, Maurice B. Reckitt, Albert Newsome, Egerton Swann and W. T. Symons. The Chandos Group (so named for the restaurant in which they met), of which these individuals formed the nucleus, came together for the first time, according to Reckitt, in May of 1926 'with the purpose of taking the social credit doctrines [of Major C. H. Douglas] upon which they agreed not as a panacea, but as an economic technique to serve as the basis of a new and eclectic social criticism and synthesis' (190).[7] The writing of *Coal*, spurred, the opening anecdote suggests, by the failure of the General Strike to effect any real changes, was their first cooperative effort.

Coal's emphasis on the national conscience, its co-authorship, and its manifesto-like introduction set the tenor for the kind of work produced in the society and politics category by the Woolfs. Echoing Martin, the book sounds a call to arms, emphasising communal action and the conjoining of 'analysis and creativeness' as a means to make of 'this mean and miserable twentieth century . . . a heroic age, an age of great culture, of a great prosperity, of a great peace' (8–9). Despite their call for collective action and for systematic reform, like Martin, *Coal*'s authors acknowledge the persistence of a line separating them and us: 'we are agreed that sympathy should go most to those who bear the brunt of our social, economic, and industrial difficulties . . .' (8). In 'The Failure of Will', Porter et al. describe 'our social segregation' as 'alarming, if we were still capable of being alarmed', and they continue: 'It is difficult to see "the other chap's point of view" if one has never set eyes on him, much less had speech with him. And how many of London's millions have ever had five minutes' talk with a miner, or even had one good look at a mining village or a mine?' (49).

'Shooting Bravely in the Unregarded Corners of this Country'

The publication of B[en] Bowker's study of the textile industry, *Lancashire Under the Hammer*, in 1928, the only book he published, signals a change of direction at the Hogarth Press away from the outsider-academic's metropolitan or southern perspective on the industrial North. The autobiographical quality of journalist Bowker's dramatic opening statement contrasts strikingly with that of Martin and Porter et al. and inaugurates a series of works in the politics and society category that feature the voices of insiders. Bowker begins:

I was born with the sour smell of tape size in my nostrils. The harsh discords of hundreds of running looms were the music of my youth. I am as cursed with cotton in my blood as any 'little-piecer' who ever lived in Oldham, or any man who ever wore a top-hat on the floor of Manchester Royal Exchange. (9)

From here, Bowker builds a romantic portrait of the rise of the cotton industry in the north, calling Lancashire men and women 'cotton proud' (13), and a tragic portrait of its demise, overwhelmed by competition from overseas. Bowker is clear about his audience: he has no need to tell Lancashire men what happened, but rather his intent is to 'enlighten the stranger' (10). He aims not to deride local men who made their fortune from the textile industry; 'they no more merit derision than a dozen Oxford and Cambridge men I have met, who all their lives have lived and still live richly out of cotton without at any time giving it an hour of their muscles or a thought of their brains.' His purpose is to prevent a second crash by showing 'the magically easy way wealth rolled in on Lancashire' and then out again (11).

Two subsequent titles, Margaret Llewelyn Davies' *Life as we have known it* (1931) and C. T. Cramp's *The Workers' Point of View: A Symposium* (1933), like Bowker's *Lancashire*, incorporate first-hand, insider accounts. Both of these pieces, like Porter's *Coal*, represent cooperative efforts. Llewelyn Davies' book consists of a collection of letters from Guildswomen, with experience as domestic servants or as miners' wives, for example, describing their daily lives, their involvement with the cooperative movement and, in a separate section, their reading. Putting front and centre the question of how to bridge the divide between the working classes and the middle classes, the collection is prefaced with an apologetic letter from Virginia Woolf to Llewelyn Davies – one of Woolf's best-known essays on the working class – in which she confesses to 'the contradictory and complex feelings which beset the middle-class visitor', to the Congress of working women, her sympathy for the women she meets inevitably 'fictitious' not 'real' (xxxi, xxx). The collection of autobiographical fragments, Woolf's letter suggests, represents Llewelyn Davies' effort to respond to this anxiety:

> Sometimes, you said, you got a letter which you could not bring yourself to burn; once or twice a Guildswoman had at your suggestion written a few pages about her life. It might be that we should find these papers interesting; that if we read them the women would cease to be symbols and would become instead individuals. (xxix)

Significantly, to Llewelyn Davies' fear that the middle-class visitor might find these fragments 'crude' and her anxiety that to 'expose [these writings] to the other eyes [might be] a breach of confidence', Woolf responds to the contrary, emphasising the importance of having working-class women speak for themselves: 'even if she [does not know how to write]' and this is unlikely, Woolf thinks, 'she has only to take her own life for subject and write the truth about that and not fiction or poetry for our interest to be so keenly roused that—that in short we cannot wait and must read the packet at once' (xxix–xxx).

Cramp's collection includes a series of articles which highlight 'the need for treatment of the worker as a human being rather than a machine', and which show 'the importance of an understanding of human motives and reactions on the part of those directing industry' ('Introductory Note'). These articles had been previously published in the National Institute of Industrial Psychology's (NIIP) journal *The Human Factor*. In his introduction, Cramp, the General Secretary of the National Union of Railways, argues that it is an opportune moment for us to hear 'the point of view of those who are the most numerous of the community'. While there are differences 'in temperament and disposition', he asserts that 'certain broad generalizations . . . can be adopted as a guide to [the worker's] general attitude towards life and the times in which he lives.' Echoing the concern voiced in Llewelyn Davies' volume that there is a divide that needs to be bridged, Cramp contrasts the impulsive way in which 'the academic socialist of the university type' examines an economic problem to the more conservative method deployed by 'an "advanced" trade unionist' (9).

While the contributions are not as raw as those included by Llewelyn Davies, most of the writers have 'written articles' or are now journalists or investigators for the NIIP, all have a background in mining or manufacturing, among them J. H. Mitchell, who 'began work underground as a haulage boy at 14' (48) and John Gibson, a plasterer with a background in a wide range of manual jobs, this information provided in biographical statements prefacing each essay. The last contribution is by former mineral-water factory worker, Yorkshireman Roger Dataller. Dataller represents a bridge between the north and south of England in his capacity as a recipient of a Miners' Welfare Scholarship to Oxford in 1928 and author of *From a Pitman's Notebook* (Cape 1925) and *A Pitman Looks at Oxford* (Dent 1933). A third title, *Oxford into Coalfield* (Dent 1934), which contains discussion of the reception of Woolf's work in Dataller's mining-village classroom, reminds us of the different kinds of networks tying Hogarth Press contributors to their writer-editors. In response to Woolf's now famous statement that ' "genius like Shakespeare's is not born among labouring, uneducated, servile people, indeed, is not born to-day among the working classes" ' (*A Room of*

One's Own qtd in Dataller 198–9), Dataller notes that while he has not 'seen' 'accomplishment in great literature', he has encountered 'the wonderful possibility of that literature nipped by economic necessity, shrivelled by domestic *misalliance*, but still shooting bravely in the unregarded corners of this country' (199).

Thomas Sharp contributed *A Derelict Area: A Study of the South-West Durham Coalfield* to the Press' Day to Day Pamphlet series in 1935.[8] Like Dataller, Sharp is motivated by a desire to provide 'the other chap's point of view'. Sharp (1901–78) knew his subject well. Born into a mining family in County Durham, after apprenticing as a surveyor he moved south to Margate and began his career as a town planner (Stansfield 150). His study of an area designated as 'derelict', one 'forsaken by the "captains of industry" who developed and owned [it]' (14), is aimed at readers 'in those comfortable parts of England, which are remote, both in space and mind, from South-West Durham' (7). In the closing section of his pamphlet, under the title 'The Future', Sharp laments misconceptions about northerners. 'For centuries all over the world the miner has been regarded as a member of a race apart from the general run of humankind, a violent, savage creature, labouring darkly in fantastic places' and he concludes that even now '[t]he miner is about as much understood as if he lived in the South Sea Islands' (41). Highlighting the degree to which literature represents an important tool in terms of shaping and changing views of the north of England, although it is often inadequate because it is outdated, Sharp describes how D. H. Lawrence's early stories about miners are used to get 'a glimpse . . . into the dark unknown' and how a miner who visits Russia or receives a scholarship to Oxford 'is regarded . . . as a living miracle, in much the same way as an Australian Bushman would be if he did the same thing' (41).

Rejecting 'Literature in the Political Manifesto Stage'

A repeat contributor to the politics and society category at the Hogarth Press, R. M. Fox (1891–1969) would have been stereotyped as just such a 'living miracle'. The Hogarth Press published three titles by Fox over ten years, the first, *The Triumphant Machine*, alongside Bowker's book in 1928, and the last, an autobiography, in 1937.[9] Raised in London, the child of a 'skilled engineering workman' and a headmistress, Fox left school at fourteen and 'was flung into industrial life', a move, he writes, motivated more by pride than money (*Smoky Crusade* 10, 9, 11). Delayed in taking up a cooperative scholarship at Ruskin College,

Oxford due to the advent of World War I, Fox became an active socialist, began to write and was jailed as a conscientious objector. In 1922 he moved to Ireland, the homeland of his wife, Patricia Lynch, young suffragist and later best known as a writer of children's fiction, and there became involved in Irish politics.

Following a similar trajectory to that described above, Fox's work at the Hogarth Press became increasingly autobiographical. *The Triumphant Machine* (parts of which had appeared in journals such as the *New Statesman* and *The Nineteenth Century and After*) is an analysis of the detrimental harnessing of man to machine in the contemporary factory. In his indictment of modern industrial practices, based on first-hand experience as a factory worker, Fox asserts that '[t]he need for beauty in industrial life is far more pressing than many realise' (5). And he calls for greater attention to what 'we may see apart from the restricted workshop arena', that is, 'a whole stream of thought finding expression in art, in literature, in drama, which stresses human values—the need for freedom, for personal expression and for beauty' (148). This first title includes an introduction by H. N. Brailsford (later himself a Hogarth Press author) in which he credits Fox with 'the gift of enabling those of us who have escaped this experience in our lives, to understand what a boy of the working-class feels as he is "broken in" to the discipline of the factory' (vii). Fox followed *The Triumphant Machine* in 1930 with *Drifting Men*, a collection of first-person literary sketches, portraits of 'rootless vagabonds' (1), immigrants and prisoners. In their marketing of the book the Woolfs highlighted the 'section on prison life . . . for the light it throws on the treatment of conscientious objectors' (Hogarth Press order form). Gerald Gould of *The Observer* noted the difficulty of the task undertaken by Fox: '[t]o write about the "underdog", the "down-and-out", is to run the risk of mawkishness on the one hand and churlishness on the other. Between these dangers', he continues, 'Mr Fox, sincere, unsentimental, clear-eyed, pitiless in delineation of fact and pitiful in understanding, keeps the true artist's way' (qtd on Hogarth Press order form).[10] Fox's autobiography, *Smoky Crusade*, appeared in 1937, alongside George Orwell's *The Road to Wigan Pier* (Gollancz) and the birth of the Mass-Observation project.[11] Confirming the Woolfs' interest in Fox's workplace experience, in a letter expressing the Press' willingness to publish the autobiography, Leonard singles out as 'excellent' the 'factory part', while recommending other topics be cut (Leonard Woolf to R. M. Fox, 9 August 1936). Heightening its documentary quality, the book is prefaced with a photograph of Fox as a young man with the title 'In the Workshop' (Fig. 8.1).

Figure 8.1 'In the Workshop'. Frontispiece for Fox's *Smoky Crusade*. Courtesy of Manuscripts, Archives and Special Collections, Washington State University. Used by permission of The Random House Group Ltd.

Opening up the socio-political to the literary side of the Press, using the more easily accessed side of the Press as a means to start talking about an arena conventionally less open to the working-class writer, in his first Hogarth Press title, which is prefaced with a poem by Irish poet A. E., Fox includes two chapters on literature. Rejecting 'literature in the political manifesto stage' as neither literature nor working class, he insists rather that '[t]he literature of the wage-earners only reaches maturity when it ceases to be pitched in an wholly aggressive key and expresses the life of the workers as something of intrinsic worth and interest apart from polemical purpose' (85). He recommends a change of venue for working-class literature in a passage that resonates with Woolf's description of fictional writer Mary Carmichael's new subjects and new spaces in *A Room of One's Own*, itself conceived in 1928 and published a year later in October 1929 (88). In so doing Fox, like Dataller, highlights the degree to which the socio-political works of the Press might be read as in conversation with Virginia Woolf's writing:

> A literature dealing with the cottage, not the hall; the tenement, not the drawing-room; the workshop, not the life of leisure—and viewing all life from this new angle—is what is meant by working-class literature. Such a literature cannot be confined to the workshop for it is not only or chiefly with the worker as a worker, but with the worker as a man or woman that we are beginning to be pre-occupied. (86)

With these comments Fox addresses the tension between the leftist, usually metropolitan, publisher's desire to see the worker produce a polemical literature or 'a literature of socialism' and the worker's preference to be represented in a broader context, or, put another way, between what the south of England wants to hear and what the north has to say.[12] In this way, Fox brings a version of the difficulty of accessing 'the other chap's point of view' (the 'two nations' problem), a central concern for the socio-political publications at the Hogarth Press, into the arena of literature in comments which usefully frame the Press' interaction with working-class fiction writers beginning in the late 1920s. Fox's assessment constitutes a challenge to the Woolfs and other London publishers, as early as 1928, to handle working-class authors in a less dogmatic way. This was a challenge he implicitly repeated when reviewing Woolf's *Orlando* (1928) for *The Irish Statesman* shortly after the appearance of his first book with the Hogarth Press. Citing a rich passage from the frozen Thames scene, Fox praises the novel for its capacity to capture 'the essential qualities of [the] centuries with their changing tones and colours'. He closes his short review of what is generally considered among Woolf's least down-to-earth pieces, perhaps making an overture to readers who might not usually read Woolf's work, with an appreciation of 'the common stuff of life' which, he suggests, the reader 'discover[s]' 'behind this pageantry of the ages'.

'Waiter Playwright', 'Soup server's startling success'

A claim of so consistent a commitment to the promotion of working-class voices is not so easily made in terms of the novels and poetry published at the Hogarth Press as it is in the politics and society category. One needs to broaden one's scope and to consider the effort to reach the 'common reader', as does Melba Cuddy-Keane in her *Virginia Woolf, the Intellectual and the Public Sphere*, to fully comprehend the Woolfs' attempts made in this regard. Competition in the 1930s for working-class fiction writers from other presses, especially those known for their left-wing politics such as Martin Lawrence, later Lawrence and Wishart (1936–), and a lack of appropriate networks before Lehmann came to the Press for the first time in 1931, meant that the Hogarth Press might not have been the first choice for a working-class writer. Several working-class fiction writers did, however, find their way to the Hogarth Press in advance of Lehmann and in advance of the Auden generation manifestoes and collections *New Signatures* (1932) and *New Country* (1933). Among the earliest were Birmingham Group novelist John Hampson (1901–55) and Welsh collier poet Huw Menai (1888–1961). The careers of these now largely forgotten writers dramatise the complications faced by the working-class writer of fiction in terms of source material, content and audience. Their publishing histories suggest the dangers run by the provincial writer courting the metropolitan press in ways that resonate with Fox's assessment of the state of working-class fiction and with the ideas voiced about the disconnect between the north and south in the politics and society category at the Press. A consideration of Hampson's and Menai's involvement with the Woolfs shows the Hogarth Press, like other metropolitan presses of the period, engaged in complex ways with questions related to the marketing and promotion of working-class writing. It reveals the Woolfs' attempts to create a space via their press from where working-class fiction writers might speak for themselves.

In 1928 John Hampson (John Hampson Simpson) submitted his first novel to the Hogarth Press under the title *Go Seek a Stranger*. Hampson's novel is a candid portrait of the trials of Alec, a gay, working-class man and an aspiring writer whose sexual orientation sees him forced from job to job and from city to city until he settles in the company of well-to-do Richard in London with a plan to embark for France; this is where the surviving fragments of the novel, now among Hampson's papers, end. Hampson's *Go Seek* was a bold choice for a first submission to the Hogarth Press at a moment when Radclyffe Hall was being prosecuted on obscenity charges for *The Well of Loneliness*. The gesture suggests that Hampson considered the Woolfs sympathetic to his politics and sensitive to his subject, their support for Hall and their condemnation of censorship in print. Previous authors published by the Press who may have indicated to Hampson that the Woolfs were open to working-class content and authors include Muir and William Plomer. The Woolfs had also published in 1927 Welsh Professor Charles Davies' *Welshman's Way*, a novella about two young men from Aberystwyth travelling to continental Europe for the first time. In a letter dated 13 October 1928, Leonard Woolf, however, found himself compelled to reject Hampson's submission, telling him nevertheless that '[the work] has interested us greatly and has such merits that we should have liked to publish', but that 'unfortunately we do not think that this would be possible under present circumstances' (Leonard Woolf to John Hampson, 13 October 1928). The Woolfs' admiration for the work is confirmed by E. M Forster, himself an admirer and later friend and advisor to Hampson, in a 1931 letter to Hampson's mentor, Irish writer Forrest Reid (103).[13]

The unpublished manuscript opens with a graphic description of an assault on sixteen-year-old Alec by two co-workers:

> Twilight crept through the dusty windows of the old basement stock room, darkening the walls.
> A dark, thin boy with straight brown hair and/sallow face stood by the counter, entering numbers into a stock-book. 'Now we've got you.'
> He turned round quickly, facing his aggressors, fearful of their intentions, and asked timidly: 'What do you want?'
> The two boys grinned at him maliciously, they came closer and with sudden resolute determination were upon him. He struggled furiously, kicking out and biting, but it was useless; in a minute they had forced him backward over a large hamper, where the stronger boy held him firmly, while the other wrenched down his trousers, daubing him lavishly with thick, evil-smelling engine oil. (1)

When Alec reports the attack, instead of sympathy, he is dismissed on the grounds that he is ' "not really the type of boy suitable for work in a factory" ' (3). Reluctant to recount the incident to his family members, who have been brought down in the world themselves and become hard as a result, Alec contemplates suicide before resolving to leave home.

Alec travels to Nottingham where he finds work in a hotel kitchen until he meets Bill, better educated and likely of a higher class than he, in the street. After Bill invites Alec to spend a week with him before he moves to Rouen for his job, Alec talks about his life including his coming to awareness of his homosexuality. Able for the first time to be himself, Alec walks and talks of books with Bill (Bill of Joyce, Huxley, Lawrence and Ronald Firbank, Alec of Compton Mackenzie, Saki, Sinclair Lewis and W. H. Hudson; Alec also reads Nordau). In Litnon (*sic*), the two men spend a glorious week together, Alec growing into his homosexual self and at the same time developing as a writer under Bill's gentle tutelage. After Bill leaves for France, Alec's next stop is Liverpool where, after escaping a second assault, this time at the hands of a drunk sailor, he secures work in a restaurant. A portion of the manuscript is missing at this point (chapters 9, 10 and 11, 64–88), but Alec appears to be working in the same restaurant, still corresponding with Bill when the manuscript resumes. Alec's co-workers have discovered his homo-sexuality and he is being pursued by Cecil whose extravagant behaviour discomfits Alec (2/90).

The closing section of Part One takes place in, for Alec, 'London at last, the city of his dreams' (6/94). In the capital, Alec attends a perform-ance of Scheherazade by the Russian Ballet and finds he recognises gay men 'hugging [the same] intolerable secret [as he]' everywhere (7/95). Having secured a good position at a hotel, Alec embarks on a quest for self-education on the streets and in the galleries and theatres. He con-tinues to write, submitting stories to magazines and a play about 'the troubles of a working-class woman' to an agent (23/111). Dramatising Hampson's own predicament as a working-class writer (and here perhaps Hampson is challenging a potential publisher not to delve into his own personal history), Alec, guessing that 'theatrical producers' would find the play's subject 'distasteful[]' 'prefer[ring] the heroines to be at least middle-class or cabaret girls', refuses to rewrite it:

> that was that, if it was produced so much the better. Pride prevented him from using his daily work to advertise his literary efforts. He knew that the newspapers would all spare lines for 'Waiter Playwright', 'Soup server's star-tling success', either he would succeed for his own merit or else die unknown. (23/111)

The first part ends with Bill's death in a car accident in Rouen.

In the closing piece of the existing manuscript, Alec moves to Five Gates in Devon as the companion of Richard. Richard is an out homo-sexual, protected by his wealth and the discretion that it allows him to maintain. The luxury of the new position, however, makes Alec uneasy and much of this last section consists of an angry attack on society's failure to accept homosexuals. An unpleasant encounter with Richard's homophobic nephew leads Alec to declare that as a homosexual he is 'more outcast than the Jews' (16/131). Richard's proposal to take Alec abroad improves his mood; however, in the closing scene of the manuscript (which ends mid sentence), Alec makes an angry departure from the theatre after he sees a music hall actor mimicking a homosexual with the question ' "what county am I representing?" '; the response, ' "Middlesex" ' (22/136).

Although not strictly working-class in origin, Hampson wrote of factory and restaurant work from first-hand experience. After his own family, formerly successfully involved in Birmingham's Theatre Royal and then in the brewery business, fell on hard times, Hampson worked 'in a wild and wide variety of jobs', 'shops, hotels, warehouses, clubs, dance-halls and munitions factories'. He also spent a short time in prison for stealing books (Harrison 207). The struggle faced by Alec in terms of his sexual orientation Hampson also knew well. Although Hampson was gay, he did marry, at the request of W. H. Auden, a German actress called Therese Giehse, friend of Erika Mann, who was in flight from Nazi Germany and needed a British passport.

Despite this initial rebuff, or encouraged by the positive spin put on this first rejection, Hampson persevered with the Woolfs, very soon afterwards submitting two other novels. The Woolfs chose to publish the second of these two submissions first, *Saturday Night at the Greyhound*, the more strictly working class of the two works which had previously been turned down by Jonathan Cape. A tightly constructed, somewhat sinister story of a family working as publicans first in Birmingham and then in rural Derbyshire, *Saturday Night* (242 pp.) became one of the Press' top sellers. Its cover was designed by Trekkie Ritchie Parsons, whose similarly styled cover for Fox's *Drifting Men* suggests the Woolfs saw a connection between the two works (see Figs 8.2 and 8.3). The Woolfs billed the book as a 'story of village life', one that 'shows Mr. Hampson's powers of story telling and character drawing'. To some degree fulfilling Hampson's fear about stereotyping and suggesting that Hampson's putative working-class status mattered to her, Virginia Woolf celebrated Hampson's success, referring to him as 'Our Cardiff waiter' in a letter to Clive Bell and as 'ravaged, exhausted, has been a bootboy, a waiter, also in prison' in another to Ottoline Morrell (*L*4 292, 347).

The working-class conditions into which Hampson's protagonist, Justin Stonetun, finds himself thrust constitute an important element of the second longer novel, *O Providence* (394 pp.); however, the young boy's awkward coming of age and his homosexuality are the

"SATURDAY NIGHT AT
THE GREYHOUND"

This is the first novel by a
new writer of great promise
and power. It is a story of
village life, the Greyhound
being the village inn. It
shows Mr. Hampson's powers
of story telling and character
drawing.

Figure 8.2 Trekkie Ritchie's dust jacket for *Saturday Night at the Greyhound*. Courtesy of Manuscripts, Archives and Special Collections, Washington State University. Used by permission of The Random House Group Ltd.

"DRIFTING MEN"

Mr. Fox's *The Triumphant Machine* was a study in industrial psychology. Here he deals with the underworld of the street agitator, with the gutter bohemians of Soho, with men and life in prison and with world wanderers; his book ranges from London to Moscow, depicting men and women who have broken loose from their moorings and have drifted physically, emotionally, and intellectually from settled ways. It gives vivid pictures of strange lives.

DRIFTING MEN

R.M. FOX

DRIFTING MEN

R.M. FOX

6/-
NET

HOGARTH PRESS

Figure 8.3 Trekkie Ritchie's dust jacket for *Drifting Men*. Courtesy of Manuscripts, Archives and Special Collections, Washington State University. Used by permission of The Random House Group Ltd.

focus of the work.[14] The Woolfs' decision to publish this more difficult novel second, only after having established Hampson's reputation with *Saturday Night*, suggests a sophisticated understanding of the market and a willingness to take a chance. After *O Providence* failed to sell as had *Saturday Night*, the Woolfs, likely guided by the market, as well as by the quality of Hampson's writing, rejected several subsequent submissions from Hampson.

His relationship in terms of primary publisher terminated with the Hogarth Press, Hampson secured homes for his subsequent novels with Heinemann, Grayson & Grayson, and Chapman and Hall (later Methuen), among others. Nevertheless his ties with the Hogarth Press continued. Hampson contributed a short story to Michael Roberts' *New Country* (1933), one of the few stories with anything to do with the working class, as Cunningham points out, and short stories and a translation to Lehmann's *New Writing* (1939), *Daylight* (1941) and *New Writing and Daylight* (1943). He also played a significant role in the London literary scene. Hampson remained in Birmingham, but acted as a liaison, connecting a network of new northern authors (among them Walter Brierley and Leslie Halward) with London publishers, including the Woolfs and Lehmann, although unsuccessfully in the former case. For their part the Woolfs continued to mentor Hampson, as did Forster and Plomer – both of whom Hampson had met via the Hogarth Press. Letters exchanged by Hampson and the Woolfs suggest that the Woolfs read drafts of later works and Hampson's *Family Curse* (1936) is dedicated 'to Leonard Woolf, with gratitude'. Thus, despite fellow Birmingham writer Walter Allen's retrospective assessment that Hampson's work suffered as a result of his contact with Bloomsbury (that the success of *Saturday Night* 'led [Hampson] to equate Bloomsbury with the world and to overrate the nature of literary success' [62]), a charge often made in terms of the provincial writer's engagement with metropolitan presses, evidence suggests that growth resulted on both sides, Hampson acquiring Forster, Plomer, Allen himself and others; the Woolfs and then Lehmann gaining access to a network of Midlands and northern writing talent.

'Better Understood in Stalingrad than in Bloomsbury'

Existing criticism on Welsh English language poet Huw Menai (Huw Owen Williams) makes only cursory mention of his Hogarth Press volume. *The Passing of Guto*, Menai's second of four publications, appeared in advance of Hampson's novels in a run of 500 copies in

1929 in Dorothy Wellesley's Hogarth Press Living Poets First Series
(No. 6). (A typical run for this series was 400–600 copies.) Menai makes
a later appearance with four poems (all from *The Passing of Guto*) in
Wellesley's *A Broadcast Anthology of Modern Poetry* in 1930, alongside
James Joyce, D. H. Lawrence, Wilfred Owen and Vita Sackville-West,
and lesser known names such as John Drinkwater, Richard Church and
Muriel Stuart. Unlike Hampson, however, Menai did not form a lasting
bond with the Woolfs or with Wellesley. Glyn Jones paints a portrait of
a headstrong man who failed to capitalise on his relationships with the
Press: 'a certain aloofness on the poet's part, a proud suspicion, I sensed,
of even a suggestion of patronage, prevented any flowering of intimacy
in that quarter' (137). Michael Dixon, citing Anthony Conran (and
echoing Allen's comments about Hampson and Bloomsbury), contends
alternatively that Menai fell victim to the faddishness of his London supporters, who dropped him when he failed to play up his colliery connection and when something more fashionable came along. Dixon suggests
that this contact with 'a relatively small, and mainly middle-class, audience' in London made inevitable Menai's subsequent marginality (18). I
want to suggest that what we see is Menai echoing Hampson's resistance
to stereotyping and, once again, the Hogarth Press, here represented
by Wellesley, negotiating between the author's desire to be read on his
own terms and the readers' expectations that he write about working-
class experience. Like Hampson's, Menai's encounters with the Woolfs
demonstrate the reach of the Press into circles conventionally viewed as
incompatible with or antithetical to its vision. Also like Hampson's, they
illustrate how networks formed in opposition to or alongside those of
the Press.

Menai published his first volume of poetry, *Through the Upcast Shaft*,
in 1920 with Hodder & Stoughton after having published individual
poems in the *South Wales News*, the *Western Mail* and the *Welsh
Outlook*.[15] In his biographical preface to the work, Ellis Lloyd extols
Menai as 'a typical product of the peasant-culture of Wales, illumined
by genius: that culture which owes little to schools and universities,
nothing to wealth, but much to kin and country' and asks '[w]ith this,
the first-born of his genius, may I claim for him his right to a recognised
place among the younger British poets of to-day?' (viii). That Menai's
status as a working miner mattered to publisher and readers is emphasised by Lloyd's continued references to Menai as 'proletarian poet' and
'working-class poet' (vii) and confirmed by his concluding lines, 'Songs
like these—songs so beautiful and musical, so brilliant with flashes of
thought—have never before been heard coming from the shaft of a
mine—not even in Wales, where the miners sing at their work' (viii), as

well as by the bracketed '(A Welsh Miner)' flanking the author's name on the title page. Especially important to Lloyd is the environment in which the work was produced rather than the subject matter of the poems themselves, and indeed very few of the poems in this first collection deal explicitly with mining ('From the Point of View of Labour' is an exception, 54–5):

> Many of these songs have come to [Menai] when engaged at his daily toil. He has shaped them in his mind and memorised them as he swung the mandril at the coal-face or adjusted the scales at the weigh-house, afterwards writing them out during his hours of leisure at his cottage. In an industrial environment which to most would be repulsive and depressing, he has seen signs and wonders. (vi)

Dixon attributes the emphasis on the mining connection in this first volume to Menai himself, suggesting it represents, along with the mining-related titles of his first and third collections, which refer to the 'upcast shaft' and 'the return' of the mine shaft, a desire to 'authenticate himself to his audience' (24); however, when Wellesley, then patron and editor of the poetry series (her own *Matrix* having appeared the previous year), followed Hodder & Stoughton nine years later in emphasising Menai's working-class status (although this time, significantly, in his own words), taking the unusual step in terms of the Press' poetry series of asking him to write 'a short account of [his] life' in order to introduce *The Passing of Guto*, Menai acquiesced only reluctantly, suggesting rather that he did not want to emphasise his mining background. He closes the first paragraph of the autobiographical introduction, in what appears to have been a typically self-deprecating fashion, with '[b]ut it seems to me there is little that is of interest to record' (7). Interestingly, when Wellesley went back to Menai for her *Broadcast Anthology*, none of the poems included were related to mining, his contributions appearing in sections titled 'The Country', 'Time and its Passing', 'Night and Sleep' and 'Romance'.

In Menai's introduction to *The Passing of Guto*, we learn of his working-class parents from North Wales, who spoke only Welsh, and of his seven years of formal education which he left aged twelve in order to sell fish in the countryside, his father having left for the South Wales coalfields to secure work. A series of jobs, Menai tells us, brought him in touch with newspapers and eventually books. After following his mother south to work in the coalmines, a transition he describes as 'stepping into another world', Menai became involved with socialist politics and during World War I began writing poetry (10). Menai suggests that the poems in the volume may indicate his current predicament, unemployed and reliant on the dole and Poor Law relief. He then closes with comments regarding influences, perhaps prompted by Wellesley, claiming no real tradition. Shakespeare and Milton have eluded him – a good thing, he avers, as, could he have understood, he might not have tried writing poetry – but he has taken pleasure in a volume of Palgrave's *Golden Treasury*, and in particular in the Wordsworth contained therein. The introduction is followed by a footnote in which the editor explains that the poet has given her permission to correct the work where needed, his poetry necessarily flawed due to the conditions laid out in the introduction. Menai only briefly mentions in his introduction a change of job which Dixon identifies as important to what he calls the poet's outsider status. Forced by unemployment to change his allegiance from 'utopian Marxist' and union activist onto the side of the employer when he became a coal weigher (the employer's representative at miners' pay time) (see *Passing* 11), Dixon contends that Menai found himself distanced from his fellow workers and 'exiled from the social world of coal production' (18–19). The debt accrued for the weighing job shapes Menai's poems.

Menai's poetry is in the tradition of Wordsworth, John Clare and W. H. Davies, a combination of pastoral, romantic and religious poetry. Although the Welsh landscape is a central feature of Menai's work, references to specific places and to the material conditions of the Welsh are sparse in the first volume. We see a shift in this regard in Menai's Hogarth Press volume where the title poem, the first of the volume, about the death of Guto, begins with the line '[h]e loved his native Wales, her language, lore,/The *Englyn*, and the pageant of the bards' (13) and we find many Welsh place names as well as several Welsh language poems. In this opening poem, very possibly in negative reaction to Wellesley's desire to emphasise his colliery connection, Menai insists on his status as poet rather than his credentials as a 'working miner'. Thus the title character of the first poem has two epitaphs, the first an awkwardly phrased tribute *written for him* in his capacity as a miner, the second, Guto's preferred tribute, a fluent ode to autumn, *written by himself*. The mining terms of the first, such as 'cogs' ('timber for holding up the roof of mines' (15)), are explained in (most likely) Wellesley's footnotes to the text.

> Guto himself has gone to join his friend
> In the last resting place—the home from home!
> And this was not his chosen epitaph:
>
> 'He lived underground, now he's dead underground,
> His "cogs" could not hold up the squeezing of age.

He knocked many "props" out, his own prop is knocked out,
He withered in earning a wage.

He turned away gas, now he's turning to gas,
A sheet he oft wound, now he's wound in a sheet;
The Jim Crow of death has bent out his breath,
And the parting is for ever complete.

He sweated the salt of his tears in work,
All life was a jest, and death but a joke;
And fashioned with pain for but little gain
Monuments that ended in smoke.'

But this more subtle one, he wrote of Autumn:
'Ripe unto seed, glory of tint, decay,
Beauty ending the breath
Of flower and leaf, beneath a sky of grey,
Autumn is Death.
And Death is Change, the changing of a coat
Shabbied by sun and rain
For one of finer fabric, one that's not
So easy to stain'. (15–16)

Not until about half way through the collection do we find mining-related poems and when we do there is a double-edged quality to the portrayal of the miner's lot. In 'Despair', Menai opens with the lament 'I cannot woo thee as I would, Queen Poesy!/Rags and hunger wreck the heart, and I can't see/Nor touch, but what is down;/I cannot stretch full height and place a crown/Upon thine head in token of my love for thee!' but closes it with the ironic stanza '[I cannot] join the tragedies that do by taverns dwell,/ Where self-respect is lost for aye . . .' (42). Similarly in 'Charity', Menai downplays the negatives of poverty when he calls into question the value of money which sees 'the millionaire,/Tied to his passion, to the ledger tied,/Until the sum of effort is multiplied,/And death for answer doth upon him stare . . .' (43). When Menai addresses mining specifically he displays an incongruous optimism and a call for harmony despite difficult times in this area hit hard by the 1926 General Strike, perhaps made necessary by his debt to Lord Rhondda (10). Thus in 'During Strike Time', the poet calls 'Brave miner mates of mine' and 'good masters' alike to contemplate the starry night, 'the shoreless Ocean of Immensity', and to 'forget the heated day,/Of passions wherein men grow quickly old;/Wasting no moments on some paltry pay,/But gathering in God's harvest of pure gold' (44).

Menai's third, longer volume *Back in the Return* was published by Heinemann in 1933. It contains poems published in a range of venues that suggest a broad popularity, among them *Time and Tide* and *The Miner*. Unlike the first two volumes, *Back* contains no biographical note. Rather, the opening lines of the first poem 'Simple Bird' celebrate anonymity and freedom from tradition: 'Nothing you know of art,/Of coterie or sect;/You empty forth your heart/And strain not for effect . . . You care not in your glee/What birds have sung before,/Content in the brief round/Of your own throat and wings . . .' (3). Again, much of the poetry has little to do with mining, except the longer title poem, 'Back in the Return', which contains sharp criticism of mining conditions: 'The mine is no romantic place—/It stinks of Hell from sump to 'face';/A honeycomb of headings, stalls,/Airways, drifts, and rubbish walls./Intake fresh, and foul Return,/Which lighted once becomes an urn/For human ashes!' (65). The decision to position this poem as part two of three, exactly in the middle of the collection (63–140; 80 of 200 pages), echoes Guto's/Menai's preference that he be remembered as poet first, while, at the same time, acknowledging his readers' desire to hear him speak as a miner about mining.

In a return to the first two volumes, Menai's fourth and final collection, entitled *The Simple Vision* (Chapman and Hall, by then part of Methuen, 1945), is prefaced with a biographical introduction authored by John Cowper Powys. Cowper Powys celebrates at length Menai's '*poetical popular poetry*' (11) and characterises the epoch which produced T. S. Eliot and the 'Between-the-Wars School' of poetry as one from which 'we are now so healthily reacting' (15).[16] In an effort to reclaim Menai, Cowper Powys, himself British but living in and writing about Wales, fetishises Menai's Welshness and the worker quality of his poetry, describing him as 'a medium through whom the emotions of thousands of men and women can flow' (13). He compares Menai to Walt Whitman and his gift to that of 'that most primordial type of all human soothsayers, the individual in an aboriginal tribe who is at once priest, clown, magician, actor, and poet' (10, 19–20).

Suggesting he overlooked or considered negligible Menai's relationship with the Hogarth Press, Cowper Powys does not mention *The Passing of Guto*. Reflecting misconceptions about the Woolfs and echoing Allen's assessment of the detrimental effect of Hampson's relationship with the Hogarth Press, in an introduction ironically not so different from that of the Hodder & Stoughton volume, Cowper Powys describes Menai in *Back in the Return* as 'giv[ing] vent to emotions that would be perhaps better understood in Stalingrad than in Bloomsbury' (24).

Proletarian fiction writers did not become a regular feature of the Hogarth Press fiction list until Lehmann returned to the Press in the late 1930s. At this point Lehmann brought with him his somewhat working-class focused journal (*Folios of*) *New Writing*, which includes information about class status in contributors' biographies prefacing each issue, as well as 1930s generation writers Edward Upward (*Journey to the Border*, 1938) and Henry Green (*Party Going*, 1939). (Lehmann characterises *New Writing* as a dialogue between those with 'a middle-class education' moving in 'metropolitan intellectual circles' and 'those who when they wrote of mines, seamen, factory worker . . . were writing from the inside', reflected in an earlier title *The Bridge* (*IMOT* 167).) The Woolfs' choices in fiction as well as the increase in the biography and letters category, at its maximum seven of twenty titles in 1937, however, suggest a desire to represent a range of voices and to reach a range of readers, which both mirrors the selections they made in terms of non-fiction and continues those in the realm of fiction.[17]

Writers and Publishers

Both Leonard and Virginia Woolf wrote about class and it is largely readings out of context of these pieces that have resulted in a tendency to ignore their contributions to the promotion of working-class voices both at the Hogarth Press and in their own writing. Statements from Leonard Woolf's humorous defence of the highbrow in *Hunting the Highbrow* and extracts from Virginia Woolf's critique of Auden generation writers' efforts to 'go over' in 'The Leaning Tower', read without attention to their work at the Hogarth Press, obscure their efforts to bridge 'the gulf' separating an old world 'divided by hedges' from a new 'world without classes and towers'.

Considered in the context of the Woolfs' careers as writers *and* as publishers, we see that *Hunting the Highbrow* is, in fact, one of a significant number of Hogarth Press publications dealing with class and one in a series focused on books and the public and on education, to a number of which Leonard Woolf contributed. Similarly, 'The Leaning Tower', first delivered in May 1940 as a lecture to the Workers' Education Association and then published in autumn 1940 in Lehmann's *New Writing*, at that time itself a Hogarth Press publication, represents the last in a series of Virginia Woolf's interrogations into the relationship between class and reading and writing, including her *Common Reader* volumes, *A Room of One's Own* and *Three Guineas*. Her essay, the central claim of which is that 'stucco suburbs' and 'expensive educations' have a role in determining who writes (Auden qtd in 'Leaning' 20), constitutes an informed assessment (whether one agrees with it or not) based on over twenty years' experience as a publisher. The fact that

Virginia Woolf felt comfortable and qualified to debate so controversial a set of issues as those addressed in her essay first at the WEA and second in a journal aimed at promoting working-class authors, a journal whose contributors included those same writers she attacks in the essay, suggests that the issue mattered to her and that she sought to do something about it.[18] That Lehmann brought *New Writing* to the Hogarth Press in 1939, judging it more appropriate to his cause than the highly political Lawrence and Wishart, its previous publisher, credits the Press and the Woolfs with a rare openness. I therefore close by seconding Lehmann when he reminds readers in his postscript to Upward, Louis MacNiece and B. L. Coombes' responses to Woolf's 'The Leaning Tower' essay, of the significance of Virginia Woolf's, and I add Leonard Woolf's, commitment to class struggles equally as writers *and* as publishers.

Notes

1. Cunningham explains that this is a phrase from the Communist Manifesto (over)used by bourgeois writers of the thirties to describe the alliance of bourgeois writers with the working classes (211). I would like to thank the National Library of Ireland (NLI) for permission to use items from their R. M. Fox collection, Roger Hubank for permission to reproduce portions of Hampson's unpublished *Go Seek a Stranger* and the Society of Authors for permission to reproduce unpublished letters by Leonard Woolf.
2. Duncan Wilson, author of a political biography of Leonard Woolf, neglects to talk about the Hogarth Press; Sebastian Spotts' collected letters includes a section on the Press; Victoria Glendinning's biography covers Woolf's work at the Press and his work in politics, but does not link the two.
3. Leonard Woolf is mistaken here. Willa was brought up in Montrose, Angus, where her father was a draper. Her family was from Shetland, although she had never been there. Willa had graduated with first class honours in classics from Glasgow University (Butter 51–2).
4. *First Poems*, 1925; *Chorus of the Newly Dead*, 1926; *Transition: Essays on Contemporary Literature*, 1926; *The Marionette*, 1927; *The Structure of the Novel*, 1928.
5. This followed John Maynard Keynes' *Economic Consequences of Mr. Churchill* in 1925. Martin also published *The Press the Public Wants* with the Hogarth Press in 1947.
6. Preceding this were Leys' *Kenya* and Thompson's *The Other Side of the Medal* about India.
7. See Jason Harding on the social credit movement, the *Criterion* and affiliated periodicals.
8. Correspondence suggests that this contribution was not solicited by Leonard Woolf and that Sharp had not intended the book for the pamphlet series (University of Newcastle upon Tyne Special Collections).

9. Undated correspondence (probably 1940?) suggests Fox approached Lehmann about a later book (NLI).
10. A quote from the *Yorkshire Post* included on the order form suggests that Fox's book was read throughout England.
11. Leonard Woolf's acceptance letter to Fox (9 August 1936), including editing suggestions, confirms that this contribution was not solicited. The Library of Leonard and Virginia Woolf at Washington State University holds a review copy of *Road to Wigan Pier*.
12. See Hilliard's chapter 'Class, Patronage and Literature'. Significantly Hilliard singles out Hogarth Press trained Lehmann as one of the few who would not sacrifice literary standards for his politics.
13. John Lehmann credits the success of *Saturday Night*, appearing shortly after his arrival, as 'smoothing [his] path a little' at the Press. Lehmann, too, expresses admiration for the rejected *Go Seek* (*Thrown* 15).
14. For a more detailed analysis of *O Providence*, see Southworth.
15. Hodder & Stoughton was by this time a successful publishing operation, doubling its 1914 sales in 1920 with its 'two-shilling "yellow jacket" novels' (Collin 147). The firm began in 1868 with an emphasis on religious works, but published in a range of subject areas, including education, translations, children's book and medical texts.
16. In 1943 Eliot published the work of Welsh poet Idris Davies at Faber & Faber. Davies' work, including his General Strike poem 'The Angry Summer', is much more consistently polemical and explicitly mine-related than the work of Menai.
17. Nineteen-thirties Hogarth Press working-class novels include Derrick Leon's *Livingstones* (1933), based on Leon's experience as a clerk in a London interior decorating shop, and Kathleen Nott's *Mile End* (1938) about Jewish garment workers, based on her experience as a social worker in London's East End. Nott was the Oxford-educated daughter of a lithographic printer, born in Camberwell.
18. Lehmann blames 'the political ties that bound Lawrence & Wishart' for their failure to 'carr[y] the project through' (*IMOT* 206).

Works cited

Allen, Walter. *As I Walked Down Grub Street*. London: Heinemann, 1981.

Bowker, B. *Lancashire Under the Hammer*. London: Hogarth Press, 1928

Butter, Peter. *Edwin Muir: Man and Poet*. New York: Greenwood Press, 1977.

Carswell, John. *Lives and Letters: A.R. Orage, Beatrice Hastings, Katherine Mansfield, John Middleton Murry, S.S. Koteliansky, 1906–1957*. New York: New Directions, 1978.

Collin, Dorothy. 'Hodder & Stoughton'. In Jonathan Rose and Patricia J. Anderson, eds. *British Publishing Houses 1820–1880*. *Dictionary of Literary Biography 106*. Detroit: Gale, 1991: 142–55.

Cramp, C. T., ed. *The Workers' Point of View: A Symposium*. London: Hogarth Press, 1933.

Cuddy-Keane, Melba. *Virginia Woolf, the Intellectual and the Public Sphere*. Cambridge: Cambridge University Press, 2003.

Cunningham, Valentine. *British Writers of the Thirties*. Oxford and New York: Oxford University Press, 1988.

Dataller, Roger. *Oxford into Coal-field*. London: Dent, 1934.

Davies, Margaret Llewelyn. *Life As We Have Known It By Co-operative Working Women*. London: Virago, [1931] 1977.

Dixon, Michael. 'Beyond the Slagheaps: The Marginality of Huw Menai'. *Welsh Writing in English: A Yearbook of Critical Essays*. Vol. 3. Cardiff: University of Wales Press, 1997: 18–41.

Forster, E. M. *Selected Letters of E.M.Forster*. Eds Mary Lago and P. N. Furbank. Cambridge: Harvard University Press, 1983–5.

Fox, R. M. *Drifting Men*. London: Hogarth Press, 1930.

—. Order form for Fox's *Drifting Men*. Held by the National Library of Ireland.

—. Review of *Orlando: A Biography* (1928). *The Irish Statesman* 8 June 1929.

—. *Smoky Crusade*. London: Hogarth Press, 1937.

—. *The Triumphant Machine*. London: Hogarth Press, 1928.

Hampson, John. *Go Seek a Stranger*. Unpublished MS. John Hampson Papers. Property of Roger Hubank, Loughborough.

—. *O Providence*. London: Hogarth Press, 1932.

—. *Saturday Night at the Greyhound*. London: Hogarth Press, [1931] 1986.

Harding, Jason. *The Criterion: Cultural Politics and Periodical Networks in Inter-War Britain*. Oxford: Oxford University Press, 2002.

Harrison, Michael, ed. *Under Thirty: An Anthology*. London: Rich and Cowan, 1939.

Hilliard, Christopher. *To Exercise Our Talents: The Democratization of Writing in Britain*. Cambridge: Harvard University Press, 2006.

Jones, Glyn. *The Dragon has Two Tongues: Essays on Anglo-Welsh Writers and Writing*. Ed. Tony Brown. Cardiff: University of Wales Press, 2001.

Lehmann, John. *In My Own Time: Memoirs of a Literary Life*. Boston: Little, Brown, 1969.

—. 'A Postscript'. *Folios of New Writing* Spring 1941: 42–6.

—. *Thrown to the Woolfs: Leonard and Virginia Woolf at the Hogarth Press*. New York: Holt, Rinehart & Winston, [1978] 1979.

Lloyd, Ellis. 'Preface'. In Menai, *Through the Upcast Shaft*.

Martin, Kingsley. *The British Public and the General Strike*. London: Hogarth Press, 1926.

—. *Father Figures: The Evolution of an Editor 1897–1931*. Chicago: Henry Regnery, 1966.

Menai, Huw. *Back in the Return*. London: Heinemann, 1933.

—. *The Passing of Guto*. London: Hogarth Press, 1929.

—. *A Simple Vision*. London: Chapman and Hall, 1945.

—. *Through the Upcast Shaft*. London: Hodder and Stoughton, 1920.

Porter, Alan et al. *Coal: A Challenge to the National Conscience*. London: Hogarth Press, 1927.

Reckitt, Maurice B. *As It Happened: An Autobiography*. London: J. M. Dent, 1941.

Rose, Jonathan. *The Intellectual Life of the British Working Classes*. New Haven: Yale University Press, 2001.

Sharp, Thomas. *A Derelict Area: A Study of the South-West Durham Coalfield*. London: Hogarth Press, 1935.

Shiach, Morag. *Modernism, Labour and Selfhood in British Literature and Culture 1890–1930*. Cambridge: Cambridge University Press, 2004.

Southworth, Helen. ' "Outside the magic (and tyrannical) triangle of London-Oxford-Cambridge": John Hampson, the Woolfs and the Hogarth Press'. In Anna Burrells et al., eds. *Woolfian Boundaries: Selected Papers from the Sixteenth Annual Woolf Conference*. Clemson: Clemson University Press, 2007.

Stansfield, Kathy. 'Thomas Sharp 1901–1978'. In Gordon E. Cherry, ed. *Pioneers in British Planning*. London: The Architectural Press, 1981: 150–76.

Willis, J. H. *Leonard and Virginia Woolf as Publishers: The Hogarth Press, 1917–41*. Charlottesville: University Press of Virginia, 1992.

Woolf, Leonard. *After the Deluge*: *As Study of Communal Psychology*. New York: Harcourt Brace, 1931.

—. *Downhill All the Way: An Autobiography of the Years 1919 to 1939*. New York: Harcourt Brace Jovanovich, 1967.

—. Letter to John Hampson. 13 October 1928. John Hampson Papers. Property of Roger Hubank, Loughborough.

—. Letter to R. M. Fox. 9 August, 1936. Held by the National Library of Ireland.

Woolf, Virginia. 'The Leaning Tower'. *Folios of New Writing* Autumn 1940. London: Hogarth Press.

—. *The Letters of Virginia Woolf*. Eds Nigel Nicolson and Joanne Trautmann. 6 vols. New York: Harcourt Brace Jovanovich, 1975–1980.

—. *A Room of One's Own*. San Diego: Harcourt Brace Jovanovich, [1929] 1981.

Chapter 9

'Oh Lord what it is to publish a best seller': The Woolfs' Professional Relationship with Vita Sackville-West

Stephen Barkway

Much has been written about the important role Vita Sackville-West played in Virginia Woolf's life: as friend, lover and, in the case of *Orlando*, muse. Woolf wrote more letters to her, nearly 450, than to any other correspondent except Vanessa Bell; however, a key facet of their relationship that has not received detailed attention is their professional one: that of a writer (Sackville-West) and her publisher (the Woolfs as owners of the Hogarth Press). Sackville-West was unique among Woolf's close friends and 'Bloomsbury', in that for seventeen years the Hogarth Press was the sole publisher of her books in Great Britain.[1] Other friends – such as E. M. Forster, T. S. Eliot, Roger Fry, Clive Bell – gave the Press the occasional book or pamphlet but no one was to become as devoted to the Woolfs' press as Sackville-West. The Press published sixteen of Sackville-West's books between 1924's *Seducers in Ecuador* and 1941's *Selected Poems*.[2]

It was quite a gamble – an emotional rather than a financial one – to associate oneself commercially with friends, especially on such traditional business terms as opposed to Roger Fry's more progressive attempts to 'employ' artists at his Omega Workshops, for example. It was a gamble that paid off, thanks to the Woolfs' and Sackville-West's mutual ability to largely keep separate the grim realities of business negotiation and personal relations: a remarkable achievement, given that the business relationship lasted the full term of Woolf and Sackville-West's friendship and was subject to tempting offers from rival publishers. One such generous offer came to Sackville-West in 1933[3] and prompted a long, letter from Leonard – who handled the majority of contract negotiations for the Press – that revealed part of his and Woolf's publishing policy. 'I do not think that any feeling of friendship really ought to influence you if your material interests are to be in any way unfavourably affected.' When Woolf had received 'tempting offers' from other publishers she, too, had to weigh up the financial options 'but that taking everything into consideration' they did not believe in the long run she would be any better off. It must be remembered that the Woolfs earned as authors and as publishers of their own books. Leonard goes on to talk about how high sales of some books subsidise less successful but worthwhile publications; how it pays publishers to 'buy' successful authors from other publishers but, although this is how the Press lost William Plomer, he is 'not prepared to adopt the system of putting large sums down as advances which means gambling on books' (Spotts 317–18).

Responding to Leonard, Sackville-West regretted giving 'the impression that it was only a feeling of friendship that kept me with the Hogarth Press . . . I am as happy as I can be with the Hogarth Press and would not change my publisher for the world' (Spotts 318 n2). Indeed, Sackville-West was one of the few authors who, lured by friendship rather than money, joined the Hogarth Press list with an already established publishing history. Together with Woolf they represented the quality of writing and type of books the Press stood for during the 1920s and 30s; they were the authors most associated with the Press in the public's eye. When 'travelling' the Press' books in the early 1930s, John Lehmann recalled a bookseller telling him: 'I hope you'll have something by Mrs Woolf or Miss Sackville-West next time you come round' (14).

Leonard was the more active administratively at the Press, so the bulk of Sackville-West's correspondence about her publications is with him. I chart her relationship with the Press, drawing on the extensive Hogarth Press archives at Reading University – much of which is previously unpublished – looking at each separate publication in chronological order (but the novels will be considered together). Their formal business relationship continued for a while in parallel with her journalistic career. Between June 1923 and November 1929, while Leonard was the Literary Editor of the *Nation and Athenaeum* (April 1923–February 1930) he commissioned from her approximately fifty reviews and articles, and on several occasions she reviewed Hogarth Press publications. Sackville-West's importance in the life of the Woolfs' Press is symbolised by the fact that in the early 1930s they gave her their Minerva platen press which they had used for many of their hand-printed books; it can still be seen at Sissinghurst.

Sackville-West's first book for the Hogarth Press, the novella *Seducers in Ecuador*, was published in October 1924, barely a year after Woolf felt comfortable enough to stop addressing her letters to 'Dear Mrs Nicolson'. Sackville-West was then under contract with William Heinemann (*Knole and the Sackvilles*, 1922; *Grey Wethers*, 1923) and she was already composing *The Land*. Looking back from the 1960s, Leonard remembered in '1924 Vita asked us whether we would like to publish a longish short story ... which no ordinary publisher would have looked at' (*Downhill* 157–8); however, contemporary evidence suggests that it was Woolf who asked Vita if she had anything she could offer the Press: 'I was hoping to see you here, partly for your own sake, partly for the sake of the Hogarth Press, which is very anxious to know if there is any serious chance that you will let it have a book' (*L3* 110).

Woolf frequently solicited manuscripts from her friends, particularly in the Press' infancy. Its early success was almost entirely down to the Woolfs' being so well connected in literary terms; they counted among their substantial network of friends some of the best writers of the day. They sensibly took advantage of the fact and this particular invitation was to prove, in time, their most lucrative of all. On 16 July 1924 Sackville-West wrote from Italy to say she was already writing her story: 'I hope that no one has ever yet, or ever will, thrown down a glove I was not ready to pick up. ... Perhaps you will be the Polite Publisher, and I shall get my story back—"The Hogarth Press regrets that the accompanying manuscript," etc.' (DeSalvo & Leaska 53).

In stark contrast to the privileged position Woolf had built for herself as her own publisher, Sackville-West was pressured to produce her story quickly in order that the Press might publish it in their autumn list. Woolf used flattery to preface a demanding deadline: 'It is very generous of you to think of giving us any of your work, and we are all very much delighted at the prospect. Is there any chance we could bring it out this autumn?' (*L3* 114). 'I like the story very very much' Woolf told Sackville-West when she first read her manuscript; 'I'm certain that you have done something much more interesting (to me at least) than you've yet done'. Woolf was 'extremely proud and indeed touched' that the Press was going to publish it (*L3* 131). Despite its title alarming the booksellers, or perhaps owing to it, *Seducers in Ecuador* sold well: 899 copies in two months (*L3* 151) and a month later Woolf was able to tell Sackville-West unashamedly: 'We are making money very comfortably out of *Seducers*' (*L3* 159); and she goes on to 'fish' for the long poem which was to be published as *The Land* by Heinemann in 1926. Almost instinctively, Woolf appreciated what a particularly attractive proposition it would be to have Sackville-West as a permanent Hogarth author. In those early months of their professional relationship we see the considerable difference in their respective positions and perspectives. While Woolf excitedly delights in the financial income, for Sackville-West *Seducers* was their 'joint progeny' (DeSalvo & Leaska 61); it was fun to be published by her friend, tantamount to collaboration. *Seducers* had clearly been written to be appreciated by Woolf; not only had Sackville-

West changed her style to appeal to Woolf, the book is dedicated to her.[4] Woolf perceived this and went so far as to say it was the 'sort of thing I should like to write myself' (*L3* 131). Sackville-West was later to write that it was 'the only one [of my novels] I might save from the rubbish-heap' (Glendinning 232) and it is a good example of how a literary press could shape and influence the work of one of its writers.

This is not to say that Sackville-West was uninterested in sales figures and income. Indeed, she cannily suggested to Leonard to defer publication from 30 October to 6 November 1924: 'has it occurred to you that the 29th is election day? I should think that any book published just then would stand a poor chance', and she enclosed a list of fifty names to whom she suggested Leonard could send circulars (HPA 424, VSW to LW, 15 October 1924). Sackville-West's mother also took sales of her daughter's books extremely seriously. Leonard was forwarded her scheme by which *Seducers* might be promoted in France, and she may have been the driving force that led him to consider an advertising campaign for the book (Spotts 289–90).

As Sackville-West was still under contract with Heinemann in 1926, her formal relationship with the Hogarth Press was temporarily unclear. She may have moaned to the Woolfs about her royalties for *The Land* (published in September) because Woolf, when sending her a further royalty check for *Seducers*, implied opportunely that she would have been better off if she had published her epic poem with them: 'See what you might have had if you had stuck to the old firm—cheques for £10 every other day perhaps; and distinction which, rightly has no price' (*L3* 253); she worked at securing Sackville-West for the Press. They would be good for each other: her name and popularity gilding the Press and in return its name would add literary distinction to hers. Perhaps by some means of transference Sackville-West was already becoming emotionally attached to the Hogarth Press, for she responded to a throwaway remark from Woolf that they might be giving it up by imploring: 'I didn't know what an affection I had for the Press till I heard it was threatened' (De Salvo & Leaska 134). Woolf was successfully luring her into the fold:

> You said you were going to finish a book in Persia. Would you let us have it? The point is I don't want to press you, if you feel, as you may, that Heinemann's has a right, and is, as maybe too, more profitable. (*L3* 266)

Clearly Sackville-West felt unable to refuse her 'idolised Virginia' anything: 'I see that I must quarrel with Heinemann for your sake; so be it' (De Salvo & Leaska 139). It was thus that Woolf secured for the Press the first of Sackville-West's two Persian travel books, *Passenger to Teheran*. Again they wanted it for their autumn list, resulting in

Sackville-West's working at a pace that Woolf marvelled at (*L3* 291, *D2* 313). In justifying her demands, Woolf quite blatantly revealed once more the financial advantage of having a book by Sackville-West to publish: 'But think of your glory; and our profit' (*L3* 284). So the prize-winning poem *The Land* was followed almost immediately by *Passenger to Teheran* in October 1926, the Press' travel book gaining from the publicity and critical attention surrounding the successful poem.

During the months following its publication, they watched the steady progress of its sales (see *L3* 304, 307, 308, 313). On the basis that all publicity is good publicity, Woolf even encouraged Sackville-West to be rude about Arnold Bennett so that he would write a defensively hostile essay (*L3* 307). By June 1927, with Sackville-West's name on the public's lips (she had been awarded the Hawthornden Prize for *The Land*), the Press determined to capitalise on their well-known author, pushing unsold copies: 'Our traveller went to Bumpus, who said they'd brought up four copies of Teheran from the cellar, put them in the window, and sold them at once' (*L3* 394).

Sackville-West's fame was at a height the Woolfs could not afford to ignore. Two months after she received her prize, Woolf begged her: 'if you've any time on your hands why not turn it to the advantage of the Hogarth Press?' (*L3* 412). Now the Press was Sackville-West's publisher of choice. In 1928 she told Woolf of her plan to translate some of Rilke's poems for the Hogarth Living Poets series[5] and inquired modestly whether Leonard 'would like a companion volume to *Passenger to Teheran*? I think he said the Press had made over it, in spite of a comparatively small sale . . . *But don't let him hesitate to turn it down if he wants to, on the score of friendship*' (De Salvo & Leaska 273, 288, emphasis added). Here are the first signs of the potentially awkward conflict: on the one hand, the author has decided to be loyal to the publisher; on the other, the author knows that the publisher will not wish to publish anything regarded as substandard. The fact that the author and publisher share a great friendship would make rejection of a manuscript potentially extremely hurtful, yet neither side would wish to be untrue, especially to themselves. They risked their friendship by entering a business relationship with one another. The Press was naturally eager to have a follow-up to the successful *Passenger to Teheran*; *Twelve Days* was published in October 1928 with a larger print run (see Appendix).

Sackville-West confided to Woolf that Harold had objected to some of the poems in her next book for the Press; she worried they were not good enough, but this may have been as a direct result of her own fears that the love poems would be interpreted as being 'Lesbian' (Nicolson

222). Sackville-West had fears, too, for the almost anorexic slimness of this little volume:

> [A]s to my own manuscript: It is, I fear, very short, and I have done what I could to pad it out by putting in a kind of index to the first lines. I have divided it, as you see, into three sections, the poems appearing to fall roughly into these groups, and I should like a blank page left between one section and the next. (HPA 420, VSW to LW, 8 August 1929)

But Leonard replied: 'Your book [*King's Daughter*] will add great distinction to the series. I left in the sonnets, because I liked them and do not think you are right in being against them. Also the book would be rather too thin otherwise' (HPA 420, LW to VSW, 18 August 1929).

Despite its size, Leonard was only too pleased to publish a book of poems by the recent winner of the Hawthornden; it was sold with a wrap-around band advertising the fact that her last poem was a prize-winner. Confident of its sales, the Woolfs produced an initial print run of 1000 copies, approximately twice the size of other volumes in the series. 'King's D. is selling well; as I know, doing them up by sixes and 12's for the youth of Oxford and Cambridge' (*L4* 101). It went into a second impression in May 1930.

However blessed the Woolfs may have felt, having now secured the popular Sackville-West for their press, nothing could have prepared them for the astonishing impact of her next novel. She seemed instinctively to have known of her projected novel's potential success – 'I've thought of a novel, and I'm going to write it this summer and make my fortune' (DeSalvo & Leaska 345) – but even she could never have dreamed of sales on such a grand scale. She told Woolf:

> I feel that for snobbish reasons alone it ought to be highly popular! I hope so, because Leonard's offer was very handsome, and I should hate to ruin the Press, towards which I feel avuncular as you know. (DeSalvo & Leaska 352)

Sackville-West's fear that *The Edwardians*, and Leonard's generous contractual offer for it, might 'ruin the Press' was ironic in retrospect, given that the novel became the Woolfs' first runaway best-seller. It sold more copies and made more money than any other book on the Hogarth Press list, including Woolf's own. Leonard wrote to her: 'V tells me that you have had an offer with regard to your novel . . . We would pay you a royalty of 15% on the first 3000 copies sold and 20% on all copies sold above that number and we would pay you an advance of £200 on the day of publication' (HPA 416, LW to VSW, 26 April 1929). Vita replied:

I am so glad that Virginia told you that I had had an offer from Heinemann with regard to my as yet unwritten, and indeed unconceived,* novel ... I need hardly say that I would very much rather publish it through the Hogarth Press, if you really think that the resources of the Press would not be too strained by the very liberal offer which you have made me.
*No longer. I started it this morning. It is about Edwardian society. (HPA 416, VSW to LW, 30 April 1929)

These exchanges suggest that Sackville-West did not yet feel comfortable enough to liaise directly with Leonard. She dropped hints to Woolf, knowing that they would get passed on to Leonard; understandably she would have felt uncomfortable negotiating a better deal with a friend face to face, having to imply that other publishers were interested in her work and making better offers. Leonard had a reputation for being dour, and this may explain why Sackville-West made this (possibly teasing) remark to Woolf earlier that same month: 'how dilatory I am, except when writing books for the Hogarth Press, and that's because I'm frightened of Leonard' (DeSalvo & Leaska 350).

At work on *The Edwardians* in France in July 1929, Sackville-West wrote to Woolf that she felt herself 'a bad novelist ... Still I peg on, and hope one day to see it all under the imprint of the Hogarth Press, in stacks in the bookshops' (DeSalvo & Leaska 358). In September she asked Woolf to 'Tell Leonard I have resumed my novel—as a publisher he will be interested to hear this perhaps' (DeSalvo & Leaska 373) and six months later the completed manuscript was sent to the Woolfs: 'A thousand congratulations from L and V on your finish. I shall read it over the weekend. Lord! What an excitement!' (*L*4 148).

Sackville-West had only two months to wait before seeing copies of *The Edwardians* 'in stacks in the bookshops'. Not that they gathered dust! It was published on 29 May in an edition of 18,000 copies, and two days later Leonard had to write to the printers, R. & R. Clark, to order 'a second impression of 8000 copies of this book. The matter is very urgent as the book is selling at the rate of nearly 1000 a day' (HPA 416). (To put this into perspective, Woolf's latest novel, *Orlando*, had an initial print run of only 5,080.) A Press advertisement in *The Times* (27 June 1930, 20) boasted 'First impression of 18,000 sold out in three weeks'. Sackville-West's reputation led to the Book Society making *The Edwardians* their Book of the Month for June; the Press thought the publication prestigious enough to issue a signed limited edition of 125 copies. Naturally the fervour and excitement surrounding the high sales were reported by Woolf to Sackville-West (*L*4 171, 178, 184); and then, keeping the momentum going on the other side of the Atlantic, the American Literary Guild chose it as their Book of the Month for

September. So on 9 August 1930, over two months after publication, Woolf was able to tell Sackville-West 'The Edwardians is still selling very well . . . I dont see any reason why we shouldnt sell 25,000; and what the sales will be in America—heaven help us—the imagination boggles, as they say' (*L4* 198).

One wonders how uneasy Woolf felt about this situation. We know she wasn't jealous of Vita's actual writing – her 'art', although she genuinely admired the poetry – but the *speed* with which Sackville-West could dash off a highly commercial novel must have been galling for Woolf as she laboured over countless revisions of her own work. Sackville-West, with apparent ease, was able to earn huge sums with very few strokes of her pen. At the same time, because the book was published by the Hogarth Press, she was also making vast sums for the Woolfs themselves. I would suggest that for someone with Woolf's moral sensitivity, she might have felt herself to be in a slightly uncomfortable position. Only a fortnight after the initial publication of *The Edwardians*, Woolf wrote in her *Diary*: 'We are very prosperous. On making up half yearly accounts, we find that we each get £425: & next year is sure, owing to the gigantic sale of The Edwardians—it verges on the 20,000. And it is not a very good book' (*D3* 305–6). A month later she told Hugh Walpole: 'the Press is flourishing, more than ever, what with Vita going into Edition after Edition' (*L4* 188); and to Margaret Llewelyn Davies: 'I agree about Vitas natural powers; the trouble is she writes with incredible ease and fills up any odd space of time by dashing off a book. This [*The Edwardians*] was done I think to wile away a few months leisure, and she has made about six thousand pounds!' (*L4* 193).

Woolf *was* honest with Sackville-West about how financially beneficial she was for them, however, though she partially veiled it under hyperbole. She wasted no time in fishing for opportunities to publish more by her friend: 'I look upon you now as the Woolf breadwinner, since it's more and more certain that my novel wont win us even a penny bun' (*L4* 210).

If we look at what Leonard wrote about these issues, and we read between the lines, we see that he and Woolf agreed about Sackville-West's importance to the Press. Candid as ever in his autobiography, he does not hide the financial advantages of having her on the Hogarth list:

> Vita was an honest, simple, sentimental, romantic, naïve, and competent writer. When she let all this go off in a novel about high life, she produced in *The Edwardians* a kind of period piece and a real best-seller. Both Virginia and Vita had been warned by friends and friendly publishers that it was madness to have their books published by such an amateurish, ramshackle

concern as the Hogarth Press, which had not the machinery to deal with a best-seller or even a seller. I have always been doubtful about this 'machinery' of publishing and was pleased to find that the machinery of the Press stood up to the strain of a best-seller. We sold nearly 30,000 copies of *The Edwardians* in the first six months, and by the end of the year the Press had made a profit of nearly £2,000 on it (*Downhill* 158).[6]

Nowhere is the 'Sackville-West-effect' more clear than in the table Leonard provided showing the Woolfs' income from the Press over a number of years: in 1924 it was £3; 1925, £73; 1926 and 1927, both £27; 1928, £64; 1929, £380 (*Downhill* 142). In 1930 it increased to £530, but in the two years in which Sackville-West's best-seller sales are reflected, the growth is astounding: in 1931 (including the first six-month sales of *The Edwardians*) it leapt up to a huge £2,373; and in 1932, with a full year of sales of *The Edwardians* coupled with the comparably successful *All Passion Spent*, £2,209. This represents a phenomenal increase in the Woolfs' annual income. Indeed, 1932 became their best-ever earning and most profitable year. If the Woolfs' other income is combined with that earned from the Press, it totalled £4,053, which translates as around £193,000 today, or not far short of $400,000.

Sackville-West capitalised on her astounding success by writing between 1931 and 1934 three more novels: *All Passion Spent*, *Family History* and *The dark island*. *All Passion Spent* did well, but not quite as well as *The Edwardians*. The quality and the public appeal lessened with each novel and sales declined similarly. That is not to say that sales were sluggish. *All Passion Spent* sold 4,000 copies before publication and it was a novel that both Woolfs thought better than *The Edwardians* (see L4 341, *Downhill* 159). With 'Sales going on uninterrupted' (*L4* 345), profits really *were* substantial, so it was with an element touching on embarrassment that Woolf told Sackville-West: 'I hear A.P.S. has beaten the Edwardians, and now if its a play, will run on and on. Oh and out of the profits—did I tell you?—I've bought a boat and a camera. Such are the blessings you shower' (*L4* 363).

Still, only six months later Leonard 'reluctantly' consented to Sackville-West's going to Ernest Benn (Cross & Ravenscroft-Hulme 81) to publish two short stories in a single ninepenny volume. Woolf felt she had to make a point to her of feeling slighted: 'you've fallen to the blandishments of Benn. I'm sorry, selfishly for the Press' (*L4* 380). Relations between author and publisher were not upset and returned to normal with *Family History*. The Press was generous with its advance, telling Sackville-West: 'I am enclosing a cheque for £400 advance on account of royalties. I think the stipulated amount was £200, but we have sold so many that I think it only fair to double it. As a matter of fact we have sold exactly 6000 copies before publication which is more than "All Passion Spent"' (HPA 418, HP to VSW, 12 October 1932).

Sackville-West's reputation in the USA was also sufficiently high to warrant exporting a quantity of the first edition to bibliophiles. Not that the extra sales were needed: the novel was selling so well that Woolf was unable to disguise her own – and the Press' – excitement in this letter to Sackville-West of 12 October 1932:

> I've just bought the 6,000th copy of Family History—6000 sold before publi-cation—my God! And my fingers are red and whealed with doing up parcels for 3 days incessantly. Miss Belsher ill—orders pouring in—we all working till 7.30—thought we were just finished—then a last batch of orders discov-ered hidden in a drawer another hours work—clerks panting—telephones ringing carriers arriving—parcels just finished in time to catch the vans—Oh Lord what it is to publish a best seller—when shall I be able to hold a pen again? But its been great fun . . .
> What fun it all is to be sure—selling 6,000. (*L5* 110)

So, although they were not runaway best-sellers like *The Edwardians*, the fast sales of these follow-up novels continued to increase the Woolfs' income substantially.

At the prospect of publishing her next novel, Woolf told Sackville-West that she and Leonard 'both shouted for joy. Our list was looking very lean and dry—now nature's plenty has descended on it. What a blessing' (*L4* 278); however, by the time he read this the third of the novels which followed *The Edwardians – The dark island –* Leonard, nothing if not astute, had perceived a decline in the quality of Sackville-West's writing. Still buoyed up by her literary success, she felt unhappy with the terms Leonard offered on the novel. Understandably there is unease in her tone as she has to ask her friends to reconsider what the book, and her contract, is worth:

> I am really sorry to have to question the contract which Miss West [Hogarth Press] has sent me. You know that I hate anything in the nature of bargaining or business-likeness, especially where you or Virginia are concerned. At the same time, you will remember that we discussed our finances with you and Virginia when you were here last year, and made it clear to you both that we had some difficulty in carrying on our life, and the education of Ben and Nigel, on what we were able to make by books or journalism.[7] I also told you that I had rejected an offer from Cassells' of £1,000 down for a novel, because I was determined to remain faithful to the Hogarth Press. I feel, therefore, that you will not think me very exacting in suggesting that you should pay me £200 when I deliver the manuscript and a further £200 on the date of publication. I quite realise that this will reduce my receipts on the 31st March 1935, when you make up my royalty account, but my need by

the autumn will be immediate, and I would therefore prefer to forego a larger royalty in March 1935.

At the same time, I observe that Harold gets 20% royalty from Constable straight away, whereas you offer me only 15% up to the first 3000 copies sold, and 20% on all copies sold above that number. I hope you won't think me very exacting if I say that I think I might expect to get, on a novel, which will presumably sell more copies than a biography, as much as Harold obtains from Constable. (HPA 415, VSW to LW, 29 June 1934)

Leonard acquiesced: 'I think you perfectly right in all your requests and stipulations, and I agree to them all. I feel a little guilty in having put the burden of suggesting them upon you' (HPA 415, LW to VSW, 3 July 1934). Sackville-West replied: 'It is very nice of you to agree so generously to my suggestions, and although I still feel rather uncomfortable about it I am most grateful to you' (HPA 415, VSW to LW, 4 July 1934).

There are not many moments like this in the correspondence, where the awful business of negotiation has to be faced square on.[8] Sackville-West, with great subtlety, let Leonard know that she knew just what her name had been worth to the Press over recent years; that she *could* have defected to a higher-paying publisher at any time, and was not going to be palmed off with a second-class contract. *The dark island* turned out to be a novel over which there were still more awkward and testing negotiations between author and publisher:

Would you approve of letting Ben [Benedict Lionel Nicolson, 1914–1978, the elder son of Sackville-West and Harold Nicolson] do the jacket for my new novel? . . . The photograph which forms part of the design is a postcard which I bought on board the 'Bremen'. . . .

I suggest also that he should draw a map to be used as an end-paper in the beginning of the book, as the geography of my Dark Island is somewhat complicated. . . . If you would pay him a small fee for his work, he would be pleased as Punch . . . I should prefer Ben to use a lettering which makes it clear that the title is spelt without capital letters, e.g. The dark island and not The Dark Island. I particularly want it spelt without capitals. (HPA 415, VSW to LW, 24 June 1934)

Leonard approved Ben's design and paid the 'usual fee' (three guineas). He advised against the unconventional lower-case initial letters for two of the three words in the title: 'I think I am just a little above the ordinary person in intelligence, and really I do not understand the difference between the title The Dark Island and The dark island' (HPA 415, LW to VSW, 27 June 1934). Sackville-West was undeterred by her publisher's preference but insisted; she was 'sorry to put an author's obstinacy in the way' (HPA 415, VSW to LW, 29 June 1934). Unfortunately, Sackville-West's separate amendments to the jacket proof were not incorporated, resulting in her specific request – that her son's name be given in full ('Benedict' instead of 'Ben') to avoid confusion with the artist Ben Nicholson – went unheeded (HPA 415, VSW to Miss West, 26 September 1934). She made some last-minute changes to four or five lines to correct the divorce story after consulting a legal friend of hers (HPA 415, VSW to Miss West, 1 August 1934) and Leonard wrote a long letter to her on receiving the manuscript, opening with how he had read it with 'considerable excitement' and that he liked 'it ever so much better than *Family History*' (HPA 415, LW to VSW, 17 July 1934). Sales of *The dark island* were significantly lower than the previous three novels, owing perhaps to the generally poor reviews: 'Vita has rather bad reviews in London: The grateful provinces adore the aristocracy' (*L5* 338).[9] By the second week after publication 4,400 of the initial print run of 10,590 had been sold but there was never a need for the Press to print a second edition.

In 1930 Sackville-West and Nicolson purchased Sissinghurt Castle and almost instantly it proved to be an inspiration for her. She wrote a poem entitled 'Sissinghurst Thursday' which was composed like a letter to Woolf. When Woolf received it she liked 'its timelessness and shade; and its air of rings widening widening till they imperceptibly touch the bank. Thats what I like best in your work' (*L4* 256), and she begged her to allow them to print it. They printed and published it themselves, a practice they performed only twice more before giving up hand print-ing for good in 1932. The final four of their hand-printed publications were all sold as signed limited editions, allowing them to charge more for very slim books which cost them considerable amounts of time and personal effort to produce. In the case of Woolf and Sackville-West they capitalised, too, on the current popularity of particular authors (this was reflected in their respective selling prices).[10] In May 1931 Leonard wrote to Sackville-West suggesting a change to the poem's title: 'I am just beginning to print *Sissinghurst* and it has struck me that it would be better to leave out on the title page "Thursday to V.W." We now have it on the first page of the poem and I think it looks a little silly on the title page. Do you agree to this?' (HPA 426, 5 May 1931). Sackville-West agreed and the poem became simply 'Sissinghurst'.

As mentioned above (see n 5) Sackville-West had first wanted to translate Rainer Maria Rilke's *Duineser Elegien* (*Elegies from the Castle of Duino*) back in 1928 when she had been living in Berlin. Her and her cousin Edward's translations became a joint project of the Hogarth Press and Count Harry Kessler's Cranach Presses, but formal agreements seem not to have been made, which resulted in some confusion. The publication was fraught with complications. The Press wrote to Kessler stating that it would 'have a much better chance here and in America if it is signed by the translators' (HPA 379, 1 April 1930), so it became a signed as well as a limited edition. The Press wanted '25 "out of series" [copies] for review & 6 for travelling' (HPA 379, 12 May 1930), but Kessler thought the proportion of free (and thus unearning copies) was too high. Owing to a misprint on the title page, Kessler advised that the bookbinder would paste in new ones. Despite its pedigree the translation did not sell well: by September 1932 only seventy copies had been sold and just three of the special edition. Leonard disowned it and regarded the Press as merely the book's distributor.

A far more positive publication for Sackville-West was her *Collected Poems*. Following a relatively poor publishing season, Woolf appealed to her friend once more: 'Do do please write us another book as soon as ever you can' (*L4* 175). Between *Family History* and *The dark island* it was just the prompt Sackville-West needed to gather together her impressive output of poetry. Although she initially found the idea of a collected edition of her poems 'pretentious', she began to make an index of those to be included – many of them previously unpublished – correctly foreseeing a book of 'over 300 pages already—quite enough for Vol I,—and that if [Leonard] really wants a collected edition of all that tripe for the autumn, he can have it' (DeSalvo & Leaska 403). There may have been some false modesty shown here because Sackville-West consistently ranked her poetry far higher than her novels. She asked Woolf to tell Leonard 'that I shall be a terrible bore to him about this edition, because it is the only book of mine I shall ever have minded about—i.e. I don't give a damn for my novels, but I do give ½ a damn for my poems' (DeSalvo & Leaska 404). She lost no time in writing to Leonard while on holiday in Perugia:

> My feeling is that I would rather have one large (i.e. important looking) volume, than two smaller ones. There is also the question of getting Heinemann & John Lane's agreement.[11] . . . If, therefore, you want to complete your autumn list before the middle of July, I suggest that you should put *Collected Poems, Vol. I*. The price I must leave to you, but I suppose it would have to be around about 10/6. (HPA 413, VSW to LW, 4 July 1933)

The following month she specified the appearance of the poems on the page: she wanted 'one poem to each page . . . even if a poem is only four lines long . . . I want the book to be as fat as possible . . . I have put *Collected Poems. Vol I*. because I would like henceforth to bring out any poems I may write in a second (and, who knows, third,) volume to match this one' (HPA 413, VSW to LW, 9 August 1933). She wrote again three days later regarding the retail price of the book: 'I rather hope that you will decide to publish at 10/6, and not at 8/6, as Nigel's little diversion[12] has cost me £200, and I am also being persecuted to pay supertax on what I earned with 'The Edwardians' two years ago!' (HPA 413, VSW to LW, 12 August 1933).

The regular trade edition was published on 16 November 1933 and was indeed priced at 10s 6d. As with *The Edwardians* there was a signed edition, limited to 150 copies, published at two guineas. Woolf memorably described its physicality as 'stately', 'like a slab of ivory engraved with steel' (*L5* 241). The volume was dedicated by Sackville-West to her mother, and she had written a dedicatory poem to be included 'but Lady Sackville objected, not wanting "to be in a book with Virginia Woolf, the author of that awful book, *Orlando*": she evidently was referring to *Sissinghurst*, the poem dedicated to VW' (Cross & Ravenscroft-Hulme 85).

The gap between the Press' publication of Sackville-West's *The dark island* and her next major book *Pepita* was caused by her writing the biography *Saint Joan of Arc* for the publishers Cobden-Sanderson[13] who had suggested the project to her. She knew she was contractually bound to give the Press her 'next book' and writing to Leonard was forced to 'appeal to you to release me from that clause', and when he consented she wrote gratefully of his reply: 'you have managed to word [it] in so tactful a way that I have no uncomfortable feeling of guilt or desertion' (HPA 415, VSW to LW, 18 & 22 January 1935). She must have possessed a lingering guilt when she sent Woolf a copy of it on publication, for Woolf was prompted to include in her reply: 'how angelically you behave to the Hogarth Press! Generous, humane, honourable . . . you're an angel about the Press: and to contradict my own theory of contemporary humanity, not one of our authors ever treats us as kindly as you do' (*L5* 50).

Cleverly the Woolfs did end up gaining a little from *Saint Joan of Arc*, and at no small cost of effort to Sackville-West. Only six days after its publication Leonard wrote to her:

> We are starting a series of biographies for children, and in the preliminary list we had down Joan of Arc. I did not say anything to you about it because I thought you would have had enough of the good woman, but it has struck me that it is just conceivable that you might be willing to do a short book like this which would not in any way compete with your great book. (HPA 419, LW to VSW, 11 June 1936)

She set to work condensing her book to a mere 20,000 words; Leonard considered her remoulded book 'quite admirable for its purpose' (*L6* 88) and in January Sackville-West apologised for returning the proofs late to the Press, owing to her getting 'them read by a child of 14, to see if there were any words etc she didn't understand, or any thing which was not clear' (HPA 419, VSW to Miss West, 1 January 1937). She was asked to cut further to meet the exact book-length requirement of 80 pages (HPA 419, HP to VSW, 6 January 1937) but upon publication of the four titles in the series (June 1937) she criticised Leonard's wording in his advertising.

> I was on the point of writing to you to suggest that surely you were making a mistake in not showing clearly on the jacket that the series was designed for children of school age. But since then I have noticed your advertisement in the New Statesman, advertising the series as being intended 'for children and adults'. Now surely no author in their senses would have dreamt of writing one of those little books in words of one or two syllables *for adults*? I hope you will not think me impertinent in suggesting that you are misleading your public in not making it clear that they are primarily meant for children, especially in an advertisement in a paper like the New Statesman, where adults are very much adults. (HPA 579, VSW to LW, 21 June 1937)

Leonard replied: 'When I read the actual books it seemed to me that while they were admirable for children of school age, like all good books written for children they also had a certain appeal for certain kinds of adults' (HPA 579, LW to VSW, 22 June 1937). Perhaps Sackville-West was right and the project did end up falling between two stools; Leonard wrote of his disappointment in not selling the books to schools 'though we sold out of the edition of the four books . . . we never got the sale we wanted and did not go on with the venture' (*Journey* 98–9).

Were the Woolfs getting impatient for the next *proper* Sackville-West title? They were unambiguous in their appeal to her: 'what I am writing to say is: for goodness sake choose your subject; whichever you will; and let us have it. What a generous and exemplary author you are compared with—but I leave a blank for fear of libel. L. says I'm to tell you we want another volume of poetry' (*L6* 40). They didn't have to wait long for Sackville-West to excitedly reveal the seeds of her new project:

> I hope that my reference to a discovery of documents has tickled your curiosity, so I will tell you what it is. It is the complete record of the depositions made by the Spanish peasants of a little village near Granada, relating to the years 1855–6 when my grandmother was staying with her mother in that village, awaiting the birth of her first child. It . . . gives a picture of Spanish life in a small country house among its vineyards, which I think could be worked up into something of real interest. My idea would be to divide the book up into three parts, rather like the design for a triptych. The first part would deal with life in the Spanish village, the second with my grandmother's life as a dancer and her connection with my grandfather, and the third would go on to the sequel of the Knole succession case and end up

with a sketch of my mother.[14] Would you approve of this as a scheme? It would quite certainly need to be illustrated with photographs which I can produce. . . .

Do tell Virginia about this and say I hope that she is envious. (HPA 422, VSW to LW, 19 June 1936)

Virginia *was* envious; she thought it a 'magnificent subject' and her 'mouth water[ed]' at the prospect (*L6* 64–5). Similarly enthused by the project, Leonard wrote eagerly: 'The book sounds better and better. How long do you think it would take for you to write it, or is it too early to begin to speak of that? Is it also too early to speak of an agreement, and if not, what would you consider to be reasonable terms?' (HPA 422, LW to VSW, 24 June 1936).

Remembering the previous time they had had to negotiate over contracts (*The dark island*, June 1934), Sackville-West was sensibly shrewd in her reply:

What a slave-driver you are, to be sure! Here am I, grinding away at your wretched biography for school children, and you are already beginning to ask me when I shall have finished the book about my grandmother, and also to talk about agreements.

. . . As regards the second point, this is an extremely delicate matter. I know that you will not think me conceited if I tell you that I feel rather like a piece of sugar with flies sitting on it—the flies in this case being your fellow publishers.

She went on to tell him of lucrative offers she had received for biographies of Rembrandt and Gertrude Bell, of her large advance for *Saint Joan of Arc*, concluding: 'But as you know, nothing would induce me to desert the old firm and I think that I had better leave it to you to make some suggestion based upon these figures which I have given you, in the certainty that we shall agree' (HPA 422, VSW to LW, 26 June 1936). Leonard foresaw the book's potential success and acknowledged the special place Sackville-West held in the list of Hogarth authors:

I must repeat what Virginia, I believe, said to you with regard to your unique merits as an author. I also feel I ought to repeat what I believe I once said before, namely, that you ought to treat it as between ourselves as a business proposition, and that if at any time you felt the slightest doubt about the advisability of continuing with the old firm you ought to give it up, without any thought of friendship. With that preliminary, the terms which we could offer would be an advance of £500 if the book were a 10/6 book, and £600 if it were above that price. (HPA 422, LW to VSW, 2 July 1936)

Leonard was keen to keep the business side of their relationship on a purely commercial footing and did not want Sackville-West to stay with the Press if she felt she could get a better deal elsewhere. It was important for the Woolfs not to exercise an emotional hold on her, not to take advantage of her loyalty to them. She must have found more material than she had initially thought and sought to delay publication of *Pepita* until the spring of 1938. Leonard insisted that it was a book 'eminently for the Christmas season, and I am sure we should lose a great deal of sale if it were not a Christmas book' (HPA 422, LW to VSW, 10 April 1937).

It is impossible to know what complications surrounded the serial rights for the book in a magazine. We know that her agent Curtis Brown had told her that she could have '£3,000 or possibly more' but in the end no serialisation in England took place and the whole episode left her feeling dejected about 'this Pepita question,—I wish she had never been my grandmother, and still more that I had never thought of writing a book about her!' (HPA 422, VSW to LW, 24 and 14 April 1937). The question raised its head again in June when the *Sunday Times* wanted the book for serialisation. She asked Woolf whether it would help or hinder the sale of a book. Woolf batted 'this business matter' over to Leonard (*L6* 137) and he replied: 'My own feeling is that it probably damages the sale of the book a little in any case, but quite a lot if the serialization really "guts" the book' (HPA 422, LW to VSW, 23 June 1937).

In July Leonard and Sackville-West corresponded about the photograph of the sole of Pepita's shoe. Once taken she thought it would make an 'amusing' and 'unusual' jacket. At first Leonard disagreed but soon changed his mind after seeing 'a rough pull of what the jacket might be if the sole is used. I don't think it looks bad, and would attract attention. I would suggest printing it on a paper rather like the one we used for the big edition of *Flush* which is a slightly toned art paper' (HPA 422, VSW to LW, 13 July 1937; LW to VSW, 28 July 1937).

In the publicity drive to promote *Pepita*, Sackville-West agreed to the Press' request to display Pepita relics under a locked glass case on the Hogarth Press stand at a book exhibition (HPA 422, HP to VSW, 1 September 1937). As the publication date of 30 October approached, Leonard's plans were suddenly thrown up into the air by a tempting offer:

The Book Society has suddenly said that they will select Pepita if we postpone publication until March or April, but that they must have my decision today. . . . It seemed to me worth while as it will mean an additional sale of about 6 or 7 thousand. It is a great nuisance in many ways as we have already travelled the book in the provinces, and we shall forego Christmas sales. (HPA 422, LW to VSW, 6 October 1937)

His letter caught up with Sackville-West on holiday in Souillac from where she replied:

1. I do not feel that the Book Society is very much of a catch any more.
2. The book has already been travelled, advertised, and announced.
3. The 6 or 7 thousand of the Book Society (which anyway would be on cheaper terms) would scarcely compensate for the loss of Christmas sales.
4. The book has already appeared in part in the New Yorker,[15] and will be out in America in November in book form.

It seemed to me on the whole that the financial advantage to be obtained from the Book Society would not be equal to the disadvantages of postponement till March.

I am afraid that my telegram will be too late to stop the acceptance of the Book Society. (HPA 422, VSW to LW, 9 October 1937)

Leonard was in time to advise the Book Society that *Pepita* would not be on the Selected List and publication went ahead as planned. Both Woolfs loved *Pepita*; Woolf told Sackville-West that she had 'read it like a shark swallowing mackerel. I think its far better than Joan [of Arc], more masterly and controlled' (*L6* 175); while Leonard 'was absolutely enthralled. It really is a superb story, and I think it comes out magnificently' (HPA 422, LW to VSW, (undated)). Sales of *Pepita* were excellent,[16] so it cannot be pure coincidence that Woolf closed her letter to Sackville-West of 26[?] December 1937 in a fashion that equated the results of its sales with luxury purchases: '12,000 copies of Pepita sold. I'm thinking of buying a fur coat' (*L6* 195). Leonard, too, was not slow to recognise the impact of the sales and in a letter to Lehmann concerning his impending purchase of a share in the Press humorously warned: 'We have done very well with Pepita. If it sells much more, our profits this year will be so large that I shall be tempted to put the price up on you!' (Spotts 330). Woolf confirmed the same to Sackville-West: 'they say its worth, The Press, £10,000. Much thanks to the noble daughter of all the Sackvilles' (*L6* 226).

In spite of the huge sales and the income generated for the Woolfs by Sackville-West's writing, her modesty persisted; she assumed nothing when she tentatively approached Leonard about her next intended book, the poem *Solitude*:

This is a very preliminary sort of letter ... to ask whether the Hogarth Press would be disposed to publish a longish poem (running to about 50 pages) by me in the autumn? ... I know poetry doesn't sell ... It would make only a small book,—a 'slim volume', in fact,—so please say frankly if you would rather I offered it to somebody else. (HPA 427, VSW to LW, 9 July 1938)

The Press was happy to proceed and Sackville-West wrote again suggesting modest terms (considering the success of *Pepita*) and how she would like the book laid out:

> I should be glad of your candid comments on my poem—and Virginia's too, if she has time to read it. I feel very dubious about it myself. Oh, terms, by the way. I don't really mind very much about this, as it won't sell anyhow. So let's say the same as Collected Poems, whatever they were. Only for God's sake don't advertise my novels at the end of it, as you did in Pepita.[17] You will realise that I want each page printed separately. ie. even though there may be only 4 lines on a page, it must still be separate. (HPA 427, VSW to LW, 19 July 1938)

Leonard read the manuscript with great enthusiasm:

> I . . . enjoyed it very much indeed. I think that besides being poetry, it is extremely moving intellectually, and I enjoy the combination of verbal dexterity with this. To me it is the best thing you've done. Its great merit is too that it talks sound common sense about the universe, which very few poets have done since Lucretius . . . I do not know whether you would or would not like a special limited edition. We had one for the Collected Poems and sold between 70 and 80 copies. I have put probable price 6s. for the ordinary edition as this is what most publishers now charge for poetry. (HPA 427, LW to VSW, 21 July 1938)

Sackville-West thought five shillings would be a preferable price and that she had: 'a completely open mind myself about a limited edition and must leave that decision to you. I had an idea that the demand for limited editions was now almost entirely exhausted, but you of course have a much better opportunity of judging this than I have. In any case does not £2.2.0 seem a very exorbitant price to charge?' (HPA 427, VSW to LW, 22 July 1938). Leonard took her advice. The 'trade' edition sold for five shillings and the limited edition for one guinea (£1.1.0; see Appendix). This was the last of her books to be published by the Press in a signed limited edition and serves as a challenge to commentators when they say that the Hogarth Press was altruistic, that its motives were pure, that the book's physicality was unimportant, that it was only the texts that mattered and so on. Leonard Woolf's qualities raised it above the other private presses set up by similar literary insiders of the day. He was prudent and economical, helping to secure the sound financial footing on which the Press was run; but he was also a shrewd businessman. It is probably coincidence that Vita and Virginia hit the acme of their respective literary careers within the same four or five years – from around 1927/8 to 1932/3 – when their public profiles were sky-high. It was no coincidence that it was during these years that their most expensive, limited, gilt-edged, vellum-spined deluxe editions were printed (with the exception of this book, *Solitude*). These were the years of huge sales and not-to-be-missed business opportunities. It was for purely commercial reasons that for the first time Woolf's books were being printed and published in signed limited editions. Her reputation was sufficient to warrant the publication of single essays smartly packaged for the well off. For example, twenty copies of *Mr. Bennett and Mrs. Brown* could be bought for the price of one copy of the signed *Beau Brummell*; and while the American presses were the main driving force behind Woolf's limited editions, the Hogarth Press, though restrained, did co-publish a signed edition of *A Room of One's Own* jointly in 1929 and famously printed and published her *On Being Ill* in 1930. Sackville-West on the other hand was a *popular* novelist, so the Hogarth Press capitalised on their coup of having an author on their list who sold in thousands. The production of signed limited editions was the exploitation of a market. By contrast with Woolf's two, the Press published no fewer than five Sackville-West titles in expensive limited editions.

In 1939 Sackville-West collected a number of her 'Country Notes' (contributed regularly to the *New Statesman and Nation*) that were published together with other occasional pieces and photographs as *Country Notes* by Michael Joseph. She sent a copy to Woolf in April 1940, and in the August wrote to her:

> I have a lot of my 'Country Notes' accumulated since Michael Joseph pub-lished them in an illustrated book. Would the Press like to reprint these unpublished ones in a cheap, unillustrated little pamphlet this autumn? say 1/- thus catching the Christmas-card sale? I shan't be in the least offended if Monsieur my publisher says no thank you. (DeSalvo & Leaska 463)

Woolf's response was quick and to the point: 'Country Notes idea enthusiastically accepted: good news already sent to John [Lehmann]: who will communicate officially' (*L6* 411). Two days later Leonard suggested the format and terms:

> We should very much like to do a cheap edition of your Country Notes, but we suggest it should be in a slightly different form . . . 2/6d book . . . a good floral design, say by Duncan Grant . . . It would make a good Christmas present, if there is a Christmas in 1940. (HPA 414, LW to VSW, 14 August 1940)

Sackville-West clarified the proposed contents of the book, but ques-tioned Leonard's idea of using Duncan Grant to decorate the cover:

> I quite realise about the gamble of publishing and agree to your terms. I wonder however if you are right in wanting a cover design by Duncan? Much

as I should like it myself, would it sell the book as well as a photograph? Does the country bumpkin who presumably will buy the book appreciate Duncan? I enclose a photograph as a suggestion. (HPA 414, VSW to LW, 19 August 1940)

Leonard agreed and suggested the title 'Country Notes in War Time' for the collection's title. Sackville-West responded: 'I think *Country Notes in Wartime* is quite a good title, unless you think people fight shy of anything to do with the war. If so, I suggest 'More Country Notes' as an alternative. I think as an act of courtesy we should advertise the 'Country Notes' published last year by Michael Joseph, 12/6, illustrated, on your fly-leaf. He advertised no less than 10 of my books published by you' (HPA 414, VSW to JL, 30 August 1940). It was published in December 1940 just in time for Christmas; by Boxing Day Woolf was able to tell her that it had already sold 1,862 copies. More importantly she went into raptures over Sackville-West's continued generosity in gift-giving. Wartime austerity had meant that her gift of 'two pounds of fresh butter' for Christmas was wonderfully welcomed and she went on to list various gifts, adding tellingly: 'Then I have to add about £2,000 from your books' (*L6* 454).

The last of Sackville-West's books to be published by the Press was her *Selected Poems*. She told Lehmann: 'I think it is a very good idea to produce selections of the Hogarth Press poets and I would be very pleased for you to do one of mine. I think I would rather make the selection myself' (HPA 425, VSW to JL, 6 November 1940), and she added several uncollected poems. As well as the last for the Press it was also sadly the only one never to be seen by Woolf; it was not published until July 1941, four months after her death.

Why, when Sackville-West had more than a dozen further books published before her own death in 1962, did this highly successful partnership between author and publisher come to an end? The answer lies with the chasm caused by *Grand Canyon*. Sackville-West had visited the Grand Canyon in the spring of 1933 and told Woolf it was 'the most astonishing thing in the world'; in June she wrote of a novel she had started which had sprung from the trip to America and 'was all about deserts and hurricanes' (DeSalvo & Leaska 394, 401). By November 1939 she had started work on it again, telling Lehmann:

I *am* trying to write a novel, but it is such a queer concern that I really don't know how to describe it. It is in two parts,—the first part takes place beside the Grand Canyon, and the second part on a wind-jammer. I hate the expression 'symbolism', but that is what it really is. I don't know if you can cast this meagre information into anything resembling a blurb for your Spring list. I call it 'a discarded novel' to myself, as I began it some years ago, put it aside, and fished it out again the other day. I'm not sure that it isn't rather a good title?[18] (HPA 613, VSW to JL, 23 November 1939)

Prophetically she had doubts about the novel and again expressed her feelings candidly about her ability as a novelist: 'I think it's bound to be a failure as a novel,—artistically, I mean, as well as financially. I simply *can't* write novels, and wish I could be jumbled up in a sack with Hugh Walpole who is what's called "a born novelist"' (HPA 613, VSW to JL, 1 December 1939). Early in 1940 Lehmann was applying pressure for delivery of the manuscript in time for publication in the autumn with an agreement already drawn up; but eighteen months later, with an extensive advertising campaign already under way, Sackville-West was uncharacteristically still struggling with it. She felt 'utterly ashamed about that wretched book. I really am doing my best but interruptions are constant. . . . I think I will give up writing and just become a farmer—that's what I feel like at the moment.' She had to apologise again at the end of the year, exclaiming that the Japanese attack on the USA necessitated fundamental changes, and anticipated publication in the spring of 1942 (HPA 613, VSW to JL, 14 August and 31 December 1941).

When the manuscript was finally delivered Leonard considered it 'not a good book'. He sent it on to Lehmann saying:

> I doubt whether, were it not by Vita, one would consider it. It would, I suppose, be difficult to refuse it and I should personally be against refusing it unless you are very certain that it is not good enough . . . The consequence is that, though I usually feel pretty certain as to what sales one should count on with a book (though of course one knows one may always very likely be wrong), here I have no idea of what one should guess at. The guess I do make is about 4000. Do you expect me to write to Vita? (HPA 613, LW to JL, 3 April 1942)

Evidently Lehmann also rejected it and expected Leonard to write to Sackville-West. What a truly unenviable task for Leonard whose rejection letter now is apparently lost but is quoted by Glendinning: 'This is one of the most unpleasant letters I have ever had to write, primarily because as an author you have always treated us so extraordinarily well that it seems almost unthinkable that the Hogarth Press should reject a book of yours' (Glendinning 318).

Her response was a measured one, generous and understanding, yet clearly hurt. It is printed here in full as it marked the end of the long and fruitful business relationship between the author and her publishers to whom she had always wished to remain loyal; its final sentence is a touching coda to the last eighteen years of shared success:

My dear Leonard

I will not pretend that I enjoyed reading your letter any more than you (I imagine) enjoyed writing it, but you could not have done otherwise.

I must consider very carefully what to do, and whether to get it published or not. I am in the awkward position of having already received a large advance on it from America.[19] I must say I was appalled to discover that you thought it could be interpreted as defeatist, when I really intended it as a cautionary tale, i.e. 'do not make peace with these people until they are thoroughly destroyed or the whole thing will start up all over again.'

Meanwhile, will you send back the copy you have as soon as possible? I have no copy myself. I need not tell you that it would grieve me to see it published under another imprint, for as you know I have resisted many lucrative bribes in the past in order to remain faithful to the Hogarth Press, but in the circumstances I must consider myself free to offer it elsewhere if I do not decide to scrap it altogether.[20]

I don't know if there is anything more to say, except that from every point of view I feel very sorry.

Yours Vita (HPA 613, 18 April 1942)

Would the Press have rejected *Grand Canyon* if Woolf herself had still been alive? I believe it would have, though the decision would have been that much more difficult to come to. Leonard's instinct has proved to be correct (critics have continued to regard it as a poor book), and after Lehmann became a partner by buying Woolf's share of the Press in 1938 such decisions were made by Leonard and Lehmann without Woolf. A year after the rejection, Leonard was adamant it had been the right thing to do, re-establishing his view of the Press' policy:

I think that the Press should not publish third-rate work either because it is a work of an established writer like Vita or because it is that of the young and 'promising' . . . I agreed at once to reject Vita's novel which was an extremely difficult and painful thing to do, especially as it was the first thing submitted by her after Virginia's death. (Spotts 344)

This history should close with Leonard's own summary of the Press' relationship with Sackville-West:

Vita was an ideal author from the publisher's point of view; she never complained when things went wrong and was extraordinarily appreciative of the publisher if they went right. This made it all the more unpleasant to have to tell her that we thought her novel not good enough for us to publish. We knew, too, that we should lose her as an author, because there were many reputable publishers who would publish this novel in order to get her 'on their list.' It was characteristic of her that she was not in the least bit hurt or resentful and the whole thing made no difference to her relationship with us. (*Downhill* 159–60)

Notes

1. Exceptions were *The Land* (Heinemann, 1926); *Aphra Behn* (Gerald Howe, 1927); *Andrew Marvell* (Faber & Faber, 1929); *The Death of Noble Godavary and Gottfried Künstler* (Ernest Benn, 1932); *Saint Joan of Arc* (Cobden-Sanderson, 1936); *Some Flowers* (Cobden-Sanderson, 1937); and *Country Notes* (Michael Joseph, 1939).
2. I am very grateful to Juliet Nicolson for granting permission to quote from previously unpublished letters from her grandmother Vita Sackville-West and to the University of Sussex, and the Society of Authors as their representative, for permission to quote from previously unpublished letters by Leonard Woolf. I was made very welcome by staff at the University of Reading, Special Collections, which houses the Hogarth Press archive.
3. Probably from Rupert Hart-Davis at Cassell; Sackville-West told Woolf that 'no temptation to leave the Hogarth Press is any temptation at all' (Glendinning 267). For the sake of clarity, in this chapter Virginia Woolf will be referred to as 'Woolf', Leonard Woolf as 'Leonard' and Vita Sackville-West as 'Sackville-West'.
4. Sproles argues that the literary influence each had on the other was 'reciprocal and profound' (5); she lays particular significance on their biographical writings (*passim*). Willis marks the influence as a key point in Sackville-West's development as a writer (105–6).
5. This project eventually manifested itself as the special, deluxe publication of *Duineser Elegien* in 1931 (see below), which was a far cry from the modest volumes in the Hogarth Living Poets series whose general editor was Vita's friend, Dorothy Wellesley. Vita contributed her collection *King's Daughter* to the series in 1929.
6. Using the Measuring Worth website calculator, and employing the most modest of its conversions – the one based on the Retail Price Index – the £2,000 the Press made on *The Edwardians* in 1930 is equivalent to £87,000 ($174,000) in today's money.
7. By contrast the Woolfs' own modest financial needs are discussed in *The Journey* (99).
8. Friction between them sometimes arose over Canadian and US rights to Sackville-West's works, with her agent often negotiating for her when US rights were invariably included in her contract with the Press. Muddles also arose because she erroneously thought Canada would be included under US rights when, being part of the British Empire, rights for Canada fell under completely different laws.
9. A Hogarth Press advertisement in *The Times* (6 November 1934, 19) calls it 'An autumn best seller' and quotes from a review in the *Manchester Guardian*.
10. *On Being Ill* (1930, 21s) would have been a great deal more expensive to bind than *Sissinghurst* (1931, 5s) being longer and with a vellum spine, marbled endpapers and a dust wrapper designed by Vanessa Bell.
11. These two publishers granted consent for the poems previously published by them in *The Land* and *Orchard and Vineyard*, respectively.
12. This may refer to Nigel's becoming seriously ill with appendicitis in July 1933 and requiring an emergency operation.

13. She had published with Cobden-Sanderson a number of occasional pieces over the years, including 'The Countryside' in *The New Forget-Me-Not* (1929) and 'Shameful reminiscence' in *Little Innocents* (1932), and she wrote the introduction to *The Annual* (c. 1930) which had been edited by Dorothy Wellesley.
14. Lady Sackville (1862–1936) had died earlier in the year. Sackville-West found the papers 'among my mother's things at Brighton. I am getting some more from the family solicitors. I thought of calling the book simply "Pepita". This would cover everything because my mother was also called Pepita until she was 18' (HPA 422, VSW to LW, 23 June 1936).
15. Unrecorded in Cross & Ravenscroft-Hulme.
16. It went into four editions by 1938 and into a 'cheap edition' in 1939 (see Appendix). When they were auditing the previous year's accounts for the Press (April 1939), Woolf told Sackville-West it was 'a very dismal matter this year, Pepita the only bright spot' (*L6* 329).
17. She confirmed her instructions to the Press in a letter to Mrs Nicholls of 8 September 1938: 'I absolutely veto any reference to my novels, so if you want to put in any review references they must relate only to my poems & travel books. I don't mind those; but my novels must be allowed to die as they deserve' (HPA 427). This underscores the fact that she regarded her novels as trifles, by comparison with her poetry and prose. After reading *The dark island*, Ben Nicolson wrote to his father: 'She is obviously a poet and not a novelist, and *All Passion* was so good only because it was so poetic' (qtd in Glendinning 274).
18. Lehmann suggested instead the title *Grand Canyon* (HPA 613, JL to VSW, 30 November 1939).
19. The advance from Doubleday, Doran had been for $5,000 (Cross & Ravenscroft-Hulme 120).
20. Curtis Brown 'first offered the book to William Heinemann who turned it down and then to Michael Joseph who shared Doubleday, Doran's enthusiasm'. Changes were made 'to remove defeatism about Britain losing the War and criticism of the USA for not having helped more' (ibid. 122).

Works cited

Cross, Robert and Ann Ravenscroft-Hulme. *Vita Sackville-West: A Bibliography*. Winchester: St Paul's Bibliographies; New Castle: Oak Knoll Press, 1999.

DeSalvo, Louise and Mitchell A. Leaska, eds. *The Letters of Vita Sackville-West to Virginia Woolf*. London: Hutchinson, 1984.

Glendinning, Victoria. *Vita: The Life of V. Sackville-West*. London: Weidenfeld and Nicolson, 1983.

Hogarth Press Archive, University of Reading, Special Collections Service, RUL MS 2750. Referenced in the text as: HPA (followed by file number).

Lehmann, John. *Thrown to the Woolfs*. London: Weidenfeld and Nicolson, 1978.

Nicolson, Nigel. *Vita and Harold: The Letters of Vita Sackville-West and Harold Nicolson*. London: Weidenfeld and Nicolson, 1992.

Spotts, Frederic. *Letters of Leonard Woolf*. San Diego: Harcourt Brace Jovanovich, 1989.

Sproles, Karyn Z. *Desiring Women: The Partnership of Virginia Woolf and Vita Sackville-West*. Toronto: University of Toronto Press, 2006.

Willis, J. H. *Leonard and Virginia Woolf as Publishers: The Hogarth Press, 1917–41*. Charlottesville: University Press of Virginia, 1992.

Woolf, Leonard. *Downhill all the Way: An Autobiography of the Years 1919 to 1939*. London: Hogarth Press, 1968.

—. *The Journey not the Arrival Matters: An Autobiography of the Years 1939 to 1969*. London: Hogarth Press, 1969.

Woolf, Virginia. *The Collected Letters of Virginia Woolf*. 6 vols. Ed. Nigel Nicolson, Assist. Ed. Joanne Trautmann. London: Hogarth Press, 1975–1980.

—. *The Diary of Virginia Woolf*. 5 vols. Ed. Anne Olivier Bell, Assisted by Andrew McNeillie. London: Hogarth Press, 1977–1984.

Woolmer, J. Howard, ed. *A Checklist of the Hogarth Press 1917–1946*. Revere: Woolmer/Brotherson, 1986.

The Hogarth Press: Vita Sackville-West's Publications

Year	Title	Number of copies printed	Retail price
1924	*Seducers in Ecuador*	1,500	4s 6d
1926	*Passenger to Teheran*	1,640	12s 6d
1928	*Twelve Days*	2,025	10s 6d
1929	*King's Daughter*	1,000	3s 6d
1930	*The Edwardians* – limited edition	150 [125]	£1 5s 0d
1930	*The Edwardians*	18,000	7s 6d
1930	2nd impression	8,000	7s 6d
1930	3rd impression	3,000	7s 6d
1931	Cheap edition	3,000	3s 6d
1931	*All Passion Spent*	12,050	7s 6d
1931	2nd impression	5,000	7s 6d
1932	3rd impression – cheap edition	4,000	3s 6d
1938	4th impression	?	3s 6d
1931	*Sissinghurst*	500	5s 0d
1931	*Duineser Elegien* Trans. of Rilke by ES-W & VS-W – special limited edition	8	£26 5s 0d
1931	*Duineser Elegien* Trans. of Rilke by ES-W & VS-W – limited edition	240 [40 not for sale]	£3 3s 0d
1932	*Family History*	12,170	7s 6d
1935	1st edition became cheap edition		2s 6d
1933	*Collected Poems Volume One* – limited edition	150	£2 2s 0d
1933	*Collected Poems Volume One*	3,045	10s 6d
1934	*The dark island*	10,590	7s 6d
1937	*Joan of Arc* (World-Makers and World-Shakers series for schools)	5,000	1s 6d
1937	*Pepita*	9,962	10s 6d
1937	2nd impression	2,926	10s 6d
1937	3rd impression	2,696	10s 6d
1938	4th impression	3,000	10s 6d
1939	Cheap edition	1,874	5s 0d

Year	Title	Number of copies printed	Retail price
1938	*Solitude* – limited edition	100	£1 1s 0d
1938	*Solitude*	3,018	5s 0d
1938	2nd impression	1,050	5s 0d
1940	*Country Notes in Wartime*	3,000	2s 6d
1941	*Selected Poems*	2,500	2s 6d

List of Contributors

Stephen Barkway co-founded the Virginia Woolf Society of Great Britain in 1998. He has been its Chair over the past twelve years and continues to serve on the Editorial Committee of the *Virginia Woolf Bulletin* to which he contributes regularly. He has edited and transcribed selections from Woolf's previously unpublished correspondence, most notably to date the forty-four letters to Christabel, Lady Aberconway (*VWB* 15), ten to Gladys Ellen Easdale (*VWB* 28) and thirteen to Winifred Holtby (*VWB* 32). He has presented papers at several Virginia Woolf Conferences and in 2007 he edited the *Virginia Woolf Daybook*.

Diane F. Gillespie is Professor Emeritus at Washington State University where she taught modern British literature. She is author of *The Sisters' Arts* and co-editor both of a volume of Julia Stephen's writings and of a selected papers volume entitled *Virginia Woolf and the Arts*. She edited *The Multiple Muses of Virginia Woolf* and, for the Shakespeare Head Press Edition of Woolf's work, she edited *Roger Fry: A Biography*. She has contributed sections to *The Gender of Modernism* and *Gender in Modernism*, both edited by Bonnie Kime Scott, and, most recently, a chapter to Maggie Humm's *Edinburgh Companion to Woolf and the Arts*. Having published numerous articles on Woolf, Bloomsbury, and early twentieth-century novelists and playwrights, she is currently creating contexts for Woolf's writing by examining her personal library.

Elizabeth Willson Gordon teaches in the Department of English and Film Studies at the University of Alberta. She specialises in twentieth-century British literature, modernism, women's writing and print culture, with a particular focus on publishing history. She has worked with the Black Sparrow Press archives as well as the Hogarth Press archives. Her recent publications include articles on Virginia Woolf and the Hogarth Press' marketing practices. In 2009 she published *Woolf's-*

head Publishing: the Highlights and New Lights of the Hogarth Press in conjunction with an exhibition at Bruce Peel Special Collections, which she curated. Her current project is *Publishing, Branding, and Selling an Icon: the Cultural Impact of the Hogarth Press 1941–2001*, which creates a literary and social history of the Press.

Mark Hussey is editor of *Woolf Studies Annual* and chair of the editorial committee, Pace University Press. Among his books are *Virginia Woolf A to Z*, *The Singing of the Real World: The Philosophy of Virginia Woolf's Fiction*, and *Virginia Woolf and War*. He teaches at Pace University in New York, where he organised the first annual conference on Woolf in 1991. Professor Hussey is presently editing *Between the Acts* for the Cambridge University Press Edition of Virginia Woolf. He is also General Editor of the Harcourt Annotated Edition of the Works of Virginia Woolf, and has edited *To the Lighthouse* for that series.

Jean Mills is Assistant Professor of 20th Century British Literature at John Jay College of Criminal Justice of The City University of New York. She has published on both Virginia Woolf and Gertrude Stein and was a winner of The Florence Howe Award for Outstanding Feminist Scholarship for her article on Gertrude Stein's 'Stanzas in Meditation'. Her most recent article on Virginia Woolf is called 'She Do The Police in Different Voices: Teaching Virginia Woolf at a Criminal Justice College', and she is currently at work on a book project based on her dissertation: *Goddesses and Ghosts: Virginia Woolf and Jane Ellen Harrison*. She has also recently created a podcast on modern art at MoMA as part of an NEH grant 'Making Objects Speak', introducing undergraduate students to museums.

Helen Southworth (editor) is Associate Professor of Literature at Clark Honors College, University of Oregon. She is the author of *The Intersecting Realities and Fictions of Virginia Woolf and Colette* (Ohio State University Press, 2004) and of articles and book chapters on a range of topics including gender and space, nationalism, publishing and periodical culture in the work of writers Virginia Woolf, Colette, John Hampson, Ford Madox Ford, George Borrow and Douglas Goldring. She is also co-editor (with Elisa Sparks) of *Woolf and the Art of Exploration: Selected Papers from the Fifteenth Annual Woolf Conference* (Clemson University Press, 2006)

Anna Snaith is a Reader in Twentieth-Century Literature at King's College London. She works in the modernist period, with particular expertise on Virginia Woolf, modernism and empire, and urban studies. Her research on Woolf has focused specifically on the 1930s, on Woolf's spatial politics and on her reading public. She has published a monograph, *Virginia Woolf: Public and Private Negotiations* (Palgrave, 2000), edited the letters Woolf received in response to *Three Guineas* (*The Three Guineas Letters*, Woolf Studies Annual, 2000) and has edited two volumes on Woolf, *Palgrave Advances in Virginia Woolf Studies* (2007) and *Locating Woolf: The Politics of Space and Place* (2007, co-edited with Michael Whitworth). She is presently editing *The Years* for the Cambridge University Press Edition of Virginia Woolf, the first, fully annotated, scholarly edition of Virginia Woolf's writing. She has published articles on many aspects of Woolf studies including her work for the Fawcett Library, *Flush* and fascism, and her early short fiction. She is also working on a monograph entitled *Colonial London: Nation, Gender, Modernity 1890–1945* (Cambridge University Press, forthcoming).

Melissa Sullivan is Assistant Professor of English at Rosemont College, where she teaches British and Irish literature. She has published articles on middlebrow writers and *Time and Tide* and on Woolf, Rose Macaulay and cultural hierarchies.

John K. Young is Associate Professor of English at Marshall University, where he studies and teaches 20th/21st-century British, American and Anglophone literatures, with particular interests in textual scholarship and narrative theory. Previous and forthcoming publications include *Black Writers, White Publishers: Marketplace Politics and 20th-Century African American Literature* and *African American Literature and Editorial Theory* (co-edited with George Hutchinson), as well as essays on Virginia Woolf as a publisher, Trinidadian novelist Robert Antoni, the Book-of-the-Month Club edition of Richard Wright's *Native Son*, Toni Morrison and Oprah's Book Club, Thomas Pynchon's publications in popular magazines, the missing last paragraph in Nella Larsen's *Passing*, and the Uniform Editions of Virginia Woolf's works.

Index

(Please note: HP-Hogarth Press; LW-Leonard Woolf; VW-Virginia Woolf)

Mussolini, Benito, 107
on the cover of *Quack! Quack!*,
199
The Political and Social Doctrine of Fascism, 119
mysticism, 35–6, 37, 76, 93, 114

Natal Witness, 132
Nation, The, 75, 84–6, 87, 88, 94, 181, 183, 207
Nation and Athenaeum, The, 235
nationalism, 115, 120, 121
Eurasian Movement, 155, 165, 167, 168
Indian, 107, 109, 110, 113, 114, 115–16
Russian, 151–4, 160–1, 172
Needham, Anuradha Dingwaney, 105
Nehru, Pandit, 123n
network study, 11, 13, 15, 16–17
networks, 19–20, 146
of commercial presses, 55
intellectual, 74, 75
international, 18, 19, 103, 104, 108, 150, 151, 154, 162, 164, 165
Kauffer and, 179, 180, 182, 203
middlebrow, 17, 53, 55, 56, 64, 65
periodical, 18, 84, 93, 94
political, 19, 119, 151
Russian émigré, 150, 172
social and literary, 17, 31–2, 104, 184, 236
working class, 20, 207, 212, 217, 223, 224
New Age, 208, 210
New Leader, 31
New Review, The, 6
New Statesman, 39, 77, 181, 207, 214, 248
New Statesman and Nation, 42
New Verse, 30
New Writing, 38, 39, 40, 70, 208, 223, 229, 230
New Writing and Daylight, 223
New Yorker, 251
Newsome, Albert, 210
newspaper advertisements, 181, 240, 248, 257n
Nichols, Norah, 15
Nicolson, Benedict Lionel, 243, 244–5, 258n
Nicolson, Harold, 6, 117, 142, 238, 244, 245
Nicolson, Nigel, 243, 247, 257n
1917 Club, 7, 151, 160–1, 162

Nineteenth Century and After (periodical), 6, 214
Nonesuch Press, The, 4, 5, 21n, 184, 185
Nott, Kathleen, *Mile End*, 69–70, 231n

Observer, The, 34, 214
Olesha, Yuri, *Envy*, 145, 146
Olivier, Lord Sydney Haldane, 106, 118
Omega Workshops, 4
Orage, A. R., 208
Orwell, George, 107, 108, 120, 123n, 124n, 214
Orwell, James, 112
Owen, Wilfred, 224
Oxford University Press, 9

pacifism, 86, 93, 104, 154, 155, 161, 162
Padmore, George, 107
Page, Ruth, 141
Palme Dutt, R., 119
Panikkar, K. M., 119
Pantheon Books, 201
Pares, Bernard, 153
Parker, Robert, 190
Parsons, Trekkie Ritchie, 197, 220, 221, 222
Partridge, Ralph, 5, 9
Patridge, Frances, 32
Pearsall Smith, Logan, 5, 7, 22n, 75, 95n, 163
Stories from the Old Testament, 74, 77–83, 89, 90, 94
Pelican Press, 22n, 183
Penguin Books, 52, 64, 194
Peppis, Paul, 14
Phelan, James, 142
Pick, Frank, 182
Pissarro, Lucien and Esther, 4
Plomer, Charles, 131
Plomer, Edythe Browne, 131
Plomer, William, 8, 9, 33, 128–46, 223, 235
biography, 130–4
The Case Is Altered, 128, 129, 132, 133, 136, 140, 141, 142–4, 145–6
I Speak of Africa, 129, 132, 140, 145
Sado, 128, 129, 132, 133, 136, 140, 141–2, 143, 144
Turbott Wolfe, 128, 129–30, 131, 134–8, 140–1, 142, 145
'Ula Masondo,' 128, 129, 139–40
poetry (Hogarth Press)
Amber Innocent (Easdale), 37, 38, 41–7
Anthology of Cambridge Women's Verse, 31

Clemence and Clare (Easdale), 34–6

Collected Poems (Sackville-West), 246–7

Collected Poems (Trevelyan), 37

A Collection of Poems (written between the ages of 14 and 17) (Easdale), 30–1

New Country (Roberts), 223

New Signatures (Roberts), 33

The Passing of Guto (Menai), 225–7

Selected Poems (Plomer), 133

Selected Poems (Sackville-West), 254

'Sissinghurst' (Sackville-West), 245

Solitude (Sackville-West), 251–2

working-class, 16, 217, 223–8

Poetry Review, The, 34

Pole, Graham, 19, 119

Political Quarterly, 207

Port of Spain Gazette, 106, 110, 111

Porter, Alan, *Coal: A Challenge to the National Conscience*, 209–10

Porter, David, 198

posters, 180, 182, 183, 184, 189–91, 198

Pound, Ezra, 17

Powell, Anthony, 39, 65

Powell, Violet, 66

Prewett, Frank, 4

primitivism, 112, 151, 156, 159–60, 169, 172

psychoanalysis, 53, 117

psychology, 64, 77, 79, 81, 82, 83, 90, 94, 115, 157, 158, 209, 212

public sphere, literary, 53, 54, 55, 56, 57, 64, 66, 70

Puffin Books, 9

Punch, 39

PWA (All-India Progressive Writers Association), 117

Rabkin, David, 130

race, and sexuality, 129–30, 136–40

racial equality, 105

racism, 114, 167

Rainey, Lawrence, 12, 13, 65

Random House, 201

rationalism, 76, 84, 115

Read, Herbert, 201

Reckitt, Maurice B., 210

religion, 74–99

    A Letter to an Archbishop (Hardwick), 74, 75, 88–90, 94, 96n

    'Questionnaire on Religious Belief,' 84–7, 88

Russian Orthodox, 167, 169–70

Stories from the Old Testament (Pearsall Smith), 74, 77–83, 89, 90, 94

Woolfs and, 76–7

Remizov, Aleksey Mikhailovich, 163–4, 165

Renan, Ernest, 77, 81, 88, 95n

Rendel, James Meadows, 31–2, 38

Rendel, Joan, 38

Rhondda, Lady, 57

Rhythm magazine, 12

Richardson, Dorothy, 8

Riding, Laura, 57

Rilke, Rainer Maria, *Duineser Elegien*, 238, 245–6

Ritchie, Alice, 196

Ritchie, Trekkie *see* Parsons, Trekkie Ritchie

Rivière, Jacques, 163

Roberts, Michael, 33, 223

Robertson, Celia, 38, 48

Robertson, J. M., 84, 86, 87

Robeson, Paul, 120

Robinson Crusoe (Defoe), 185

Rose, Jacqueline, 138

Rose, Jonathan, 21n, 207

Rosenbaum, S. P., 22n, 87

Rossetti, Christina, 30, 35, 39

Runyon, Damon, 6

Russell, Bertrand, 65, 71n

Russell, Patricia, 71n

Russia, 119

Russian nationalism, 151, 155, 165, 167, 168

Russian Revolution (1917), 151–2, 153–4, 160–1, 172

Russian translation, 150–73

Rutherford, Mark (Hale White), 31

Rylands, George (Dadie), 9, 198, 199

Sackville, Lady, 247, 258n

Sackville-West, Edward, 108

Sackville-West, Vita, 6, 7, 8, 16, 31, 70–1n, 142, 224, 234–56

    All Passion Spent, 242, 258n

    on *Amber Innocent*, 42

    biography series for children, 247–8, 249

    Collected Poems, 246–7, 252

    The dark island, 242, 243, 244–5, 247, 258n

    The Edwardians, 144, 239–42, 247, 257n

    Family History, 33, 144, 242, 243